MODERNIZATION, DEMOCRACY, AND ISLAM

MODERNIZATION, DEMOCRACY, AND ISLAM

Edited by Shireen T. Hunter
and Huma Malik

Foreword by Ahmedou Ould-Abdallah

Published in cooperation with the Center for Strategic and
International Studies, Washington, D.C.

PRAEGER

Westport, Connecticut
London

Library of Congress Cataloging-in-Publication Data

Modernization, democracy, and Islam / edited by Shireen T. Hunter and Huma Malik ;
foreword by Ahmedou Ould-Abdallah.
    p.   cm.
    "Published in cooperation with the Center for Strategic and International Studies,
Washington, D.C."
    Includes bibliographical references and index.
    ISBN 0–275–98511–3 (alk. paper)—ISBN 0–275–98530–X (pbk. : alk. paper)
    1. Islamic countries—Politics and government.   2. Democratization—Islamic countries.
3. Political culture—Islamic countries.   4. Islamic countries—Civilization.   5. Islam and
politics.   I. Hunter, Shireen.   II. Malik, Huma.   III. Center for Strategic and International
Studies (Washington, D.C.)
    JQ1852.A91M63   2005
    320.917'67—dc22   2004017541

British Library Cataloguing in Publication Data is available.

Library of Congress Catalog Card Number: 2004017541

ISBN: 0–275–98511–3
       0–275–98530–X (pbk.)

First published in 2005

Praeger Publishers, 88 Post Road West, Westport, CT 06881
An imprint of Greenwood Publishing Group, Inc.
www.praeger.com

Printed in the United States of America

The paper used in this book complies with the
Permanent Paper Standard issued by the National
Information Standards Organization (Z39.48–1984).

10 9 8 7 6 5 4 3 2 1

Contents

Part II: From Within and Without: Factors Influencing Modernization and the Development of Democracy in the Muslim World

Part III: Case Studies

Foreword

Debate about Islam is not new in the West. But in the last few years, there has been a proliferation of writings on Islam. In particular, since September 11, 2001, much has been said and written on terrorism and its connection to Islam. Islam has become the subject of hundreds of books, articles, and conferences, thus providing opportunities for instant "specialists" to add their fresh "expertise" to the established knowledge of academics, travelers, and seasoned diplomats who have lived and worked with and among Muslims.

No doubt, some valuable work has been done on Islam, Islamic culture, and Islamic values. But a great many works are one-sided, inflammatory, and infused with emotions and ideological undertones. Indeed, at present impartiality seems a rare commodity when discussing Islam, and most discussions have become politicized and subjective. However, a fundamental question remains: namely, how to live with the more than 1.2 billion Muslims spread throughout the world.

Modernization, Democracy, and Islam is a remarkable contribution to the ongoing debate about Islam, Islamists, and Muslims. This wide-ranging book, incorporating politics, history, economics, and development issues, makes commendable efforts to explain intricate issues and their interconnections. It does so in a noncontroversial manner, educating readers and reminding them to put things into their multiple contexts. This approach, however, does not excuse or defend governments in the Muslim world. On the contrary, Muslim leaders are invited to note that "after more than five decades of efforts at modernization, the Muslim world still lags behind not only the advanced Western countries but also a number of East Asian states." The book goes further with an analysis of the "Muslim world's modernization and democracy gap." The consequences of this deficit, including its security implications, have become a preoccupation for policy makers, especially among major countries, notably the United States, and in many leading circles in the Muslim world.

Although there is an overall consensus on the reality of the gap in modernization and democratization between Muslim states and Western countries, the explanation of its root causes and possible solutions poses immense problems. Stereotypes, including within Muslim countries, do not help address the structures that nurture this gap. It is important that physical, psychological, or verbal terror, whatever the source, is not minimized in this book. However, the book's major focus is to determine the conditions most favorable to international peace and security, and those must include economic development.

The book frequently reminds us of the imperative today to put analyses of Islam into proper historical, economic, and geographical contexts. Hence, it makes a considerable effort to rescue history from the new experts and historians of Islam. Culturalists and other orientalists may not be totally wrong in their views on why Islamic countries are lagging behind, but they are invited "not to ignore the diversity of the modernization process" and are reminded that "traditions, including religious, have survived in modern Western societies and in some cases, such as that of the United States, are becoming stronger." On democratization, the book recalls that "Britain was the only country where modernization and democratization was an indigenous phenomenon, accomplished in relative peace over a period of more than two hundred years." In contrast, in neighboring France, the democratic evolution was marked by violence. Consequently, we are advised to have a "less insular" and a "less abstract" debate on Islam and democracy. Comparisons between other cultures and democracy, on the one hand, and historical contexts, on the other, are indispensable to scientific assessments of the evolution of cultures. Modernity and democracy, too, were not linear processes. The book is full of very interesting demonstrations of the correlations among past events now ignored or minimized, though critical in their time.

No doubt, this method helps us understand some historical developments and puts them in proper perspective. Colonization and other foreign presences have made local populations more aware of the necessity to defend and, thus, reorganize their own religious and cultural systems. Rejection, adaptation, or integration of the colonizers' models were debated, and the return to an idealized historical form of government has often been seen in the modern world as a shield against foreign or modern intrusion.

The book concludes with a set of concrete recommendations. It notes that cultures and values are not immutable, as changes in economic and social structures very often lead to cultural transformation. Indeed, reform is possible if a number of mutually reinforcing actions are undertaken at different levels. The general principles—for instance, respect for human rights and transparency—should be upheld over a significant period of time. At the national level, human capital is to be built or strengthened in a sustained manner with a culture of tolerance and inclusion. Finally, mature democracies, with high stakes at the security level in a stabilized world, should support modernization in a consistent manner.

Indeed, in this era of mass communication, universal values should defeat double standards, and serious efforts should be organized to strengthen the credibility of the international community and thus help to address the root causes of misunderstanding among cultures and regions. Terrorists, nihilists, and all those promoting any form of totalitarianism in approach or in action could then be defeated.

Ahmedou Ould-Abdallah
Special Representative of the UN Secretary-General for West Africa

Preface

The fall of the Berlin Wall on November 9, 1989, followed by the fall of the Communist regimes in Eastern Europe, and finally the collapse of the Soviet Union in December 1991, generated an optimistic mood regarding the future of international relations, especially in the West.

It was expected that the Soviet Union's collapse, which had validated the superiority of the Western liberal model of economics and politics and confirmed its universal application, would lead other countries to embrace this model. It was also expected that the Soviet collapse would free funds for economic and social development—the so-called peace dividend.

This optimism was further strengthened by the victory of the U.S.-led international coalition in the Persian Gulf War of 1990–91 to reverse Iraqi aggression against Kuwait, and later buttressed by the Oslo process resulting in the Palestinian-Israeli Agreement of 1993.

Sadly, however, events took a different turn. The Soviet Union's collapse unleashed centrifugal tendencies in the Balkans and the former Soviet Union and led to conflicts in Bosnia, Kosovo, and Chechnya, plus intra- and interstate conflicts in the Caucasus and Central Asia.

The Soviet Union's withdrawal from Afghanistan, instead of bringing peace and security, led to a devastating civil war and to the emergence of the Taliban with their reductionist reading of Islam and their intolerant attitude toward the West and a good part of the Muslim population. Meanwhile, the Bosnian and Chechen wars, both involving Muslims, became breeding grounds for new generations of Muslim militants. They also generated widespread resentment among Muslims because of the international community's perceived inaction toward these conflicts. Meanwhile, the prospects for the Arab-Israeli peace dimmed after the assassination of Israel's prime minister Yitzhak Rabin in 1995. Modernization and democratization, in large swaths of the Islamic world and beyond in the developing world, were casualties of these developments. Instead of greater aid and other efforts to help the developing world, much of the international community's attention in the 1990s was absorbed by events in Russia and the Balkans and the state of Russo-Western relations.

The fact that history after all did not end with the Soviet Union's demise also led to a search for new and overarching paradigms that could explain the future shape and direction of international relations. This search resulted in the promulgation of the "clash of civilizations" thesis by Samuel Huntington.

The attacks on the World Trade Center and Pentagon on September 11, 2001, by terrorists belonging to the extremist Muslim organization Al-Qaeda appeared to validate the clash of civilizations thesis. However, it soon became clear that as abhorrent and inhuman as these acts were, they reflected the deep and multidimensional—economic, social, political, and cultural—crisis of the Muslim world resulting from its significant deficiencies in modernization and democratization. These attacks also alerted the international community, especially the United States, to the global ramifications of these deficiencies. The events of September 11 were also a wake-up call for Muslim states that, unless they undertook fundamental reforms, extremism would attract more followers. Immediate actions of the international community under the U.S. leadership understandably were to dismantle the Taliban's and Al-Qaeda's power base; hence the military operations in Afghanistan and a global effort to eliminate transnational terror networks.

The Afghan intervention in October 2001 was followed by the removal of Saddam Hussein's regime in March 2003 by the United States and its coalition of a number of European and Asian countries. As a result of these interventions, the United States and the international community at large became directly involved in the process of state and nation building, modernization, and democratization in Afghanistan and Iraq. The post–September 11 developments also shifted international attention to the persisting problems of underdevelopment and authoritarianism in the Muslim world. It was in recognition of this situation and its inherent risks that in March 2004 the United States unveiled a long-term action plan to promote democratization and modernization in the Greater Middle East, and sought support from the Group of Eight for this ambitious project.

The experiences of the past few years in Afghanistan and Iraq have demonstrated the dilemmas inherent in the processes of state and nation building and democratization, including the tension between the imperatives of order and freedom. In short, the international community has had to deal with the same types of problems and dilemmas that have bedeviled the developing countries for the past fifty years and, in some cases, for more than a century.

Meanwhile, in response to U.S. actions, many Muslim countries, notably in the Arab world, have started to take some steps toward an opening of the political sphere.

At this important juncture where both Muslim countries and key international actors seem determined to address the issues of modernization and democratization in the Muslim world, it is important that lessons of the past be put to good use. One important lesson, as Alexander Gerschenkron noted forty years ago, is that advanced countries will not succeed in their efforts to help developing nations if they ignore the latter's particularities and the nature of their shortcomings.

It is therefore hoped that this book, by explaining the factors behind the Muslim world's modernization and democratization deficit and by providing some broad suggestions on how to overcome existing obstacles, will be of benefit to those in the United States, the Muslim world, and elsewhere who are endeavoring to give a new impetus to modernization and democratization in the Muslim world. Some of the conclusions of this book are also valid for other developing countries.

This book, resulting from the work of a study group that met twice, in May and July 2003, would not have been possible without the generous support of the Carnegie Corporation of New York. Huma and I would therefore like to express our personal thanks, as well as that of the Center for Strategic and International Studies (CSIS), for this support. We would also like to express our own and CSIS's gratitude to the LUSO-American Foundation for the additional support they gave to this project. Our thanks also goes to all participants in the study group and contributors to this volume. We would also like to thank our interns, Celeste Allred, Sarah Islam, and Mariya Amelicheva. Shireen Hunter would also like to thank her husband, Robert Hunter, for his support during the preparation of this book.

Shireen T. Hunter
Director, Islam Program
Center for Strategic and International Studies

1

Introduction

Shireen T. Hunter

At least for the past fifty years, there have been sustained efforts at modernization in the Muslim world. In parts of the Islamic world, the beginnings of a modernization process date to the mid-nineteenth century, if not earlier. Yet the
Muslim world lags behind not only the advanced Western countries in every aspect of modernization but also such East Asian countries as Taiwan, South Korea,
Singapore, and China. Moreover, in regard to the socioeconomic indicators of
modernization, Muslim countries fare poorly even when compared to the more
advanced of the Latin American countries. No doubt, there are differences among
Muslim countries in terms of their record of success in modernization; there are
even a few success stories, notably that of Malaysia. By and large, however, the
Muslim world's modernization record is disappointing. The following figures
provide a glimpse of the magnitude of the Muslim world's modernization deficit.
For example, out of forty-six countries with a majority Muslim population, seventeen are in the category of LDCs (least developed countries)[1] and twenty-two
are in the category of developing countries[2] (Table 1.1). The combined gross domestic product (GDP) of the Muslim majority countries with a total population
of 1.17 billion in 2002 was $1.38 trillion,[3] or a fraction of the $10.11[4] trillion of
the European Union, which has a population of only 370 million.[5]

Except for those in oil-producing countries, per capita incomes in the Muslim
world remain low even in the case of the most advanced countries, such as
Malaysia and Turkey, with $3,500 and $2,500, respectively[6] (Table 1.2). The
Muslim world's share in international trade is a meager 6.86 percent.[7] This figure would be even lower if oil exports were excluded.

The economies of most Muslim countries are not diversified, and levels of industrialization and the share of industry as a percentage of GDP, as well as the
share of exports,[8] remain low[9] (Table 1.3). Similarly, although the share of agri-

Table 1.1
Levels of Development for Muslim Majority Countries

LDCs*	Low Income (per capita GNI less than US$745)	Lower Middle Income (per capita GNI US$746–2,975)	Upper Middle Income (per capita GNI US$2,976–9,205)	High Income (per capita GNI greater than US$9,206)
Afghanistan	Afghanistan	Albania	Lebanon	Bahrain
Bangladesh	Azerbaijan	Algeria	Libya	Brunei Darussalam
Burkina-Faso	Bangladesh	Djibouti	Malaysia	Kuwait
Chad	Burkina-Faso	Egypt	Oman	Qatar
Comoros	Chad	Iran	Saudi Arabia	United Arab Emirates
Djibouti	Comoros	Iraq		
Gambia	Gambia	Jordan		
Guinea	Guinea	Maldives		
Maldives	Indonesia	Morocco		
Mali	Kyrgyz	Palestine		
Mauritania	Mali	Syria		
Niger	Mauritania	Tunisia		
Senegal	Niger	Turkey		
Sierra Leone	Nigeria	Turkmenistan		
Somalia	Pakistan			
Sudan	Senegal			
Yemen	Sierra Leone			
	Somalia			
	Sudan			
	Tajikistan			
	Uzbekistan			
	Yemen			

Sources: LDCs: Office of the High Representative for the Least Developed Countries, "Landlocked Developing Countries and Small Island Developing States," http://www.un.org/special-rep/ohrlls/ldc/list.htm. Income level: World Bank Group, *World Development Indicators 2003* (Washington, DC: World Bank, 2003).

*LDC criteria: Per capita GDP below US$900 for inclusion but above US$1,035 for graduation; weak human assets based on health, nutrition, and education indicators; high economic vulnerability based on instability of agricultural exports, inadequate diversification, and economic smallness; and a population below 75 million. It is important to note that criteria are subject to change. In fact, the 2003 review of the least developed countries by the United Nations Committee for Development Policy was based on the inclusion threshold of a three-year (1999–2000) average of US$750 and the threshold for graduation of US$900: United Nations, Committee for Development Policy, "Fifth Session, 7–11 April 2003," Economic and Social Council, Official Records, Supplement 13, 2003, http://www.unescap.org/MDG/LDC.asp.

Table 1.2
Per Capita Income

Country	Per Capita GNI ($)	Country	Per Capita GNI ($)
Afghanistan	n.d.	Palestine	930
Somalia	n.d.	Syria	1,130
Iraq	n.d.	Morocco	1,190
Sierra Leone	140	Turkmenistan	1,200
Niger	170	Albania	1,380
Tajikistan	180	Egypt	1,470
Chad	220	Iran	1,710
Burkina-Faso	220	Algeria	1,720
Mali	240	Jordan	1,760
Gambia	280	Tunisia	2,000
Nigeria	290	Maldives	2,090
Kyrgyzstan	290	Turkey	2,500
Sudan	350	Malaysia	3,540
Bangladesh	360	Lebanon	3,990
Comoros	390	Libya	7,570
Mauritania	410	Oman	7,720
Guinea	410	Saudi Arabia	8,460
Pakistan	410	Bahrain	11,130
Uzbekistan	450	Kuwait	18,270
Senegal	470	Brunei Darussalam	19,210
Yemen	490		
Indonesia	710	Qatar	19,844
Azerbaijan	710	United Arab Emirates	20,530
Djibouti	900		

Source: World Bank and United Nations Development Programme, *Human Development Report 2003* (New York: United Nations Development Programme, 2003). All data are for 2002, except for those of Bahrain, Brunei-Darussalam, Kuwait, Libya, Oman, Qatar, Saudi Arabia, and United Arab Emirates, which are for 2001.

Note: n.d. = no data available.

culture in total GDP of many Muslim countries has declined, agriculture still employs a very large percentage of the population in most Muslim countries. While urbanization has increased in the Muslim world, it has been largely the result of the impoverished rural population moving to the cities rather than the consequence of large-scale industrialization. In terms of other socioeconomic indicators of modernization, the Muslim world presents an equally depressing picture. The level of illiteracy, especially among women, as well as unemployment, particularly among women and the young, is very high. Indeed, the extremely inadequate level of the incorporation of the female population in national life and the persistence of a glaring gender gap in relation to every index of socioeconomic and political progress represent some of the greatest failures of modern-

Table 1.3
Measures of Industrialization

Country	GDP by Sector 2001			Labor by Sector 1980-82		
	Agriculture (%)	Industry (%)	Services (%)	Agriculture (%)	Industry (%)	Services (%)
Afghanistan	n.d.	n.d.	n.d.	76.0	10.5	14.0
Albania	50	23	26	n.d.	n.d.	n.d.
Algeria	10	55	36	48.0	19.5	32.5
Azerbaijan	17	46	36	n.d.	n.d.	n.d.
Bangladesh*	23	25	52	50.0	15.5	34.5
Burkina-Faso	38	21	41	92.5	2.5	5.0
Chad	39	14	48	88.5	3.0	8.0
Egypt*	17	33	50	32.0	17.0	51.0
Gambia	40	14	46	85.5	6.5	9.0
Guinea	24	38	38	91.5	1.5	7.5
Indonesia	16	47	37	54.5	14.5	31.0
Iran	19	33	48	n.d.	n.d.	n.d.
Iraq	n.d.	n.d.	n.d.	41.5	17.5	41.5
Jordan	2	25	73	n.d.	n.d.	n.d.
Kuwait[†]	1	52	47	1.0	19.5	79.5
Kyrgyz*	38	27	30	52.5	11.0	36.0
Lebanon	12	22	66	16.5	25.0	58.5
Libya	n.d.	n.d.	n.d.	39.5	16.0	44.5
Malaysia*	9	49	42	17.0	31.0	52.0
Mali	38	26	36	89.0	1.5	9.5
Mauritania	21	29	50	72.0	6.5	22.0
Morocco*	16	31	53	6.0	36.0	58.5
Niger	40	17	43	6.5	49.0	45.5
Nigeria	30	46	25	n.d.	n.d.	n.d.
Oman[†]	3	58	39	38.0	27.0	35.0
Pakistan	25	27	52	n.d.	n.d.	n.d.
Saudi Arabia[†]	6	50	43	35.0	11.0	54.5
Senegal	18	27	55	82.0	5.5	12.5
Sierra Leone	50	30	20	72.5	12.0	15.5

Table 1.3 (continued)

Somalia[†]	65	n.d.	n.d.	79.5	7.0	13.5
Sudan	39	19	42	77.0	6.5	16.0
Syria	22	28	50	n.d.	n.d.	n.d.
Tajikistan	29	29	41	n.d.	n.d.	n.d.
Tunisia	12	29	60	43.0	31.0	26.5
Turkey*	14	26	61	53.0	17.5	29.5
Turkmenistan	29	51	20	n.d.	n.d.	n.d.
United Arab Emirates[†]	2	64	35	2.5	23.5	74.0
Uzbekistan	34	23	43	n.d.	n.d.	n.d.
Yemen	16	50	35	79.0	10.0	11.0

Source: World Bank Group, World Development Indicators 2003 (Washington, DC: World Bank, 2003), 46–48, 190–92.

Note: n.d. = no data available.
*Labor statistics are for 1998–2001.
†GDP sector statistics are for 1990.

ization in the Muslim world (Tables 1.4 and 1.5). Further, the pattern of income distribution is highly skewed in favor of the small, rich minorities, and the percentage of population living at or below the poverty line remains very high (Table 1.6).

Also, with the exception of Malaysia, the level of the Muslim world's integration in the global electronic and communication network remains very low. For example, in the Arab world there are fewer than 18 computers per 1,000 people, as compared to the global average of 285 in the developed countries.[10] Other Muslim countries do not fare much better in comparison (Table 1.7).

The Muslim world's record in establishing democratic governments and building the institutions and practices necessary for such a system, at both the state and the society levels, is equally disappointing. In fact, over the past fifty years the majority of Muslim countries have lived under different types of authoritarian or semitotalitarian regimes or both. At certain times, disorganized popular movements have supported these regimes, which, by manipulating nationalist or religious sentiments or by using external threats, have managed to strike a "populist bargain." The underpinning of this bargain has been the government's promise to ward off external threats and to provide economic prosperity in exchange for the delaying of democratic rule. However, most Muslim governments have failed to deliver on their part of the bargain. Therefore, today most of the exist-

Table 1.4
Illiteracy Rates, 2001

Countries	Youth (15–24 years) Male (%)	Female (%)	Adult (above 15 years) Male (%)	Female(%)
Afghanistan	n.d.	n.d.	n.d.	n.d.
Albania	1	3	8	22
Algeria	6	15	23	42
Azerbaijan	n.d.	n.d.	n.d.	n.d.
Bangladesh	43	60	50	69
Burkina-Faso	53	75	65	85
Chad	25	38	47	64
Egypt	23	36	33	55
Gambia	33	49	55	69
Guinea	n.d.	n.d.	n.d.	n.d.
Indonesia	2	3	8	17
Iran	4	8	16	30
Iraq	40	70	45	76
Jordan	1	1	5	15
Kuwait	8	6	16	20
Kyrgyz	n.d.	n.d.	n.d.	n.d.
Lebanon	3	7	8	19
Libya	0	6	9	31
Malaysia	2	2	8	16
Mali	52	74	63	83
Mauritania	43	59	49	69
Morocco	23	40	37	63
Niger	67	86	76	91
Nigeria	10	15	27	42
Oman	0	3	19	36
Pakistan	28	57	42	71
Saudi Arabia	5	9	16	32
Senegal	40	57	52	71
Sierra Leone	n.d.	n.d.	n.d.	n.d.
Somalia	n.d.	n.d.	n.d.	n.d.
Sudan	17	27	30	52
Syria	4	20	11	38
Tajikistan	0	0	0	1
Tunisia	2	10	18	38
Turkey	1	6	6	23
Turkmenistan	n.d.	n.d.	n.d.	n.d.
United Arab Emirates	12	5	25	20
Uzbekistan	0	0	0	1
Yemen	16	51	32	73

Source: World Bank Group, *World Development Indicators 2003* (Washington, DC: World Bank, 2003).

Note: n.d. = no data available.

Table 1.5
Unemployment Rates

Countries	Youth (15–24 years), 2001			Total Work Force, 1998–2001			By Level of Education, 1997–99		
	Male (%)	Female (%)	Total (%)	Male (%)	Female (%)	Total (%)	Primary (%)	Secondary (%)	Tertiary (%)
Albania	n.d.	n.d.	n.d.	15.8	20.9	18.0	n.d.	n.d.	n.d.
Algeria*	46.0	14.0	39.0	n.d.	n.d.	n.d.	n.d.	n.d.	n.d.
Azerbaijan	n.d.	n.d.	n.d.	1.0	1.4	1.2	6.7	30.8	62.5
Bangladesh	11.0	10.0	11.0	n.d.	n.d.	n.d.	n.d.	n.d.	n.d.
Egypt	14.0	37.0	20.0	5.1	19.9	8.2	n.d.	n.d.	n.d.
Gambia	n.d.	n.d.	n.d.	15.3	12.2	13.8	3.9	32.4	60.8
Indonesia*	9.0	9.0	9.0	n.d.	n.d.	6.1	38.3	47.9	9.2
Jordan	n.d.	n.d.	n.d.	11.8	20.7	13.2	n.d.	n.d.	n.d.
Kyrgyz	n.d.	n.d.	n.d.	n.d.	n.d.	n.d.	33.4	55.7	10.9
Malaysia	n.d.	n.d.	n.d.	n.d.	n.d.	3.0	n.d.	n.d.	n.d.
Morocco	16.0	15.0	15.0	20.3	27.6	22.0	n.d.	n.d.	n.d.
Niger*	1.0	n.d.	1.0	n.d.	n.d.	n.d.	n.d.	n.d.	n.d.
Pakistan	11.0	29.0	13.0	4.2	14.9	5.9	n.d.	n.d.	n.d.
Palestine	n.d.	n.d.	n.d.	n.d.	n.d.	14.1	n.d.	n.d.	n.d.
Syria†	n.d.	n.d.	n.d.	3.8	3.8	3.9	n.d.	n.d.	n.d.
Tajikistan	n.d.	n.d.	n.d.	n.d.	n.d.	n.d.	10.6	83.2	6.3
Tunisia	n.d.	n.d.	n.d.	n.d.	n.d.	n.d.	n.d.	33.7	4.1
Turkey	21.0	18.0	20.0	7.6	6.6	8.3	n.d.	n.d.	n.d.

Source: Youth unemployment: United Nations Development Programme, *Human Development Report 2003*, 232–36. Total unemployment and unemployment by education: World Bank Group, *World Development Indicators 2003* (Washington, DC: World Bank, 2003), 50–52.

Note: n.d. = no data available.
*Youth unemployment data are for 1990.
†Data are for 1980–82.

Table 1.6
Income Distribution

Country	Share of Income		Country	Share of Income	
	Lowest Twenty Percent (%)	Highest Twenty Percent (%)		Lowest Twenty Percent (%)	Highest Twenty Percent (%)
Afghanistan	n.d.	n.d.	Mauritania	6.4	44.1
Albania	n.d.	n.d.	Morocco	6.5	46.6
Algeria	7.0	42.6	Niger	2.6	53.3
Azerbaijan	7.4	44.5	Nigeria	4.4	55.7
Bangladesh	9.0	41.3	Oman	n.d.	n.d.
Burkina-Faso	4.5	60.7	Pakistan	8.8	42.3
Chad	n.d.	n.d.	Saudi Arabia	n.d.	n.d.
Egypt	8.6	43.6	Senegal	6.4	48.2
Gambia	4.0	55.2	Sierra Leone	1.1	63.4
Guinea	6.4	47.2	Somalia	n.d.	n.d.
Indonesia	8.4	43.3	Sudan	n.d.	n.d.
Iran	5.1	49.9	Syria	n.d.	n.d.
Iraq	n.d.	n.d.	Tajikistan	8.0	40.0
Jordan	7.6	44.4	Tunisia	5.7	47.9
Kuwait	n.d.	n.d.	Turkey	6.1	46.7
Kyrgyz	9.1	38.3	Turkmenistan	6.1	47.5
Lebanon	n.d.	n.d.	United Arab Em.	n.d.	n.d.
Libya	n.d.	n.d.	Uzbekistan	9.2	36.3
Malaysia	4.4	54.3	Yemen	7.4	41.2
Mali	4.6	56.2			

Source: World Bank Group, *World Development Indicators 2003* (Washington, DC: World Bank, 2003), 64–66.

Note: n.d. = no data available.

ing regimes rely more on coercion or popular apathy or a combination of the two for their survival rather than on popular acceptance. Meanwhile, a facade of democracy in the form of regular elections, in the course of which the incumbent elites are returned to power, often without any competition and with large majorities of 80 or 90 percent of the votes cast, is maintained. Even in a country such as Turkey, with the longest-functioning democracy in the Muslim world, the democratic process has often been interrupted by military coups d'état, and the elected leaders have operated under the watchful eye of the military.

Despite the emergence of encouraging spots, such as Senegal, Mali, Bangladesh, and Malaysia, plus Indonesia's efforts to consolidate its democracy in the post-Suharto era, the Muslim world's democracy deficit is very large and the challenge of democratization remains daunting.

Table 1.7
Communication Infrastructure in Select Countries

	Daily Newspapers (per 1,000 people), 2000	Personal Computers (per 1,000 people) (2001)	Internet Users (thousands), 2001	Telephones (per 1,000 people), 2001	Mobile Phones (per 1,000 people), 2001
Afghanistan	5	n.d.	n.d.	1	n.d.
Albania	35	7.6	10	50	88
Algeria	27	7.1	60	61	3
Azerbaijan	27	n.d.	25	111	80
Bangladesh	53	1.9	250	4	4
Burkina-Faso	1	1.5	19	5	6
Chad	0	1.6	4	1	3
Egypt	31	15.5	600	104	43
Gambia	2	12.7	18	26	41
Guinea	n.d.	4	15	3	7
Indonesia	23	11	4000	35	31
Iran	28	69.7	1005	169	32
Iraq	19	n.d.	n.d.	29	n.d.
Jordan	75	32.8	212	127	167
Kuwait	374	131.9	200	240	445
Kyrgyz	27	n.d.	151	78	5
Lebanon	107	56.2	300	195	212
Libya	15	n.d.	20	109	9
Malaysia	158	126.1	6500	196	314

Table 1.7 (continued)

Mali	1	1.2	30	4	4
Mauritania	0	10.3	7	7	42
Morocco	28	13.7	400	41	164
Niger	0	.5	12	2	0
Nigeria	24	6.8	115	5	4
Oman	29	32.4	120	90	124
Pakistan	40	4.1	500	23	6
Saudi Arabia	326	62.7	300	145	113
Senegal	5	18.6	100	25	31
Sierra Leone	4	n.d.	7	5	6
Somalia	1	n.d.	1	4	n.d.
Sudan	26	3.6	56	14	3
Syria	20	16.3	60	103	12
Tajikistan	20	n.d.	3	36	0
Tunisia	19	23.7	400	109	40
Turkey	111	40.7	2500	285	302
Turkmenistan	7	n.d.	8	80	2
United Arab Emirates	156	135.5	976	340	616
Uzbekistan	3	n.d.	150	66	2
Yemen	15	1.9	17	22	8

Source: World Bank Group, *World Development Indicators 2003* (Washington, DC: World Bank, 2003); ITU.

Note: n.d. = no data available.

GLOBAL IMPLICATIONS

Clearly, the Muslim peoples have suffered most from the modernization and democratization shortcomings of their countries. However, the adverse consequences of these shortcomings have not been limited to the Muslim peoples. Rather, some of these consequences, such as increased risks of political instability, the radicalization of social and political discourse (including Islamic extremism), civil war, and state breakdown, have entailed risks for other states and the international community. The civil wars in Algeria, Afghanistan, Somalia, and Sudan, along with the growth of more destructive terrorist activities—exemplified by the tragic events of September 11, 2001—illustrate the adverse global implications of these twin deficits. In the case of Afghanistan and Iraq, the risks posed to international security resulted in external military intervention led by the United States, as well as U.S. and international involvement in state and nation building in these two countries.

More than forty years ago, Alexander Gerschenkron argued, "The paramount lesson of the twentieth century is that the problems of backward nations are not exclusively their own. They are just as much the problems of the advanced countries."[11] This is even more true today. Therefore, the modernization and democratization shortcomings of the Muslim world are—or at least should be—of concern to the entire world, especially in view of the strategic importance of a significant part of the Muslim world, stretching from the Caspian Sea to the Persian Gulf, largely because of its vast energy reserves, upon which the prosperity of the industrialized world and the health of the international economy rest.

IDENTIFYING THE CAUSES: THE CULTURALIST THESIS

In light of the foregoing, it is not surprising that in the past fifteen years the issue of identifying the principal causes of the Muslim world's poor performance in modernization and democratization has been the subject of renewed interest, analysis, and debate, both in the West and in the Muslim world. By far the most influential thesis, which has emerged in the West, is the one based on religious and cultural factors and the specificities of Islam as a religion and as a sociopolitical order.

The most prominent representatives of the culturalist thesis are Samuel Huntington and Bernard Lewis.[12] However, they draw on a long tradition of Western culturalist thinking on these issues. Indeed, the question of the relationship between culture and modernization, and that between culture and democratization, has been a subject of inquiry for more than a century.

Max Weber provided the clearest connection between cultural, notably religious, characteristics of a society and modernization, by ascribing the rise of the modern capitalist system to the Protestant ethic, as developed by John Calvin and those inspired by him. Within the Christian world, Weber saw Catholicism as an impediment to economic modernization along capitalist lines.[13] Weber's view of

Islam and other Asian religions was even harsher. He thought them to be in-compatible with modernization, and not merely in economic spheres, as illus-trated by the following: "For the various popular religions of Asia, in contrast to ascetic Protestantism, the world remained a great enchanted garden. . . . No path led from the magical religiosity of the non-intellectual classes of Asia to a ra-tional, methodical control of life."[14] Weber thought Islam particularly incompat-ible with rational thinking: "Islam, in contrast to Judaism, lacked the requirement of a comprehensive knowledge of the law and lacked that intellectual training in casuistry which nurtured the rationalism of Judaism."[15] Later developments, how-ever, proved Weber's cultural determinism unjustified.

Indeed, the full-scale modernization of the non-Protestant zones of Europe—some quite late—and the economic transformation of Japan and other East Asian countries seriously eroded the validity of the cultural determinist thesis. The his-torical process of modernization, including that in Europe, also showed that cul-tural changes are as much the result of modernization as they are its cause. Southern Europe provides the best example of economically induced cultural changes.[16] The process of modernization, both in Europe and in non-Western countries, also demonstrated how the timing of modernization affected both the character of its principal agents and its results, giving rise to different types of modernization, including the socialist version, as best exemplified by the former Soviet Union. This is why Gerschenkron rejected the Marxist view, "according to which it is the history of advanced or established industrial countries which traces the road of development of the backward countries," and warned that "in several very important respects the development of a backward country may, by the very virtue of its backwardness, tend to differ fundamentally from that of an advanced country."[17]

Indeed, disparities in the level of modernization observable in Europe today are the consequence of differences in the starting point and the pattern of evolu-tion of their modernization processes. It also became clear that, beyond a few countries in Western Europe, notably England, France, and possibly Holland, modernization has been essentially an imitative process that has elicited varying responses from indigenous societies. However, even in England and France, as well as in Germany, there were many critics of modernization, especially its al-leged despiritualizing dimensions.[18] Over time, this type of response, ranging from emulation and synthesis to rejection or selective emulation, show remark-able similarities across cultures, further questioning the thesis that responses to the challenge of modernization are determined by cultural peculiarities. More-over, the latecomers to modernization, especially non-Western countries, have been vulnerable to the impact of the external environment and exogenous forces. European modernization was facilitated by its outward expansion, beginning in the late fifteenth century, and reached its height in the nineteenth century. The outside world provided Europe with vast resources and places for migration, which eased demographic pressures and somewhat mitigated the less desirable socioeconomic consequences of modernization. European countries also achieved their progress within a neutral or favorable external environment. For example, the European Community—now the European Union—contributed to Europe's stability and greatly accelerated the modernization and democratization of countries such as Italy, Spain, Portugal, Greece, and Ireland—all either Catholic or Orthodox Christian countries. Meanwhile, the North Atlantic Treaty Organization (NATO) provided the security umbrella under which Europe's reconstruction and modernization could take place. The security shield provided by the United States to countries such as Japan, Taiwan, and South Korea also helped their modernization and eventual democratization. In the case of the Muslim countries, by contrast, the external environment for the past two centuries has been unfavorable and has acted more as a hindrance than as a help to their modernization. By the mid-nineteenth century, nearly all of the Muslim world was colonized or was under great-power tutelage. Nor did this state of dependency and vulnerability to external forces and pressures end with the end of colonialism. The dynamics of the cold war era, in particular, produced many distortions in the development process of significant numbers of Muslim countries. Particularly, the political imperative of the cold war and the requirements of East-West rivalry hampered the Islamic world's democratization. In short, factors such as colonialism, the fallout of the cold war, and great-power policies have often been serious hindrances to modernization, especially as they have interacted with domestic dynamics; these factors have been an even greater obstacle to democratization.

Yet, despite a strong body of historical evidence showing that modernization is a complex process and its course is affected by a multiplicity of factors, the frustration caused by many failures of modernization in the non-Western and, especially, the Muslim world led to a strong revival of the culturalist thesis in the early 1990s, a perspective that is still popular and influential.

MODERNIZATION, DEMOCRACY, AND CULTURE

The relationship between modernization and democracy is ambiguous and depends largely on how the term "modern" is defined. In one definition of "modern," no society can be considered completely modernized without a democratic form of government. In other words, by this definition democracy is an integral part of the modernization package.

Yet the history of both European modernization and that of the non-Western world provides ample examples of societies that acquired many features of a "modern" society, such as industrialization, urbanization, secularization, delineation of public and private spheres, and the transformation of traditional patterns of socioeconomic relations and values, without becoming democracies. Nazi Germany and the Soviet Union are the best examples of modernization without democratization, thus raising the question whether such societies can be considered modern—or whether there are different types and degrees of modernity. In other words, are there multiple modernities? Meanwhile, as with modernization, early on a link was established between cultural and religious traits and values and prospects for democracy. In this context, Roman Catholicism, Orthodox Christianity, and Asian cultures and religions—with their emphasis on order, hierarchy, and the primacy of the community over the individual—were considered less conducive to democracy. As with modernization, Protestantism was viewed as providing a more propitious environment for the growth of democracy. The following quote from Martin Seymour Lipset illustrates this point: "Historically, there have been negative relationships between democracy and Catholicism, Orthodox Christianity, Islam, and Confucianism; conversely, Protestantism and democracy have been positively correlated."[19] Earlier, in his famous article in *Foreign Affairs* in 1993, Samuel Huntington declared that Islam and Confucianism are incompatible with democracy.[20] However, during the ascendancy of developmentalist thinking (1960s to mid-1970s) regarding the modernization of the underdeveloped parts of the world, a more optimistic view in respect to the prospects for the modernization of the less developed world prevailed. During this period, it was assumed that modernization eventually would lead to democratization, even if these countries had first to go through an authoritarian phase to achieve rapid modernization.[21] The dynamics of the cold war and the East-West competition for the hearts and minds of the third world countries enhanced the propensity to be optimistic regarding the prospects of modernization and democratization in the non-Western world. Consequently, in this period, cultural factors were given less weight in determining the course and spread of modernization compared to other, notably economic, variables.

In some cases, such as Spain under Franco, Chile under Pinochet, plus Taiwan, South Korea, and Singapore, authoritarian systems did achieve considerable levels of modernization. However, in the overwhelming majority of developing countries, authoritarianism did not result in modernization, at least not to a sufficient degree, and it certainly hampered the development of institutions, structures, and patterns of behavior necessary for a democratic form of government.

In the 1980s, the transition to democracy of a number of countries in Latin America and Africa, some with low levels of modernization, challenged the thesis that democratization is not possible without an advanced level of modernization and undermined the theory of the authoritarian road to modernization.

However, many of these new democracies remain fragile, and their future viability is threatened by daunting social and economic problems. These trends and countertrends also illustrate the difficulties involved in defining the concept of "modern" and the nature of the relationship between modernization and democracy.[22] Moreover, the concept of democracy itself has evolved, and different definitions have emerged, thus making the task of establishing a causal relationship between modernization and democracy more difficult. To illustrate, the liberal democracy of the present-day Western world would be unrecognizable from the perspective of the early democracies of the late-eighteenth- and nineteenth-century Europe and United States.[23]

In the West, the evolution of democracy has involved a broadening of its scope so as to incorporate groups that were previously disenfranchised, such as non–property owners, women, and ethnic, racial, and religious minorities. The concept of what constitutes basic individual rights has also been enlarged. In the non-Western world, most democracies fall short of this liberal model, hence the questions: Are there different types and levels of democracy, and what is their validity? Also, can there be intermediary stages of democracy as judged against the ideal of liberal democracy? Is progress toward liberal democracy linear, or can there be reversals in this process? European history, best exemplified by the rise of Fascism and Nazism in the 1920s and 1930s, shows that dramatic reversals are possible.

Be that as it may, the fact that a significant number of non-Western countries, notably those in the Muslim world, did not take part in the so-called third–wave democratization of the 1980s[24] once more brought to the fore the role of culture in helping or hindering democracy, as well as the thesis that some cultures are particularly inimical to democracy. For example, Seymour Martin Lipset, one of the early proponents of a close linkage between socioeconomic indicators and prospects for democracy, wrote that "cross national historical evaluations of the correlates of democracy have found that cultural factors appear even more important than economic ones."[25] However, as with modernization, the actual experience of many countries belonging to non-Protestant cultures shows that culture is not an insurmountable barrier to democratization. Thus, once deeply Catholic, European countries such as Italy, Spain, Portugal, and Ireland now have democratic systems, and other Catholic majority countries such as Poland, Hungary, and the Czech Republic have also established democratic governments since the late 1980s. Greece, an Orthodox Christian country, has made a successful transition to democracy. Many Latin American countries with large Catholic populations have also established democratic systems.

Meanwhile, the process of democratization in Taiwan and South Korea shows that Confucianism is not a hindrance to democracy. Even in the Muslim world, there are examples of democratic forms of government, notably in Turkey, Malaysia, Mali, Senegal, and Bangladesh—albeit with many weaknesses and vulnerabilities. In short, the historical evidence does not support a culturally deterministic explanation for failure in either modernization or democratization in the Muslim world and elsewhere.

To point out the limitations of the culturalist thesis is not to suggest that cultural factors do not play a role in the process of modernization and democratization. They do. But while in some cases religion sanctifies certain cultural practices not rooted in religion, it is not the main determinant of either modernization or democratization. For example, regarding gender issues, the patriarchal culture is more of an inhibiting factor than religion per se. Therefore, noting the limitations of the culturalist thesis is to stress the point that other factors play equally important roles in these processes. Furthermore, it is a reminder that cultural patterns are not immutable; they do change in response to economic changes and external influences.

Therefore, the purpose of this volume is: (1) to identify those factors that have collectively been responsible for the Muslim world's poor record of modernization and democratization; (2) to show how similar factors have affected the course of both processes in non-Muslim countries; (3) to assess the relative role of cultural factors; and (4) to suggest some remedies to the obstacles to modernization and democratization in the Muslim world.

The basic methodology throughout the study is historical and comparative. The study is divided into three parts. Part I deals with broad thematic issues, such as the relationships between modernization and culture, between modernization and democratization, and among modernization, democratization, and gender, plus the question of Islam and its relation to modernity and democracy. It also addresses the question of various responses to the challenge of modernity in non-European countries, including Muslim countries, thus establishing patterns of similarity across cultures.

Part II looks into the impact of both internal factors—such as the size and scale of the military and its role in society and politics and the economic structures of society—and external factors—such as colonialism, great-power rivalry, intervention, and aspects of international economic and trading systems—on the process of modernization and democratization.

Part III consists of a number of case studies, showing how particular types of interactions among these factors in different regional and national contexts have affected the process and outcome of efforts at modernization and democratization.

The conclusion brings together the insights provided in different chapters and identifies the most important themes to be considered in any analysis of the twin processes of modernization and democratization in the Muslim world, and it puts the cultural factors in a proper perspective. These broad themes and lessons drawn from the case studies, in turn, suggest possible remedies and lines of action—both for Muslim countries and for key external actors, notably the great powers and international institutions—most likely to help advance the Muslim world's modernization and democratization. It also draws attention to those actions that could create future problems in achieving these goals and therefore should be avoided.

NOTES

1. United Nations, "List of Least Developed Countries (as of December 2003)," http://www.un.org/special-rep/ohrlls/ldc/list.htm. For the 2003 criteria for the least developed countries, see United Nations, Committee for Development Policy, "Report on the Fifth Session, 7–11 April 2003," Economic and Social Council, Official Records, Supplement 13, 2003, http://www.unescap.org/MDG/LDC.asp. Thresholds for inclusion in the list of least developed countries are population less than 75 million; per capita gross national income (GNI) less than US$750 million; human assets index (HAI) less than 55; and economic vulnerability index (EVI) greater than 37. A country must meet the last three criteria for inclusion. Thresholds for graduation from the list of least developed

countries are per capita GNI greater than US$900; HAI greater than 61; and EVI less than 33. A country must meet at least two of the criteria for graduation.

2. Asli Guveli and Serdar Kilickaplan, "A Ranking of Islamic Countries in Terms of Their Levels of Socio-Economic Development," *Journal of Economic Cooperation* 21, no. 1 (2000): 97–114, annex 3: Socio-Economic Development List.

3. World Bank Group, "Data by Country," http://www.worldbank.org/data/country data/countrydata.html. GDP information excludes Afghanistan, Iraq, and Somalia because no information was available. All data are for 2002 except when not available; then the most recent data available were used: Bahrain (2001), Brunei Darussalam (1998), Kuwait (2001), Libya (1998), Qatar (1998), Saudi Arabia (2001), United Arab Emirates (1998).

4. European Union, "Eurostat Yearbook 2003," http://europa.eu.int/comm/eurostat/ Public/datashop/print-product/EN?catalogue=Eurostat&product=freeselect3-EN&mode=download. U.S. dollar equivalent was calculated using current market value on November 3, 2003, with the universal currency converter at http://www.xe.com/ucc/ convert.cgi.

5. European Commission, "General Publications," http://europa.eu.int/comm/publi cations/booklets/eu_glance/14/index_en.htm.

6. World Bank Group, "Data by Country."

7. World Trade Organization, "Trade Statistics, Historical Series, Merchandise Trade, and Commercial Services Trade Table," http://www.wto.org/english/res_e/statis_e/ statis_e.htm#worldtrade. This number was calculated by summing the merchandise and commercial services exports for each Muslim majority Organization of Islamic Conference (OIC) country and dividing the total by the total world merchandise and commercial services exports. All data used are the most recent available. All merchandise exports data are for 2002 except for those of Djibouti (2001). All commercial services data are for 2001 except for those of Jordan, Malaysia, Morocco, Tunisia, and Turkey (2002); Algeria, Brunei, Burkina-Faso, Chad, Comoros, Djibouti, Gambia, Mali, Mauritania, Niger, Nigeria, Senegal, Sierra Leone, Syria, and Yemen (2000); and Libya and Uzbekistan (1999). No service exports data are available for Afghanistan, Lebanon, Qatar, Somalia, Turkmenistan, and United Arab Emirates.

8. World Bank Group, *World Development Indicators 2003* (Washington, DC: World Bank, 2003), 202–4.

9. Ibid., 46–48.

10. United Nations Development Programme, "Creating Opportunities for Future Generations," *Arab Human Development Report 2002* (New York: United Nations Development Programme, 2002).

11. Alexander Gerschenkron, *Economic Backwardness in Historical Perspective* (Cambridge, MA: Belknap Press of Harvard University Press, 1962), 29–30.

12. Samuel P. Huntington, *The Clash of Civilizations and the Remaking of World Order* (New York: Touchstone Books, 1996); Bernard Lewis, *What Went Wrong? Western Impact and Middle Eastern Response* (New York: Oxford University Press, 2002), and "The Roots of Muslim Rage," *Atlantic Monthly*, September 1990.

13. Max Weber, *The Protestant Ethic and the Spirit of Capitalism,* trans. Talcott Parsons (London: Unwin University Books, 1974).

14. Weber, *Protestant Ethic*, 21; for Weber's view on Islam, see his *The Sociology of Religion*, 5th ed. (Boston: Beacon Press, 1969), 263–65.

15. Weber, *Sociology of Religion*, 265–66.

16. Ibid.

17. Gerschenkron, *Economic Backwardness*, 6–7.

18. Stuart Hall et al., eds., *Modernity: An Introduction to Modern Societies* (Cambridge, MA: Blackwell Publishers, 1996).

19. Seymour Martin Lipset, "The Social Requisites of Democracy Revisited," *American Sociological Review* 59, no. 1 (February 1995): 5.

20. Samuel P. Huntington, "The Clash of Civilizations?" *Foreign Affairs* 72, no. 3 (Summer 1993).

21. Daniel Lerner, *The Passing of Traditional Society: Modernizing the Middle East* (Glencoe, IL: Free Press, 1958).

22. Hall et al., *Modernity*.

23. On the evolution of the concept of democracy, see David Held, *Models of Democracy* (Cambridge: Polity Press, 1987).

24. Samuel P. Huntington, *The Third Wave: Democratization in the Late Twentieth Century* (Norman: University of Oklahoma Press, 1993), 281.

25. Lipset, "Social Requisites," 6.

I

Thematic Issues

2

Culture and Development

Heather Deegan

THEORIES OF CULTURE AND DEVELOPMENT

The interconnection between Islam and culture in Muslim countries has been held as detrimental to their economic, social, and political development. To assess the validity of this thesis requires an understanding of how cultural forces operate within a society and the extent to which religion informs traditional patterns of life. For more than a century eminent analysts have striven to explain and understand the relationship between development and cultural change. They have asked whether some cultures are more conducive to development than others. Can economic progress take place without a massive shift in societal values and behavioral patterns? Does development inevitably erode primordial loyalties and encourage a new cultural enlightenment based on communication and interests? The thrust of their argument suggested that there was, indeed, a strong link between culture and development. Using a comparative approach, often closely patterned on Western models of development, these analysts identified a process of modernization against which a country's progression could be charted. The model assumed many guises but tended to coalesce around certain characteristics, namely, rationalization, national integration, social stratification, economic change, and political autonomy.[1] As defined by Samuel Huntington, political autonomy implied the development of organizations and procedures that transcend interests of particular social groups.[2]

It was assumed that as countries developed, their populations would shift toward the adoption of scientific knowledge and evolve from subsistence farming to commercial agricultural production and industrialization. Such changes involved great social and cultural alteration, thus marking a break in established norms of social and economic life, including the erosion of familial, kinship, religious, and cultural ties regarded as restrictive traditional forces.[3] For some, political participation was seen as necessary to development, thus distinguishing the traditional society from a modernizing state.[4] Others believed that initially a more authoritarian system would be more conducive to economic development. "Development first, democracy later" was the theme.[5]

Inevitably, attitudes toward social activities and societal change would vary among different cultures depending on their values and beliefs. Also, societies were comprised of structures whose "cultural systems" exercised organized patterns of influence over the whole community, sometimes irrespective and independent of particular individuals.[6] In general, then, cultural factors could serve as an overall integrative function in society. Yet often a complex relationship existed between culture and a social structure. According to Emile Durkheim, societal values constituted the component that reached the highest level of generality, for they were "conceptions of the desirable society that are held in common by its members."[7] Values and norms were specified within the cultural system and determined the manner in which "people behave as they are expected to in a given situation."[8] Yet modernization as a complex process of social change had the capacity to dislodge previous cultural systems and value structures.[9]

The requirements and outcome of development—improved literacy rates, expanding economies, exposure to mass communications—subjected a society's institutional framework to continual challenges to adapt to rapidly developing productive forces. Economic modernization was intended to eliminate traditional beliefs, ways of life, and patterns of authority. The process presented difficulties, particularly in traditional societies where value systems tended to be "prescriptive."[10] A prescriptive system was characterized by "the comprehensiveness and specificity of its value commitments and by its consequent lack of flexibility. Motivation is frozen . . . through commitment to a vast range of relatively specific norms governing almost every situation in life." Whereas in a modern society a degree of flexibility had to be introduced in economic, political, and social spheres, in "prescriptive" societies a religious system would attempt to regulate all those areas. "Thus, changes in economic or political institutions—not to speak of family and education—in traditional societies tended to have ultimate religious implications."[11] In certain societies, notably those in the Muslim world, it was believed that traditional culture was synonymous with religion and rested "everywhere on an Islamic basis."[12]

The relationships among religion, tradition, and development became more complicated during the second half of the twentieth century when the dynamics of modernity—social, economic, and political progress—combined, for the first time, as imperative challenges. It was at this stage that analysts claimed cultural forces could inhibit modernization in certain societies. R. B. Bellah argued that a society's value system or culture must "change from a prescriptive type to a 'principial' mode" for economic, political, and social change to occur. What distinguished prescriptive and principial societies were their belief systems. In a principial state the religious system would not attempt a detailed regulation of all aspects of economic, political, and social life. Religion would not disappear from the culture of a society, but its function would alter: "In modern society there is a differentiation between the levels of religion and social ideology which makes possible greater flexibility at both levels."[13] Such separation allows social, economic, and political reformers to engage with secular ideas without being regarded as cultural religious heretics.

CULTURAL FACTORS AND THE PROCESS OF DEVELOPMENT

To what extent, then, has there been a specific culture regarded as propitious for development as compared to others, viewed as inhibiting or hindering forces? Max Weber argued that a dynamic religion could cause radical change in societal and economic structures. The energetic spirit of modern capitalism was powerfully influenced by the values of Protestantism. Economic rationalism, Weber believed, derived from the religious revolution of the sixteenth century. The term described an economic system based neither on custom nor on tradition, but "on the deliberate and systematic adjustment of economic means to the attainment of the objective of pecuniary profit."[14] Far from there being an "inevitable conflict between moneymaking and piety," the two were united under the "Protestant ethic." In particular, Calvinism, based on the teachings of John Calvin, encouraged religious rationalism in the context of spiritual values and objectives.[15]

Protestantism differed markedly from Roman Catholicism and those religious orders based on vows of obedience, poverty, and chastity. Within Catholicism, the church would mediate to the believer through a papal intermediary and through the sacraments, especially penance. In Protestantism there was no such mediator, a trait that contributed to a strong sense of individualism and a consciousness that the power of God worked through the person. The individual, therefore, had to fulfill "God's will" not through a life of contemplative prayer but through diligence, self-discipline, and work. This activity provided, Weber argued, the religious basis of capitalism.[16] Within the sociology of religion, then, "Calvinistic Protestantism transformed Western culture towards an anti-magical, disciplined life-world."[17] Weber's hypothesis continued to attract much attention years after its presentation and influenced numerous studies measuring "culture" and the role of religion.[18]

For Bryan Turner, the Protestant ethic argument raised two major issues. First, rationality was tied to modernity, in that for a society to become modern it had to "undergo and embrace the disciplines of goal-directed rational conduct." Second, a clear division was drawn between a progressive Christian West and a retarding Islamic Orient.[19] Certainly, Weber had little regard for Islam as a modernizing religion, but he was equally critical of Catholicism. Friedrich Engels also noted the unchanging nature of Muslim societies and their economic conditions, despite periodic mass uprisings.

Ernest Gellner believed the strength of Islam rested not only in its commitment to a "firmly delineated divine message," which provided a firm social framework, but also in the way it did not "sacralize" daily life: "Islam may be socially demanding but it does not abolish the dualism which saves the sacred from being compromised by the profane."[20] Yet it must be acknowledged that less than fifty years ago Roman Catholicism observed very strict duties, including daily prayers at 6 a.m. Judaism has rigorous devotional practices, and Orthodox Christianity as practiced in Greece calls for the celebration of saints.

Gellner, however, distinguished between "high" and "low" Islam, which, although at times generating conflict, had generally "interpenetrated and tolerated each other in peaceful détente." The high culture of Islam developed from its scriptural, scholastic, puritanical, urban, and merchant background, whereas its low or folk culture was expressed in communities and brotherhoods springing up around Muslim saints. The high form presented a normative image of the religion that society would endeavor, but often fail, to uphold.[21] At a societal level, religious continuity depends on the extent to which belief and ritual patterns are passed on to each generation as a process of acculturation.[22] Religion then becomes an important and meaningful connection between generations and provides individuals with methods of confronting and dealing with life's problems.

Religious phenomena, according to Durkheim, were naturally arranged in two distinct categories: beliefs and rites.[23] The objective of religion was to raise humans above themselves and to instruct them to lead better lives than they would otherwise follow if left to their own individual whims.[24] Durkheim regarded religion as a necessary and vital force in maintaining social stability and an indispensable means of social constraint, because religion was a "social act," in which rites and ceremonies assumed social significance. These processes symbolically tied individuals to their kinship community. Yet, for Gellner, Islam was "trans-ethnic" and "trans-social" and did not "equate faith with the beliefs of any one community or society."[25] In short, it was universal. The strength of interactions among religion, culture, and society depends on the nature of religion and the type of society. Religious belief and practice tends to vary according to a society's size and mobility. As societies urbanize or industrialize, and as different class structures emerge and are exposed to altered value systems, the relationships among religion, culture, and society change. However, Gideon Sjoberg, in his examination of traditional and transitional societies, found that although differences existed between folk and feudal communities, both had "sacred-value orientations" that at times made them resistant to progress.[26]

CHANGE AND RESISTANCE

The issue of assumed resistance to change is interesting because over the years seemingly negative cultural factors have changed or been overcome. One classical example is that of Italy's postwar economic development. Studies of 1950s Italy highlight the negative and extreme backwardness of peasant culture in parts of the country. This was due to "the inability of the villagers to act together for their common good or, indeed, for any good transcending the immediate, material interest of the family."[27] Equally, the dominance of the Catholic Church on Italian peasant society made it "defensive and inward looking."

From the nineteenth century, the church had intervened in society through rural banks, co-operatives, charities, education programs, and youth work, thus becoming a dominant social force. Yet the 1960s and 1970s witnessed "a profound social revolution" and an "economic miracle."[28] By 1970, Italian per capita income, which had lagged far behind that of the northern European countries, had reached 60 percent of that of France and 82 percent of that of Britain, yet religion continued to be an important element in Italian culture. So, how did this happen? First, there was massive internal migration: 15.5 million Italians changed their place of residence between 1952 and 1962, and the young spearheaded this migration to the North of the country. Often, kinship ties were used initially for housing and support, and urban accommodation became better than rural provision. However, one significant dynamic of Italian economic development was the desire of the young to "escape from the oppression of the extended family."[29]

The internal migration to urban areas boosted the number of local entrepreneurs and contributed to the buildup of small-scale industrialization. These economic developments ultimately had an impact on social areas—divorce, for example—and although the church did not shift on that issue, John XXIII's papacy was liberalizing in its ecumenicalism. So an amalgam of economic and social changes led to a significant shift in the cultural paradigm of Italy in a relatively short period of time. Also, Spain's and Portugal's emergence from authoritarian governments in the 1970s and Ireland's economic progress during the 1980s took place against the backdrop of the social and cultural influence of the Catholic Church. However, although religion was a powerful force in all those societies, there was a clear distinction between the realms of church and state, and Roman Catholicism did not presume to have an "alternative" economic model. Rather, its contemporary "liberation theology" tended to be little more than an attempt to contain the social impact of capitalism. In fact, the perspective of Pope Leo XIII's encyclicals, published from 1878, on unbridled capitalism was censorious: "A small number of very rich men have been able to lay upon the teeming masses of the laboring poor a yoke little better than that of slavery itself." Yet the church was equally critical of socialism on the grounds that it denied ownership of property. The encyclicals covered a range of topics, including civil society, antisocialism, and human freedom and demonstrated instructively the church's renewed engagement with social and political thought.[30] While remaining faithful to its doctrine, it had loosened its grip on the cultural and social realms. But it must be recognized that other external factors were also especially important. The Marshall Plan and the European Community both spearheaded and consolidated the economic progress of southern Europe and Ireland.

Similarly, Greek Orthodox Christianity had communitarian tendencies, which could be regarded as a hindrance to development. Traditionalist value systems, expressed in the primacy of familial relations, the importance of village communities, the role of religion, and the modesty of women, were long established features of Greek society. Cultural change in Greece has been regarded as slow, not really taking off until the late twentieth century, despite the fact that considerable economic progress had taken place at least two decades earlier. Greece's economy thrived from the 1960s with rapid urban change, increases in consumerism and tourism, and a general embourgeoisement. In Greece's case a clear paradox exists. Whereas strongly held sentiments about family and community are attitudes conventionally considered detrimental to socioeconomic growth, the expansion of Greece's urban areas was significant. During this period, however, cultural sentiments shifted only marginally, with no "fundamental changes" in the "central personal values of popular culture."[31] The village community cohabited well with industrializing urban society, and sacred beliefs did not stifle social change. Other internal and external factors played a part in economic development. First, the church recognized the transition Greece's social order was experiencing and chose not to prevent economic and social development.[32] Second, Greece's accession to the European Community in 1981 established it economically and politically.

More recently, attention has focused on the progress of Asian nations and China's development potential. In particular, the so-called Asian values, namely, the emphasis on discipline and social cohesion and the existence of a powerful work ethic have been viewed as key factors in the area's development. The rise of East Asia has also challenged "deep-rooted conceptions of economic development, political modernization, social integration and cultural change."[33] Certainly, there have been considerable shifts in academic opinion and explanation as to the reasons for the region's growth. Recent scholarship has viewed Confucian beliefs as instrumental in developing a functional equivalent of the Protestant ethic. While emphasizing the values of community and family, Confucians did not do so at the expense of individuality, as exemplified by the Confucian calling "Establish others for the sake of establishing oneself; enlarge others for the sake of enlarging oneself," and by stressing the importance of education.[34] If these notions of self-improvement are functional equivalents of a work ethic in Protestantism, then Asian economic growth presents a challenge to Weber's belief of instrumental rationality and received judgments on traditionalism and modernization.

Some have questioned whether "Asian values" are compatible with liberal democracy. With the emphasis on discipline and order, authoritarian regimes have been a feature of the region, but Francis Fukuyama argues that social stratification can take place through educational achievement and the emergence of a middle class capable of providing "a durable basis for democratic transition."[35] Yet during the early twentieth century, China was held as an example of rigid traditionalism, and Confucianism was regarded as a complete way of life that "stood for reaction and obscurantism."[36] Other analysts found cities in South and Southeast Asia to be agglomerations of folk society unlike their Western counterparts.[37]

In sum, other socioreligious cultures and traditional societies, once regarded as resistant to change, over time have not hindered development.[38]

IS ISLAM ANTIDEVELOPMENT?

The transformation of non-Protestant Christian societies, plus those of a number of Asian countries, with religious and cultural traditions perceived as hindering development, has raised the question of whether Islam is antidevelopment. It has been argued that far from providing an impetus for future change and development, Islamic society has followed a cyclical process of movement from "central authority supported by tribal federation, through urban impiety and degeneracy to the crisis which renews the impulse of tribal revolt and thus instantiates a new central authority."[39] Like Weber, Karl Marx considered religion to be closely associated with the economic structure of society but in a different way.[40] Whereas Weber believed religious ideas could change an economic system, Marx regarded religion as a by-product of economic conditions. Historical materialism rendered "otherworldly" religions redundant. Where religiosity continued to flourish, it did so because of social needs. Once the social factors that produced those needs were removed, religion would lose its function.

Both Weber and Marx regarded "Oriental" or "Asiatic" societies as economically stagnant. Thus, a contrast was drawn between a dynamic, modernizing West and a retarded and static Orient. Ali Mazrui contested these views by concentrating on the issues of production and distribution. He argued that despite Marx's apparent focus on the "factors of production," he was more concerned with distribution. As Mazrui argues, as in Islam, "two of its five pillars are concerned with distribution and consumption." The Islamic tax of *zakat* was intended to distribute funds to the poor and needy, while the prohibition of Ramadan curtailed consumption.[41] No doubt nascent forms of capitalism can be found in early Islam in the context of profit and mercantilism. Trade has been a core activity within Islamic societies since its early days and was regarded as "an honorable profession by Muhammad."[42] However, the Qur'an prohibits *riba*, which is generally taken to include all forms of interest payment. Yet, in this, Islam's view is similar to those of mediaeval Christianity and Judaism. More recent and instructive are the parallels between Pope Leo XIII's encyclicals and Abu'l-A'la Mawdudi's critique of the social consequences of capitalist development: "No opportunity is left in these days for small industrialists and agriculturalists to earn their livelihood freely. Everyone is compelled to accept the lot of slaves, servants and laborers of these financial princes and captains of industry."[43]

Yet neither wished to adopt socialism, which was criticized as denying spiritual development and prohibiting the ownership of property. Communism, as a political system, was also viewed as concentrating economic and political power in the hands of a small minority. Consequently, neither favored secular Marxism. Meanwhile, similarities in their views suggest that Islam, as interpreted over time, shares many principles with other religions. It partly shares Calvin's pursuit of profit but remains critical of capitalism in true Jesuitical tradition. It defends trade and mercantilism but places barriers to their development. It condemns socialism but regards itself as socially and economically just. Far from Sayyid Qutb's notion of Islam "as a modern ideology capable of absorbing all scientific and technological innovations without being tainted with their philosophical substratum," at closer inspection Islam appears more contradictory.[44] The contested interpretations of the relationship between Islam and capitalism, especially among Muslims, prompted the seminal study by the neo-Marxist Maxime Rodinson in 1966. He concluded that "the correlation between Islam and any particular economic system has emerged as being very largely inconclusive." Certainly, the notion that Islam basically opposed capitalism was nothing more than a "myth," while Muslim societies' passing attraction to socialism was not related to the "precepts of Islam."[45] Regarding accusations that Islam encourages fatalism and inaction, Rodinson's response is succinct; the sacred writings of Judaism and Christianity contain "much, if not more, to justify that attitude than can be found in Islam."[46]

Nevertheless, some Muslim economists see Islamic economics as offering an alternative vision. Whereas the fundamental concept of neoclassical economics rests on the individual operating within economic rationalism, the Islamic approach is supposed to consider wider issues, including "social, ethical and religious circumstances, inclinations and beliefs" of people. As Masudul Choudhury explains, the notion of "ethico-economics" or "humanomics" cannot be viewed in the sense of economic maximization.[47]

This claim rather obscures the fact that apart from certain "ethical" investment proscriptions, for example, eschewing alcohol manufacturing companies, Islamic economics has failed to produce wealth and social justice, as evidenced by the case of Iran. In certain states, numerous Islamic investment companies (IICs) have been established. In Egypt alone, more than 100 such companies exist, with an estimated deposit value of US $2.3 billion.[48] These institutions convey political overtones: "The IICs are the economic symbol of rising Islamic tendencies in Egypt. The shift in the ideological makeup of Egyptians toward Islam has made them ready to deposit their money in the IICs. They use non-usurious concepts of economics and Islamic symbols. They open their speeches and their advertisements with Qur'anic verses."[49]

Islamic groups "propagate the idea of an independent Islamic economy," and these companies play an important role.[50] However, the attraction of these organizations to the wider Muslim society may indicate not only the powerful cultural appeal of religion but also popular disenchantment with governmental institutions and those affiliated with the ruling classes.

The extent to which Islamic approaches to development can be successful is open to question. It is claimed that a deep ambivalence exists within Islamic economics toward modern capitalism: "Capital in itself is not the root of the problem . . . only by placing capital within its comprehensive view of life, Islam restores its productive and useful function in society: man becomes a trustee of God delegated to undertake certain activities and refrain from others."[51] Yet such alleged uneasiness may not be accurate, as demonstrated recently in an interesting multivariate study by Marcus Noland. Noland examined the economic impact of Muslim communities in certain nations in which they were weighted for their "population share" and "distance from Mecca."[52] He found in his econometric analysis that at either "cross-country or within-country level," Islam did not appear to be a "drag on growth or an anchor on development. If anything, the opposite appears to be true."[53] While it has been argued that because Islam cannot be "relegated to some unobtrusive corner of society" it has to be replaced in order for countries to develop, it is becoming apparent that more prosaic reasons may explain slow and hesitant economic development of some parts of the Muslim world.[54] Factors that played such an important role in the development of the West and, more recently, Japan have failed to emerge, particularly in the Arab Muslim world.

Some analysts, however, have pointed to the existence of cultural inhibitors, that is, despite the claims of Islamic economic purists, no activated work ethic actually exists in the Arab world as distinct from the wider Muslim region.[55] So while Muslims in Malaysia and elsewhere work diligently, their coreligionists in the Middle East are less willing to engage in manual labor. This suggests that factors other than an all-pervading homogeneous Islamic culture are at play. Economies buoyed by oil rentierism or indirectly through remittance payments have become distorted and malfunctioning. According to the findings of a UN report, the creation of "productive jobs" together with the provision of "better education and improved health care" would make a significant contribution to development in a number of Muslim countries.[56] As Noland makes clear, "If one is concerned about economic performance in predominantly Muslim regions or countries, conventional economic analysis may yield greater insight than the sociology of religion."[57]

CULTURE VERSUS OTHER FACTORS IN DEVELOPMENT

There is no doubt that there are profound structural weaknesses in the economies of the Middle East and North Africa (MENA). The low level of investment flows to the region has occasioned predictions that, far from improving, the situation could actually deteriorate during the coming decade with much of the region sliding "to the bottom of world development tables."[58] What role does culture play in this economic stagnation? If culture is understood by four clusters of meaning—ethics and beliefs, collective social development, arts and self-expression, and a general way of life—certain significant features emerge.[59] Most important is familism and the dominance of the paterfamilias, which restrict social and economic mobility for the young and for women. When these traditions are sanctioned by orthodoxy, their impact is felt in all four areas of cultural definition, as well as in the economy. A good example of this is the low level of female participation in the labor force in the MENA region.[60] (See Chapter 7 in this volume by Valentine Moghadam.)

Cultural traditionalism, then, significantly hampers the emergence of developed patterns of economic behavior. Yet cultural and religious structures and patterns of behavior do not always inhibit economic progress. In Italy's development in the 1970s, just such features were apparent, but the young rebelled through internal migration and employment, unleashing a socioeconomic transformation that ultimately changed the country's cultural environment. Similar traditional loyalties have not prevented Asian countries, including predominantly Muslim nations such as Malaysia and Indonesia, from developing. Around 60 percent of MENA's population is estimated to be under the age of twenty-five years, but their experience differs from that of young Italian malcontents in that migration means either working in an oil-rich country or permanently moving overseas, thereby depleting the area of potential innovators. The general cultural environment of the MENA region also fails to recognize the full economic contribution that young women can make to the overall benefit of society. It is expected that the role of women, religion, and family will, to some extent, remain unchanged. Yet this situation does not exist in all regions with Muslim communities, such as Southeast Asia. Noland factored into his econometric study of Muslim communities in Malaysia and elsewhere a control for "any possible negative impact of Islam on female educational attainment" and still found a positive coefficient.[61]

It is the varied nature of development within different Islamic societies that is interesting. In Iran significant numbers of women are both highly educated and engaged in professional employment. Yet overall the economy remains restricted because of the policies of the religious elite. In Pakistan, of $25 billion worker remittances, little was invested in productive sectors.[62] A contradiction seems to exist, then, in that although traditionalism can operate as an obstacle to individual expression, religious leaders have recognized the important role the young can play in furthering their own political agenda. Radical Islam has courted young men and women, playing on their frustrations and disaffection with existing governments. So while cultural traditionalism is expressed in the acceptance of conservative norms of behavior, extremist religious groups desire more radical, antimodern changes to society. This dichotomy may rest in the cultural tensions in parts of the Muslim world in that a distinction exists between two components: new is exciting versus old is good. While new technology is desired and utilized by political elites, homegrown entrepreneurialism in the MENA region is in short supply. Although Islam presumes it has a complete model for life, in reality it contains a set of principles that do not comprise a blueprint for the modern world.

Over the long term, the Islamic religious-socioeconomic agenda suited the age in which it was conceived 1,400 years ago. To revisit texts and beliefs of any religion of that time will produce doctrinal documents appropriate for that era; some may appear prescient, others reactionary, but the important factor is that they are all historical positions. Economic and political modernization in the West hinged upon developments in printing and communication; agricultural and industrial revolutions based on technical innovation and invention; massive increases in manual labor and productivity; greater knowledge and education for the masses; and the inculcation and consolidation of consumer demand. In the recent economic growth of East Asia, similar factors have been decisive. Yet the family continues to serve as a vital institution for "social cohesiveness, moral education, spiritual growth and capital formation."[63]

One crucial factor in the emergence and development of early capitalism was the economic freedom induced by changing interpretations of Christianity. Today, other religions have adjusted to economic development. The assumed dichotomy between tradition and modernity is no longer clear-cut. Primordial ties such as familism and religion still feature prominently in the public space of a range of different countries. It seems no longer possible to relegate them into the background as residual cultural forces symbolizing emotional attachments to the past. Assumptions of retarding cultural forces inevitably hindering development require reexamination. It is not in the interests of a clearly differentiated Muslim world to be mired in the past. However, cultural forces are not the only ones determining this situation. The political environment is interlinked with the economic sphere. Moreover, today, notions of culture are not simply an amalgam of beliefs, values, and customs but include wider dimensions and features such as literature, lifestyle, media, artistic expression, philosophy, public arena, human rights, personal choice, and identity. It is in these areas that the Muslim world's cultural paradigm shift should occur. If that were to happen, new cultural forces could forge development and political change.

CONCLUSION

Is Islamic culture holding back development in the Muslim world? This question cannot be answered without raising three points. First, "Islam" should be unlinked from "culture." Culture, as expressed in much of the Muslim world, is essentially a form of traditionalism that has been apparent in numerous other non-Muslim states. Traditional behavior patterns, invariably informed by piety and often regarded as resistant to change, have mutated into different cultural articulations over time. Cultural traditionalism cannot be regarded as an immutable and permanent obstacle to socioeconomic and political change. Islam's interaction with traditionalism, however, is complicated because the religion does not operate purely at a social and collective level. It also assumes economic and legal powers. These Islamic economic restrictions can combine with autocratic and bureaucratic political environments to suppress development and market-led expansion in *some* Muslim states.

Second, there is economic and cultural variation within the Muslim world. Attitudes to labor and competitive advantage in Malaysia are different from those in Middle Eastern states. Islamic influences are neither homogeneous nor absolute.

Third, economic stagnation seems linked to the traditionalist constraints placed on young people. Modernity and democracy are powerful global forces that cannot be ignored, and it is clear that the instruments of development have to be absorbed over time. However, flawed international perceptions and notions of Islamic and Muslim cultural exceptionalism should not be permitted to undermine movement toward real and meaningful change.

NOTES

1. Samuel P. Huntington, "Political Development and Political Decay," *World Politics* 17, no. 3 (April 1965): 386–405; Karl W. Deutsch, *Nationalism and Social Communication* (New York: John Wiley & Sons, 1953).

2. Huntington, "Political Development."

3. Neil J. Smelser, "Mechanics of Change and Adjustment to Change," in Jason L. Finkle and Richard W. Gable, eds., *Political Development and Social Change* (New York: John Wiley & Sons, 1966), 29.

4. Daniel Lerner, *The Passing of Traditional Society: Modernizing the Middle East* (Glencoe, IL: Free Press, 1958), 48–50.

5. Jagdish Bhagwati, *The Economics of Underdeveloped Countries* (London: Weidenfeld and Nicolson, 1966), 53. See also the later, updated version: "The New Thinking on Development," *Journal of Democracy* 6, no. 4 (October 1995): 50–64.

6. R. Billington, S. Strawbridge, L. Greensides, and A.Fitzsimons, *Culture and Society* (Basingstoke: Macmillan/Palgrave, 1991), 4.

7. Kurt H. Wolff, ed., *Essays on Sociology and Philosophy by Emile Durkheim* (Columbus: Ohio State University Press, 1960), 122.

8. Talcott Parsons, *The Structure of Social Action* (New York: Free Press, 1968).

9. Deutsch, *Nationalism and Social Communication,* 35.

10. Robert N. Bellah, "Religious Aspects of Modernization in Turkey and Japan," in Finkle and Gable, *Political Development*, 188.

11. Ibid., 189.

12. Denkwart A. Rustow, "The Politics of the Near East," in Gabriel Almond and James Coleman, eds., *The Politics of Developing Areas* (Princeton, NJ: Princeton University Press, 1960), 453.

13. Ibid.

14. Max Weber, *The Protestant Ethic and the Spirit of Capitalism* (London: Unwin University Books, 1974), 43.

15. Ibid., 123.

16. Ibid., 157.

17. Bryan S. Turner, *Orientalism, Postmodernism, and Globalism* (London: Routledge, 1994), 11.

18. David C. McClelland, *The Achieving Society* (New York: John Wiley & Sons, 1976); Geert Hofstede, *Culture's Consequences: Comparing Values, Behaviours, Institutions, and Organisations Across Nations*, 2nd ed. (Thousand Oaks, CA: Sage Publications, 2001); Peter L. Berger, "The Desecularisation of the World: A Global Overview," in Peter L. Berger, ed., *The Desecularisation of the World: Resurgent Religion and World Politics* (Grand Rapids, MI: William B. Eerdmans, 1999).

19. Turner, *Orientalism, Postmodernism, and Globalism.*

20. Ernest Gellner, introduction to Akbar S. Ahmed and Hastings Donnan, *Islam, Globalization, and Postmodernity* (London: Routledge, 1994), xiii–xiv.

21. Ibid., xi.

22. Milton J. Yinger, *The Scientific Study of Religion* (New York: Macmillan, 1970), 155.

23. Emile Durkheim, *The Elementary Forms of Religious Life* (London: George Allen and Unwin, 1976), 42.

24. Ibid., 41.

25. Ernest Gellner, *Muslim Society* (Cambridge: Cambridge University Press, 1993), 101.

26. Gideon Sjoberg, Folk and Feudal Societies, quoted in J. Finkle and R. W. Gable, *Political Development and Social Change* (New York: John Wiley and Sons, 1966), 46.

27. Paul Ginsborg, "Family, Culture, and Politics in Contemporary Italy," in Zygmunt G. Baranski and Robert Lumley, eds., *Culture and Conflict in Post War Italy: Essays on Mass and Popular Culture* (Basingstoke: Macmillan, 1990), 23.

28. Ibid., 32.

29. Ibid., 35.

30. "Rerum Novarum, 7," as cited in Brian C. Cox and Anthony E. Dyson, eds., *The Twentieth Century Mind: History, Ideas, and Literature in Britain* (Oxford: Oxford University Press, 1972), 170.

31. Jim F. Campbell, "Traditional Values and Continuities in Greek Society," in Richard Clogg, ed., *Greece in the 1980s* (New York: St. Martin's Press, 1983), 204.

32. K. Ware, "The Church: A Time of Transition," in Clogg, *Greece in the 1980s*, 226.

33. Silke Krieger and Rolf Trauzettel, eds., *Confucianism and the Modernization of China* (Mainz, Germany: Hase & Koehler Verlang, 1991), 39.

34. Ibid., 10, 37.

35. Francis Fukuyama, "Confucianism and Democracy," *Journal of Democracy* 6, no. 2 (April 1995): 20–33.

36. William Theodore De Bary, Wing-Tsit Chan, and Chester Tan, eds., *Sources of Chinese Tradition* (New York: Columbia University Press, 1964), 2:151–52.

37. Gideon Sjoberg, "Folk and 'Feudal' Societies," and Philip M. Hauser, "Some Cultural and Personal Characteristics of the Less Developed Areas," both cited in Finkle and Gable, *Political Development*, 46–49 and 56, respectively.

38. Luigi Guiso, Paola Sapienza, and Luigi Zingales, "People's Opium? Religion and Economic Activities" (NBER Working Paper 9237, National Bureau of Economic Research, Cambridge, MA, 2002); Leonard Dudley and Ulrich Blum, "Religion and Economic Growth: Was Weber Right?" *Journal of Evolutionary Economics* 11, no. 2 (2001); Robert J. Barro and Rachel McCleary, "Religion and Economic Growth" (NBER Working Paper 9682, National Bureau of Economic Research, Cambridge, MA, 2003).

39. Simon Bromley, *Rethinking Middle East Politics* (Cambridge: Polity Press, 1994), 26.

40. Alasdair MacIntyre, *Marxism and Christianity* (London: Pelican Books, 1971), 83.

41. Ali A. Mazrui, *Cultural Forces in World Politics* (London: James Currey, 1990), 78–79.

42. Ibid., 75.

43. Imam Sayyid Abul A'la al-Mawdudi, *The Economic Problem of Man and Its Islamic Solution* (Lahore, Pakistan: Islamic Publications, 1978), and *The Islamic Way of Life*, 11th ed. (Lahore, Pakistan: Islamic Publications, 1979), as cited in Youssef M. Choueiri, *Islamic Fundamentalism* (London: Pinter Publishers, 1990), 117.

44. Sayyid Qutb's writings were a response to Egyptian nationalism: he had been educated in the United States. See Choueiri, *Islamic Fundamentalism*, 120.

45. Maxime Rodinson, *Islam and Capitalism* (London: Allen Lane, 1974), 186, 155, 181.

46. Ibid., 95.

47. Masudul Alam Choudhury, *Islamic Economic Co-Operation* (London: Macmillan, 1989), 88.

48. Abdel Monem Said Aly, "Privatization in Egypt: The Regional Dimensions," in Iliya F. Harik and Denis Sullivan, eds., *Privatization and Liberalization in the Middle East* (Bloomington: Indiana University Press, 1992), 58; Sami Zubaida, "The Politics of the Islamic Investment Companies in Egypt," *British Society for Middle Eastern Studies* 17 (1990).

49. Aly, "Privatization in Egypt," in Harik and Sullivan, *Privatization and Liberalization*, 53.

50. Ibid.

51. Choueiri, *Islamic Fundamentalism*, 119.

52. Marcus Noland, "Religion, Culture, and Economic Performance" (International Economics Working Paper WP03-8, Institute for International Economics, September 2003), 21.

53. Ibid., 26–27.

54. Richard H. Pfaff, "Disengagement from Traditionalism in Turkey and Iran," in Claude E. Welch, Jr., ed., *Political Modernization* (Belmont, CA: Wadsworth Publishing, 1967), 105.

55. Raphael Patai, *The Arab Mind* (New York: Charles Scribner's Sons, 1973), 276.

56. The Economic and Social Commission for Western Asia, *Impact of Economic Reform Policies on Poverty in Selected ESCWA Member Countries: Egypt, Jordan, and Yemen* (Beirut: ESCWA, 1998), 70.

57. Marcus Noland, "Religion, Culture, and Economic Performance," 27.

58. Clement Henry and Robert Springborg, *Globalisation and the Politics of Development in the Middle East* (Cambridge: Cambridge University Press, 2001), 2.

59. Peter W. Preston, *Political/Cultural Identity: Citizens and Nations in a Global Era* (London: Sage, 1997), 39.

60. World Bank Group, "Gender and Development in the Middle East and North Africa: Women and the Public Sphere," overview to *Middle East and North Africa Development Report* (Washington, DC: World Bank, 2003), 1.

61. Noland, "Religion, Culture, and Economic Performance," 26.

62. Maleeha Lodhi, "Back to the Future," *The World Today*, November 1999.

63. Krieger and Trauzettel, *Confucianism*, 40.

3

Responses to Modernization: Muslim Experience in a Comparative Perspective

Timothy McDaniel

Throughout much of the Muslim world over the last twenty-five years, the slogan "Islam is the answer" has become ubiquitous. The "question" to which it is the answer is, Why, after a variety of experiments in social change over nearly a century, do Muslim societies remain economically underdeveloped, poor, and politically repressive, albeit to varying degrees? Since the mid-1970s the answer for many Muslims has become increasingly clear: The problems of the Islamic world derive from its rejection of its heritage, and a return to Islamic values—an Islamic state, Islamic law, and Islamic culture—will resolve these problems.

In much contemporary Western scholarship, too, Islam has also become the "answer"—not as the solution to contemporary challenges but as the explanation for the Muslim world's socioeconomic and political ills and its anti-Westernism. This contemporary Western "answer" has many variations—Islam supports authoritarianism, undermines freedom, nurtures aggression, oppresses women, and reinforces premodern hierarchies—and, consequently, it poses a host of further questions. Ultimately the presumed cause—Islam—becomes impossible to specify analytically, and the presumed effects—dimensions of the Muslim world's development and democracy deficit—vary so greatly that this answer is no more compelling than its Muslim counterpart.

Despite their very different answers to the question of the Muslim world's development and democracy deficit, Islamic and liberal Western analyses share a common assumption: that it makes sense to treat a religion, or a religiously based civilization, as the master key to understanding historical change in the modern world. It is this underlying postulate that this chapter questions by looking at the patterns of non-Western responses to modernity for more than a century. It will show that "Islam's" ideological role in Muslim societies is neither unitary nor without close parallel in other non-Western societies where outcomes have been very different.

This is not to deny the force of religion in Muslim and other societies. But its role needs to be understood in terms of complex webs of influence and causation among many other economic, social, and political conditions, and not as some ultimate prime mover. Further, because religion is inevitably both cause and effect, it, too, will take different forms and have different roles across Muslim societies. Thus, through an examination of types of non-Western responses to Western modernity, this chapter suggests that, with respect to the explanation of contemporary dilemmas in modern societies, "Islam" is neither the right question nor the right answer.

THE QUESTION OF MODERNITY

Common sense tells us that distance, either in time or in space, gives perspective, which is necessary for understanding. This is why historians are often suspicious of "contemporary history." Understanding, they feel, requires the kind of distance unavailable to contemporaries. Behind this view lies a naive empiricism—perspective and distance will provide a "correct" picture, unsullied by the prejudices of the time. But, in fact, as noted by Max Weber, perspectives frame all social and historical reality.

Contemporaries, observing various aspects of the "birth of the modern," lacked clarity born of perspective. How many of them had any idea that a "modern society" was slowly coming into being? What they saw were individual processes, some of them perhaps seen as revolutionary in their time, but hardly adding up to an entirely new form of society. Moreover, events that now seem revolutionary—the Protestant Reformation or the English revolution of the seventeenth century—were considered by many of their participants as a return to the essence of past truths. Martin Luther wanted a return to the authentic teachings of the New Testament. The Puritans, too, saw themselves as the renewers of ancient truths. Other changes, such as the "putting out" system, a forerunner of capitalism, and the invention of new forms of bookkeeping, did not appear as dimensions of a new form of society. The emergence of aggressive secularism in early modern Europe was a movement self-consciously modern in its opposition to what it saw as clerical obscurantism. The gradual development of the territorial state was also seen by contemporaries as novel.

Perhaps, then, twentieth-century observers can better see the nature of the "modern" in what seemed at the time a congeries of unconnected events. But for those reflecting on this long and complex history, perspective has its dangers, especially when it is enveloped in the search for system and the assumption of teleology. From such a perspective "modern society" is seen as a set of interlocked traits mutually reinforcing one another. For example, the separation between church and state is considered necessary for the rise of the modern territorial state. A similar functionalist narrative is that the reemergence of legal consciousness, in the same period, favored the rise of new economic forms that would culminate in modern capitalism, thus requiring the legitimation of profane affairs. Other changes in family and social relations and the emergence of new forms of knowledge can also be adduced as necessary and interdependent factors in a grand synthesis.

Methodologically, a huge problem undermines this kind of interpretation: there is only one case of an indigenous emergence of modern society—Western Europe. Therefore, it is methodologically impossible to separate what might be a necessary dimension of modernity from European particularities. Yet this dilemma has not prevented the historical and social scientific thinking, adducing countless numbers of necessary traits, prerequisites, obstacles to modernity, and inevitable sequences of change.

Consequently, modernization becomes Europeanization. Is this wrong? Here, too, there is the problem of inference based on one case. The hypothesis can be neither proved nor disproved. Can any conclusions be drawn about what Jones called "the European miracle" for the nature of modernity and the implications for non-Western society?[1] How far does the systemic and functionalist analysis of the emergence of modern European society hold as a general model for modernity in other societies?

For decades, there have been intellectual challenges to a singular modernity pioneered by a monolithic "Europe," including Alexander Gerschenkron's classic theory of the importance of timing and "backwardness" for shaping different forms of modernity.[2] The pioneers of European modernization—England and France—despite their differences, operated on a basically liberal model because a large number of indigenous factors facilitated growth without an overall design. But for late modernizers, such as Germany and especially Russia modernization was a conscious plan of catching up. "Catching up" meant achieving many of the same goals already achieved by the more-advanced countries—industrialization, urbanization—but the means to the end had to be different, because the societies were so disparate. Germany was more "advanced" than Russia and could rely on the conscious direction of banks. In Russia, conscious direction could come only from the state, which becomes the agent of modernization.

Same ends, different means? This was hardly possible, for the means necessarily affected social, economic, and political outcomes at every turn. Thus, not only does the experience of the "backward" countries show that there may be various routes to modernity; it also suggests that there may be different forms of modernity, at least at certain levels of development. The tragic elements in modern German and Soviet societies suggest that there are limits and immense drawbacks to their illiberal and statist versions of modern society. Their failures have given validity to the idea that there may be only limited variants of advanced modern society, which do not include modernizing dictatorships.

Gerschenkron's overall logic was taken up by a large number of scholars studying non-Western countries, who used his central methodological perspective, namely, that modernity was not a unitary phenomenon in either its genesis or its outcomes. These depended on timing, sequencing, institutional settings, international contexts, and the like. Therefore, the Western pattern could not be seen as a functional and prescriptive model for all other societies.

This effort to separate the idea of modernity from its moorings in Europe also had significant cost. The very idea of modern society now lost any conceptual unity. If, as modernity in the Soviet Union indicated, it did not require a developed civil society, could modern society still be defined by the partial independence of society from the state? Similarly, if Japan could industrialize and militarize under the mobilizing ideology of a revived Shintoist national identity, should secularism be a defining trait of modernity? Further, if the Japanese experience showed the efficacy of state planning in a quasi-capitalist economic structure, was market rationality based on private calculations so fundamental to a modern economy? In general, was the functionalist model of modern society anything other than a projection of the specificities of Europe onto the rest of the world?

Such questions have bedeviled attempts to develop historically sensitive theoretical analyses of social change in non-Western societies. The choice often seems to be between good history with weak analytical power to generalize and imaginative theory with few roots in historical specifics. Unfortunately, the passage of time has not helped produce a clear view of what modernity is, or decide whether a unified view of it is possible. Consequently, when attempts are made to theorize about the nature of modernity, there is a sense that behind the pretense of universality there is hidden an implicit Western model.

NON-WESTERN SOCIETIES AND THE SCHEMATIZATION OF MODERNITY

If the passage of time has not yet given the dispassionate perspective prized by historians, it is perhaps forgivable that some postmodernists are willing to argue that modern society has never really been modern. Possibly more perspective can be gained, not by the glance across centuries, but through the gaze of contemporary non-Western societies. From this vantage point, distant not in time but in overall social experience, the nature of modernity seems as simple as to an unapologetic advocate of the Europe-as-modernity school. For just as the advocate of European exceptionalism tends to schematize Europe and to identify it with modernity, so do non-Western thinkers attempting to unravel the secrets of Western success (or failure) stereotype and simplify. Seldom do they attempt to grapple with the complexities discussed above, notably that the West is not unitary. There is, instead, "the West and the rest of us," a polar opposition that threatens to schematize both sides. The West, as ideal type, is identified with Western history, and a series of stereotypes, good or bad, emerges to interpret reality. The counterpart of this is the simplification of the other side as some equally undifferentiated reality—whether as a "dependent" world, a "traditional" world, or some other type.

In the age of authentic imperialism, when Western countries were achieving ascendancy over the rest of the world, most non-Western countries showed little interest in the detailed understanding of what was behind the new imbalance of power. Bernard Lewis maintains that, while, beginning in the early modern period, Western investigators were interested in the Muslim world, there was almost no reciprocal interest.[3] Similarly, when the Jesuits were studying the intricacies of Chinese culture, the Chinese were fascinated by their clocks. By the late eighteenth and early nineteenth centuries, intellectual awareness both of the wealth of the Europeans and of the profound problems of China was high but remained within a purely Chinese orbit. Moreover, Confucian scholars who delved into China's problems with a critical eye could risk their lives, which made it impossible to take the West as a model and analyze the factors behind its success.[4] Pre-Meiji Japan was isolationist and provincial, and only in the Meiji period did Japanese nationalism incorporate a Westernist outlook.

Another reason for non-Western thinkers' sterile response to modernity, often called "Occidentalism," was that the phenomenon that they should have been studying in Western history, namely, the emergence of a relatively autonomous society and sphere of public participation, was opaque to them. With rare historical exceptions (Sung China comes to mind), there were few parallels to these cardinal traits of modern Western society. Traditional Islamic, Japanese, Chinese, or Russian cities shared traits that distinguish them from the Western pattern: weakness or lack of corporate organizations, limited overall urban solidarity, and strong patterns of government control. A nuanced view of modern society in its Western incarnation would have required an imaginative leap into a world of substantial self-organization and complicated interconnections among various parts of society. The nature of the Western legal tradition and the subtle relations among state and social groups would have required reflection. But the thinkers, concerned with the state as the source of national strength, could not see the importance of these phenomena, let alone comprehensively analyze them.

No wonder, therefore, that statesmen and scholars in non-Western countries could think of the West only as a set of stereotypes. They also thought of their own societies in terms of polar oppositions, whether good or bad. In fact, it is often easier to discuss non-Western ideas of the West and modernity than to actually analyze the roots and nature of modernity. For while the latter theme is full of paradox and complexity, the former often is formulaic, along the lines of "the West and the rest of us."

While non-Western views of modernity are frequently formulaic and lacking in empirical subtlety, they are not uniform. The impact and example of the West has divided thinkers into competing camps, creating one of the many new sources of cleavage that emerged as a consequence of the challenge of modernity. These responses, while variable, have to do more with a logic of opposition—opposition to both the West itself and to internal opponents—than with the complexities of Western society. Because such views tend to be schematic, it is justified to attempt to schematize them for purposes of comparison. The following two distinctions are especially useful: First, to what degree were nonintellectual thinkers positive about modern society? Second, what was their stance to their own culture—did they reject its central values and institutions in the name of modernity, or did they consider their own societies as providing a viable foundation for the future? Taken together, these distinctions produce the following matrix:

	Relation toward their own societies	
	−	+
	− Revolutionary innovation	Integralism
Relation to modernity		
	+ Westernism	Synthesis

These categories are not exact. For instance, the main example of revolutionary innovation is Marxism. The Marxist tradition had an ambivalent relation to modernity, even in its capitalist dimension. Nonetheless, the fundamental Marxist stance toward modern Western society was negative, and so, although the classification necessarily lacks nuance, it is not inaccurate.

Major advocates of all of these positions can be found in virtually all non-Western societies and civilizations. Therefore, it is erroneous to identify either societies or religions with any particular response. Neither civilizations nor religions can be thought of as causes explaining responses to modernity. Rather, they are the somewhat inchoate matrix out of which diverse responses are chiseled to meet the Western challenge. In this diversification of tradition, culture becomes schematic and ideological. It also becomes a tool for mobilization and a weapon for action. The variables relevant for explanation are not of Confucianism, Islam, or the Russian idea, but ideological constructions such as "modern-text" reformist Confucianism, Islamic modernism, or Slavophilism—quasi ideologies built upon but not in any way identical to a culture, civilization, or religion. Within any broad cultural tradition, a multiplicity of such visions compete with each other across time and place.

Revolutionary Innovation

This first category includes all those who are deeply critical of their own societies' cultures, institutions, and shortcomings, including helplessness before the great powers. It was particularly hard for colonized countries to avoid these indictments. When these were combined with a hostility to the West largely because of the effects of colonialism, the obvious alternative was some form of revolutionary innovation. In the twentieth century, anarchism and communism were the main representatives of revolutionary agendas, although they now seem archaic. Throughout much of the century these ideologies, particularly communism, became popular in places where no Marxist-style proletarian class existed. Nonetheless, the many-sided appeal of Marxism as an attack on both the domestic status quo and the hypocritical West can be seen in the example of Ho Chi Minh, who became a Marxist-Leninist by reading Lenin on imperialism. In Asian countries, Marxism was partially assimilated to Asian cultures by intelligentsias confronting the challenges of peasant societies.

Revolutionary Marxism had significant impact in only a few Muslim countries, notably Iran and Indonesia. Elsewhere it was handicapped by social structures that could not generate either worker radicalism (as in Russia) or peasant communism (as in many Asian countries). The leftist alternative in most Muslim countries was a contradictory amalgam of socialism, militarism, and nationalism—for which the term "revolutionary innovation" is hardly appropriate.

Integralism

Integralism takes refuge in the image of a superior culture rooted in the past but also seen as the most authentic and realistic solution for present ills. In various forms, it has been one of the most widespread responses to modernity in non-Western countries. Its most famous example is Russian Slavophilism, which as either an explicit doctrine or a set of fundamental cultural assumptions has deeply influenced Russian society for the past 150 years, including in the late Soviet period as exemplified by Alexander Solzhenitsyn's ideas.[5] Slavophilism originated in the middle of the nineteenth century, as a reaction to Western modernity, which, especially through state policy, was seen to be corrupting native ideas and institutions. In response, a group of young thinkers developed an alternative ideology based on certain aspects of Russian tradition, such as the peasant commune, with its cooperative structure. They emphasized the spirituality of the Russian Orthodox Church and demanded a state that promoted not progress but an integrated society based on native spirituality and communal practices. Russia did not lag behind, they proposed; rather, Europe was going down the path of proletarianization and class polarization. Russia could avoid these ills and pioneer a more humane version of modern society.

Slavophilism displays the contradictions of integralism. Posing as a reclamation of native traditions, it is an ideological and highly distorted vision of the past. The traditional Russian peasant commune was as much patriarchal and oppressive as communal and liberating. The Orthodox Church was as linked to the autocratic state as to the popular culture. Moreover, Slavophilism was influenced by theories of German idealism and by the works of German philosophers such as Johann Fichte and Friedrich Schelling.[6]

Integralisms in many other parts of the world have similar traits. The contemporary Hindu nationalist movement has attempted to ideologize Hinduism by singling out those texts of Hindu scriptures most suitable to serve as the basis of a kind of fundamentalism and by systematizing doctrine and distinguishing itself from its adversaries, whether Hindus or followers of other religions, and rupturing Hindu tradition of acceptance in favor of a militant doctrine.[7] Such patterns of ideological closure and intolerance are also characteristic of such integralist responses to modernity as Meiji Shintoism. Such movements, allegedly representing tradition, are detrimental to any society, except when they have little influence, as in the cases of Julius Nyerere's African *ujamaa,* Mariategui's Incan communalism, and many varieties of Confucian revivalism.[8]

The most important contemporary example of integralism is Islamic fundamentalism—not a unified phenomenon, but a congeries of ideological versions of Islamic religion. They are ideological because they seek to systematize by creating a set of clear truths out of what is a complex and somewhat inchoate tradition; they reject history in the interest of principles; and they anathemize as unbelief or heresy everything that does not fit their catechism. Like Slavophilism, many of their ideas are derived from modern philosophies or ideologies, as reflected in the works of Ali Shariati, and even Abu'l-A'la Mawdudi, because they are not pure evocations of tradition but schematic responses to modernity. As in Slavophilism, the world is defined in terms of a polar opposition between an authentic tradition and a barbarian assault on the native truths. The appeal to authenticity ensures that Islamic integralism will have a personal religious appeal as well as an ideological attraction as a solution to the problems of contemporary society. Like Slavophilism, then, it looks both backward and forward in an apotheosis of truth, and, also like Slavophilism, it is as much myth as history.[9]

Like Slavophilism, Islamism, too, emerges more from its oppositional stance to the West than from a reading of Islamic history and culture: The West separates church and state; thus, Islam fuses them (not at all true historically). The West is materialistic; Islam is spiritual. The West is unequal; Islam will redeem the poor.

Westernism

A key factor stimulating integralism in non-Western countries is the widespread popularity of pro-Western ideas. Because it is not easy to define either the West or modernity, the Westernizers have a selective vision of their meaning. Secular intelligentsias emphasizing the societal dimensions of Westernization hope for a liberation of society from tradition and governmental tutelage. They favor pluralism, civil liberties, and democratic forms of association and political life. Cultural elites may be drawn to those aspects of modernity emphasized by Daniel Bell, such as the emphasis on novelty and individual creativity. These are in tension with the kinds of Westernization favored by political elites, focused on strengthening the state apparatus, thus enabling it to penetrate society and to promote economic modernization. At times, these different elites coalesce; however, ultimately their ways part, as exemplified by the fate of pro-Western intellectuals who supported Reza Shah in Iran. Rulers such as the Pahlavi shahs or Kemal Ataturk may share a hostility to traditional cultural forms with modernist intellectuals, but they attack tradition in the name of a regimentizing modernization rather than a liberating modernity.

Westernism has two fundamental weaknesses: First, it usually takes root among elites cut off from the masses. The masses are acquainted with certain aspects of modernity from their own experience—the modern factory, the foreign-owner plantation—but this does not lead to an assimilation of modernity as a project. Therefore, modernity often has to be imposed in extremely non-Western ways.[10] Second, because of such pacts with the devil, partisans of modernization become divided against themselves. Consequently, modernity loses even that modest measure of coherence that it possessed in its European cradle. Modernity appears to many as nothing more than hypocrisy and a guise for other projects, including the accumulation of power.

Synthesis

Finally, there are attempts at synthesis, selecting what is regarded as the best in the indigenous society and combining it with the most positive features of modernity. Such attempts at synthesis are appealing because as the Chinese Cultural Revolution and Boris Yeltsin's attempts to repudiate the Russian past show, cultural iconoclasm is fraught with danger and history cannot be ignored. Moreover, some form of modernity is an imperative, hence the attraction of some form of selective borrowing—something along the lines of "Western technology, Chinese spirit," to take one famous example. Yet, few serious attempts have been made at such synthesis, and they have turned out to be artificial on the programmatic level.

Examples include Kang Youwei's attempt to modernize Confucianism to meet the challenges of China at the turn of the twentieth century and the Russian Socialist Revolutionaries' commitment to the modernization of Russia on the basis of revitalized agrarian institutions. Here only two cases, which clearly display the main drawbacks of such a strategy, will be discussed. The first is that of Jamal al-Din al-Afghani, the influential nineteenth-century Islamic reformer.[11] He embraced modernity, but not as a Western contribution. Rather, modernity had many sources, including the Islamic contribution. The Europeans claimed the mantle of innovation, but in fact the streams that made up modern society were multifarious. The world of Islam was now behind, reduced to a passive position in international civilization. But this was not because of any innate inferiority, as the past clearly showed, but because of the stranglehold of a rigidified tradition, including that imposed by the religious class, that distorted the authentic nature of Islam. Islam should abandon present-day superstitions and rigidities, and renew itself as a vital partner in modernity. In short, Afghani tried to combine the best features of Islamic tradition and modernity in a superior synthesis.

Afghani's ideas inspired a significant intellectual movement of Islamic modernism and reform. He was also influential with some of the political elite, who were impressed with his efforts to strengthen the position of Islamic states and his anticolonial stand. But despite this surface modernism, Afghani's activities represented an older pattern, the effort to realize change through teachings and contacts with elites. On this level, it was easier to promote ideas of synthesis, but by the same token, Afghani was unable to create mass movements or mobilize large publics. The future belonged not to such as he, but to leaders such as Hasan al Banna, the integralist founder of the Muslim Brotherhood, who could speak to and organize masses. Banna's consistent Muslim integralist message was more accessible to the masses than Afghani's syncretism.

Early Meiji Japan provides another example. To create a synthesis of Western progress and Japanese ideas, Meiji elites initiated a two-pronged campaign of cultural change—one part reactionary, one part Westernizing—and the two never fit together. The result was, in the expression of Marius Jansen, "a failed cultural revolution."[12] Early Meiji reformers' dualistic policy derived from their delicate position: they had just overthrown the Tokugawa regime on the basis of loyalty to the emperor, but they were also committed to strengthening and modernizing Japan. Moreover, except for the appeal to imperial restoration, they lacked legitimacy. From this dilemma their initial policy followed: to promulgate, with the help of Shinto priests and other enthusiasts, a version of imperial Shinto as official ideology. As Jansen explains, "The invocation of the theocratic pretensions of a state headed by a ruler descended from the sun goddess provided important support for consensus and centralization. And there was cultural politics involved, in terms of the proper ideological foundations for the new state."[13]

The purpose of this new authority based on a hoped-for traditional consensus was Japan's modernization. Consequently, the same government that promoted a Shinto revival, based on the primitive spirit world of ancient Japan, sent "learning missions" abroad to obtain whatever was necessary for the country's modernization. "Initially American education, British industrialization, French jurisprudence, and German representational institutions held particular promise."[14] No wonder the Shinto cultural revolution failed. In short, while synthesis expresses an ideal marriage of old and new, in practice it usually means contradiction, because the disparate native and Western elements inevitably clash.

IMPLICATIONS

Examples of reactions to Western modernity discussed here lead to two general conclusions with some theoretical implications. First, each society or region has had multiple reactions to the challenge of modernity. Examples of Islamic integralism, Westernism, and synthesis were noted. It would also have been possible to discuss patterns of revolutionary innovation. Similarly, China and Japan had no homogeneous response to these issues. Indeed, virtually all major societies have experienced some form of all four responses to Western modernity, albeit in different degrees.

The point is important, for it challenges a common strategy of analyzing social and cultural change that I will call teleological reductionism. The logic is as follows: an end point of cultural or social change is chosen—peasant communism in Russia (Barrington Moore); populist Maoism in China (Theda Skocpol); Islamic ideology (Bernard Lewis)—and this end point is interpreted as the outcome of deep-seated cultural or structural patterns. The first error is the often arbitrary identification of an outcome: In what sense, for example, was the Maoism of the Cultural Revolution more of an outcome than the Soviet-style bureaucratism of 1950s or 1980s China? Why the assumption that some form of Islamic ideology is the "natural" response to modernity in Islamic countries? What happened to the Nasserist outcome of the 1950s and 1960s? Are there ever really outcomes that were both inevitable historically and exclude other alternatives in the future?

Hence the need to relativize and historicize the identification of outcomes themselves, and particularly the definition of these outcomes in terms of a single response to the challenges of modernity. Islamism is not the answer, for there is no single question, and no completely valid answer to any one of the multiple questions raised by modernity. Only an ideologized version of culture looks at history as a one-dimensional challenge and response. Here is a more recent example: In present-day Muslim countries there appears to be a revival of Westernizing ideas in response to the perceived failures of Islamism. In the West there is much talk of reformist and liberal Islam. Some authors see this new democratic tendency as "the" solution rooted in both Islam and modernity. Yet one must be skeptical of such conclusions.

Second, there are significant continuities across highly diverse societies. For example, Slavophilism, Islamism, Confucian revivalism, and Incan socialism have a great deal in common. They are all rooted in their societies' pasts. But they are also ideological answers for their countries' futures in the modern world.

Much the same can be said for the other cells in the matrix: all of them can embrace a wide variety of cases—diverse on the surface, but in fact united by a similar logic in response to a threatening and promising modernity. If it is true, therefore, that there is a family resemblance among societies, cultural and societal reactions to modernity should not be treated in the traditional way. What appears to be the "Russian" or "Arab" or "Chinese" response is actually more than this: a local version, with its important specificities and historical trajectories, of more generalized patterns. In this sense, the world is globalized with cognate patterns of experience. But this globalized world is exceptionally cosmopolitan. Globalization means not homogeneity but a multiplicity of questions and answers, rooted partly in common patterns but also in a cross-national dialogue of possibilities.

In summary, all four ideal-type responses can generally be found in the experiences of major non-Western countries. Therefore, any kind of mechanical essentialism that identifies a particular society with a separate and unified cultural response to modernity should be rejected. Rather, continuous historical change (and not fixed end points) must be the analytical postulate. And patterns within particular societies must be related to transnational issues, such as common imperatives of modernity and the diffusion of cultural models across societies.

BUT NOT ALL COWS ARE BROWN

While internal diversity and transnational parallels are emphasized, the salient traits of particular societies should not be ignored. Cultural responses to modernity may be typologically similar across different countries, but the relative significance of different orientations for societies and social change varies significantly. For example, there are versions of integralism in Turkey, but in the past century Westernism has been more influential. Until recently in Russia, different versions of revolutionary innovation competed with quasi-Slavophile integralism as dominant models, while syncretic responses have not been popular, as exemplified by the failure of Mikhail Gorbachev's vision. Therefore, as suggested by Weber, one must look for "elective affinities" between ideas and empirical patterns of social and political change.

Only some fragmentary hypotheses can be offered here, based on the Weberian assumption of classes and status groups as the bearers of characteristic ideal orientations. In this respect, the affinity between state actors and either Westernism or synthesis should be noted. In general, political elites must take seriously the imperatives of modernity if their countries are to maintain their positions in the international system. Although revolutionary innovation in its Communist form offers a model of modernization and state power, it is unacceptable to status quo elites. Integralism, meanwhile, can serve to legitimate state power but is unable to envision a competitive version of modernity, particularly regarding the role of the state, because integralist images of the state are generally archaic and unworkable in the modern age.

However, the Westernizing vision of political elites is often limited to the augmentation of state power, and they find other elements of modernization less appealing, except beyond their contribution to societal development. For example, both Kemal Ataturk and the Pahlavi shahs improved women's positions, but largely for instrumental goals.

The early Meiji rulers saw the advantages of synthesis: traditional legitimation used to support an iconoclastic modernization. The reform process under the dowager empress, the "last stand of Chinese conservatism," represents the same impulse.[15]

Secular intelligentsias tend to be advocates of either revolutionary innovation or Western modernity, although integralism and synthesis are also possibilities. Western modernization, with its relative absence of purges and class cleansing, offers more stable choices. But in this case, too, there are limits to their scope of action because of the underdeveloped state of the civil sphere. This situation means that the most realistic choice is usually service to the state through the professions. Since most of the secular intelligentsia chooses some kind of linkage to the state, it becomes further alienated from a societal base, thus weakening the appeal of their ideas among the masses, as can be seen in many contemporary Islamic societies.

The bearers of integralist visions are rarely state actors, unless an integralist movement seizes power, as in Iran. Even then the purity of the integralist stance among state actors weakens, as they confront practical problems of governance. Integralism can even become a convenient cover for pure realpolitik, as has happened in Iran. Historically, integralist movements have rarely gained power because often they do not know how to organize a mass base. In those cases, when integralist leaders are able to mobilize large numbers, the movement's strength is sapped by the compromises necessary to gain influence. This dilemma has been apparent in the history of the Muslim Brotherhood, where participation in mass politics has weakened the ideological drive of many of its followers. That is why, initially, Mawdudi did not want his Jama'at-i Islami to participate in political life.

Further, it is generally difficult for integralists to gain much support among political elites because the elites are suspicious of their antimodern tendencies and also recognize that such movements often only involve an intellectual elite.

Another weakness of integralists is that they alienate the traditional religious leadership, thus further eroding their ability to gain support among the masses. The Russian Orthodox Church was generally suspicious of the Slavophiles, despite many ideological affinities. The traditional religious hierarchy has also been by and large hostile toward the Islamists. In Iran many leading traditional clerics have been against the ideologization of Islam and the involvement of religious leaders in politics.

As a solution to complex problems, Islamic fundamentalism is therefore much weaker than it seems. It is racked by internal fissures and relies on a contradictory social base. When it operates as a large-scale movement within the context of national states, it tends to become reformist and less interested in the ideal of an Islamic state. By contrast, it takes revolutionary form as a movement of uprooted youth or as a transnational network of radicals disconnected from their own societies. It may be premature to pronounce the defeat of Islamic fundamentalism, but it is legitimate to emphasize its fragmented and incoherent state.[16]

The attempt at synthesis is found often enough in theory, but seldom in practice, because state elites, while espousing more traditionalist ideas, mainly engage in the pragmatic tasks of staying in power. Moreover, over time, the true believers are either purged or remain as an impotent opposition. For these reasons, efforts to imbue Western modernity with indigenous ideological content have made little impact on modern society.

In sum, the strength of any ideological response to Western modernity within a particular society will depend largely on the weight of the typical social bearers of these ideas. In general, where there is a relatively large secular intelligentsia and a more independent public sphere, Westernizer ideals will be more prominent. By contrast, when there is still a substantial traditional intelligentsia connected to strategic parts of the social structure such as the merchant class, as in Iran, or other types of traditional middle class, integralism is far more likely. Synthesis is usually the work of reformist intelligentsia but rarely connects itself to a social base. Revolutionary innovation is a phenomenon born of significant modernization of both culture and the social structure. Thus, the weight of any ideological response to Western modernity requires not just an analysis of the ideas but a sociological perspective connecting them to key sectors of the society.

CONCLUSION: THE NONLIBERAL NON-WEST

Non-Western countries have had no choice but to define themselves through contrast and comparison with Western societies, the first and perhaps only models for the meaning of modernity itself. Through this process of comparison, historical experience, both Western and non-Western, becomes schematized, and there emerge standard responses to the Western challenge across non-Western countries: the four possibilities discussed throughout the text. Beyond these variations in response, there has also, at least until recently, been a very widespread rejection in third world countries of the most revolutionary elements of the Western experience—the culture of individualism, the free-market economy, and the liberal state. In this respect, Gerschenkron's insight that modernization has a history and a structure illuminates far more than the economist's claim that there is a single logic for modern economies and societies. Perhaps this latter claim is true in principle, but it fails to illuminate the actual history of modernity. For, as Gerschenkron explained, late modernizing countries have different actors and resources, and they face a different international environment. As a result of these differences, for most of the past century virtually everywhere in the non-Western world there have been calls for a regulated economy, shared culture, and limited political competition. These limitations on liberalism have been supported both out of a sense that they correspond better to indigenous traditions and also because they are presumed to provide a better model for progress.

The corollary of a skeptical view of liberalism has been the emergence of swollen states throughout much of the non-Western world, best exemplified by communist Russia. Such states have shown that they are capable of substantial development and modernization up to a certain point. But they are handicapped by inefficiency, lack of innovation, and inability to stimulate and capitalize on individual initiative and creativity. The experience of the Soviet Union suggests that they are unable to lead their countries into the modern technological age. The question in contemporary China is whether a mixed Communist system will be able to do better.

Such thoroughly statist models of modernization have been quite rare in non-Western countries. The more general pattern is for swollen states to coexist with some form of capitalist structure and with a society with some degree of autonomy, as found in countries as diverse as Mexico, Indonesia, Egypt, Malaysia, and Taiwan. The success of such patterns of modernization varies enormously. Several East and Southeast Asian countries have performed extremely well, at least until recently, while others, such as Egypt and Pakistan, have done poorly.

The key determinant of success seems to be whether such an authoritarian state can coexist with a dynamic capitalist class. In all of the success stories, the state has not prevented, and may have even encouraged, the emergence of significant entrepreneurship.

Indeed, intellectuals and political leaders in several of these countries claim that their modernization has not been "partial." Such a judgment, they say, takes

Western history as a normative model for modern society. Figures such as Lee Kuan Yew of Singapore and Mahathir Mohammad of Malaysia argue that their own East Asian model of society is superior.

The theoretical issue raised is the same discussed earlier: to what extent is modernity a system of interlocking changes based on Western historical experience? Or are there variants of modernity that depart from the more liberal Western model? In all of this debate, is it possible to separate fact and value? That is, is there such a thing as a value-neutral concept of modernity, or are different visions culturally relative? These are old questions to which there have been few satisfactory answers.

In the less successful pattern of partial modernization, swollen states have not been able to coexist with a relatively dynamic capitalist structure, either for ideological reasons such as Arab "socialist" regimes or because the state provides the main opportunities for advancement, thus depriving the private sector of talent and resources. Lacking the kind of purely statist system of the Communist countries, with their associated social and ideological models, such countries have little or no foundation for modernization.

Interesting exceptions to the general pattern of state hypertrophy in non-Western countries are the Islamic Republic of Iran and Afghanistan under the Taliban, which have more or less systematically attempted to create a relatively consistent Islamic version of society. Unlike statist ideals, traditional Islamic political values, as interpreted by many contemporary Islamist leaders, favor a consultative government based on rule by morally pure, not professionally qualified, people. The goal is to protect Islamic beliefs and the Islamic community internally and externally, but not to exercise tutelage over society, as have third world developmentalist states.

This contemporary version of an ancient model is incompatible with modern bureaucracies and modern democracy, based on open electoral competition, legislation, and administration by experts. Iran "solved" this problem by creating a kind of dual government, with one set of institutions based on Islam—the supreme religious authority and various councils of religious experts—and a set of parallel democratic institutions based on a president, elections, and a parliament. In theory, both sets of institutions would be compatible, since democratic processes would operate within the general consensus represented by the religious leaders. Instead, there has emerged an unwieldy political system with an inchoate structure, great internal conflict, and a lack of clear loci of authority and decision making, and hence, an inadequate model for a modern state. The Iranian experience shows that the ancient model of moral guidance based on poorly institutionalized personalism is irrelevant to the modern world. Late-nineteenth-century Confucianism had much the same weakness in China. The model lacked reality even in classical Islam, where the ideal religious model was soon displaced by imperial structures.

The Afghan political structure under the Taliban was not so divided against itself. There was no attempt to incorporate modern political structures within a system of religious guidance. In fact, based on some version of the pristine Islamic society, politics was reduced to policing morality, internecine warfare, and engagement in commercial activities. There was no bureaucracy, no defined set of political procedures, and no institutionalized form of popular participation in politics. There was only rule by self-proclaimed morally pure people whose goal was to Islamicize the society. The latter task was seen not as political but as moral and social.

These differences between Islamic Iran and Islamic Afghanistan, as well as among societies throughout the Muslim world, indicate that Islam can be neither "the" question nor "the" answer. Instead, as both a religion and the cultural foundation of broader civilization, Islam generates many questions and many answers. It is not the prime mover, but both cause and effect in complex chains of relationship with a host of other aspects of modern society. Finally, it is both part of modernity, as the different schema built upon it in contemporary society demonstrate, and as a transcendental monotheistic religion, standing in judgment of all human institutions. What a mistake, then, to try to identify religion with society or to claim that religion can determine society. Given the complexity of forces to which people are subject in their social relations, there can be Islamic ideals, but no Islamic (or Christian or Buddhist) society.

SOME HOPE?

Notwithstanding its limits, synthesis may still have a future in the Muslim world. However, to be viable such syntheses should not be of competing schematic paradigms (integralism and Westernism, for example) but of concrete practices: pragmatic compromises that attempt to learn from history, both Western and Muslim, rather than simplistically categorize it. Only in this way can such frequently found oppositions in the Muslim world—religion versus secularism; Islam versus the West; private interest versus the state; and perhaps even men versus women—be superseded. But to advocate such pragmatic synthesis means to change the terms of the discussion, and urge that non-Western responses to the West be based on Western experience and not on a hypothetical "West" absolutely opposed to the "rest of us." Such a rethinking would require radical reorientations among those who idealize the West and those who celebrate the non-Western "other." Global demythologization is the challenge of the hour, for only out of it can come deeper understanding of the past and the possibilities for the future.

NOTES

1. Eric L. Jones, *The European Miracle,* 2nd ed. (Cambridge: Cambridge University Press, 1987).

2. Alexander Gerschenkron, *Economic Backwardness in Historical Perspective* (New York: Praeger, 1965).

3. Bernard Lewis, *Islam and the West* (New York: Oxford University Press, 1993).

4. Jonathan Spence, *The Search for Modern China* (New York: W. W. Norton, 1990), 143–47.

5. Aleksander Solzhenitsyn, ed., *From Under the Rubble* (Chicago: Regnery Gateway, 1981).

6. On Slavophilism, including the influence of German philosophy on it, see Abbott Gleason, *European and Muscovite* (Cambridge, MA: Harvard University Press, 1972).

7. Daniel Gold, "Organized Hinduisms: From Vedic Truth to Hindu Nation," in Martin Marty and Scott Appleby, eds., *Fundamentalisms Observed* (Chicago: University of Chicago Press, 1991).

8. Julius Nyerere, *Ujamaa: Essays on Socialism* (London: Oxford University Press, 1968); the important Peruvian intellectual Jose Carlos Mariategui formulated his ideas on indigenous socialist traditions in the Andes in *Siete Ensayos de Interpretacion de la Realidad Peruana* (1928; Mexico, D.F.: Serie Popular Era, 1988); several varieties of Confucian reformism are examined in Joseph Levenson, *Confucian China and Its Modern Fate* (Berkeley: University of California Press, 1968).

9. Wilferd Madelung, *The Succession to Muhammad: A Study of the Early Caliphate* (Cambridge: Cambridge University Press, 1997).

10. Tim McDaniel, *Autocracy, Modernization, and Revolution in Russia and Iran* (Princeton, NJ: Princeton University Press, 1991).

11. Nikki Keddie, *Sayyid Jamal al-Din "al-Afghani": A Political Biography* (Berkeley: University of California Press, 1972).

12. Marius Jansen, *The Making of Modern Japan* (Cambridge, MA: Harvard University Press, 2000), 349.

13. Ibid., 350.

14. Ibid., 360.

15. Mary Wright, *The Last Stand of Chinese Conservatism* (Stanford, CA: Stanford University Press, 1957).

16. Gilles Kepel, *Jihad* (Cambridge, MA: Harvard University Press, 2002); Oliver Roy, *L'islam mondialisé*, Series: Couleur des idees (Paris: Seuil, 2002).

4

Development and Democracy: The Muslim World in a Comparative Perspective

Mehran Kamrava

The issue of the relationship between development and democracy has been debated among development experts, political scientists, and sociologists for the past fifty years. However, tensions between development and democracy go back to earlier times. They were apparent in the case of many European countries that were latecomers to the process of modernization. Furthermore, Europe was the birthplace of nondemocratic models of development best exemplified by Nazi Germany and the Soviet Union. The process of development in European countries has culminated in the establishment of democratic forms of government, albeit fairly late in the case of south and east European countries.

In the non-Western world, until recently, development had not led to democratization, with postwar Japan (with its unique conditions) being the exception. Some developing countries have had democratic governments, such as India. Others in Latin America and East Asia, such as Taiwan, Korea, and Chile, have made a transition to democracy. Malaysia, a Muslim country, has achieved an impressive level of development while maintaining a fairly democratic form of government. Turkey is another, though less impressive, example of development within a more or less democratic system. Other Muslim countries, especially those in the Middle East, have neither achieved significant levels of development nor established democratic governments.

The question thus arises, To what extent have the development strategies of Muslim countries, especially those in the Middle East, contributed to their failure to democratize. To answer this question, it is necessary to first address the following issues: (1) What are the principal dilemmas faced by developing countries in balancing development and democracy? (2) What form of development is more conducive to democracy? (3) What features of the patterns of development in the Middle East have been most detrimental to the process of democratization? Based on the answers, conclusions will be drawn as to what changes in development strategies are needed to encourage movement toward democratization.

ECONOMIC DEVELOPMENT AND STATE POWER

By nature, *developing* countries feature processes of economic development that are inimical to democratic openings and face what Eva Bellin has called the "developmental paradox."[1] According to Bellin, "by sponsoring industrialization, the [authoritarian] state nurtures the development of social forces ultimately capable of amassing sufficient power to challenge it and impose a measure of policy responsiveness. In short, the very success of the state's strategy leads to the demise of the state's capacity to dictate policy unilaterally."[2] Societal autonomy and the empowerment of social actors in relation to the state are key to the onset of pressures for democratization. Developing states foster economic and industrial processes that constrain the autonomy of social actors in the short run while, in the long run, they enhance their prospects for empowerment and autonomy from the state.

While this developmental paradox may in the long term foster conditions that favor democratic openings, it is not a natural by-product of economic development, but rather a specific outcome of developmental processes unleashed by "developmental states." Chalmers Johnson defines developmental states as those that combine the market rationality of capitalist economies of states like the United States with the ideological-plan economies of states similar to that of the former Soviet Union. "In the plan rational [i.e., developmental] state, the government will give greatest precedent to industrial policy; that is, to a concern with the structure of domestic industry and with promoting the structure that enhances the nation's international competitiveness."[3] Japan, South Korea, and Taiwan are paradigmatic cases of successful developmental states. Elsewhere in the developing world, only Chile and to a much lesser extent Argentina and Brazil approximate the model of developmental states.[4] In the rest of the developing world the dynamics of economic transformation and development have been decidedly different. Notwithstanding regional and other differences in patterns of development, in the developing world the dynamics have been such that they have enabled the state to survive the pressures emanating from the forces unleashed by the development process. A partial exception is South Africa, although its democratic transition was due as much to the relentless struggle of the African National Congress (ANC) as to the results of economic development, especially the rise of a small but articulate middle class of black revolutionaries.[5]

For a relationship between economic development and democratization to occur, two key, interrelated developments are needed: first, the emergence of a sizable middle class that is financially autonomous from the state; second, and concomitant with the first, development of a private sector that also retains a meaningful level of economic and political autonomy from the state. By definition, the middle classes outside of the civil service (i.e., financially autonomous from the state) belong to the private sector. But there are also important qualitative differences between the two, namely, in levels of economic power and organizational resources. Their natural overlappings notwithstanding, the two groups serve the process of democratic opening in two distinct ways: *subjectively* by the middle classes and *objectively* by the private sector.

The subjective ways in which the middle classes help the cause of democratization are through their explicit or implicit support for nonstate initiatives and non-state-dictated sources of identity, especially as represented through professional associations and nongovernmental organizations (NGOs). While such activities by the middle classes, if permitted by the authorities, ultimately erode the institutional, objective bases of the state, they also help spread the ideals of self-empowerment, political independence (from the state), local activism, and civic responsibility in society. In short, the middle classes are critical components of civil society, so long as they have the political autonomy and the financial and organizational resources necessary to mobilize themselves into professional associations and other civil society organizations.[6]

This is not to imply that the oppositional potential of the middle classes is largely subjective and devoid of direct institutional significance. On the contrary, through NGOs and professional associations, the middle classes directly challenge the functions and performance of state institutions in specific areas, such as in the provision of particular services. Nevertheless, these middle class–driven organizations contribute to the larger societal context and atmosphere within which democratic openings occur rather than serve as the actual catalysts for authoritarian withdrawals. The defection of the private sector from the "authoritarian bargain," however, can be directly consequential for the overall strength and the institutional integrity of the state. Authoritarian states rely on authoritarian bargains of various kinds, many of which revolve around the incorporation and complicity of the private sector. For the private sector's defection to be politically consequential it needs to have formidable economic muscle and organizational and financial strength and, even if it initially owed its good fortunes to the state and its corporatist largesse, it must break away from the state and become politically autonomous.

This is precisely what happened in South Korea, where a highly underdeveloped and resource-starved economy began to turn around in the mid-1960s, as the country's policy makers switched from import substitution to an export-led policy of growth. This shift had two additional consequences. First, it required the establishment of a number of trade barriers to *some* imports; instead of simply encouraging exports as an engine of economic development, policy makers exploited the country's "comparative advantage" and continued to allow for the import of goods that would have been costly to produce domestically.[7] In practice, this meant a close level of cooperation between state leaders and policy makers and private sector investors and industrialists. Second, unlike Brazilian and Taiwanese industries, Korean firms—especially in the automotive sector—have been reluctant to rely on international subcontractors and instead have manufactured most components of their products in-house.[8] While this was costly in the short run, in the long run it has resulted in Korean firms emerging as more independent and, overall, more powerful. Gradually, by the late 1980s, they began to pull out of the state's authoritarian bargain.

Hence, much depends on the viability and resilience of the bargain struck between authoritarian state leaders and key social actors whose financial and organizational resources the state needs to co-opt. Even if the bargain does not explicitly co-opt these resources, it needs to mollify their potential for political opposition if it is to persevere. In observing authoritarian bargains, one can see why they unraveled in predemocratic South America, and to a lesser extent in East Asia, especially in South Korea and Taiwan, while they continue to persevere in the Muslim world, especially the Middle East.

In Brazil and Argentina, the state adopted the import-substitution industrialization (ISI) strategy for development, through which it sought to placate middle-class demands for consumer durables and directly targeted benefits to domestic and international investors.[9] From about the 1950s to the late 1970s the bargain worked, as military-led states fostered impressive industrial growth, kept the middle classes economically content, and held the domestic opposition at bay through indiscriminate repression. But because of inadequate domestic exports and lack of other natural resources to finance ISI, Brazil and Argentina resorted to massive international borrowing, which by the early 1980s led to balance-of-payment and debt crises.[10] The structural adjustments that were subsequently dictated by the so-called Washington Consensus alienated the very groups that were once the beneficiaries of ISI—the middle classes and the investors—resulting in the unraveling of their authoritarian bargains.[11] Argentina, suffering from internal discord and lack of cohesion, resorted to one last desperate measure to rally middle-class support when it invaded the Falkland Islands in 1982. But its failure only precipitated its collapse and the retreat of the ruling generals. Similarly, hasty withdrawals from power occurred in Bolivia and Peru, as well as in the Philippines, followed subsequently by elections. In Brazil and Uruguay, the military's exit from power under more favorable economic and political circumstances better positioned it to negotiate the terms of its withdrawal, having already committed itself to some political liberalization before the elections of the mid-1980s.[12]

In East Asia, meanwhile, developing states were able to foster what some observers have called "conservative coalitions." According to David Waldner, "conservative coalitions are narrowly based coalitions supporting collaboration between the state and large business; significant segments of the population are excluded from these coalitions, and deliberate efforts are made to maximize side-payments to popular classes."[13] The South Korean and Taiwanese state elites (and the Japanese elites before them) enjoyed high levels of internal cohesion. Against a backdrop of deep-seated economic nationalism,[14] these elites devised economic policy without significant pressure from the popular classes.[15] Following the

Japanese model, the Taiwanese and South Korean states devised elaborate agencies, as well as formal and informal mechanisms, to promote the growth and success of the private sector: Korea's Ministry of Trade, Industry, and Energy (originally called the MTI) and Taiwan's Council for Economic Cooperation and Development (later renamed Council for Economic Planning and Development—CEPD) successfully replicated the work of Japan's Ministry of International Trade and Industry (MITI).[16] So long as the state's policies resulted in the growth of private sector capital, the private sector remained ambivalent toward democratic reform. However, when "the state began to cut back on its sponsorship of private sector capital and the latter's need for state support also declined . . . the private sector began to exhibit remarkable enthusiasm for political reform and democratization."[17] By the early 1990s, both the South Korean and Taiwanese states, and to some extent the Thai state, could be considered democratic.

STATE POWER IN THE MIDDLE EAST

The situation in the Middle Eastern states has been different. The pattern of development in the Middle East has been such that it has reinforced state power and prevented the emergence of autonomous nonstate actors. In addition, Middle Eastern states differ from East Asia and Latin American countries in three significant ways: (1) they initially lacked elite cohesion; (2) they have relatively easy access to economic resources; and (3) they have comparatively low levels of globalization. Together these variables have enabled the state to strike authoritarian bargains that so far have withstood major challenges by undergoing only minor modifications. Consequently, much of the Middle East remains a bastion of authoritarianism.

First, unlike the states of East Asia, the Middle Eastern states had little or no initial elite cohesion. This was a product of the region's colonial legacy, both Ottoman and European, which encompassed the whole of the Middle East from modern-day Turkey in the East to Morocco in the West. In most places, lasting well into the late 1940s, colonial domination impeded the ability of indigenous political institutions to emerge independently and to become consolidated. When independence came abruptly after the end of the World War II, political aspirants competed for dominance and hegemony by seeking to cultivate support among specific social groups. As Waldner maintains, "Intense elite conflict impels one of the competing elite factions to incorporate a mass base: the state bargains with popular classes, exchanging material benefits for popular support."[18]

Incorporating the masses into the political process might have undermined the state's economic performance, but it also gave it a facade of street democracy that masked, albeit often unsuccessfully, its innately authoritarian nature. At the very least, it balanced out the grievances of the groups excluded from the bargain (e.g., workers and peasants) with support from those who were included (e.g., civil servants). As many of the once inclusionary states aged over time, they resorted less and less to street theater to keep up democratic pretenses. However, they could not significantly reduce the high levels of side payment to their constituents in society. Indeed, over time, a relationship of mutual dependence has emerged between the state and certain key societal constituents, with neither being able to break out of the relationship. Precisely who these societal groups are differs among Middle Eastern countries. In general, however, the middle classes are uniformly targeted for incorporation, especially through the expansive civil service and state-owned enterprises.[19] Other targeted groups include organized labor, especially in Algeria and Egypt,[20] or wealthier members of the private sector, as in Iraq[21] and Turkey.[22]

Second, Middle Eastern states are able to rely on rentier economies, based largely on oil. (See Chapter 10 in this volume by Giacomo Luciani.) Rentierism has given Middle Eastern states extractive autonomy from society by enabling them to provide for the population without demanding much in direct taxation. More important, Middle Eastern states have been able to avoid the vulnerabilities of debt-ridden Latin American states by continually financing the incorporation of dependent groups. The recurrent economic recessions of the 1980s and the 1990s failed to completely dislodge the rentier underpinnings of Middle Eastern economies. For the most part, Middle Eastern economies either rely on rent revenues directly—such as through those derived primarily from the export and sale of oil, as is the case in the Arabian peninsula—or do so indirectly—through foreign aid, tourism, and remittances by expatriate workers, especially in resource-poor countries such as Morocco, Egypt, and Jordan.[23] Nevertheless, the significant decline in rent revenues did necessitate certain economic liberalization measures.[24] Ultimately, the once-fractured state elites have become more cohesive, and half-hearted measures at economic liberalization have not been followed up by meaningful political liberalization.[25]

Third, there have been lower levels of globalization in the Middle East as compared to other regions of the developing world, except for Africa. There is a strong correlation between high levels of economic and normative globalization and the prospects for democratic transitions.[26] The overwhelming majority of Middle Eastern states rank consistently low on all indicators of globalization. Outside the oil sector, foreign direct investment has been lower in the Middle East than in East Asia or Latin America.[27] The main reasons include weak domestic markets, uncompetitive private sectors, and strong opposition from those who see globalization as a threat to their countries' cultural, religious, and national identity, and to their national interest and autonomy.[28] More important is the threat posed by globalization to the authoritarian power structures, because globalization requires transparency in economic transactions, free flow of information, a credible banking system, and the empowerment of civil society.[29]

That is why in most Middle Eastern states leaders have viewed globalization with skepticism, at best allowing it in a slow and controlled manner, as illustrated by restrictions imposed on information technology.[30] Presently the potential that globalization would erode authoritarianism in the Middle East seems unlikely and hence, as long as authoritarian rule remains the norm in the Middle East, the prospects for the region's globalization to the level of Latin America and East Asia appear bleak.

In sum, economic development has a paradoxical relationship with democratization. There is no linear relationship between industrial development and democracy. The causal relationship between the two is far more nuanced and context-specific.[31] If in the process of economic development, the middle classes and the private sector gain autonomy from the state on the one hand and organizational and financial resources and strength on the other, they can emerge as powerful actors in the push for state accountability and democratization. This is what happened in East Asia and Latin America and has not happened in the Middle East and in many other parts of the Muslim world.

CIVIL SOCIETY AND DEMOCRACY

Philip Oxhorn defines civil society as

a rich social fabric formed by a multiplicity of territorially and functionally based units. The strength of civil society is measured by the peaceful coexistence of these units and by their collective capacity simultaneously to *resist subordination* to the state and to *demand inclusion* into national political structures. The public character of these units allows them to justify and act in open pursuit of their collective interests in competition with one another. Strong civil societies are thus synonymous with a high level of "institutionalized social pluralism."[32]

As such, "because they are self-constituted, the units of civil society serve as the foundations for political democracy."[33]

Juan Linz and Alfred Stepan similarly define civil society as "that arena of the polity where self-organizing groups, movements, and individuals, relatively autonomous from the state, attempt to articulate values, create associations and solidarities, and advance their interests."[34] However, they argue, civil society is a tremendously helpful but ultimately insufficient element of democratic transitions. They maintain, "At best, civil society can destroy a nondemocratic regime." For democratic transition—and especially democratic consolidation—to occur, civil society needs to be politicized and transformed into what Linz and Stepan call "political society." Political society may be defined as "that arena in which the polity specifically arranges itself to contest the legitimate right to exercise control over public power and the state apparatus."[35]

A subtle but important distinction needs to be drawn between *civil society* and *civil society organizations* (CSOs). CSOs are the constituent members of civil society, what Oxhorn calls "a multiplicity of territorially and functionally based units."[36] They are the various individual groups and organizations whose collective efforts over time, and the effects of the horizontal and often also the organic links that develop among them, make it possible for civil society to emerge.[37] Frequently, CSOs are issue-specific and issue-driven, and as such have a strong sense of corporate identity. They are also politically, institutionally, and financially independent from the state. In fact, they often come into existence as the very result of the state's inability, or unwillingness, to perform those functions on which societies rely: its inability to ensure physical security, for instance, or its lack of sufficient attention to spreading literacy or giving people job skills. Therefore, the emergence over time of CSOs and later of civil society is contingent on the nature and extent of the relationship between the state and the larger society.

A democratic transition will not be possible until an authoritarian regime is confronted with a crisis of power. Consequently, CSOs, and even civil society, are, in themselves, inconsequential if they do not directly weaken state power. The CSOs and civil society give social actors a sense of empowerment and self-actualization, but this does not amount to the institutional weakening of the state and a vacuum of official power. By itself, therefore, civil society does not lead to democratization. The existence of civil society is not even a prerequisite for democratic transition. However, where it does exist, civil society greatly assists the transition to democracy and its consolidation, as pointed out by Linz and Stepan. Nevertheless, civil society also provides the larger societal and cultural context within which collapsing governments are replaced by democratic ones.

CIVIL SOCIETY IN THE MIDDLE EAST

CSOs or other similar "units" of civil society have historically existed in Middle Eastern societies, whether in the form of politically autonomous *ulama* or in the form of merchant guilds. In contemporary times, CSOs have proliferated in the form of informal religious gatherings, cultural groups, private or semiprivate educational institutions, and professional associations.[38] However, they have operated in highly hostile political and economic environments. As a result, these groups have been largely fragmented and unable to form mutually reinforcing ties and institutional links. Therefore, CSOs in the Middle East have largely failed to bring about civil society, or "political society," in Linz and Stepan's formulation.

There are two primary reasons for this: (1) the state's suspicion toward any manifestations of social autonomy because they fear that it may erode their ability to maintain their coercive relationship with society and (2) the pattern of state-dependent economic development through which the state curtails or makes dependent the powers of private capital. Financial dependence undermines the resources and possibilities available to social groups and seriously impedes their ability to act independently.

The Middle Eastern states' hostility to civil society has varied depending on the precise nature of the state's relationship with society. Some states have tended to have highly coercive relationships with their societies, allowing the least degree of financial autonomy to the market forces and the middle classes, and exhibit the greatest hostility toward independent groups and organizations. Consequently, civil society organizations are least developed in such states as Algeria, the Sudan, Libya, Yemen, Syria, and Iraq.[39]

Others, while suspicious of and therefore repressive toward CSOs and independent associations, foster economic conditions that are more conducive to the initial appearance and growth of middle-class-based groups. In Tunisia, for example, there is "a large educated middle class, a society relatively unfragmented by ethnic cleavage, a vast network of associations that are training citizens in civisme and civility, and an increasingly independent class of private entrepreneurs."[40] These are all ingredients of civil society. Nearly the same conditions exist in Egypt. However, both the Tunisian and Egyptian states have employed a variety of legal and repressive tools to either suppress independent associational activities or ensure their continued dependence on the state.

Others, including Arab monarchies, differ in the degree of their willingness to allow associational life. In recent years, Morocco, Jordan, and Kuwait have made positive changes in this direction by permitting the formation of professional associations and allowing them some limited breathing room.[41] However, Morocco has been unwilling to loosen its grip on such powerful CSOs as the Moroccan Workers Union (UMT) and the General Union of Moroccan Workers (UGMT) and to enable them to act independently.[42] Even traditional monarchies such as Saudi Arabia, Bahrain, Qatar, Oman, and the United Arab Emirates are moving, however slowly, toward greater democratic opening, especially after 2002.

From a comparative perspective, by far the most robust manifestations of civil society are found in the Middle East's few, and limited, democracies. Iran, Turkey, and Lebanon all feature political systems that have more limits placed on them in their interactions with society than any of the other states in the Middle East. Moreover, they have given rise to financial and social circumstances that make the growth of CSOs more of a possibility than is the case elsewhere. However, even in these countries civil society or even CSOs are not completely unhindered in pursuit of their goals. Periodic press crackdowns and imprisonment of journalists are common in Iran; Turkish political parties suspected of inadequate Kemalist credentials are routinely banned; Lebanon's associational life is often a victim of the country's confessional mosaic.[43]

In sum, in the past decade, there has been an unprecedented explosion of CSOs and of associational life in the Middle East, often accompanied by or a by-product of half measures toward democratization. Activists, scholars, and intellectuals in the region openly discuss and debate the merits of civil society and its relationship with social pluralism and democracy.[44] If civil society is an ideal to strive for, significant progress has been made, insofar as the preparatory groundwork is concerned. But there is still a long road ahead. CSOs in the Middle East remain largely embryonic in development and evolution and are closely monitored and harassed by the state. The middle classes, meanwhile, remain largely dependent on the state either directly or indirectly, and their ability to articulate political demands is highly circumscribed. Only when civil society in the Middle East succeeds in tipping the balance of power in favor of society and away from the state can it become a force for democratization.

CONCLUSION

Democracy is ultimately a question of balance of power between state and society, which results when a state's powers are held in check by procedures and institutional mechanisms grounded in and supported by society. Authoritarian states seek to ensure their longevity by fostering ruling bargains with key social and economic actors in which the state's resort to repression is complemented with some form of legitimacy, no matter how narrow and superficial. So long as the ruling bargain holds and the balance of power remains unchanged, with the state as the dominant actor holding social groups dependent on it for its largesse, a transition to democracy is unlikely to occur.

Political authoritarianism in the Middle East owes its longevity to the continued ideological and institutional cohesion of authoritarian elites, on the one hand, and their ability to perpetuate authoritarian ruling bargains that incorporate or pacify potentially oppositional social actors, on the other. Particular patterns of economic development and specific developmental outcomes may in the long run erode authoritarian ruling bargains and lead to defection from them by key social groups. This occurred in East Asia and South America, but by and large it has not taken place yet in the Middle East.

Democratic transitions do not become possible unless and until democratic bargains and pacts are struck between departing incumbents and incoming elites. Pacts that are based on implicit or explicit understandings over an emerging set of rules of the game are key to sustaining new democracies. A simple collapse of the authoritarian elite is more likely to lead to their replacement by another group of authoritarian elite, not to genuine democratization. This is what happened when Romania and the Soviet Union collapsed. Overthrowing authoritarian elites is an insufficient precondition for democratization, as the overthrow of the Iranian monarchy in 1978–79 demonstrated. Far more necessary is the existence of competing groups throughout the polity, within both the institutions of the state and the strata of society, among whom a consensus emerges regarding the mutually beneficial nature of democracy. In eastern Europe, South America, and East Asia, such a consensus developed when state leaders bankrupted themselves institutionally and economically, and social actors felt powerful enough to engage them in negotiations. For the time being, except in some instances, the development of similar predicaments do not seem likely in the Middle East. Leaders remain economically and institutionally powerful relative to society, and social actors find it hard to place demands on the state. Unless and until this uneven balance of power changes, by among other things the perusal of an economic development strategy that ultimately erodes the state's power, the prospects for democratic transition in the Middle East remain unpromising.

NOTES

1. Eva Bellin, *Stalled Democracy: Capital, Labor, and the Paradox of State-Sponsored Development* (Ithaca, NY: Cornell University Press, 2002), 4.

2. Ibid.

3. Chalmers Johnson, *MITI and the Japanese Miracle: The Growth of Industrial Policy* (Stanford, CA: Stanford University Press, 1982), 18–19. For more on Johnson's concept of the developmental state, see Chalmers Johnson, "The Developmental State: Odyssey of a Concept," in Meredith Woo-Cumings, ed., *The Developmental State* (Ithaca, NY: Cornell University Press, 1999), 32–60.

4. Guillermo O'Donnel, *Modernization and Bureaucratic-Authoritarianism: Studies in South American Politics* (Berkeley: Institute of International Studies, University of California, 1973).

5. James DeFronzo, *Revolutions and Revolutionary Movements,* 2nd ed. (Boulder, CO: Westview Press, 1996), 291–332.

6. This important point will be explored in greater detail in the next section.

7. Youn-Suk Kim, "Korea and the Developing Countries: Lessons from Korea's Industrialization," *Journal of East Asian Affairs* 11, no. 2 (1997): 426.

8. Ibid., 427.

9. Patrice Franko, *The Puzzle of Latin American Economic Development,* 2nd ed. (Lanham, MD: Rowman & Littlefield, 2003), 59–61.

10. John Waterbury, "The Long Gestation and Brief Triumph of Import-Substituting Industrialization," *World Development* 27, no. 2 (1999): 334–35.

11. Stephan Haggard and Robert R. Kaufman, *The Political Economy of Democratic Transitions* (Princeton, NJ: Princeton University Press, 1995), 33.

12. Ibid., 69.

13. David Waldner, *State Building and Late Development* (Ithaca, NY: Cornell University Press, 1999), 138.

14. Meredith Woo-Cumings, "Introduction: Chalmers Johnson and the Politics of Nationalism and Development," in Woo-Cumings, *Developmental State*, 6.

15. Waldner, *State Building,* 4.

16. Linda Weiss, *The Myth of the Powerless State* (Ithaca, NY: Cornell University Press, 1998), 55–59.

17. Bellin, *Stalled Democracy,* 163.

18. Waldner, *State Building,* 36.

19. Alan Richards and John Waterbury, *A Political Economy of the Middle East,* 2nd ed. (Boulder, CO: Westview Press, 1996), 210–11.

20. Marsha Pripstein Posusney, *Labor and the State in Egypt: Workers, Unions, and Economic Restructuring* (New York: Columbia University Press, 1997).

21. Marion Farouk-Sluglett and Peter Sluglett, *Iraq Since 1958: From Revolution to Dictatorship* (London: I. B. Tauris, 2001), 242.

22. Waldner, *State Building,* 71–72.

23. Richards and Waterbury, *Political Economy of the Middle East,* 16–21.

24. Iliya Harik and Denis Sullivan, eds., *Privatization and Liberalization in the Middle East* (Bloomington: Indiana University Press, 1992). According to Henry and Springborg, Middle Eastern and North African states "face a major crisis because they can no longer deliver the goods. As the rents evaporate, they must tax more and presumably be

subjected to greater accountability." Clement Henry and Robert Springborg, *Globalization and the Politics of Development in the Middle East* (Cambridge: Cambridge University Press, 2001), 76.

25. Bahgat Korany, Red Brynen, and Paul Noble, eds., *Political Liberalization and Democratization in the Arab World,* vol. 1, *Theoretical Perspective* (Boulder, CO: Lynne Rienner, 1995); Bahgat Korany, Red Brynen, and Paul Noble, eds., *Political Liberalization and Democratization in the Arab World:* vol. 2, *Comparative Experiences* (Boulder, CO: Lynne Rienner, 1998).

26. Jale Simensen, "Democracy and Globalization: Nineteen Eighty-Nine and the 'Third Wave,'" *Journal of World History* 19, no. 2 (1999): 394–95.

27. World Bank Group, *2003 World Development Indicators* (Washington, DC: World Bank, 2003), 312.

28. Henry and Springborg, *Globalization,* 19.

29. Ibid., 20–21.

30. Joshua Teitelbaum, "Dueling for *Daʿwa*: State vs. Society on the Saudi Internet," *Middle East Journal* 56, no. 2 (2002): 222–39.

31. After looking at the relationship between capitalist development and democracy in Europe, Latin America, and the Caribbean, Rueschemeyer, Stephens, and Stephens come to the conclusion that "factors such as dependent development, late and state-led development, international political constellations and events, and international learning, all conspired to create conditions in which the combination of causes and thus the paths to democracy (and dictatorship) were different in different historical contexts and in different regions." Dietrich Rueschemeyer, Evelyne Huber Stephens, and John D. Stephens, *Capitalist Development and Democracy* (Chicago: University of Chicago Press, 1992), 284.

32. Philip Oxhorn, "From Controlled Inclusion to Coerced Marginalization: The Struggle for Civil Society in Latin America," in John A. Hall, ed., *Civil Society: Theory, History, Comparison* (London: Polity Press, 1995), 251–52.

33. Ibid., 252.

34. Juan J. Linz and Alfred Stepan, *Problems of Democratic Transition and Consolidation: Southern Europe, South America, and Post-Communist Europe* (Baltimore: Johns Hopkins University Press, 1996), 7.

35. Ibid., 8.

36. Oxhorn, "From Controlled Inclusion," 251.

37. This is not to imply that whenever there is a cluster of CSOs they will necessarily lead to civil society.

38. Saad Eddin Ibrahim, "Civil Society and the Prospects for Democratization in the Arab World," in Augustus Richard Norton, ed., *Civil Society in the Middle East* (New York: E. J. Brill, 1995), 51–52; Hooshang Amirahmadi, "Emerging Civil Society in Iran," *SAIS Review* 16, no. 2 (1996): 87–107.

39. Henry and Springborg, *Globalization,* 123.

40. Eva Bellin, "Civil Society in Tunisia," in Norton, *Civil Society,* 147.

41. An example is the Kuwaiti government, which has made allowances for a CSO named the University Graduates' Society.

42. Thierry Desrues and Eduardo Moyano, "Social Change and Political Transition in Morocco," *Mediterranean Politics* 6, no. 1 (Spring 2001): 36.

43. Andrew Rigby, "Lebanon: Patterns of Confessional Politics," *Parliamentary Affairs* 53, no. 1 (2000): 169–80.

44. Mehran Kamrava, "The Civil Society Discourse in Iran," *British Journal of Middle Eastern Studies* 28, no. 2 (2001): 165–85; Fethullah Gülen, "A Comparative Approach to Islam and Democracy," *SAIS Review* 21, no. 2 (2001): 133–38; Salwa Ismael, "Democracy in Contemporary Arab Intellectual Discourse," in Korany, Brynen, and Noble, *Political Liberalization*, 1:93–111.

5

Islam and Modernity: Are They Compatible?

Tamara Sonn

Modernity is an equivocal term. In the West, where the term developed, "modernity" is often confused with "modernism," although the two are not synonymous. "Modernity" generally refers to the sociopolitical transformation of Europe that accompanied the scientific and technological developments ensuing from the Enlightenment. That transformation resulted from a shift from reliance on religion as the basis of political legitimacy to a reliance on democracy, and was accompanied by the separation of church and state and the emergence of secularism. "Modernism" refers to a philosophical approach to certainty that relies primarily on reason rather than revelation. It began with Descartes' effort to overcome doubt by identifying self-evident principles, but it is usually identified with Kant's critical analysis of epistemological, ethical, and aesthetic judgments. This intellectual approach to certainty is recognized as the basis for the development of modernity. However, in everyday usage, the meanings of "modernism" and "modernity" are merged. This is particularly evident in the Islamists' discussion of modernity. The Arabic term *ʿasriya* is commonly used to translate "modernity" and "modernism."

   In Islamic discourse, modernity/modernism often includes modernization, as well as scientific and technological development. But overall Islamic discussions of modernity focus on the fundamental issues of rationalism, secularism, and democracy. Islamic attitudes toward democracy are discussed elsewhere in this work. (See Chapter 6 in this volume by John O. Voll.) This discussion will focus on Islamic discourse on rationalism and secularism. It will demonstrate that, while there are no inherent barriers in Islam to these elements of Western modernity, the expressions of these phenomena are not necessarily identical in Western and Islamic societies. In particular, Islam's ideology and historical experience result in distinctly Islamic approaches to secularism.

RATIONALISM*

Muslim Brotherhood ideologue Sayyid Qutb (d. 1966) describes modernity as responsible for stripping humanity of its spirituality and its values and reducing human beings to the level of animals—perhaps rational, but animals nonetheless. In his words:

There is no doubt that man has attained great conquests by virtue of science. He has made immense progress in the field of medicine and treatment of physical diseases. In the same way, man has also made tremendous progress in the field of industrial products. But despite all these, the question arises what man has actually got out of these struggles and progress? Have they caused any spiritual growth? Has he gained the wealth of peace, comfort and satisfaction? The answer to all these questions is nothing but an emphatic 'No.' As a result of his material progress, instead of getting peace and ease, man is confronted [by] troubles, restlessness and fear.[1]

In Qutb's analysis, the root of this modern malaise is the replacement of the guidance of revelation with the dictates of human reason. This negative appraisal of modernity is predicated on the assumption that Western rationalism relies solely on reason and rejects faith. As such, it is seen as excessive intellectualism, the "de-spiritualization" of humanity. In Islamist discourse, the antidote to this essentially inhuman rationalism is Islam's deep spirituality, which does not preclude reason but subordinates it to faith. In this perspective, Islamic values keep reason in its proper place: in the service of faith. Although Sayyid Qutb's analysis is typical of modern Islamist discourse, other Islamic analyses reflect a more nuanced view of rationalism.

FAITH AND REASON IN TRADITIONAL VIEWPOINTS

Rationalism has a variety of connotations in Western philosophy, beginning with classical Greek efforts to avoid the seemingly arbitrary and unpredictable results of sense-based knowledge. This was to be achieved by relying on unchanging rational principles instead of empirical observation for certainty. This kind of extreme rationalism also appeared in the early modern period, again in the search for bases of certainty. By this time, sense perception was even more demonstrably imprecise. It had led people to think, for example, that the moon is a source of light and that the sun revolves around the earth, notions that had been demonstrated to be false by scientific means. Therefore, thinkers such as Descartes wanted to base all knowledge on unquestionable mathematical principles, avoiding sense data altogether.[2]

But what is commonly known in the West as "rationalism" is of a less radical

---

*This section is excerpted from my "Modernity, Islam, and the West," in Zafar Ishaq Ansari and John L. Esposito, eds., *Muslims and the West: Encounter and Dialogue* (Islamabad: Islamic Research, 2001), 216–31.

sort. Mainstream rationalism claims that sense perception provides the data upon which reason operates to give us knowledge of the world around us. To distinguish reliable propositions from unreliable or doubtful ones, modern rationalist philosophers distinguished among kinds of propositions or truth claims, and identified ways of reasoning. Kant distinguished between concepts derived from observation and those he believed were prior to experience (a priori), or simply part of the way human beings think. He said that we automatically perceive the things we observe in nature as being causally connected. For example, we assume that motion is caused in a formerly stationary object by the input of energy, even though we cannot observe the transfer of energy. Such a priori judgments, he believed, can be generally considered reliable, just as analytic statements can be. Analytic judgments are those derived from the very definition of the subject about which they are made—for example, that anything with size also has shape. By contrast, we must be more careful of synthetic statements that put together two elements not causally or essentially related.

In this way, rationalism seeks to avoid the uncertainties of mere opinion. But in its modernist phase, rationalism sought as well to supersede clear fallacies taught by religious authorities, such as geocentrism. As such, it can be seen as a reaction to a premodern order in which religion had political authority. This politicized religious authority tried to maintain its central role by denying the validity of any truths other than those propagated by the church. The rationalists, generally, were seeking a basis of certainty whereby human beings could argue authoritatively against those imperious powers who used religion to justify their control.

Because of this, rationalism is often judged to be antireligious and atheistic and therefore utterly lacking in morality. However, rationalism did not seek to supplant religious truth as such, much less the moral certainty that comes with it. Kant argued that the primary moral ideas of goodness and duty are innate and that the first principles of morality are self-evident. The paradigm of his "rational morality" is his categorical imperative: "Act only on that maxim which you can at the same time will to be a universal law." In other words, do only those things based on principles you believe should be followed by everyone. Furthermore, although Kant claimed that knowledge of the existence of God and the afterlife cannot be demonstrated on the basis of empirical knowledge, he believed that they must be assumed "as conditions of the full realization of the goals of morality."[3] Kant could not imagine a moral world without God and the afterlife.

This attitude toward the respective spheres of faith and reason reflects the traditional Christian approach. In the view of thirteenth-century theologian Thomas Aquinas, morality is perfectly reasonable. It does not have to be reasoned, because it is revealed; however, there is nothing in revelation that is repugnant to reason. Aquinas held that human beings are rational. Reason equips us to arrive at truth. Some truths can be reached through ordinary experience and reasoning about that experience. Among these truths are that God exists and that God is good and provides for us. But there are important religious truths that cannot be arrived at through reason. These have been revealed through scripture. We may then reason about these revealed truths, and we will find that they are not contrary to reason. But we would never have been aware of them had it not been for revelation. Therefore, reason and revelation are complementary, and both are necessary for human life.

The complementarity of faith and reason is also the traditional Islamic position. The question of the relationship between revealed truth and truths attainable by the human mind was already under discussion by the twelfth century. Andalusian philosopher Ibn Tufayl (d. 1185) wrote the story of Hayy ibn Yaqzan, who, abandoned on a desert isle—without benefit of revelation and using only his human faculties of observation and thought—came to an awareness of the one God.[4] An influential earlier philosopher, Abu Hamid Muhammad al-Ghazali (d. 1111), had argued that reason is insufficient for human happiness; revelation is necessary because human reason is inadequate to determine what is ultimately in the best interest of human beings. Ibn Tufayl's contemporary, Ibn Rushd (d. 1198) argued against al-Ghazali, saying that revelation is necessary for those unable to engage in higher philosophy, but that God has granted some people greater intellectual abilities; all people have the responsibility to pursue knowledge to the best of their abilities, and that includes philosophers. Ibn Rushd was perhaps the greatest influence on medieval Christian philosophy. However, many of his conclusions concerning revelation, including the equivalence of the philosophical intellect with that of Prophet Muhammad, like those of his great Iranian predecessor Ibn Sina (d. 1037), were condemned by mainstream Muslim theologians.

Nevertheless, the value of reason in human life was a dominant value in Islam from the earliest times. Fourteenth-century legal scholar Abd al-Rahman Ibn Mohammed Ibn Khaldun, taking inspiration from al-Ghazali, claimed that faith and reason are both necessary for a balanced human life. The ultimate goal of the Islamic community is justice, he said. Scriptures tell us that God established the Muslim community and commissioned Muslims—as his stewards—to spread justice throughout the world.[5] To do that, Ibn Khaldun says, people were given reason. Reason is necessary to achieve the goals established through revelation. Ibn Khaldun criticizes people in his era who take a passive attitude toward establishing justice or rely on fortune-tellers to predict the future. Instead, people should use reason to understand their religion and the world, and to therefore be able to establish Islamic values in the world's ever-changing circumstances. He says in *The Muqaddimah* that people's ability to think is what distinguishes them from animals. It allows human beings "to obtain their livelihood, to cooperate to this end with their fellow men, and to study the Master whom they worship, and the revelations that the Messengers transmitted from Him."[6]

As part of their commitment to justice and a healthy society, therefore, people should develop the sciences. Like Thomas Aquinas, Ibn Khaldun believed that there are some things in revelation that cannot be elucidated through reason. The study of rational arguments that support basic beliefs—such as the oneness of God—is important as a means to defend religious truths from those who try to lead others astray. But people should not try to find comprehensive explanations for the whole of existence, as the Greek philosophers did. That kind of study is bound to lead to frustration and even despair, because the human mind is by nature limited. Therefore, people should concentrate on things they can understand. Ibn Khaldun describes empirical science as the kind of understanding of their environment that human beings can develop through observation and reasoning in an orderly way. Pursuit of this kind of science has obvious practical uses that promote human well-being. Of all sciences, however, law is the most important, because it details the ways to promote justice and prevent injustice. This is why the great Islamic thinkers of the medieval world claimed that the pursuit of science is a religious duty.

In these formulations, Islam places greater emphasis on the need for reason than does Christianity. For Aquinas, people may engage in rational pursuits, but this process is not necessary since revelation tells us what we need to know. In Ibn Khaldun's view, people must reason to determine how to carry out the divine mandate of *khilafah* (stewardship). But both views limit the use of reason regarding divinity. The proper sphere of reason is the practical.

Clearly then, the role of reason in classical Islamic formulations does not differ significantly from that in classical Christianity. Interestingly, the misunderstanding of the role of reason in modern Western society by some Islamists is perhaps as profound as Aquinas' misunderstanding of the role of reason in Islam. Among Aquinas' major works is his critique of non-Christian ideas, primarily those of Muslims, the *Summa Contra Gentiles*. There he complains that this is a "difficult business" because, among other problems,

the Mohammedans and the pagans . . . do not agree with us in accepting the authority of any Scripture, by which they may be convinced of their error. Thus, against the Jews we are able to argue by means of the Old Testament, while against heretics we are able to argue by means of the New Testament. But the Mohammedans and the pagans accept neither the one nor the other. We must, therefore, have recourse to natural reason, to which all men are forced to give their assent. However, it is true, in divine matters the natural reason has its failings.[7]

Muslims reading this passage would be very surprised to find that they do not recognize the authority of scripture. What could Aquinas have been talking about? In fact, Aquinas was criticizing not Islamic thinkers as such, but Islamic philosophers, specifically Ibn Sina and Ibn Rushd. Rather than accept that reason sometimes is incapable of understanding revelation, as Aquinas did, these philosophers adhered to the "dual truth" hypothesis. In their view, both reason and revelation are sources of truth, but when revelation conflicts with the results of reason, revelation should be understood metaphorically.

This position was rejected by the mainstream Islamic religious scholars. In Christianity, because the philosophers were the mainstream religious scholars, Aquinas assumed that Ibn Sina and Ibn Rushd represented mainstream Islamic religious thought and concluded that Muslims do not recognize the authority of scripture. But in Islam, the mainstream religious scholars were the *fuqaha'*, the legal scholars. They were the ones who used reason to guide society on questions about how best to implement the commands given in revelation.

Viewed in this light, it is clear that reason and revelation are complementary in both Christianity and Islam. This is true in classical and modern Christianity, as it was in classical Islam. But is it true in modern Islam?

REASON AND RELIGION IN MODERN ISLAM

When Western observers hear the condemnations of modernity emanating from twentieth-century Islamists, they tend to doubt it. Closer examination of those condemnations indicates that it is not reason as such—or even modernity, as it is understood in the West—that is being condemned, but the actions of Western countries that colonized the Muslim world. Islamist condemnations must be recognized as protests against imperialism and the continued problems of post-colonial life, which are also blamed—rightly or wrongly—on the West. Virtually all of the Muslim world was colonized, and this is the dominant reality in its modern history; developments in twentieth-century Islamic thought can be viewed as a series of efforts to deal with its results.

Prior to World War I, Islamic reform efforts were characterized by appeals to Islam's inherent rationality and commitment to science and learning. A prominent proponent of this perspective was Jamal al-Din al-Afghani (d. 1897). Islamic reformers particularly resented the European rationalization of their imperialism on the basis of claims that Islamic culture was backward and unscientific. Afghani noted that it was Islam's commitment to learning that had produced the highest scientific culture in the Middle Ages. Scholars in the Muslim world had pulled together the ancient traditions of Greece, Egypt, Mesopotamia, India, and China, revising and developing them, and then transmitted them to Europe. According to Afghani, science "is continually changing capitals. Sometimes it has moved from East to West, and other times from West to East." Science does not belong to any single culture; it is a world heritage to which various communities have contributed at various times. Noting Muslims' major contributions to science, Afghani concludes that Europeans are mistaken when they claim that Islam is inherently unscientific or backward. In fact, he says, of all the major religions Islam is the most supportive of science.

Afghani recognized that Muslims had lost their commitment to learning and their scientific spirit. He believed that they had passed it on to the Europeans, leading to the latter's dominance over Muslims. Afghani was particularly critical of religious scholars who cautioned people about science and mistakenly "divided science into two parts. One they call Muslim science, and one European science." They did not even recognize their own scientific heritage when confronted with it in modern form. They thought it was all foreign. He concludes, "Those who forbid science and knowledge in the belief that they are safeguarding the Islamic religion are really the enemies of that religion. The Islamic religion is the closest of religions to science and knowledge, and there is no incompatibility between science and knowledge and the foundation of the Islamic faith."[8]

Egyptian religious scholar Muhammad Abduh (d. 1905) also encouraged Muslims to revive their spirit of intellectual independence, and cautioned against traditionalism. He said that "traditionalism can have evil consequences as well as good and may occasion loss as well as conduce gain. It is a deceptive thing, and though it may be pardoned in an animal, is scarcely seemly in man."[9]

According to Abduh, it was intellectual creativity that within a few centuries had allowed the Islamic community to become one of the world's major political and cultural forces. But when Muslims began to simply imitate their ancestors, elevating tradition to the status of virtue, they lost their intellectual vigor and fell into obscurity and became easy prey for more energetic forces. Abduh noted that the universe is inherently rational. He described rationality as a reflection of divine unity. Rejecting the tendency to split the world into the spiritual (religious) realm and the physical (nonreligious) realm, Abduh insisted that the divine is revealed through all creation. Based on the Qur'anic command to "read the signs" and "seek knowledge," Abduh considered the exercise of reason to be essential to the practice of Islam. Failure to exercise one's reason was a religious failing.

The stress on reason and science in nineteenth-century Islamic reform movements was accompanied by an optimism that was lost in the aftermath of World War I. Instead of gaining independence and progress, those Muslims who supported the European war effort remained under colonial rule or great-power influence. This disappointment caused a backlash against the earlier reform efforts and eroded the Muslims' admiration for the European culture of Enlightenment. Some Muslim leaders embraced Soviet-style militant socialism. But on the popular level a more indigenous approach to cultural and political empowerment, based on Islamic symbols and values, had greater appeal and led to the emergence of a movement variously called fundamentalism, Islamism, and political Islam. Because of the failure of the earlier "foreign" models of reform, this movement called for their replacement with Islam.

This indigenous approach favors radical transformation of society, and its ultimate goals are similar to those of the earlier movements: independence, peace, and prosperity. But the means advocated to achieve these goals are different. In contrast to World War I movements that stressed an identity based on rationality and cultural sophistication vis-à-vis Europe and tended to deny major cultural differences between Islam and the West, Islamism calls on people to recognize their unique Islamic identity and stresses that Islam provides solutions to all their problems. Islamists' popular appeal derives from their insistence that Islamic teachings, norms, institutions, and coping mechanisms are both necessary and sufficient to produce a just society.

There are two identifiable strains of Islamist discourse. One phase stands in stark contrast to the confident optimism of its reformist predecessors. It is defensive, bordering on xenophobic, characterized by deep distrust of a stereotypical "West" that seems bent on undermining and even destroying the Muslim world. It blames virtually all of the Muslim world's problems and shortcomings on the West. Islamism acknowledges the need for revising Islamic law to suit changing realities and criticizes traditional religious leaders for passivity in the face of oppression, but it does not offer a detailed program. Rather, Islamist discourse is utopian. Its hallmark is the claim that Islam is the solution to all problems, from moral to social, political, economic, and environmental. It is not concerned with the details of achieving power or running governments. This kind of Islamist discourse can be characterized as concerned primarily with consciousness-raising. Its main goal is to motivate people to assert their unique Islamic identity in a world dominated by the globalizing West.

Another strain of Islamist discourse is more self-critical, rational, and practical. It recognizes the positive role of reason in Islam and stresses the need to exercise it. For example, Iran's president Muhammad Khatami espouses reform and development in the context of what he calls a total transformation of society.[10] He notes that Iran, like all Islamic societies, is still struggling with economic, social, and political underdevelopment. While admitting the legacy of colonialism as one of the sources of these problems, Khatami maintains that the persistence of underdevelopment is the responsibility of Islamic societies themselves. In contrast to those Islamists who totally reject Western society, he says that Western societies have positive strengths and achievements, and identifies modernity specifically as something Muslims should try to emulate. Thus, Khatami's approach differs from the earlier Islamist ideology. Modernity, he points out, is not a rejection of religion in favor of godless reason but rather is merely a rejection of the "autocratic and whimsical rulers." Two essential elements of modernity, he says, are freedom and reason. Freedom is necessary for people to be able to use reason as God intended it to be used: to examine societies and find out what is necessary to remedy their problems. "Transformation and progress require thought," he says.[11]

Algerian reformer Mohamed Arkoun also bemoans the negative effect that defensive, militantly anti-Western activists have had on Islam's present intellectual climate. He speaks of their "intellectual poverty" and considers their views a deviation from Islam's intellectual traditions. He says, "There is a need to encourage and initiate audacious, free, productive thinking on Islam today." The task now, as it has always been, is to "integrate . . . new disciplines, new knowledge, and new historical insights into Islam."[12] Similarly, Moroccan philosopher Mohammed ʿAbed al-Jabri calls upon Muslims to examine their intellectual and scientific heritage. They must distinguish between the content of that knowledge, by now quite outdated, and the process of developing that knowledge. That process—the "intellectual enterprise" of thinking, examining information, developing new knowledge—is an essential part of Islam's tradition. Those wishing to assert an authentic Islamic identity vis-à-vis the West, he says, would do well to reactivate that intellectual enterprise.[13] Iranian intellectual and reformer Abdolkarim Soroush agrees. He traces the roots of modernity, including secularism, to the use of reason. Human beings were created with reason, and reason demands freedom: "We are impassioned about freedom and consider it the *sine qua non* of humanity because reason and freedom are inextricably intertwined."[14] "Our mission as rational human beings is to search actively for the truth."[15]

In sum, while antirational viewpoints appear in some Islamic discourse on modernity, they do not represent an essentially Islamic position on the subject. Understanding of basic Islamic teachings on the human responsibility to exercise reason, along with both classic discussions of the role of reason in society and the broad range of contemporary discourse on the subject, reveals that Islam cannot be construed as an impediment to rationality. Just as in Western heritage, faith and reason are seen as complementary in Islam.

SECULARISM

In Europe's modernity, the reliance on reason was accompanied by the development of secularism. Reason was considered the secular (Latin *saecula*, concerned with the temporal realm) replacement for the eternal (Latin *aeterna*, outside the temporal realm) authority of church authorities, and demanded the separation of religion and state. In premodern Europe, from December 25, 800, when Charlemagne was crowned emperor of Rome by Pope Leo III, religious officials played critical roles in legitimating government. Church and state worked together in a kind of mutual empowerment. Both, therefore, were implicated in the atrocities of the old regimes, and both vigorously resisted the transition to democratic legitimation of government. Because of their antidemocratic stance, removal of religious officials from politics was critical to the success of democratization. The institutionalized church was not only antidemocratic but unquestionably religiously exclusivist, as illustrated by the long history of Europe's religious warfare. It was therefore necessary to isolate it from political power to safeguard both democracy and pluralism. In the case of France, which endured a bloody, revolutionary break from church-legitimated authority, the insistence on laicism remains particularly strong.

Must secularism therefore be considered an essential component of modernity and its concomitant democratization? Some modern Islamic thinkers condemn secularism. Fazlur Rahman equates secularism with atheism and attributes the atrocities of colonialism to the West's secularism. For him it is "the bane of modernity."[16] Abdolkarim Soroush, a proponent of democracy, likewise rejects secularism. He says:

It is amazing that some consider the democratization of the religious government contingent upon the secularization of religion and religious law. Liberal democracy draws inspiration and strength from the authentic axiom that states: human beings are naturally free and unique. . . . Is the religious society not, by nature, plural and pluralistic? . . . Belief is a hundred times more diverse and colorful than disbelief. If the pluralism of secularism makes it suitable for democracy, the faithful community is a thousand times more suitable for it. . . . We no longer claim that a genuinely religious government can be democratic but that it cannot be otherwise.[17]

This view reflects the attitude of the majority of Muslims who, according to a 2003 Pew Global Attitudes Poll, favor both democratization and a greater role for Islam in politics. Such assertions appear confusing from the Western viewpoint, where pluralism demanded secularism. But Islamic ideology and historic experiences differ from those of the premodern West, resulting in uniquely Islamic approaches to pluralism in the modern world.

ROOTS OF PLURALISM IN ISLAM

Religious pluralism is rooted in the Qur'an's explicit acceptance of religious diversity: "For each of you [religious communities: Jews, Christians, Muslims] we have appointed a law and a ritual. If God had willed it, he could have made you all one religious community. But [he has not] so that he may test you in what he has given you. So compete with one another in good works" (5:48 cf. 11:118). Muslims are told: "[The People of the Book—i.e., Jews and Christians] are not all alike; some of them are upstanding, reciting God's signs in the night watches, bowing, believing in God and the Last Day, bidding good and forbidding evil, and competing with one another in good works. They are righteous" (3:109–10). Therefore, the Qur'an says, "Do not argue with the People of the Book unless it is with something that is better, except with such of them who do wrong. And say: We believe in what has been revealed to us and revealed to you. Our God and your God are one, and to him we surrender" (29:46). Rejecting exclusivism, the Qur'an exhorts all monotheists to work together for the common good: "O People of the Book [Jews, Christians, Muslims], let us come together upon a formula that is common among us, so that we may serve only God" (3:64).

The normative model established by Prophet Muhammad—the Sunna—confirms this acceptance of pluralism. When the newly formed Muslim community moved from Mecca to Medina to escape religious persecution there, Prophet Muhammad dictated a constitution to guide intercommunal relations. In the constitution, Muhammad said, "The Jews . . . are a community along with the believers. To the Jews their religion and to the Muslims theirs."[18] The constitution then confirmed that the various tribes would cooperate in mutual support and loyalty, but that each group was free to practice its religion. Only those who were disloyal to the community would lose their rights.

Based on the Qur'an and the example of the Prophet, Islamic legal scholars institutionalized religious freedom. That included the freedom of non-Muslims to live according to their own laws of religious practice and personal status, although in civil and criminal matters they were bound by Islamic law. Non-Muslims were treated differently in matters of taxation and sometimes in regard to social practices. At times they were required to wear distinctive clothing and to put a mark on their houses and keep them shorter than Muslims' houses. Nevertheless, Islam maintained its essential pluralism, and because Islamic sources accepted the validity of other revealed religions, Islamic political theory protected the rights of non-Muslims to practice their respective religions.

ROOTS OF EXCLUSIVISM IN ISLAMIC THOUGHT

Despite that essential pluralism, hostility toward the West stemming from the colonial experience and postcolonial condition has raised questions about pluralism in modern Islamic thought. This hostility often takes on an ideological caste in contemporary Islamist discourse, where an elision is made between the degenerate nature of Western society and secularism itself. In many cases, secularism is construed in such a way as to make it utterly and hopelessly immoral. In an article entitled "Toward a More Comprehensive and Explanatory Paradigm of Secularism," Egyptian scholar Abdulwahab al-Masiri rejects the definition of secularism as "the separation of church and state," although he acknowledges that this definition has "gained currency." He claims that secularism, "if defined in a complex way," is "a total world outlook, a weltanschauung, a comprehensive paradigm" that "operates on all levels of reality through a large number of implicit and explicit mechanisms"; it is "the underlying and over-arching paradigm in modern Western civilization, and in all modernities for that matter." Ultimately, al-Masiri says, secularism is the paradigm accounting for a staggering array of problems, which he characterizes as "the crisis of modern civilization."[19]

This attitude was reflected in the views of early Islamists such as Abu'l-A'la Mawdudi (d. 1978). Some legal scholars in colonial India had determined that as long as Muslims were free to practice their religion under British rule, the territory remained Muslim.[20] Mawdudi rejected this view. Assuming the classical identity of Muslims as those living subject to an Islamic state, he viewed Muslims as a special community that must keep itself separate from non-Muslims, characterized generally as nonbelievers. Mawdudi believed that this was necessary to preserving Muslims' religious and cultural identity. However, there are many Islamic voices that challenge this exclusivism on Islamic grounds.

ISLAMIC ARGUMENTS FOR PLURALISM AND DEMOCRACY

Sheikh Rachid Ghannouchi, the exiled leader of Tunisia's al-Nahda Party, is one of these voices. He argues in favor of Muslims' participating in non-Muslim governments. He says that Islam has given Muslims the responsibility to protect certain essential human rights through the ages and in whatever circumstances. He cites fourteenth-century Andalusian legal scholar al-Shatibi's list of the essential human rights to be protected by any Islamic government: religion, life, family, wealth, and the mind (or reason). Ghannouchi insists that in all historical circumstances, the critical issue for Muslims is "the fulfillment of the needs of humans and serving their best interests."[21] It would be ideal, he says, to live in a truly Islamic government. But since that is not possible today, Muslims must work with what is available, and that is what he calls "power-sharing." Ghannouchi bases his claim on another essential Islamic principle, *shura*, which he defines as the authority of the community. Muslims must work with whoever is willing to help achieve essential goals, such as "independence, development, social solidarity, civil liberties, human rights, political pluralism, independence of the judiciary, freedom of the press, or liberty for mosques and Islamic activities."[22] He cites a number of authoritative examples from Islamic history, notably Joseph, who, abandoned by his brothers, ended up in the pharaoh's government. What made this Islamic? It was that he was acting out of a sense of duty "to rescue many nations that were threatened by famine and drought. He did not wait for the Egyptian people to renounce paganism and embrace his monotheistic religion." Instead, he followed his duty to work for the well-being of all people.

Therefore, Ghannouchi concludes that "the community of believers may participate in any alliance aimed at preventing injustice and oppression, at serving the interests of mankind, at protecting human rights, at recognizing the authority of the people and at rotating power-holding through a system of elections. The faithful can pursue all these noble objectives even with those who do not share the same faith or ideology."[23] Dismissing the conclusions of Mawdudi, he says, "A just government, even if not Islamic, is considered very close to the Islamic one, because justice is the most important feature of an Islamic government, and it has been said that justice is the law of God."[24] Therefore, "The best option for such minorities is to enter into alliances with secular democratic groups. They can then work towards the establishment of a secular democratic government which will respect human rights, ensuring security and freedom of expression and belief—essential requirements of humanity that Islam has come to fulfill."[25]

European Muslim scholar Tariq Ramadan takes this argument farther. Rather than justifying Muslim participation in just non-Muslim governments merely as a temporary phenomenon resulting from the lack of a truly Islamic government in the present era, Ramadan views it as a historic development consistent with Islamic principles. Ramadan rejects the notion that there is an ideal form of Islamic government and identifies essential components of any Islamic government. He says that revelation (the Qur'an and Sunna) provides both essential principles and examples of how to implement those principles in specific historic contexts. But as those contexts change, so must the means of implementation. The roots of Islamic jurisprudence, *usul al-fiqh*, provide the means to do that. They "make clear that Islam allows us to consider its intrinsic possibilities for adaptation to space and time."[26] Islam's principles constitute a way of life that not only can but must be lived in all contexts. Fiqh has prescribed the methodology, *ijtihad*, for devising ways of accommodating changing circumstances while maintaining fidelity to Islamic principles.

Among the accommodations required by the present age is jettisoning the archaic bifurcation of the world into Muslim and non-Muslim spaces (*dar al-islam* and *dar al-harb*). Like Ghannouchi, Ramadan offers pertinent examples of Muslims living under non-Muslim rule during the time of Prophet Muhammad. He does not dispute that in the Prophet's time these were temporary arrangements. But, unlike Ghannouchi, Ramadan believes that there is no reason to make the same requirement today, as it would be "a methodological mistake," not accounting for today's realities.[27] For example, it would allow no space for European converts to Islam. Rather than requiring Muslims who live under secular European law to consider themselves in exile or diaspora, Ramadan insists that "there is absolutely no contradiction . . . between their citizenship and their being Muslims; the law allows them to act in this sense, their faith commands it."[28]

Why then do some Muslims claim Islam is opposed to secular democracy? Ramadan says it is because they are failing to take into consideration differences in the historical circumstances in which Islam and Western democracies developed. In the latter case, it was necessary to develop political institutions independent of religious authorities because of the oppressive coercive authorities the institutionalized church had supported. But this is not the case in Islamic history. Because religious authorities were not affiliated with coercive power for the most part, Muslims were never required to separate themselves from it.

Ramadan concludes that Islam is completely opposed to theocracy and adds that although there is no unique model of Islamic government, basic principles have been provided, which he calls "a framework to run pluralism."[29] For example, Islamic government must be conducted through consultation and, as Ghannouchi claims, also requires freedom of conscience. This is based on Ramadan's reading of the Qur'an's prohibition of compulsion in matters of religion (2:256). Thus, he says, people must have the right to choose their leaders, express their opinions, and live—male and female, Muslim and non-Muslim—under equal protection of the law. The exact forms taken by government must adapt to the circumstances.

Egyptian-American legal scholar Khaled Abou El Fadl largely agrees. He recognizes that Islamist arguments against secular democracy turn on the question of sovereignty. In that discourse, democratic government replaces divine sovereignty with human sovereignty and therefore cannot be considered consistent with Islam. But to Abou El Fadl, this reasoning is faulty. First, it is strictly reactionary. It is used by people who want to distinguish themselves from the West; if Western government is based on popular sovereignty, many Islamists insist that Islamic government cannot be. But beyond that, this argument is not based on a thorough understanding of classical Islamic principles. In Abou El Fadl's analysis, Islamic tradition is pluralistic and incorporates a number of concepts comparable to those of modern secular democracies. To illustrate: Early Muslim jurists "agreed on the notion that government exists by contract—'*aqd al-khal-*

ifa—between the ruler and the ruled."[30] They differed on the status of this contract but agreed that there must be popular approval of the government. This is confirmed by the concept of *bayah* or pledge of allegiance in the classical Islamic thought. Finally, both the Qur'an and the Sunna call for *shura*, government by consultation.

The major difference between Ramadan's and Abou El Fadl's analyses is revealed in Abou El Fadl's understanding of the notion of sovereignty. For him, it is critical to distinguish between God's eternal and immutable will, and human efforts to articulate that will into practical codes of law. Going back to a distinction insisted on by medieval jurists such as Ibn Taymiyya and al-Juwayni, Abou El Fadl identifies the former as *Shari'a* and the latter as *fiqh*. The notion of divine sovereignty is unassailable in Islam, but that does not mean that legal codes based on the divine will as revealed in the Qur'an and exemplified in the life of Prophet Muhammad are likewise flawless. Abou El Fadl says, "The Islamic tradition, like any other tradition, is determined by human agents and constructed in a variety of ways to mean a variety of things in a variety of contexts in various periods of history."[31] He cites a hadith in which the fourth Caliph Ali said that the Qur'an is "but ink and paper, and it does not speak for itself. Instead, it is human beings who give effect to it according to their limited personal judgments and opinions."[32]

The idea that God is the sole legislator is therefore "a fatal fiction that is indefensible from the point of view of Islamic theology," because as Abou El Fadl insists, it assumes that some human beings have perfect access to the divine will.[33] As perfect a guide as the Qur'an is, it does not regulate everything human beings will ever do. It gives guidance for all aspects of life, but specific rulings for specific contexts, aside from the basic regulations presented in revelation, are left for human beings to extract. They must be guided by the Qur'an's principles, and these have been articulated by jurists through the ages. Abou El Fadl identifies justice and mercy as foremost among them. No human being or group of human beings can claim to have direct access to the divine will other than through the guidance of revelation. Whether through an advisory body of jurists, as in the Middle Ages, or an elected assembly of representatives, as in a modern democracy, people must struggle to implement a social order that is both just and merciful. Because it is administered by human beings, it must be recognized as fallible and therefore must remain flexible. But to the extent that it is successful in establishing justice and mercy, it will reflect divine sovereignty. As Abou El Fadl puts it, "Principles of mercy and justice are the primary divine charge, and God's sovereignty lies in the fact that God is the authority that delegated to human beings the charge to achieve justice on earth by fulfilling the virtues that approximate divinity."[34]

What constitutes a just and merciful government in today's world? For Abou El Fadl, as for Ghannouchi, it is one that protects the basic human rights identified by Islam's classical jurists. Traditional interpretations of these rights, however, are no longer tenable. For example, early scholars interpreted the protection of religion as the prohibition of apostasy on punishment of death, and the protection of mind or reason as the prohibition of alcohol. Nowadays, those interpretations would not achieve a just and merciful society. Those rights must be "re-analyzed in light of the current diversity of human existence." In particular, he calls for equal rights for all citizens. Any government that does these things reflects the divine mandate. By recognizing the human responsibility for articulating, executing, and adjudicating that government, divine sovereignty remains intact. In other words, "Democracy . . . offers the greatest potential for promoting justice and protecting human dignity, without making God responsible for human injustice or the degradation of human beings by one another."[35]

These scholars agree not only that Islam is compatible with secular democratic principles, but that Islamic principles demand secular democracy in today's world, although they disagree on the details of the working of democracy. Ramadan says that the role of the scholars may now be taken up by elected assemblies, while Abou El Fadl believes that the scholars should remain an identifiable body and advise Muslim voters. However the details are worked out, these views are typical of such modern Muslim thinkers who call for political participation with non-Muslims to achieve Islamic goals of justice and mercy and who believe that in order for a government to conform to Islamic principles, it must fully and equally protect the rights of Muslims and non-Muslims. That is, as Soroush says, they believe a government does not have to be secular to protect religious pluralism, but it has to be pluralist to be Islamic.

CONCLUSION

This discussion has argued that there are no essential impediments in Islam to the development of either rationalism or secularism, key components of modernity. Just as in Christian thought, out of which modern rationalism grew, Islamic thought reflects a conviction that faith and reason are complementary. Both Christians and Muslims hold that reason is of limited use when confronted with divinity. But there is nothing inherently antirational in either their classical or modern thought. Indeed, the free and energetic exercise of reason is a characteristic component of Islamic heritage. However, Western and Islamic experiences of pluralism have diverged in critical ways. Unlike premodern Western law, classical Islamic law protected pluralism. As a result, the West's modernity stresses the separation of religion and politics, while voices of modern Islam find that separation unnecessary. While pluralism is considered essential to modern Islamic democracies, secularism as such is not.

In 1992, Francis Fukuyama's *The End of History* raised the question of whether it is possible to imagine modernity in ways different from the Western model.[36] As Emmanuel Todd summarizes Fukuyama's position, the goal of history is "the universalization of liberal democracy."[37] Others argue that there can be many "modernities." John Voll, for example, has argued that it is a mistake to equate modernity with "the West." He describes modernity as "a phase of world history" characterized by "set processes that brought an end to the traditional lifestyles of medieval civilizations." These processes were set in motion by industrialization and, in fact, follow organically from industrialization. Western Europe pioneered these processes, but they have no exclusive control over them. In that sense, Voll concludes that identifying modernity as "Western" would be like identifying writing as Sumerian. Instead, he says, modernity can take a variety of forms, "which will be shaped by the broad cultural traditions of the humans involved."[38] That is just what Islamic modernity is doing. It appears that Islamic countries are developing their own models of modernity, ones that value the role of reason and are pluralist, but also religious.

NOTES

1. Sayyid Qutb, *Islam: The True Religion,* trans. Ravi Ahmad Fidai (Karachi, Pakistan: International Islamic Publishers, 1981), 25–26.

2. Rene Descartes, "Meditations," in Rene Descartes, *The Philosophical Writings of Descartes*, 1st and 2nd ed., trans. J. Cottingham, R. Stoothoff, and D. Murdoch (Cambridge: Cambridge University Press, 1985).

3. Henry E. Allison, "Kant," in Ted Honderich, ed., *The Oxford Companion to Philosophy* (Oxford: Oxford University Press, 1995), 437.

4. Translated into Latin, this work became a model for later Christian philosophers, as well.

5. The reference here is to two fundamental tenets in Islam, *amanah* and *khilafah*. The former is based on the Qur'an's description of creation wherein God entrusts the world to human beings (33:72). The second refers to the Qur'an's designation of human beings as God's representative or stewards on earth (2:30; 6:165).

6. Abd al-Rahman Ibn Mohammad Ibn Khaldun, *The Muqaddimah,* trans. Franz Rosenthal (Princeton, NJ: Princeton University Press, 1974), 333.

7. Saint Thomas Aquinas, *Summa Contra Gentiles,* trans. Anton C. Pegis (Notre Dame, IN: University of Notre Dame Press, 1975), 1:62.

8. Nikki R. Keddie, *An Islamic Response to Imperialism: Political and Religious Writings of Sayyid Jamal al-Din "al-Afghani"* (Berkeley: University of California Press, 1983), 103–7.

9. Muhammad Abduh, *The Theology of Unity,* trans. Ishaq Musaʿad and Kenneth Cragg (London: George Allen & Unwin, 1966), 39–40.

10. Mohammad Khatami, *Islam, Liberty, and Development* (Binghamton, NY: Institute of Global Cultural Studies, Binghamton University, 1998), 3.

11. Ibid., 11.

12. Mohamed Arkoun, "Rethinking Islam Today," in Charles Kurzman, ed., *Liberal Islam: A Sourcebook* (New York: Oxford University Press, 1998), 205–7.

13. Mohammed ʿAbed al-Jabri, *Arab-Islamic Philosophy: A Contemporary Critique,* trans. Aziz Abbassi (Austin: University of Texas Center for Middle Eastern Studies, 1999).

14. Mahmoud Sadri and Ahmad Sadri, trans. and eds., *Reason, Freedom, and Democracy in Islam: Essential Writings of ʿAbdolkarim Soroush* (Oxford: Oxford University Press, 2000), 88.

15. Ibid., 90.

16. Fazlur Rahman, *Islam and Modernity: Transformation of an Intellectual Tradition* (Chicago: University of Chicago Press, 1982), 15.

17. Sadri and Sadri, *Reason, Freedom, and Democracy,* 144–45.

18. For the entire text of the Constitution of Medina, reportedly dictated by Muhammad, see W. Montgomery Watt, *Islamic Political Thought: The Basic Concepts* (Edinburgh: Edinburgh University Press, 1968), 130–34.

19. Delivered at the University of South Florida, Tampa, Spring 1995.

20. Majid Khadduri, *War and Peace in the Law of Islam* (Baltimore: Johns Hopkins University, 1955; New York: AMS Press, 1979), 157, where he references Abdur Rahim, *Principles of Muhammadan Jurisprudence* (Madras, 1911), 396–97; William W. Hunter, *The Indian Musalmans* (London: Trübner, 1871), 120–25.

21. Rachid Ghannouchi, "Participation in Non-Islamic Government," in Kurzman, *Liberal Islam,* 91.

22. Ibid.

23. Ibid., 93.

24. Ibid.

25. Ibid., 94.

26. Tariq Ramadan, *To Be a European Muslim* (Leicester: Islamic Foundation, 1998), 65.

27. Ibid., 126.

28. Ibid., 175.

29. Tariq Ramadan, "The Notion of Shura: Shura or Democracy?" http://max211. free.fr/articles/anglais/articles-shorra.htm.

30. Ethics and Public Policy Center, "Islam's Forgotten Heritage: A Conversation with Khaled Abou el Fadl," June 24, 2003, http://www.eppc.org/programs/islam/publications/ pubID.1588,programID.36/pub_detail.asp (accessed October 3, 2003).

31. Ibid.

32. Khaled Abou El Fadl, "Islam and the Challenge of Democracy," *Boston Review* (April–May 2003), http://www.bostonreview.net/BR28.2/abou.html (accessed October 2, 2003).

33. Ibid.

34. Ibid.

35. Ibid.

36. Francis Fukuyama, *The End of History and the Last Man* (New York: Free Press, 1992).

37. Emmanuel Todd, *After the Empire: The Breakdown of the American Order* (New York: Columbia University Press, 2003), 9.

38. John O. Voll, "The Mistaken Identification of 'The West' with 'Modernity,' " *American Journal of Islamic Social Sciences* 13, no. 1 (Spring 1996): 1–6.

6

Islam and Democracy: Is Modernization a Barrier?

John O. Voll

Does religion represent an obstacle to modernization and democratization? Does religion pose a threat to democracy if a democratically elected government becomes a "theocracy"? Does the majority rule of democracy threaten the liberty and freedom of other members of a society? If the majority imposes its will on minorities, is that a departure from democracy in general or from "liberal" democracy? Does modernization strengthen or inhibit democratization and individual liberty? These broad questions are being debated in many different contexts around the world. They provide a framework for looking at the experience of Muslim societies and the relationships between Islam and democracy.

Tensions between democracy and liberty have deep historical roots and are presently visible around the world. The rise of what Fareed Zakaria calls "illiberal democracy" is an important product of these tensions.[1] "It appears that many countries are adopting a form of government that mixes a substantial degree of democracy with a good deal of illiberalism [restriction of individual liberties]."[2] Religion can play a role in defining and imposing this "illiberalism." These developments occur within a global context shaped by the interaction between local politics and the policies of the United States. "Countries are often deciding how best to move along the path to democracy. And the United States is constantly formulating policies to deal with countries as they move—or slip—along that path."[3] This provides an important framework for studying the case of the Muslim world, since "nowhere are these tough choices between order and instability, liberalism and democracy, and secularism and religious radicalism more stark" than in the Muslim world today.[4]

Major tensions within societies and in international relations are created by different understandings of the threats and possibilities of democratic participation by religious movements. Many leaders and policy makers who support democracy in principle often fear that the actual operation of democratic processes could result in authoritarian rule by an elected majority. Fears generated in the West by the electoral victories of the Islamic Salvation Front in Algeria in 1990–91 and by the Turkish military's ending of the government of Necmettin Erbakan in 1997 attest to this underlying ambivalence. In discussions regarding the nature of Iraqs' post–Saddam Hussein government, in 2003, prominent American political leaders expressed similar fears. Senator Richard Lugar stated that the United States could not accept "a popularly elected theocracy in Iraq."[5] Implicit in all of these responses is an assumption that an Islamic state, even if democratically established, would be transformed into an illiberal and undemocratic theocracy.

The underlying question in such discussions is whether Islam is a barrier to democracy, especially the liberal variety. Consequently, in the broader context of debates about the nature and future of democracy, the subject of Islam and democracy often receives special attention.

Over the past decade, a standard format has emerged in the argumentation about Islam and democracy. In this format some definition is given of "Islam" and of "democracy," and then it is argued how those definitions are either complementary or contradictory. Depending on the interpretations of the analyst, it is concluded that either Islam and democracy are compatible or they are not. It is important to understand the main outline of the "standard debate." But it must be realized that at the beginning of the twenty-first century, this debate takes place within the broader context of debates about the future of democracy. Often, discussions of Islam and democracy take on an insular character, as if the experiences of democracy in other societies and cultures are irrelevant to the Muslim experience of democracy. Broadening the scope of discussion to an examination of the ambiguous relationships between democracy and modernity can suggest different perspectives. One perspective is that, possibly, major obstacles to democratization in the Muslim world involve less "Islam" than "modernization." Modernization may have been a major barrier to democratization.

ISLAM AND DEMOCRACY: THE STANDARD FORMAT

The standard format of recent discussions on Islam and democracy echoes older debates within the Muslim community and among non-Muslim scholars of Islam. In the early twentieth century, discussions of the relationship between democracy and Islam were part of the broader debates regarding modernization, and democracy was still a contested subject in many Western societies.

Within the Muslim world, conservative* Muslim thinkers argued that Islam and democracy were incompatible because of, first, the Islamic concept of the absolute sovereignty of God. They believed that ideas of the sovereignty of the

---

*In this chapter the term "conservative" refers to those people and groups who resist change in the existing social or ideological order and *not* to radical reactionaries or fundamentalists.

people in a democracy contradicted this fundamental principle. Second, in Islam the law was defined and promulgated by God and God's law, the *Shari'a*, could not be altered by elected parliaments. Third, the concept of parliaments as sources of law was seen as blasphemous.

Some less conservative, and even radical, thinkers in the middle of the century also maintained these views. Abu'l-A'la Mawdudi, distinguished between the "deen" (*din*, "religion" as faith and practice) of democracy and the "deen" of Islam: "What is the meaning of *Deen* of the masses? Only this that the common people of a country are its paramount sovereign; that they should be governed by the *Shari'a* which they themselves have framed; and that all the inhabitants of that country should affirm obedience and servitude to their own democratic authority."[6] This is contrasted with the "deen" of Islam: "The basis of this *Deen* is that Allah alone is the Owner of the land and Sovereign of all human beings. Thus, He alone must be obeyed and served, and all affairs of man's life must be conducted according to His *Shari'a*. This principle of Allah being the supreme authority specified by Islam has only one and no other aim that only Allah's writ must run the world."[7] Kalim Siddiqui has identified "democracy" as one of the modern ideologies of political unbelief: "The great political *kufr* [unbelief] of the modern world is nationalism, followed closely by democracy ('sovereignty of the people'), socialism ('dictatorship of the proletariat'), capitalism and 'free will.' All political systems based on one or more of these ideas, emotions or philosophies are part and parcel of *kufr*."[8]

Some non-Muslim scholars hold similar views. Elie Kedourie wrote, "The idea of representation, of elections, of popular suffrage, of political institutions being regulated by laws laid down by parliamentary assembly, of those laws being guarded and upheld by an independent judiciary, the ideas of the secularity of the state . . . all these are profoundly alien to the Muslim political tradition."[9] Earlier in the 1950s, Bernard Lewis also wrote that

the political history of Islam is one of almost unrelieved autocracy. . . . There are no parliaments or representative assemblies of any kind, no councils or communes, no chambers of nobility or estates, no municipalities in the history of Islam; nothing but the sovereign power, to which the subject owed complete and unwavering obedience as a religious duty imposed by the Holy Law. . . . For the last thousand years, the political thinking of Islam has been dominated by such maxims as "tyranny is better than anarchy" and "whose power is established, obedience to him is incumbent."[10]

In short, one side of the debate in the standard format considers Islam as basically incompatible with democracy on theological grounds, because it is in conflict with the sovereignty of God, and on the grounds of the basically authoritarian vision presented by the body of teachings developed over a millennium by Muslim scholars.

The other side of this debate asserts that Islam, rightly understood, is compatible with democracy. There were conservatives who affirmed this position. An older introduction to Islam, reprinted from "al-Azhar Official Organ," concluded a description of Qur'anic verses relating to political and social life in the early Muslim community with the statement "Such were the principles on which the political system of Islam was grounded. It was thoroughly democratic in character. It recognized individual and public liberty, secured the person and property of the subjects, and fostered the growth of all civic virtues."[11] Ahmad Shawqi al-Fanjari, an Egyptian writer, compiled a list of democratic rights and liberties found in the major writings of earlier Muslims and concluded that "what is called freedom in Europe is exactly what is defined in our religion as justice ('adl), right (haqq), consultation (shura), and equality (musawat). . . . This is because the rule of freedom and democracy consists of imparting justice and right to the people, and the nation's participation in determining its destiny."[12]

Contemporary Muslim thinkers continue this line of analysis, leading to the conclusion that "Islamic doctrine, as embedded in the text and traditions, is conducive to democratic thought in many compelling ways," and the "greatest periods of Islamic rule have been precisely those in which Islam's structural and intellectual developments were the most democratic."[13] Some, like Rachid Ghannouchi, argue that in the conditions of the contemporary era, "pluralistic parliamentary democracy" is "the ideal instrument to put God's Shari'a into practice."[14] This principle of divine sovereignty is maintained by arguing that democracy provides a system for avoiding having a single human individual or class claim sovereignty. Such thinkers argue that

democracy is the spirit of the Islamic governmental system, even though they reject its philosophical assumptions about the people's sovereignty. . . . Since the Qur'an commands Muslims to conduct their affairs through mutual consultation (shura) and grants the privilege of khilafah [representative agency] to the entire Muslim community rather than to a single individual or a specific group or class of people, the resulting shura and selection of a ruler must be based on the free will of the Muslim masses.[15]

Some ideologically radical groups extend this opposition to hierarchical structures that claim sovereignty, and see Islam as the foundation for revolutionary populist democracy. The People's Mujahedin Organization of Iran (PMOI) argued that "from time immemorial, the Towhidi [monotheistic] Prophets have been in the forefront of the most authentic and selfless revolutionary populists of history. . . . The Towhidi Prophets were the heralds of the rule of the people."[16] In this radical perspective, the rise of the "bourgeois system of class relations" created a structure of class domination of the masses even though it was called democracy. "As great anti-imperialist struggles take shape with an anti-exploitative content, the true meanings of populism and democracy have become revived and these concepts have their content once again restored."[17] In this perspective, contemporary radical democracy is rooted in the teachings of the monotheist prophets.

The distinguishing characteristic of the debate about Islam and democracy is its assumption that each of these great concepts is singular in its ultimate definition. In much of this debate, these unitary definitions are tied to particular historic constructions and specific forms. In general terms, not just in relation to Islam, "for people in the West, democracy means 'liberal democracy,' " a combination of "constitutional liberalism" and various forms of liberty with political democracy ("the rule of the people"), although the freedoms involved in "constitutional liberalism" have "nothing intrinsically to do with democracy."[18] Many in the West believe that democracy is a distinctively and exclusively Western phenomenon with specific requirements. Non-Western societies that democratize should follow Western patterns and models. Similarly, for many Muslim and other scholars, the definition of "Islam" is tied closely to the vast intellectual and societal structures developed as the historical manifestation of Muslim faith and tradition over a millennium and a half. This historic tradition becomes the norm, and if that tradition is authoritarian or autocratic, then that is the definition of Islam itself. Consequently, in many ways the debates become circular because the conclusion depends more on the initial definition than on analysis.

ISLAM AND DEMOCRACY: CONTESTED CONCEPTS

An alternative to the standard format is emerging. Its intellectual roots go back many years, but it has received more attention in the past decade. The starting point is the recognition that both democracy and Islam are not easily defined in monolithic terms.

Democracy is increasingly recognized as an "essentially contested concept."[19] Such concepts involve disputes "which are perfectly genuine: which, though not resolvable by argument of any kind, are nevertheless sustained by perfectly respectable arguments and evidence."[20] In fact, scholars (and some activists) recognize that democracy can take many apparently contradictory forms, reflected in terms such as "illiberal democracy,"[21] "semi-authoritarian democracy,"[22] and "cyberdemocracy,"[23] as well as more familiar terms such as "radical democracy,"[24] "consociational democracy,"[25] and "associative democracy."[26]

Similarly, Muslim and non-Muslim scholars and observers stress that Islam is not monolithic. John L. Esposito urges that people ask the question "Whose Islam?" since Islam is always presented through the voices and perspectives of Muslim groups and individuals.[27] The South African scholar Ebrahim Moosa notes that "there are many 'islams' with a small 'i,' and many Muslims with differences in terms of their practices and their understandings, since each person or Muslim community appropriates the discursive tradition differently."[28] There is a sense that the highly visible presentation of Islam by contemporary militant radicals, which presents "the powerful image of a single eternal Islam," forecloses the possibility of an understanding of the full range of the way the revelation has been viewed and implemented by humans.[29]

Consequently, there has been a growing emphasis on the rich and deep repertoire of concepts and symbols presented in the Qur'an, the experience of the early Muslim community, and Islam's basic principles,[30] which allows a wide range of possible definitions of fundamental concepts and specific terminologies.

Indeed, it is possible to build, as medieval Muslim thinkers did, an edifice of authoritarian political theory. But this was not limited to the Muslim world. All medieval civilizations were nondemocratic in their vision of political authority. The patriarchal forms of monotheistic theology supported the conceptualization of the human political order on the pattern of divine order, with one sovereign ruler and a hierarchical society. However, Islam contains symbols and concepts upon which a theory of Islamic democracy can be built.[31]

Some contemporary Muslim intellectuals argue that Islam should not be identified with any particular political program or ideology, because doing so places limits of time and place on its universal message. Nevertheless, it is important that Islam be maintained as the foundation for whatever programs are advocated.[32] Within the circumstances of the early twenty-first century, this argument can mean that a democratic system is the most appropriate Islamic political system and that the old authoritarian theories and systems, even if valid in their time and place, are un-Islamic, or even anti-Islamic, options for Muslim societies.[33]

Today, democracy is advocated and supported globally, and few major leaders or intellectuals oppose it. In fact, "For the vast majority of the world, democracy is the sole surviving source of political legitimacy. . . . Democracy has gone from being a form of government to a way of life."[34] Yet according to many observers, these trends have had only limited results in the Muslim world, thus raising the question of the relationship between Islam and democracy to one of great interest to policy makers and scholars. This question cannot be usefully answered within the limiting conceptual framework of the old standard format.

MODERNIZATION, DEMOCRACY, AND ISLAM

Throughout the world, democratization occurs in the context of continuing modernization and is viewed by many as a vital part of the whole structure of modernity. Therefore, a discussion of Islam and democracy must be placed in the broader contexts of modernity and global modernization. An older line of analysis, too, places the specific question of democracy's failure in the Muslim world within the framework of modernization (and modernization theory), which is independent from the cultural-ideological arguments of the "standard format." The modernization theorists attribute the Muslim world's lack of success in democratization to its insufficient socioeconomic modernization.

In the 1950s, Charles Issawi wrote: "In the Middle East the economic and social soil is still not deep enough to enable political democracy to strike root and flourish. What is needed is not merely constitutional or administrative reforms. . . . What is required is a great economic and social transformation which will strengthen society and make it capable of bearing the weight of the modern state."[35] Yusif A. Sayigh, too, concluded that "it is only through development and the concomitant break of the old rigid system that a solid foundation for political democracy can be laid."[36]

In sum, according to this perspective, the more modernized a country, the more promising its prospects for the establishment and maintenance of a democratic system. Like the "standard format" discussions, this line of analysis is based on a monolithic definition of "modernization/modernity" and "democracy." Rather than recognizing democracy as an essentially contested concept, modernization theory tended to define it in terms of liberal democracy as practiced in modern Western countries and saw it as part of the package of elements that defined modern society; the end point of the process of modernization.

Daniel Lerner's *The Passing of Traditional Society: Modernizing the Middle East* identified the elements of this unitary modern package as urbanization, industrialization, secularization, democratization, education, and media participation and concluded that they were interdependent and "in some historical sense, they *had to* go together."[37] This tightly correlated package placed democratization and secularization together in the processes of modernization, concluding that the "top policy problem, for three generations of Middle Eastern leaders, has been whether one must choose between 'Mecca and mechanization' or if the two can be compatible. The main issue has been, not whether, but *how* one should move from traditional ways toward modern life-styles. The symbols of race and ritual fade into irrelevance when they impede living desires for bread and enlightenment."[38] In this perspective, to the extent that "Islam" limits the secularization of society, it also limits its modernization and democratization. But it concludes that obstacles posed by Islam (or religion in general) will inevitably "fade into irrelevance." The question was how soon.

Modernization, as a precondition for democratization, is still an important part of the discussions of Islam and democracy. In examining the prospects for a democratic system in Iraq in 2003, Minxin Pei, after noting the postwar democratization and reconstruction of Germany and Japan, observed, "I think we're going to have big trouble ahead. Germany and Japan were developed, modern societies, but developing countries like Iraq have so many internal characteristics that aren't conducive to that kind of change."[39] Context and preconditions are important in any assessment of the prospects for democracy in any society. But in this perspective, the key element is economic development as a part of modernization, since neither Germany nor Japan had any real tradition of democratic rule.

Like the concepts of democracy and Islam, the concept of modernization has been redefined in significant ways in recent scholarship. As articulated by scholars such as Daniel Lerner, modernization was a linear process that ultimately led to the creation of basically similar societies. However, "the fact of the great institutional variability of different modern and modernizing societies—not only among the transitional, but also among the more developed, even highly industrialized societies—became progressively more and more apparent."[40] Instead of the anticipated homogeneous world of a single mode of modernity, there has been a "continual development and formation, constitution, and reconstruction of a multiplicity of cultural programs of modernity and of distinctively modern institutional patterns, of multiple modernities."[41]

In the contexts of multiple modernities, it is increasingly recognized that religion has not faded into irrelevance. It has, instead, assumed in many instances increased importance, and many scholars have been rejecting the older assumptions of inevitable secularization. Peter Berger, one of the most important proponents of "secularization theory" in the 1960s, recently concluded that the "whole body of literature by historians and social scientists loosely labeled 'secularization theory' is essentially mistaken."[42]

Islam's resurgence and its continuing significance in all realms of public life has greatly contributed to this reassessment. The newly observed significance of religion does not represent a victory of tradition over modernity or the triumph of a Luddite conservatism. Instead, it reflects the evolving and complex nature of modernity itself, with the movements of religious resurgence being as modern as their secular ideological counterparts. The Islamic resurgence of the late twentieth century (and other religious movements) is the product of modernization in as much as it might be a response to it. In this perspective, "the best way to understand the contemporary world, including the upsurge and reconstruction of the religious dimension on the contemporary scene," is within the paradigm of multiple modernities.[43]

Within this context, the question of the relationships among Islam, democratization, and modernization must be reexamined. Modernization has been taking place within the Muslim world while Islam's role remains significant. However, if these concepts and processes are seen as complex, contested, and multi-definitional, then it is important to specify "what Islam" is being discussed. Since Muslim majority societies have been experiencing significant modernization, the symbol-concept repertoire of Islam has not been a barrier to modernization. However, the Islam of historic authoritarian institutions and medieval intellectual formulations has reinforced normal societal conservatism, thus impeding modernizing reforms. Modernizing reforms have, however, received strong support from other modes of Islamic articulation, including those of early Islamic modernists such as Muhammad Abduh. Similarly, modernization has not eliminated Islam's importance.

Despite modernization, democratization has been unsuccessful in much of the Muslim world, especially the Arab region. A study on the Arab world concluded: "There is a substantial lag between Arab countries and other regions in terms of participatory governance. This freedom deficit undermines human development and is one of the most painful manifestations of lagging political development."[44] This raises the question Are there specific barriers to democratization in the contemporary Muslim world?

The most common line of analysis in dealing with this issue in the Muslim world is to ask the questions with which this essay began: What is the relationship between Islam and democracy? Are they compatible? The conclusions drawn from those debates are inconclusive. However, many observers see no inherent or essential aspect of Islam that would make it incompatible with democracy. Certain forms of Islam may present barriers to democracy in specific times and places, but if modernization has transformed most Muslim societies, then why has not democracy followed? This question forces a reexamination of the old modernization theory assumptions about democracy as part of the tightly correlated package of modernity. It may be that just as secularization is not necessarily a part of that package, so, too, democratization might be a separable part of the processes. Under some circumstances, it might be that modernization actually becomes a barrier to democratization, or at least to liberal democracy.

MODERNIZATION AS A BARRIER TO LIBERAL DEMOCRACY

The history of modernity and modern societies reflects that liberal democracy is not an inevitable or essential part of "the modern." Some of the most technologically modern societies of the past century, such as Nazi Germany and Communist Russia, were not liberal democracies. There is a major tension within modernity between authoritarian centralization and libertarian equality. The roots of "illiberal democracy" go back to the beginnings of political modernity. Already in the mid-twentieth century, J. L. Talmon noted that "concurrently with the liberal type of democracy there emerged from the same premises in the eighteenth century a trend towards what we propose to call the totalitarian type of democracy.... The tension between them has constituted an important chapter in modern history, and has now become the most vital issue of our time."[45]

Modernization programs in the non-Western world also reflect this tension. Within the Muslim world, the initial major reform programs of Westernization and modernization were primarily those that created more effective administrative structures, stronger military capacities, and more centralized communication systems. "The cumulative effect of reform and modernization was, paradoxically, not to increase freedom but to reinforce autocracy."[46] By the twentieth century, "the emergence of the modern secular state was one of the most important corollaries of the integration of the Middle East" into the global world system,[47] and the repressive apparatus of this modern state had the capacity to limit the political participation of the bulk of the population.[48] In short, the modern secular state as it emerged in the Muslim world was not a liberal democracy. It was a centralized, authoritarian political system, although the ruling elites frequently framed their policies and goals in democratic terms. They have been examples of what Talmon termed "totalitarian democracy" and Zakaria calls "illiberal democracy."

The experiences of Muslim societies with Western imperial rule contributed to the authoritarian nature of modernizing regimes in the Muslim world. Despite its rhetoric of the "civilizing mission" and, later, preparation for self-government and independence from colonial rule, even when indirect, imperial rule was authoritarian. "Western colonization . . . was in large part an act of state-sanctioned violence. On the crudest level, [domestically] liberal [Western] regimes forcibly 'pacified' native peoples who resisted colonization. On a more subtle level, their rule rested on a set of coercive practices that violated their own democratic values."[49] Examples of this behavior in the Middle East included the crushing of the "revolutions" at the end of World War I in Egypt (1919) and Iraq (1920) and the suppression of the Syrian General Congress (1920).

The colonial institutions reinforced the authoritarian dimensions of political modernization throughout the Muslim world. After independence, the dual heritage of authoritarian reformism and autocratic imperialism shaped the emerging political systems of the Muslim world. Although emerging political systems, monarchical and republican, identified themselves as "democratic" and representing the "will of the people," and the original political systems were structurally similar to Westminster or American models, by the second half of the twentieth century they were replaced by either military regimes or one-party states. The emergence of such "authoritarian democracies" was tied relatively closely to the agents of modernization and was not a reversion to more "traditional" political habits. They were similar to Talmon's "modern totalitarian democracy," rested partly on popular enthusiasm, and were "thus completely different from absolute power wielded by a divine-right King, or by a usurping tyrant."[50]

By the 1960s, military rule had become a common replacement for the parliamentary regimes of early independence, and the military was considered a major agent of modernization.[51] (See Chapter 8 in this volume by Elizabeth Picard.) Many observers and participants saw this new phenomenon as a stage in the processes of modernization and therefore as a stage in the development of effective democratic systems, and so they viewed the military as "the spearhead of modernization in politics, economics, and society."[52]

Moreover, the theory of "the authoritarian road to democracy" maintained that a period of political stability and economic development was necessary before "democratic" institutions could be fully established. The vehicle providing the control for this period of transition was seen most appropriately as "the military."[53]

From the present vantage point it appears that the "authoritarian road" of the 1960s resulted in continued authoritarianism with a democratic facade. The power of the "new" authoritarians, who have now been in power for almost half a century, is based on the power given to the state and the coercive instruments of the state by modernization. This ruling elite emerges as one of the barriers to liberal democracy rather than the vehicle for its realization.

ISLAM, MODERNITY, AND DEMOCRACY

The two conflicting dimensions of political modernity discussed by Talmon—the totalitarian and the liberal—remain crucial features of the struggles to define the future of political systems throughout the world. In these struggles, the tension is not between democracy and nondemocracy. Scholars recognize that we "live in a democratic age."[54] In this context, the battle is not between totalitarianism and liberalism; it is between totalitarian (or "illiberal") democracy and liberal democracy.

This conflict takes special forms within the Muslim world. In the debates about the compatibility of Islam and democracy, one important consideration is whether democracy should be defined in fundamentally Western terms. As noted earlier, some Islamic scholars and intellectuals argue that Islam has within its historic and theological repertoire of symbols and concepts the resources to create democratic discourses and to provide the foundations for systems of Islamic democracy. What such a development demands is a transcending of two major barriers in the contemporary sociopolitical contexts of the Muslim world: (1) the theologically static authoritarian political traditions of historic-medieval Muslim society and (2) the authoritarian legacies of modernization and imperialism. This is a stunningly difficult challenge, but, given the emergence of mass politics and the overwhelming support for the creation of systems that involve the real political participation of the people in governance, it is a challenge that must be faced.

The efforts in mid-2003 to construct a new political order in Iraq provide an important case in which some of the fundamental issues are highlighted. There was fear that the active participation of the Shi'a majority in democratic elections might result in the establishment of a theocracy. This stark dichotomy presented by some U.S. policy makers and political leaders between democracy and theocracy is based on the assumption that Islamic democracy is an oxymoron and a euphemism for theocracy. This is an artificially imposed polarity based on a conviction that Muslim societies' historic authoritarian political traditions are so deeply embedded in Islamic civilization that change or development in this area is impossible. (Similar views were held regarding Catholicism until recently.) It also makes the same assumption made by the Islamic fundamentalists that if something does not fit within the pattern of the medieval canonical synthesis of Islamic thought as reflected in the medieval definitions of the *Shari'a*, it is not "authentically" Islamic. In this way, intellectual and political reformulations of the basic Islamic symbols and concepts are often derided by both "fundamentalists" and Western secular scholars, as being artificial attempts at syncretism between Western modernity and Islam.

Within the framework of the stark dichotomy, there is no alternative for Muslims other than secular-liberal democracy or theocracy. In practice, such alternatives have been defined and even tried, but the forced conceptual polarity makes it difficult to see their potential strengths.

Currently the most important experience of trying to combine Islam and democracy is in Turkey. Discussions of the contemporary political situation in Turkey attempt to push the Turkish experience into the Procrustean bed of *either* secular democracy *or* domination by religious parties that will lead to theocracy. This conceptualization can lead to serious misjudgments in policy and diplomacy, as exemplified by the U.S. effort in March 2003 to pressure Turkey into accepting the

American plan for the Iraq war. A senior Turkish analyst, M. Akif Beki, noted that "the Bush administration failed to see that its request was coming at a juncture in Turkish history, as the military and political establishment [the old advocates of thoroughly secular republicanism] turn away from the West while the country's Muslim traditionalists embrace Western democratic values."[55] The evolving Turkish political system is working to create a synthesis that brings together the secularist-republican tradition with an emerging Islamically based vision that embraces Western democratic values as an authentic expression of Islam.

To assume that the Justice and Development Party (JDP) represents a secret move for the long-term establishment of a theocracy in Turkey is to present a conspiracy theory that shows little knowledge of the JDP leadership, program, and history. It also assumes that it is not possible to have a democratic system that is built on or utilizes Islamic principles. In the past, the strong and doctrinaire secularism embedded in the original (and successful) authoritarian road to democracy prevented an Islamic democratic synthesis in Turkey. However, that modernization-created obstacle is being mitigated by the changing views of the older military-political establishment. The experience of the JDP government in its first years of existence gives some basis for arguing that the Islamic-democracy synthesis may be possible.

Iran is a less successful example of efforts to synthesize Islam and democracy. Nevertheless, compared to secular authoritarian regimes of the Middle East Iran has a good deal of public participation in politics. The ideas of the Iraqi leader Ayatollah Muhammad Baqir al Sadr represent another effort at synthesis. Thomas Melia found in Afghanistan that "Afghans also do not believe that there is any incompatibility between Islam and democracy; they believe they can and should have both. Indeed, the Koran was cited as authority for the notion that people should choose their rulers and everyone should be treated equally, regardless of their status or religion."[56] Melia noted that a number of studies of Muslim attitudes in many regions "echo" his findings in Afganistan.[57] Muslims, in other words, are convinced that there is an Islamic democratic alternative that is a copy of neither Western-style secular-liberal democracy nor the theocracy of Islamist extremists.

However, there are obstacles to recognizing the appeal of such alternatives, deriving from the *modern* conceptualization of the relationship between religion and politics in the context of the contemporary world. The imposition of the secular-versus-theocracy dichotomy itself becomes a barrier to forms of democratization that have any possibility of acceptance by the general population within the Muslim world.

At the beginning of the new century, in a world in which the desecularization of modernity and the emergence of multiple modernities are important features, it is important to recognize that the processes and conceptualizations involved in modernization as they were understood in the past may themselves create barriers to democratization in the Muslim world. Modernization created institutions and modes of operation that strengthened the power of authoritarian tendencies.

The most "modern" institutions, such as the military, often became the enabling institutions for continuation of authoritarian political regimes that utilize rhetorical democratic devices.

There are significant dangers if the choices in the Muslim world are defined in essentialist and simplistic terms as being between secular-liberal democracy and a fundamentalist theocracy. Abdullahi An-Na'im defined these dangers clearly:

Advocates of secularism for Islamic societies are clearly motivated by objections to the agenda of Islamic fundamentalists; they fear the disastrous consequences of that form of political Islam for national politics and international relations. Ironically, however, their advocacy of secularism may in fact strengthen what they are opposing. If presented with European secularism as the only alternative to the so-called Islamic state and application of *Shari'a*, Islamic societies will clearly prefer the latter, however serious its conceptual faults and practical difficulties. . . . Whenever Islamic societies exercise their right to self-determination by choosing their own system of government, the outcome is unlikely to favor European conceptions of secularism.[58]

Sayyed Abdol Majeed al-Khoei, the Shi'a cleric who was murdered in Najaf in April 2003, also stated that "if we want to evaluate suitability, or unsuitability, of secularist plans vis-à-vis Muslim countries, a careful revision and scrutiny is necessary for Muslim problems in a way that is altogether different from dealing with those known in Europe. If secularism means a precondition that excludes religion, this is unacceptable. . . . But if secularism is secularism without a precondition excluding religion, it will then mean pluralism. . . . There is no objection to that."[59]

Thus, the challenge is to define a democratic system that does not have the precondition of excluding religion.

CONCLUSION

The imposed choice between a secular and a fundamentalist future is a modern choice that has significant embedded dangers, but the choice is almost inherent in the nature of modernity as generally understood. To the extent that the imposed dichotomy is an inherent part of modernity, modernity becomes an obstacle to democratization. Ultimately, the resolution of the paradoxes, dilemmas, and contradictions may come from transcending the conceptualizations of modernity itself as they have been understood in the past two centuries. Both the actual processes of modernization and the conceptual agendas of modernity may have represented barriers to democratization in the Islamic world.

This understanding of the issues changes the frame of reference of the debates about Islam, democratization, and modernization. "Islam," "democracy," and "modernity" are all contested terms. In many discussions, it is assumed that there is a fixed and single definition of each of these terms. If one accepts the absolutist definitions of extremist Muslim radicals or of Eurocentric secularist fundamentalists, then there is no need for discussion. In the old standard format of the debates about the relations between Islam and democracy, the answers were simple and depended on the definitions rather than analysis. However, the more recent conceptualizations of the issues can recognize that while Islam as defined by radical reactionaries may not be compatible with democracy, Islam and democracy are compatible in the faith and aspirations of most Muslims in the contemporary world.

In the concrete contexts of contemporary Muslim societies, there are many obstacles to creating participatory democratic societies. Some of them are the result of deeply rooted institutions and attitudes. Yet some of the most authoritarian regimes in the Muslim world, such as that of Saddam Hussein in Iraq, were neither traditional Muslim regimes nor Islamist in program. They were the products of modernization. In the form and experience of modernization in the Muslim world, modernization itself may have been a barrier to creating a successful synthesis of Islam and democracy.

NOTES

1. Fareed Zakaria, "The Rise of Illiberal Democracy," *Foreign Affairs* 76, no. 6 (November–December 1997): 22–43; Fareed Zakaria, *The Future of Freedom: Illiberal Democracy at Home and Abroad* (New York: W. W. Norton, 2003).

2. Zakaria, "Rise of Illiberal Democracy," 24.

3. Zakaria, *Future of Freedom*, 117.

4. Ibid., 118. Zakaria's actual final words in this passage are "more stark than in the Middle East today." However, since he discusses Muslim majority countries outside of the Middle East, like Indonesia, I have used the term "Muslim world."

5. *Meet the Press with Tim Russert,* MSNBC News, April 20, 2003.

6. S. Abul A'la Maududi, *Khutabat (Fundamentals of Islam)*, 2nd ed. (Chicago: Kazi Publications, 1977), 257.

7. Ibid., 258–59.

8. Kalim Siddiqui, "Primary Goals and Achievements of the Islamic Revolution in Iran," in Kalim Siddiqui, ed., *Issues in the Islamic Movement, 1983–84 (1403–04)* (London: Open Press, 1985), 13.

9. Elie Kedourie, *Democracy and Arab Political Culture* (Washington, DC: Washington Institute for Near East Studies, 1992), 5, as quoted in Zakaria, *Future of Freedom,* 123.

10. Bernard Lewis, "Communism and Islam," in Walter Z. Laqueur, ed., *The Middle East in Transition* (New York: Frederick A. Praeger, 1958), 318–19.

11. Ahmad A. Galwash, *The Religion of Islam: A Standard Book*, 5th ed. (Cairo: Imprimerie Misr, 1958), 1:105.

12. Ahmad Shawqi al-Fanjari, *Al-Hurriyat al-Siyasiyyah fi al-Islam* (1973), as quoted in Hamid Enayat, *Modern Islamic Political Thought* (Austin: University of Texas Press, 1982), 131.

13. Ahrar Ahmad, "Islam and Democracy: Text, Tradition, and History," *American Journal of Islamic Social Sciences* 20, no. 1 (Winter 2003): 35–36.

14. "Ghanoushi on Past and Present Despotism in Muslim Countries," *islam21* 3 (December 1997): 16.

15. Mumtaz Ahmad, "Islamic Political Theory: Current Scholarship and Future Prospects," in Mumtaz Ahmad, ed., *State Politics and Islam* (Indianapolis, IN: American Trust Publications, 1986), 4.

16. "Towhidi (Divinely Integrated) Populism Versus Vulgar Populism," *Mojahed* 1, no. 6 (June 1980): 51.

17. Ibid.

18. Zakaria, *Future of Freedom*, 17–18.

19. Jan-Erik Lane, *Constitutions and Political Theory* (Manchester: Manchester University Press, 1996), 244.

20. W. B. Gallie, *Philosophy and the Historical Understanding* (London: Chatto & Windus, 1964), 158.

21. Zakaria, *Future of Freedom*.

22. Marina Ottaway, *Democracy Challenged: The Rise of Semi-Authoritarianism* (Washington, DC: Carnegie Endowment for International Peace, 2003).

23. Elaine Ciulla Kamarck and Joseph S. Nye, Jr., eds., *Governance.com: Democracy in the Information Age* (Washington, DC: Brookings Institution, 2002).

24. Chantal Mouffe, ed., *Dimensions of Radical Democracy: Pluralism, Citizenship, Community* (London: Verso, 1992); C. Douglas Lummis, *Radical Democracy* (Ithaca, NY: Cornell University Press, 1996).

25. Arend Lijphart, "Introduction: The Belgian Example of Cultural Coexistence in Comparative Perspective," in Arend Lijphart, ed., *Conflict and Coexistence in Belgium*, Research Series 46 (Berkeley: University of California, Institute of International Studies, 1981), 1–12.

26. Paul Q. Hirst, *Associative Democracy: New Forms of Economic and Social Governance* (Amherst: University of Massachusetts Press, 1994).

27. John L. Esposito, *Islam and Politics,* 4th ed. (Syracuse, NY: Syracuse University Press, 1998), xx.

28. Ebrahim Moosa, *Islam and Cultural Issues* (Victoria: University of Victoria, Centre for Studies in Religion and Society, 2002), 7.

29. Mohammed Arkoun, *Rethinking Islam: Common Questions, Uncommon Answers,* trans. Robert D. Lee (Boulder, CO: Westview Press, 1994), 7–8.

30. John L. Esposito and John O. Voll, *Islam and Democracy* (New York: Oxford University Press, 1996), chap. 1.

31. Enayat, *Modern Islamic Political Thought*, 125–39.

32. See for example some of the lines of analysis presented by Abdolkarim Soroush in Mahmoud Sadri and Ahmad Sadri, eds. and trans., *Reason, Freedom, and Democracy in Islam: Essential Writings of Abdolkarim Soroush* (New York: Oxford University Press, 2002), passim and especially chaps. 8 and 9.

33. "The People Are One Community: An Islamic Theology of Religions for the Twenty-First Century," in Abdulaziz Sachedina, *The Islamic Roots of Democratic Pluralism* (New York: Oxford University Press, 2001), 40–49.

34. Zakaria, *Future of Freedom*, 13–14.

35. Charles Issawi, "Economic and Social Foundations of Democracy in the Middle East," in Laqueur, *Middle East in Transition*, 33, 49. Reprinted from *International Affairs* 32, no. 1 (1956): 27–42.

36. Yusif A. Sayigh, "Development and Democracy," in William R. Polk, *The Development Revolution: North Africa, the Middle East and South Asia* (Washington, DC: Middle East Institute, 1963), 124.

37. Daniel Lerner, *The Passing of Traditional Society: Modernizing the Middle East* (New York: Free Press, 1958), 438.

38. Ibid., 405.

39. Quoted in Tom Zeller, "Building Democracy Is Not a Science," *New York Times*, Sec. 4, 3, April 27, 2003.

40. Shmuel N. Eisenstadt, "Introduction: Historical Traditions, Modernization, and Development," in Shmuel N. Eisenstadt, ed., *Patterns of Modernity*, vol. 2, *Beyond the West* (New York: New York University Press, 1987), 4.

41. Shmuel N. Eisenstadt, "The Reconstruction of Religious Arenas in the Framework of 'Multiple Modernities,' " *Millennium: Journal of International Studies* 29, no. 3 (2000): 592.

42. Peter L. Berger, "The Desecularization of the World: A Global Overview," in Peter L. Berger, *The Desecularization of the World: Resurgent Religion and World Politics* (Grand Rapids, MI: William B. Eerdmans, 1999), 2.

43. Eisenstadt, "Reconstruction of Religious Arenas," 592.

44. United Nations Development Programme, *The Arab Human Development Report 2002: Creating Opportunities for Future Generations* (New York: United Nations Development Programme, 2002), 2.

45. Jacob L. Talmon, *The Origins of Totalitarian Democracy* (New York: Frederick A. Praeger, 1960), 1.

46. Bernard Lewis, *What Went Wrong? Western Impact and Middle Eastern Response* (New York: Oxford University Press, 2002), 53–54.

47. Philip S. Khoury, "Islamic Revivalism and the Crisis of the Secular State in the Arab World: An Historical Appraisal," in Ibrahim Ibrahim, ed., *Arab Resources: The Transformation of a Society* (London: Croom Helm, 1983), 215.

48. Ibid., 221–22.

49. Alice L. Conklin, "Colonialism and Human Rights: A Contradiction in Terms? The Case of France and West Africa, 1895–1914," *American Historical Review* 103, no. 2 (April 1998): 419.

50. Talmon, *Origins of Totalitarian Democracy*, 6.

51. Dankwart A. Rustow, "The Military in Middle Eastern Society and Politics," in Sydney N. Fisher, ed., *The Military in the Middle East* (Columbus: Ohio State University Press, 1963), 9.

52. Ibid., 6.

53. Manfred Halpern, *The Politics of Social Change in the Middle East and North Africa* (Princeton, NJ: Princeton University Press, 1963), 223.

54. Zakaria, *Future of Freedom*, 13–14.

55. Glenn Kessler and Philip Pan, "Missteps with Turkey Prove Costly," *Washington Post,* Sec. A, 1, March 28, 2003.

56. Thomas O. Melia, "What Muslims Want: In Afghanistan, and Elsewhere—Democracy," *Georgetown Journal of International Affairs* 4, no. 1 (Winter–Spring 2003): 158.

57. Ibid., 160.

58. Abdullahi A. An-Na'im, "Political Islam in National Politics and International Relations," in Berger, *Desecularization of the World*, 119–20.

59. Sayyed Abdol Majid Al Khoei, "Islam and Secularism," *islam21* 3 (December 1997): 14–15.

7

Is Gender Inequality in Muslim Societies a Barrier to Modernization and Democratization?

Valentine M. Moghadam

Since the 1990s, studies have appeared suggesting that a distinctive pattern of values and behavior sets the Muslim world apart from, and sometimes in collision with, the West. These studies are based on culturalist arguments and emphasize the constraining impact of Islamic orthodoxy in the Muslim world's intellectual, technological, scientific, and economic progress.[1] Others cite as principal culprits "petro Islam" and Islamist movements such as those in Afghanistan, Algeria, Egypt, Sudan, and elsewhere.[2] Samuel Huntington, the best-known proponent of the culturalist explanation, has argued that modernization, interdependence, and democratization—instead of resulting in convergence and increased cooperation among nations—have resulted in a growing divergence that is likely to culminate in a clash of civilizations. He is particularly concerned that the demographic surge of the Islamic world, which he sees as a source of strength, is a threat to the West.[3]

Scholars have also argued that Muslim societies are the most resistant to gender equality, which, in turn, has slowed their progress. David and Richard Landes attribute the Muslim world's lagging behind the West to the "slow evolution of Islamic societies' treatment of women."[4] Ronald Inglehart and Pippa Norris believe that the cultural fault line dividing the West and the Islamic world relates to gender relations, the position of women, and attitudes toward sexuality. They maintain that on issues of gender and sexuality, "Muslim nations have remained the most traditional societies in the world." Thus, they assert that despite surveys showing that Muslims favor democracy, their lack of "commitment to gender equality and sexual liberalization" means that "democracy may not be sustainable in their societies."[5]

It is, of course, possible to challenge these perspectives, at least by pointing out that the Islamic world is too vast, diverse, and divided to be treated as an undifferentiated unit. Nevertheless, it is reasonable to posit that (1) gender inequality in many Muslim societies has been a barrier to modernization and development and (2) continued resistance to women's economic and political emancipation and full participation can hinder the future progress of many Muslim countries. Empirical research shows that in many Muslim countries, women have been locked into a patriarchal family unit, and this has been economically and socially costly for those countries. By contrast, those Muslim societies that have made a commitment to women's rights and their enhanced participation in the national life are likely to perform better in terms of economic, social, and political indicators.[6]

This chapter's focus is gender inequality, modernization, and democratization in the Middle East and North Africa (MENA) because the region's oil economy, neopatriarchal states, and prevalence of Islamic family law have imparted a distinctive pattern of economic development, state-society relations, and gender relations to the MENA region. The rise of Islamist movements in the 1980s further challenged women's legal status and social positions in many MENA countries. But this chapter also refers to the case of other Muslim countries and occasionally compares them with non-Muslim countries at similar stages of development or similar income levels.

The main thesis of this chapter is that (1) women's economic marginalization in the MENA region has contributed to the slow pace of its economic and social development; (2) women's marginalization from formal politics has been due to the neopatriarchal and authoritarian nature of the region's governments and their resistance to democratization; and (3) by the late twentieth century, women in the Muslim world, and especially in the MENA region, had emerged as the main agents of modernization and democratization.

First, a methodological and conceptual note is in order. It is difficult to establish the direction of causality between gender equality or its lack, and modernization, development, and democratization. Certainly there are interconnections: economic development seems to correlate with women's economic participation, and higher levels of economic development appear to correlate with gender equality. The relationship between gender and modernization, similarly, works both ways; the more modernized a society, the more extensive women's rights and their participation in the public sphere. By contrast, the relationship between gender equality and democratization is less straightforward. For example, women's political participation was higher under communist regimes and much lower under the new democratic regimes in Eastern Europe and Russia.[7] It is possible, though, that gender equality provides a more conductive environment for democratization. A cross-national study by Inglehart, Norris, and Welzel shows that although "democratic institutions, by themselves, do not guarantee gender equality," the "rising emphasis on gender equality [does] improve the chances that democratic institutions will emerge and flourish."[8]

GENDER PATTERNS IN THE MUSLIM WORLD

Conventional wisdom holds that women's legal status and social position are worse in Muslim countries than in other societies. Current interpretations of Islamic theology and law emphasize women's roles as wives and mothers, and render them legal minors and dependents of husbands or male kin.

In the late twentieth century, Muslim societies were characterized by higher-than-average fertility and maternal mortality rates and high rates of population growth.[9] This was accompanied by high rates of illiteracy among the adult female population, gender disparity in education, and low rates of female labor force participation, especially in the MENA region and in the Muslim states of South Asia. In 1980, women's share of the labor force was the lowest in the Middle East and North Africa (23 percent) and highest in the communist economies of Eastern Europe and the Soviet Union, including Muslim Central Asian republics. In 1990, women's participation in administrative and managerial jobs, clerical and service jobs, sales work, and production was lowest in South Asia, West Asia and the Middle East, and North Africa. In 1997, women's share of the labor force in MENA had increased to about 27 percent, but it was still the lowest of any region in the world, including South Asia, where women's share was 33 percent.[10] In 2000, adult female illiteracy and maternal mortality were the highest in sub-Saharan Africa, South Asia, and the MENA region. A woman's estimated lifetime chance of dying in pregnancy or childbirth was 1 in 55 in MENA and 1 in 54 in South Asia but only 1 in 157 in Latin America and the Caribbean and 1 in 283 in East Asia and the Pacific.[11]

In the 1970s and 1980s, a large literature linked the high rates of fertility, low literacy, high maternal mortality, and limited labor force participation in Muslim countries to the low status of women. This lower status was, in turn, attributed to the prevalence of Islamic law and norms. The continued importance of values such as family honor and modesty meant that women's participation in nonagricultural or paid labor carried a social stigma, and gainful employment was not perceived as part of women's role.[12]

Since the 1980s, the issue of women's rights in the Muslim world has been tied to Islam's cultural and political reassertion and particularly to the emergence of Islamist movements. Critics and advocates of Islam hold sharply divergent views on this matter and have produced a literature on this issue that may be categorized as either "misery research" or "dignity research." The former focuses on the oppressive aspects of Muslim women's lives, while the latter shows the strength of women's positions in their families and communities. Secular feminists describe adherence to Islamic norms and laws as the main impediment to women's advancement.[13] Freda Hussein has raised counterarguments based on the concept of "complementarity of the sexes" in Islam. She distinguished "authentic Islam" from "pseudo-Islam" and maintained that the former is emancipatory. Other Muslim feminists emphasize the egalitarian and emancipatory content of the Qur'an, which they maintain has been hijacked by patriarchal interpretations since the early Middle Ages.[14] Finally, those identifying most with Islamic law are convinced that Islam provides all the necessary rights for humankind and womankind and that Islamic states go the farthest in establishing these rights.[15]

This emphasis on the status of women *in Islam* does little to satisfy social science inquiry because Islam is experienced, practiced, and interpreted quite differently over time and space. As the Tunisian sociologist Abdelwahab Bouhdiba has shown, Islam is fundamentally "plastic"; hence, there are many varieties of Islam.[16] A sociological survey of attitudes toward religion and society in Egypt, Kazakhstan, Indonesia, and Pakistan confirms the existence of significant variations in religiosity, which ranges from extremely orthodox in Pakistan to syncretic and flexible in Indonesia, to nonreligiosity in most of Kazakhstan.[17] Therefore, to understand Islam's social implications for the status of women, it is necessary to look at the broader sociopolitical and economic order within which these implications are realized. To illustrate: there are Tunisian female lawyers, judges, parliamentarians, cabinet ministers, and political activists. In Muslim Senegal, the majority of women are not veiled, and they dress in the traditional African fashion. Malaysian women fully participate in their country's economic development and are employed in the export-manufacturing sector in large numbers. By contrast, Saudi women lack all these advantages. In short, whether the content of the Qur'an is inherently conservative and hostile toward women or egalitarian and emancipatory, although not irrelevant to social science inquiry, is less central or problematical than is often assumed.

Women's economic and political participation, at high levels, is increasingly seen as a measure of their advancement and of a country's efforts toward gender equality in decision making. There is also the perception that women in high-level positions in the executive, legislative, and judiciary can be effective advocates for women's rights. Available data for the year 2000 shows that on the three major measures of women's empowerment—the female share of seats in parliament, administrators and managers, and professional and technical workers—Malaysia ranked the highest among Muslim countries, followed by Eritrea and Senegal. Central Asian countries usually rank better than MENA or South Asian countries. Turkmenistan showed a 26 percent female share of parliamentary seats.[18]

However, the appointment of Central Asian women to ministerial or subministerial positions in the post-Soviet era has been lower than in other Muslim countries. In terms of parliamentary seats, Malaysia and Turkey stand out. Turkey and Senegal have the highest proportion of subministerial positions occupied by women. Pakistan and Bangladesh have had women prime ministers, but the vast majority of women in these countries fare poorly on social and gender indicators, including parliamentary representation. On the whole, the conservative Gulf Arab states, followed by other conservative Arab countries, Iran, and Turkey rank the lowest in the gender equality measure (GEM). Progress, however, should be noted. In the summer of 2002, Algeria's president Abdelaziz Bouteflika appointed five women to his cabinet, an unprecedented number; meanwhile, the introduction of a parliamentary gender quota in Morocco led to an 11 percent female share following the elections of November 2002. The same occurred in Senegal, when women won 19 percent of parliamentary seats in the 2002 elections. In Iran, women's share of parliamentary seats remains low, even though they emerged as an important political constituency in the 1990s, especially within the reform movement.

GENDER AND DEVELOPMENT

A World Bank report, *Engendering Development,* contains a useful survey of recent empirical studies on the relationship between gender equality and economic development.[19] According to these studies, greater gender equality and improved educational opportunities for women are associated with positive development outcomes. Empirical evidence shows that improving women's education and lessening the gender gap in education, distributing income within households toward mothers, and increasing women's control over fertility improve the health of children. Although the relationship between gender equality and the rate of economic growth is subject to debate, several studies show that gender equality in education has a positive impact on the rate of economic growth.[20] These findings are especially relevant in the case of South Asia, sub-Saharan Africa, and the MENA region, where gender gaps in education, although narrowing, are still wide, and low rates of economic growth have been prevalent. According to one analyst, Stephen Klasen, gender inequality in "employment representation" also affects the rate of growth.[21] Representation is measured by the growth of the female share of both the labor force and the working-age population in the formal sector of the economy. Klasen also finds a positive correlation between income growth and these measures, thus suggesting that greater equality in employment representation might contribute to economic growth.[22] This finding, too, is especially relevant to the Arab region, Iran, and Pakistan, which show both low growth rates and continued low levels of female participation in the formal labor force.[23]

The contrast between Iran and Malaysia is instructive (see Tables 7.1 and 7.2). Malaysia's female labor force participation and share of the labor force in various economic sectors have been consistently higher than those of Iran. Malaysia has actively encouraged increases in female labor force participation, especially for Bumiputera (Muslim Malay) women. In the late 1980s, Malaysian women constituted over 42 percent of the workforce, compared with barely 9 percent in Iran. In 2000, their participation rates were above 48 percent, compared with 29 percent in Iran. Iran's oil-based gross domestic product (GDP) is higher than Malaysia's ($105 billion compared to $90 billion), but because of higher population its GDP per capita is lower. Moreover, the level of GDP per capita in Iran has stagnated over the past twenty years, while Malaysia's has increased, indicating the effectiveness of Malaysia's developmentalist strategy over Iran's Is-

Table 7.1
Percentage of Women in the Labor Force by Sector (female share), Late 1980s

	Total	Agriculture	Manufacturing	Finance	Trade	Services
Iran	8.9	8.1	14.5	9.2	1.7	13.6
South Korea	36.6	44.9	36.2	28.2	41.5	29.4
Malaysia	42.7	38.5	41.4	29.9	29.0	44.6
Indonesia	33.1	31.6	44.8	16.9	47.9	31.0

Source: International Labor Organization, *Yearbook of Labor Statistics, Retrospective Edition on Population Censuses* (Geneva: International Labor Organization, 1991), table 2A.

Table 7.2
Socioeconomic Gender Comparisons, Iran and Malaysia, 2000

	Female Economic Activity Rate (%) (as % of male rate)	Female Share of Paid Labor Force (%)	Gender Development Index (GDI) (rank)	Estimated Earned Income, Female (PPP* US$)	GDP per Capita Annual Growth Rate, 1990–2000 (%)
Iran	29.0 (37)	12	83	$2,524	1.9
Malaysia	48.4 (61)	42	54	$5,711	4.4

*Purchasing Power Parity

Source: United Nations Development Programme, *Human Development Report 2002* (New York: United Nations Development Programme, 2002), tables 12, 22, 25.

lamist strategy. Growth rates have been negative or low in the Arab countries, as well as in Iran. In 1990–2000, GDP per capita annual growth rate was 0.7 percent among the Arab states, compared with 5.7 percent in East Asia and the Pacific, 1.7 percent in Latin America and the Caribbean, and 3.3 percent in South Asia.[24]

The MENA countries also fare badly on literacy and educational attainment figures. In the early 1990s, oil-rich MENA states lagged behind Malaysia (and even a poor country, Vietnam) on educational attainment, especially for the adult population, and registered wide gender disparities (see Table 7.3). These differences have not disappeared in the intervening decade. The data in Table 7.4 show that the Arab region continues to lag behind other regions in adult female literacy, except South Asia.

The foregoing suggests that countries such as Malaysia, Vietnam, South Korea, China, and others that invested in women's education and encouraged their eco-

Table 7.3
Mean Years of Schooling for Individuals Twenty-Five Years of Age and Older, Early 1990s

MENA Country	Males	Females	Other Developing Countries	Males	Females
Algeria	4.0	0.8	Argentina	8.5	8.9
Egypt	3.9	1.9	Chile	7.8	7.2
Iran	4.6	3.1	China	6.0	3.6
Iraq	5.7	3.9	Colombia	6.9	7.3
Jordan	6.0	4.0	Malaysia	5.6	5.0
Kuwait	6.0	4.7	Mongolia	7.2	6.8
Lebanon	5.3	3.5	Philippines	7.8	7.0
Libya	5.5	1.3	Sri Lanka	7.7	6.1
Morocco	4.1	1.5	Thailand	4.3	3.3
Saudi Arabia	5.9	1.5	Uruguay	7.4	8.2
Tunisia	3.0	1.2	Viet Nam	5.8	3.4

Source: United Nations Educational, Scientific, and Cultural Organization, *Education for All: Status and Trends 1994* (Paris: United Nations Educational, Scientific, and Cultural Organization, 1994).

Table 7.4
Gender Inequality in Education, 2000

	Adult Literacy, Women Fifteen Years of Age and Older (%)	Women's Literacy as Percentage of Men's Literacy
Arab States	50.1	68
East Asia and the Pacific	79.4	86
Latin America and the Caribbean	87.4	98
South Asia	43.8	66
Sub-Saharan Africa	53.6	77
Central and Eastern Europe and the CIS	98.3	99

Source: United Nations Development Programme, *Human Development Report 2002* (New York: United Nations Development Programme, 2002), table 24, 233.

nomic participation have been able to face the challenges of globalization and have benefited from its opportunities, including foreign direct investment (FDI). In contrast, levels of FDI flow to the MENA region have remained low. Moreover, the impact of available FDI on women's economic participation is limited because it is not directed toward sectors where female labor is likely to grow. The MENA countries' trade performance is also below that of other regions, and its information and communication technology (ICT) links are also among the weakest in the world.[25]

THE DISTINCTIVE CASE OF THE MIDDLE EAST AND NORTH AFRICA

MENA countries are characterized by high (though declining) fertility rates, gender gaps in literacy, limited access for women in paid employment, and underrepresentation in the political system. Despite urbanization, sizable rural populations remain in the large MENA countries and have resulted in a lower average age at first marriage and higher rates of marriage and fertility compared to countries at similar stages of development.[26]

Access to education has improved greatly over the past few decades, so the illiteracy rate among the MENA region's young people (ages fifteen to twenty-four) is half that of the adult population. However, illiteracy remains widespread among women, the poor, and rural populations, reflecting the social inequalities of MENA countries such as Egypt, Morocco, and Yemen. Overall, the MENA region's illiteracy rates are often higher than those of other countries with comparable per capita incomes. Moreover, the gender gap in literacy has persisted and in most countries is as wide among young people as it is in the adult population. More than 40 percent of the region's female adults (age fifteen and older) are illiterate, double the rate for men. In the Arab countries, women's illiteracy is not expected to be eliminated until 2040, about fifteen years after the expected date for the elimination of male illiteracy.[27]

Female labor force participation rates and occupational shares are growing in a number of countries, but for the region as a whole they remain among the lowest in the world.[28] Women's share of the labor force increased between 1980 and 1997, especially in Jordan, Kuwait, Oman, Saudi Arabia, and the United Arab Emirates, where previously it had been almost negligible. The 1990s also saw increases in women's employment in Turkey, Egypt, Iran, and Algeria, largely in the teaching and health professions, and to a lesser extent in sales and services. Some of these increases were due to rising educational attainment and declining household budgets in a post–oil boom era, which increased women's involvement in the formal and informal sectors of the economy. In addition, improved enumeration techniques yielded higher percentages of women in agriculture and in urban informal occupations.

However, a study of Arab women's economic participation by the Tunis-based Center of Arab Women for Training and Research (CAWTAR) notes that in a number of countries there has been a trend to encourage women to withdraw from the labor force, partly due to male unemployment, and that this runs counter to global trends. The 1990s also saw increased levels of female unemployment. At the beginning of the twenty-first century, the CAWTAR report showed, adult female illiteracy rates remained high, and the gap with men wide, particularly in Egypt, Morocco, and Yemen. And women's participation in administrative, managerial, and decision-making positions, in public and private sectors, remained low.[29] In 2000, Egyptian and Turkish women's share of high-level administrative and managerial posts was about 10 percent, despite much higher economic activity rates (35 percent for Egyptian women and nearly 50 percent for Turkish women).[30]

Women in the Middle East have always been involved in political movements (e.g., independence, national liberation, socialist, and feminist movements), but their presence in formal political structures (e.g., political parties, parliaments, governments) is a more recent phenomenon and of limited scope. Except for Turkey, where women were given the right to vote in 1930, other countries granted women voting rights in the 1950s (Egypt, Lebanon, Syria, Tunisia), the 1960s (Algeria, Iran, Libya, Morocco, the former People's Democratic Republic of Yemen), or even later (Iraq). Their limited political participation, therefore, is due partly to the relative novelty of elections, especially for women, and partly to the patriarchal gender system. Although women are found in the rank and file and leadership of political parties (e.g., in Algeria, Morocco, Tunisia, Turkey), nowhere have they reached a critical mass, and their appointment to party or government positions has been largely a form of tokenism.

To what can these patterns of women's educational, employment, and political participation be attributed? Here we can identify economic, political, legal, and cultural barriers. During the era of booming oil prices (1960 to mid-1980s), capital-intensive technologies and relatively high wages for men were the main hurdles for the greater involvement of women in the labor force. With a few notable exceptions, most employed women were found in the professions, largely concentrated in the public sector, as teachers, doctors, nurses, adminstrators, and so forth.[31] A smaller share work in factories, but MENA working-class women generally lack the educational qualifications of factory workers in countries such as China, Vietnam, and especially Central and Eastern Europe.

Political obstacles include the nature of the state. The region's political systems have been described as "authoritarian-socialist" (Algeria, Iraq, Syria), "radical Islamist" (Iran and Libya), "patriarchal-conservative" (Jordan, Morocco, Saudi Arabia), and "authoritarian-privatizing" (Egypt, Tunisia, Turkey). Hisham Sharabi introduced the umbrella term "neopatriarchal state," which is a useful concept to help explain gender inequality, incomplete modernity, and stalled democratization.[32] For Sharabi, "The most advanced and functional aspect of the neopatriarchal state . . . is its internal security apparatus, the *Mukhabarat*. . . . In social practice ordinary citizens are not only arbitrarily deprived of some of their basic rights but are virtual prisoners of the state, the objects of its capricious and ever-present violence. . . . It is in many ways, no more than a modernized version of the traditional patriarchal sultanate."[33] In the 1990s, there was a process of political liberalization or quasi democratization in some countries (notably Turkey) and the emergence of vibrant democratic movements in others (notably Iran). But MENA states remain authoritarian, and citizen participation is limited.[34]

In the neopatriarchal state, unlike in liberal or social democratic societies, religion is bound to power and state authority; moreover, the family, rather than the individual, constitutes the underpinning element of the community. The neopatriarchal state and the patriarchal family reflect and reinforce each other. In some cases, modernizing or revolutionary states have undermined patriarchal structures, or attempted to, through legislation aimed at weakening traditional rural landlord or tribal structures. Yet most states have been ambivalent about transforming the role of women and the structure of the family. Rather, they have sought to achieve the contradictory goals of economic development and strengthening of the traditional male-dominated family. The latter reflects a bargain struck with more conservative social elements, such as religious leaders.

Legal frameworks and cultural attitudes also matter. Cross-national research on world values shows that countries with a higher degree of religiosity are less likely to be egalitarian, modernized, or democratic.[35] Within the MENA region there is a variable mix of religion, legal frames, and political structures. Turkey is the only country where there is a constitutional separation of religion and the state, while Tunisia is a de facto secular state. Islam is not a state religion in Syria, and the Syrian constitution guarantees freedom of religion and worship and grants women "every opportunity to participate effectively and completely in political, social, economic, and cultural life." Consequently, urban, educated, and professional women enjoy a degree of freedom comparable to, for example, that of women in some of the Latin American countries. Yet it is difficult to reconcile women's rights with current interpretations of Islamic law (*Shari'a*), which remains unfavorable to women with regard to marriage, divorce, and inheritance. In addition, most of the region's population engages in a high level of religious observance.

Shari'a law informs the family laws—also known as personal status codes—that are in place in all countries except Turkey and to lesser extent Tunisia.[36] Republican Turkey's family law was not based on Islam, but was, nevertheless, quite conservative, until the women's movement forced changes in 2001. Tunisia modernized its family law immediately after independence, and further reforms toward more gender equality in the family were adopted in 1993. Elsewhere, family laws place women in the legal status of a minor, dependent on their father, husband, or other male kin and disadvantaged in the areas of marriage, divorce, child custody, and inheritance. Muslim family laws require women to obtain the permission of fathers or husbands for employment, obtaining a loan, starting a business, or undertaking business travel. Because start-up capital for entrepreneurial purposes generally comes from family wealth, unequal inheritance laws and norms disadvantage women in the business sphere.

Muslim family laws reflect and reinforce patriarchal gender relations, or what I have termed the "patriarchal gender contract." This is a set of social relationships between men and women predicated on the male breadwinner–female homemaker ideal, in which the male has direct access to wage employment or control over the means of production and the female is largely economically dependent on male members of her family.[37] The patriarchal gender contract determines the type of occupations and professions considered suitable for women and is codified in law. This patriarchal gender contract has perpetuated the gender gaps in literacy and educational attainment and has led to the development of curricula and teaching materials that are often gender-biased, reinforcing attitudes denying women full and equal participation in society. The mass media, which are influential in shaping values and attitudes, often suffer from and perpetuate the same biases.

The patriarchal gender contract is behind the region's unsustainable demographic explosion, which has made it very difficult for states to attain development goals, including the eradication of illiteracy and the alleviation of unemployment and poverty. But, it also has been challenged by the "modernizing women" of the region.

MODERNIZING WOMEN

Despite limitations and barriers to their advancement, MENA women have emerged as the main agents of modernization and democratization in the region.[38] In response to the rise of Islamism, and in order to address the problem of second-class citizenship and economic marginalization, women in the MENA region have formed dynamic movements and organizations. Using a variety of legal and discursive strategies, including secular and Islamic feminism, MENA women have been challenging the patriarchal gender contract to expand women's civil, political, and social rights and to empower women economically and politically.

The Arab women's movement took off at a regional preparatory meeting for the Beijing Conference in November 1994, organized by the United Nations Economic and Social Commission for West Asia (ESCWA), held in Amman in November 1994. The meeting produced a bold document calling for women's rights.[39] The global women's rights agenda and the United Nations (UN) conferences of the 1990s—especially the 1994 International Conference on Population and Development, held in Cairo, and the 1995 Fourth World Conference on Women, which convened in Beijing—created a favorable environment that allowed the proliferation of women's organizations and women-led NGOs. During the 1990s, seven types of women's organizations emerged: service organizations; worker-based organizations; professional associations; women-in-development (WID) nongovernmental organizations (NGOs); research centers and women's studies institutes; women's auxiliaries of political parties; and women's rights or feminist organizations. All are contributing to the development of civil society in the region, although the feminist organizations probably are doing so most consciously.[40] The WID NGOs have an important function in fulfilling the developmental objectives of civil society: decentralized, participatory, and grassroots use of resources. In Bahrain, "women's voluntary associations form an integral part of civil society," responsible for "initiating all organizations for the handicapped as well as modern education."[41]

In Iran, women have formed a large number of NGOs that provide social services, address the problems of Afghan female refugees, and educate the public on environmental concerns. Groups focusing on women workers are few but are likely to grow as more women enter the workforce. There are also region-wide women's organizations and networks such as the Arab Women's Solidarity Association, the Arab Human Rights Organization, the Magreb-Mashrek Gender Link Information Project (GLIP), the Women's Court, and the Permanent Arab Court to Resist Violence against Women. These regional and national groups have some involvement with transnational feminist networks such as Women Living Under Muslim Laws, the Sisterhood Is Global Institute, and the Women's Learning Partnership.[42] These organizations encourage women to run in national elections, support women's involvement in local elections, and insist that more women be appointed to ministerial and subministerial positions. Moroccan women's organizations were behind a ten-year-long campaign for the reform of family law, which was finally accomplished by a royal commission and a parliamentary majority in January 2004.

The rise of the women's movement is the result of changes in the characteristics of the female population. Rising educational attainment and smaller family size among middle-class women has enabled them to engage in civic and political activities. Although fertility rates are high in some countries (Saudi Arabia, Yemen, Palestine), elsewhere they are declining and are as low as 2.3 children per woman in Iran, Turkey, and Lebanon. Enrollment rates for girls at the primary and secondary school levels are rising and are nearly at par with those of boys. Less is known about the quality of female education. Some research shows that in many Arab countries government cutbacks have resulted in crowded classrooms, fewer qualified teachers, and poor instructional materials in the state-owned schools.[43] But women are more likely than men to enroll in universities. In 2003, more than 50 percent of college students in Bahrain, Iran, Jordan, Kuwait, Lebanon, Qatar, and Saudi Arabia were women; the rate for Libya, Morocco, Palestine, and Tunisia was more than 40 percent. Women are also increasingly studying subjects such as engineering, medicine, law, commerce, finance, mathematics, and computer sciences. Such graduates are contributing significantly to the modernization of their countries, among other things by challenging a male-centered and reductionist reading of Islam. They are also more likely to form women's and other civil society organizations, as well as professional associations.

Additionally, MENA women have been contributing to modernization and democratization through literary and media efforts, including the publication of books and journals and the production of films. Both secular and Islamic feminists contribute to these publications.

Around the world, women's rights activists have evinced an ambivalence to the state. While being wary of the state, they still engage with state agencies and officials. This is an approach that I call "critical realist," and it is an approach also found among MENA women's organizations. MENA feminists are aware of the neopatriarchal and authoritarian nature of the state and how it reinforces their subordinate status, while also recognizing the reality of the state as an unavoidable institutional actor. They therefore pressure the state to improve their legal status and social positions, to live up to its commitments, and to implement the international conventions that it has signed, such as the United Nations Convention on the Elimination of All Forms of Discrimination against Women (CEDAW) and the Beijing Declaration and Platform for Action.

CONCLUSIONS

Past failures by neopatriarchal states in the Middle East and North Africa to invest in women's literacy, education, and economic participation have led to an unsustainable demographic explosion, high unemployment, a small tax base, an uncompetitive labor force, growing impoverishment, civil unrest, and an inability to meet the challenges posed and opportunities offered by globalization. Women's economic and political marginalization has hampered socioeconomic development and democratization. At the same time, those middle-class women who were beneficiaries of modernization have promoted values of modernity, democratization, equality, and rights-based development through their involvement in women's and other civil society organizations.

Samuel Huntington is incorrect to suggest a clash of values between the Islamic and the Western world. Indeed, a number of scholars from the world polity–world culture school of sociology have posited a worldwide isomorphism in values and institutions, including such developments as the extension of political rights to women, the adoption of international conventions, and the proliferation of nongovernmental organizations, including human rights, women's rights, and environmental organizations.[44] In almost every Muslim country, educated and employed women have formed women's rights organizations, have become involved in trade unions and professional associations, and have helped change family relations from patriarchal to egalitarian. This is true also of the MENA region, where educated and employed women are challenging patriarchal gender relations and family laws and the neopatriarchal state.

Sociological surveys (e.g., the World Values Survey), opinion polls (e.g., Zogby International), and academic studies such as the comparative study of value orientations in Egypt, Jordan, and Iran concerning religion, gender, and politics, by Mansoor Moaddel, have found that large sections of the modern middle class in Muslim societies hold values and beliefs regarding gender relations and democratization that would be familiar to their counterparts in North America, Latin America, and Europe.[45] In Iran, for example, the increasingly more liberal social values and the emergence of a movement for political reform, democratization, and separation of religion and politics and law is partly due to the experience of two decades of authoritarian Islamism, plus the growth of an educated middle class with access to international information. Democratization in Turkey—even with its Islamic inflection—is an outgrowth of the changing nature of state-society relations and of new forms of political contestation as well as a growing adherence to European-style concepts of human rights and political rights. The changes in gender policies and norms are similarly a function of both internal dynamics and external influences.

Not all Muslim countries, however, are undergoing changes in gender policies, practices, and norms. These countries also remain among the least modernized, developed, and democratized members of the Islamic world. In sum, gender inequality is certainly an obstacle to modernization and democratization, but the oppression of women is also a function of limited economic development and of the persistence of weak, corrupt, and authoritarian regimes.

NOTES

1. David Landes, *The Wealth and Poverty of Nations: Why Some Are So Rich and Some So Poor* (New York: W. W. Norton, 1998); Milton Viorst, *In the Shadow of the Prophet: The Struggle for the Soul of Islam* (New York: Doubleday, 1998); Daryush Shayegan, *Cultural Schizophrenia: Islamic Societies Confronting the West* (Syracuse, NY: Syracuse University Press, 1997).

2. Olivier Roy, *The Failure of Political Islam* (Cambridge, MA: Harvard University Press, 1994); Gilles Kepel, *Jihad: The Trail of Political Islam* (Cambridge, MA: Harvard University Press, 2002); Paul Berman, *Terror and Liberalism* (New York: W. W. Norton, 2002).

3. Samuel P. Huntington, *The Clash of Civilizations and the Remaking of World Order* (New York: Simon and Schuster, 1996).

4. David S. Landes and Richard A. Landes, "Do Fundamentalists Fear Our Women?" *New Republic*, September 29, 2001.

5. Ronald Inglehart and Pippa Norris, "The True Clash of Civilizations," *Foreign Policy* (March–April 2003): 65. Inglehart and Norris include attitudes not only toward male-female equality but also toward "sexual liberalization," or attitudes toward homosexuality, as an indicator of tolerance.

6. Massoud Karshenas and Valentine M. Moghadam, "Female Labor Force Participation and Economic Adjustment in the MENA Region," in Mine Cinar, ed., *The Economics of Women and Work in the Middle East and North Africa* (Amsterdam: Elsevier/JAI Press, 2001), 51–74; Valentine M. Moghadam, *Women, Work, and Economic Reform in the Middle East and North Africa* (Boulder, CO: Lynne Rienner, 1997); and Valentine M. Moghadam, *Modernizing Women: Gender and Social Change in the Middle East*, 2nd ed. (Boulder, CO: Lynne Rienner, 2003).

7. Valentine M. Moghadam, ed., *Democratic Reforms and the Position of Women in Transition Economies* (Oxford: Clarendon Press, 1993).

8. Ronald Inglehart, Pippa Norris, and Christian Welzel, "Gender Equality and Democracy," *Comparative Sociology* 1, nos. 3–4 (2003): 329.

9. John Weeks, "The Demography of Islamic Nations," *Population Bulletin* 43, no. 4 (December 1988).

10. United Nations, *The World's Women 2000: Trends and Statistics* (New York: United Nations, 2000).

11. United Nations Development Programme, *Human Development Report 2002* (New York: United Nations Development Programme, 2002), 27, 233.

12. Nadia Youssef, "The Status and Fertility Patterns of Muslim Women," in Lois Beck and Nikki Keddie, eds., *Women in the Muslim World* (Cambridge, MA: Harvard University Press, 1978), 69–99; Fatima Mernissi, *Beyond the Veil: Male-Female Dynamics in Modern Muslim Society*, rev. ed. (Bloomington: Indiana University Press, 1987); Julinda Abu Nasr, A. Khoury, and H. Azzam, eds., *Women, Employment, and Development in the Arab World* (The Hague: Mouton/International Labor Organization, 1985); Ruth Leger Sivard, *Women . . . A World Survey* (Washington, DC: World Priorities, 1985); Ester Boserup, "Economic Change and the Role of Women," in Irene Tinker, ed., *Persistent Inequalities: Women and World Development* (New York: Oxford University Press, 1990).

13. Juliette Minces, *The House of Obedience: Women's Oppression in Algeria* (London: Zed Books, 1982); Haleh Afshar, "Women, State, and Ideology in Iran," *Third World Quarterly* 7, no. 2 (April 1985): 256–78; Mai Ghoussoub, "Feminism—or the Eternal Masculine—in the Arab World," *New Left Review* 161 (January–February 1987): 3–13; Haideh Moghissi, *Feminism and Islamic Fundamentalism: The Limits of Postmodern Analysis* (London: Zed Books, 1999).

14. Freda Hussein, ed., *Muslim Women* (London: Croom Helm, 1984); Asma Barlas, *Believing Women in Islam: Unreading Patriarchal Interpretations of the Qur'an* (Austin: University of Texas Press, 2002); Riffat Hassan, "Rights of Women within Islamic Communities," in John Witte, Jr., and Johan D. van der Vyver, eds., *Religious Human Rights in Global Perspective: Religious Perspectives* (The Hague: Martinus Nijhoff, 1996); Azizah Al-Hibri, "Islam, Law, and Custom: Redefining Muslim Women's Rights," *American University Journal of International Law and Policy* (1997).

15. This is a widespread view among Islamist women and has been expressed at international women's meetings by delegations from Sudan and the Islamic Republic of Iran. See Moghadam, *Modernizing Women*, chaps. 3 and 6.

16. Abdelwahab Boudiba, *Sexuality in Islam* (London: Routledge and Kegan Paul, 1985).

17. Riaz Hassan, *Faithlines: Muslim Conceptions of Islam and Society* (Karachi, Pakistan: Oxford University Press, 2002).

18. The United Nations Development Programme's (UNDP) annual *Human Development Report* includes measurements for women's status and gender equality, such as the gender empowerment measure and the gender development index.

19. World Bank Group, *Engendering Development: Toward Gender Equality in Rights, Resources, and Voice* (Washington, DC: World Bank, 2001).

20. Elizabeth M. King and M. Anne Hill, eds., *Women's Education in Developing Countries: Barriers, Benefits, and Policies* (Baltimore: Johns Hopkins University Press for the World Bank, 1993); Moghadam, *Women, Work, and Economic Reform*, chap. 2.

21. Stephen Klasen, "Does Gender Inequality Reduce Growth and Development? Evidence from Cross-Country Regressions," *World Bank Policy Research Report on Gender*

and Development (Working Paper Series 7, World Bank Development Research Group/Poverty Reduction and Economic Management Network, November 1999).

22. Ibid., 28.

23. Bangladesh's GDP per capita growth rate of 3.0 in 2000 may be attributed to foreign direct investment (FDI) in the textiles and garments sector, which has relied heavily on female labor in recent years.

24. UNDP, *Human Development Report 2002,* 193.

25. *Finance and Development*, special issue, "The Middle East on the Threshold of Change," March 2003; and Center for Arab Women for Training and Research (CAWTAR), *Globalization and Gender: Economic Participation of Arab Women* (Tunis: CAWTAR and UNDP, 2001).

26. UNDP, *Human Development Report 2002*; Moghadam, *Modernizing Women*, 133–34. A notable exception to the regional pattern is Tunisia, which has had a more conductive legal framework and economic environment for women's participation.

27. UNDP, *The Arab Human Development Report 2002: Creating Opportunities for Future Generations* (New York: UNDP, 2002), 52.

28. Moghadam, *Modernizing Women*, chap. 2. The participation rate refers to the proportion of the (female) population of working age that is economically active or participates in the labor force. Participation rates are usually age-specific. Labor force shares refer to the proportion of an occupation, a profession, or some other employment category that is male or female.

29. CAWTAR, *Globalization and Gender: Economic Participation of Arab Women*, Arab Women Development Report (Tunis: CAWTAR, 2001).

30. UNDP, *Human Development Report 2002,* tables 23 and 25.

31. In Lebanon, most employed women are found in the private sector. Morocco and Tunisia are distinctive for their larger shares of working women in the manufacturing sector.

32. Hisham Sharabi, *Neopatriarchy: A Theory of Distorted Change in Arab Society* (New York: Oxford University Press, 1988).

33. Ibid., 45.

34. Alan Richards and John Waterbury, *A Political Economy of the Middle East,* 2nd ed. (Boulder, CO: Westview Press, 1996); Clement M. Henry and Robert Springborg, *Globalization and the Politics of Development in the Middle East* (Cambridge: Cambridge University Press, 2001).

35. Inglehart, Norris, and Welzel, "Gender Equality and Democracy."

36. In the Jewish state of Israel, family law is based on the Halacha and supervised by the rabbinate. Nevertheless, a higher proportion of Israeli women are active in employment and in political participation than is the case elsewhere in the region. I believe that the chief reason for the difference lies in level of economic development and in the democratic polity.

37. Moghadam, *Women, Work, and Economic Reform.*

38. This may also be the case in Afghanistan, although more time is needed to see the extent of women's political participation and cultural influence.

39. For an elaboration, see chapter 8 in Moghadam, *Women, Work, and Economic Reform.*

40. Nadje Al-Ali, *Secularism, Gender and the State in the Middle East: The Egyptian Women's Movement* (Cambridge: Cambridge University Press, 2000); Nemat Guenena and Nadia Wassef, *Unfulfilled Promises: Women's Rights in Egypt* (Cairo: Population Coun-

cil, 1999); Fatima Sadiqi, "Aspects of Moroccan Feminism," in Fatima Sadiqi et al., ed., *Mouvements féministes: Origines et orientations* (Fes, Morocco: Centre d'Etudes et de Recherches sur la Femme, 1999), 195–214; Valentine M. Moghadam, "Engendering Citizenship, Feminizing Civil Society: The Case of the Middle East and North Africa," *Women and Politics* 25, nos. 1–2 (2003): 63–87.

41. Mounira Fakhro, "Civil Society and Non-Governmental Organizations in the Middle East: Reflections on the Gulf," *Middle East Women's Studies Review* 11, no. 4 (January 1997): 1–3.

42. I elaborate on this in my forthcoming book, *Globalizing Women: Gender, Globalization, and Transnational Feminist Networks* (Baltimore: Johns Hopkins University Press).

43. UNDP, *Arab Human Development Report 2002*.

44. John Boli and George M. Thomas, "World Culture in the World Polity," *American Sociological Review* 62, no. 2 (April 1997): 171–90.

45. Mansoor Moaddel and Taghi Azadarmaki, "The Worldviews of Islamic Publics: The Cases of Egypt, Iran, and Jordan," *Comparative Sociology* 1, nos. 3–4 (2002): 299–319.

II

**From Within and Without:
Factors Influencing Modernization
and the Development of
Democracy in the Muslim World**

8

The Role of the Military

Elizabeth Picard

In the examination of the evolving role of the military in the economic and political life of the Middle Eastern countries and their popular image, the principal hypothesis of this chapter is that changes in those areas are rooted in recent history and are the result of certain watershed events. These events are the imperial conquest of the Middle East, the process of colonization and decolonization, and the impact of the bipolar international system of the post–World War II era and the East-West rivalry.

For most of the past fifty years, using a Weberian perspective, intellectuals and governments ascribed to the military a leading role in the modernization process. They viewed it as the main tool of a "new middle class" bound to give an impulse to national development; therefore, this chapter will analyze the military's role in light of the formation of Middle Eastern states and the transformation of their societies.[1]

Within this broad context, this chapter assesses the role of the military establishments in the reform process by looking at their recent record outside the purely military domain, and by examining their influence on, and participation in, the current attempts at modernization and democratization in the Middle East,[2] and offers some hypotheses about the military's future role in view of the new global security priorities. In doing so, it focuses on some common features of the military in the Middle East—defined here as the region stretching from Morocco to Pakistan—and brings out the specific combination of domestic and international constraints that shapes the role of the military in politics in the Middle East Muslim states.

Clearly, the armed forces in Muslim countries share certain broad characteristics with other militaries in the world, such as social conservatism and resistance to invention and innovation, dealing with practical and ethical issues according to strongly inculcated models, and valuing discipline and obedience rather than autonomy and consultation.[3] Moreover, in the case of all militaries from Latin America to Southeast Asia, their collective practice and institutional structures shape the pattern and character of their approach to public life and politics. Similarly, in nearly all cases the militaries' intervention in the political arena involves maintaining law and order and often suspending the rule of law and using oppression.

Nevertheless, each country and its military have their own specific characteristics and dynamics. Therefore, this chapter examines five concrete cases: Algeria after the suspension of the electoral process in 1992, Egypt under general Hosni Mubarak (1981–), the military-Ba'thist regime in Syria (1970–), Turkey since the third military coup (1980–), and Pakistan under General Zia ul-Haq (1977–88) and General Pervez Musharraf (1999–). This chapter also briefly refers to the case of post–civil war Lebanon and Iran.

The discussion in this chapter distinguishes among political, social, and economic spheres of the military's intervention, while being cognizant of a close interrelation among them. It also advances the thesis that the new international security context, wherein the global struggle against extremist Muslim groups has supplanted the struggle against communism, forces the regional regimes to submit to international rule or to the superpowers' interests. Consequently, a new kind of governance is emerging wherein private interests compete with public interest in the shaping of national politics, thus blurring the boundaries between domestic and international realms and between public and private spheres. This situation creates new opportunities for the military to participate in economic and political life and in the debate about political liberalization.

ARMED FORCES AND THE DEFINITION OF NATIONAL IDENTITY

From the beginning, in the postindependence states of the Middle East, newly created or reorganized military establishments were instrumental in defining the state's identity by erecting and defending its boundaries against external enemies and internal separatist movements. The military also participated in the invention and defense of notions such as patriotism and indivisibility of the state and in the promotion of national ideologies such as Arabism and Turkism, with their mythologies, historical roots, and heroes. When in power, the military, more than the civilian leaders, emphasized national unity and the consolidation of the state's national identity and demanded full allegiance to the state. Despite their diverse ethnic, sectarian, and regional affiliations, and notwithstanding their frequent rhetorical references to larger identities such as Arabism, Pan-Turkism, or even Pan-Islamism, most of the ruling officers promoted nation-state identity. By attempting to acquire a monopoly on the legitimate use of force on the national territory and by displaying national symbols and using authoritarian practices, they placed their political ambitions within the framework of the new nation-state. In Turkey, the military, which rules behind the civilian facade, succeeded in gaining popular support on two crucial occasions, namely, during the Turkish military intervention in Cyprus (1974) and during the American attack against Iraq in 2003, by taking a strong nationalist stand.[4] Hafez al-Assad's long rule contributed to the routinization of state-society relations and the internalizing by most Syrians of a sense of Syrian national identity and common national interest within state boundaries.

The military has used conscription as the main instrument of political socialization. Conscription has to some degree contributed to modernization by enabling young provincial draftees to come into contact with other regions of their country and with their fellow citizens. By stressing the practice of a national *koine* transcending various languages and dialects, conscription has contributed to cultural homogeneity, which is a decisive factor in nation building. During their military service, young conscripts become literate and learn basic skills, such as driving.[5] For many rural Egyptians, this experience is often their first and only encounter with education. In countries plagued by a high level of unemployment,[6] military training is helpful in finding employment, as shown by the cases of Egypt and Turkey.

Meanwhile, young recruits are supposed to be socialized to common values, such as patriotism, in order to consolidate national identity and promote national unity as opposed to parochial loyalties. However, in most cases, the recruits' perception of their countries' leadership (the "state" or the "regime") has not been enhanced by their experience with the military, especially in those countries where the military plays a central role in running the government. On the contrary, they often became aware of a resistance to change within the military and of their role in perpetuating authoritarianism. They also resent the huge gap between the military and their original environment in terms of power, resources, identity, and loyalty. This has meant that the militaries' success in enhancing a transcendental national identity has been at best limited.

Social Cleavages and Military Factions

Military establishments in Middle Eastern countries often reflect the existing cultural and social cleavages while contributing to their deepening and perpetuation. Rivalries and feuds among military elites of the Muslim world coupled with various cleavages and competing alliances result in costly and endless series of plots and coups. The imperial tradition had long routinized the organization of professional or mercenary armed forces according to social segmentation and solidarity based on family, clan, and tribal affiliations, and mid-nineteeth-century attempts to impose universal conscription were cut short by the colonial conquests. With the exception of Turkey, the Muslim world's armies and police forces fell under the control of European colonial administrations that recruited their personnel according to ethnic criteria. In the process, they often invented or reinvented these identities for the purpose of societal control, as illustrated by the assigning of special roles to "warrior" ethnic groups such as the Punjabis in British India, the Assyrians in Iraq, and the Druze in Syria, or by recruiting from among religious minorities, especially Christians, or from certain regions, such as the Kabyle *harkas* in French Algeria. Local attempts to impose universal conscription on the basis of a newly adopted citizenship in the mid-nineteenth century were prevented by colonial policies.

After World War II, another attempt at reforming the armed forces was frustrated because minority groups clung to their privileged positions.[7] Thus, recruitment and promotions during the years of state-centered development (1950s–1980s) was done on the basis of primordial solidarities. This trend was accentuated after independence because the military career represented a main venue for upward social and economic mobility. Fifty years later, certain ethnic, sectarian, and regional groups are still overrepresented in the armed forces of many Muslim countries, notably the Punjabis in Pakistan,[8] the Alawites in Syria,[9] and the Oujda group in Algeria.[10] In terms of technical modernization of the military, such an imbalance has been costly because it has resulted in the duplication of equipment, depriving some units of certain kinds of weapons, competition among units at the expense of national security, promotion of incompetent officers, and the predominance of personal networks over experience and skill in the formation of army general staff.

Segmentarity and tribalism within the Middle Eastern armed forces hinders democratization in two ways: First, the logic of *ʿasabiyya* (primordial solidarity)[11] encourages ethnic- and sectarian-based factions to take control of civilian power either by overt military coup or by forming a secret or shadow military organization to supervise the government. Once this goal is achieved, important national security decisions are taken principally in light of the interests of a minority group even at the expense of national interest. Pakistan's involvement in the Soviet-Afghan and Afghan civil wars and Syrian intervention in Lebanon (1976) are examples of such decisions.[12]

Second, *ʿasabiyya* allows social groups to promote their parochial interests within the military enterprises by favoring members of their own community in appointments to high positions, obtaining economic advantages from the state for their regions, and having privileged access to domestic and external rent. In this way, the military brings societal divisions into the core of the state, and instead of being the neutral instrument of a civilian leadership and the protector of national territory from external threats, it encourages and facilitates dissent, secession, and irredentism, and, consequently, regional instability. The Syrian army best exemplifies this kind of struggle for power, which for Syria began in the early 1960s and continued during Hafez al-Assad's rule.[13] Rivalry among senior Algerian officers played an equally important role in prolonging the country's civil war, which began in 1992.[14]

Turkey is an exceptional case, where the military establishment recruited mainly from rural Anatolian lower and middle classes and was able to maintain strong loyalty to the Kemalist state among them. While the armed forces did not systematically exclude Kurdish elements, the latter had to prove to be fully Turkicised and had to make clear their allegiance to Kemalist nationalism and their commitment to the country's indivisibility. This relative homogeneity of the Turkish military has been the key to its strength on the domestic scene. Nevertheless, on occasions it has been a threat to democracy, as was the case from 1984 to 1998, when army commanders were the strongest advocates of and primary actors in the war against Kurdish autonomist movements, mainly the PKK (Kurdistan Workers' Party). They insisted on a military solution to the conflict and opposed the granting of cultural rights to the Kurds, sometimes against the wishes of civilian leaders, such as Prime Minister Turgut Özal. This emphasis on military power, plus the imposition on the whole society of a preformatted political culture further alienated the Kurds.[15] Unlike the case of Latin America in the 1980s and 1990s, it is unlikely that factionalism within most Middle Eastern armies would lead to democratic bargains, thus facilitating a transition to democracy.

Armed Forces and the Islamic Alternative

Most of the armies in the Middle East were set up and grew in symbiosis with nationalist doctrines, combining commitment to modernization and secularization with loyalty to the young nation-state. Even Pakistan, whose national identity is based on Islam, promoted a modern nationalist doctrine. Under General Muhammad Ayub Khan (1958–1969), the 1962 constitution did not emphasize Islam; instead, the issue of democracy versus military dictatorship dominated the political discourse.[16] In Algeria until the early 1980s, the debate about social and economic choices was conducted within an essentially secular context.[17] And finally, Assad's Syria provided the most violent example of opposition to Islamist movements by crushing the Hama revolt in 1982.[18] In fact, nearly everywhere the armed forces were originally the most committed supporters of secularist nationalism. However, this doctrine did not survive the military setbacks and the poor performance of state-centered development policies, although, at least officially, most of the higher military command and officers who perform civilian and political roles still subscribe to it. Military heads of state such as Assad and Mubarak made concessions to social re-Islamization by engaging in public expressions of faith, opening the public space to religious actors (Islamic nongovernmental organizations [NGOs] and television preachers),[19] and allowing parliaments to promote conservative Islamic legislation. Yet security priorities enforced by the military and the military's policies when in power were rarely favorable to political Islam, as shown by the examples of Turkey, Egypt, and Algeria. Pakistani president Zia ul Haq, who engaged in an Islamization experiment, was an exception.

President Zia was representative of a generation of officers recruited in the Punjabi middle class, known for its conservatism and religious orthodoxy.[20] In the Middle East, he had peers among the 1980s classes of the Turkish military academies whose cadets came from conservative low- and middle-income families in Central Anatolia[21] and among several post–Camp David Egyptian officers.[22] Indeed, even some of the Free Officers who carried out the Revolution of 1954, including Anwar Sadat, were close to the Muslim Brethren.[23] The new generation that joined the armed forces after the Arab-Israeli wars of 1967 and 1973 and after the erosion of Nasserism was socialized in a re-Islamized milieu that substituted Islamism to deceptive secular nationalism.[24] Little is known about Islamic influence since the suppression of the Hama revolt in 1982 within the Syrian armed forces. But it is possible that junior Sunni officers favor a political overture toward conservative Islamic groups as an alternative to Bashar al-Assad's sectarian-based regime. In Algeria, too, it is difficult to measure the degree of influence of Islamism within the military establishment, especially among young army cadres. However, in the early 1990s, senior officers hinted at possible Islamist tendencies within recruits in technical branches who had not been trained in military academies.[25]

Traditional antagonism of Middle Eastern armies toward leftist and Marxist ideologies and their struggle against them is another reason for the influence of Islamism among the armed forces. This was particularly the case in Turkey in the 1980s and early 1990s.[26] It was less so in the pro-Soviet Ba'thist regimes of Syria and Iraq, although both suppressed the Communist militants until their complete marginalization in the 1980s. Thus, the affinity between military ethics and Islamic values was reinforced by a tactical convergence of interests against a common enemy.

The most far-reaching Islamization of the military occurred in postrevolutionary Iran. The imperial army was heavily purged and saved from total destruction only because of the outbreak of the Iran-Iraq War. New recruits, however, underwent Islamic indoctrination. Meanwhile, the Islamic regime created the Sepah-E-Pasdaran-E-Enghblab (The Guardian Army of the Revolution—referred to in the West as the Islamic Revolutionary Guard Corps, or IRGC), which has emerged as a second army. As protectors of the Islamic Revolution, the IRGC have an implicit political role although they remain under the authority of Ayatollah Khamenei, the commander in chief of the armed forces.[27] In Lebanon's case, the national army, reunified and reorganized by Commander In Chief Michel Aoun, combines a clear trend toward secularism with a strong tendency to interfere in domestic security matters. Paradoxically, it represents more of a danger to democracy than Hizbullah, the Shiite militia. This is because Hizbullah, since 1992, has transformed itself into a large civilian party, fully participating in the national consociational political game.[28]

In some Middle Eastern countries, the re-Islamization of the armed forces can cause tensions between senior officers who are more Westernized and enjoy a high social and economic status and middle and junior officers who have less income and lower status. This differentiation could adversely affect prospects for democratization in two ways: First, combined with communal cleavages, it might lead to intramilitary dissent and confrontation, resulting in a reinforcement of authoritarian military rule.[29] Second, the possibility of an alliance between the Islamists and part of the armed forces cannot be ruled out. Should this happen, it, too, would reinforce authoritarian and conservative rule.

THE STATE AND THE NEW SECURITY AGENDA

It is generally assumed that the state's monopoly over the legitimate use of violence and the implementation of defense and security missions by national armed forces are necessary for the strengthening of the modern state. However, recent experiences of Muslim countries challenge this thesis. Rather, because of continuing low-intensity conflicts and the emergence of new transnational security issues,[30] it has become clear that: (1) war is a burden that hampers modernization of the state; (2) the institutionalization or the shadow presence of security agencies behind the government runs counter to the aim of state building; and (3) the definition and implementation of security priorities by the military contribute to the longevity of authoritarian rule.

The Cost of War

In the Middle East, excessive military spending compared to resources allocated to economic and social needs, including health and education, has been a major reason for the Middle East's poor record in human development.[31] In recent years in Pakistan, the military budget has represented around 30 percent of the state budget. Moreover, military spending has escaped both economic austerity measures and public accountability.[32] In Algeria, the military has succeeded in obtaining the lion's share of the national budget, plus the revenues from oil and gas exports. Meanwhile, the poor performances of national armed forces in interstate conflicts and in the suppression of domestic unrest, despite large military budgets and substantial foreign military assistance, have been undermining the rationale for huge military spending.[33] Local attempts at developing independent military industries, such as the foundation of the Arab Military Industry in Cairo in the wake of the Gulf War (1991) and Iran's effort to build up its arms industry, have had little impact on developing civilian industries. It is unlikely that arms industries could solve the Middle East's underdevelopment problem, because civilian technology and management must be free from military influence and supervision in order to respond to complex social requirements.[34]

The "cost of war" extends far beyond the financial dimension.[35] Giving priority to national defense and security may lead local regimes toward noneconomic strategies, such as rejecting the benefits of international trade and aiming for economic autarky, as the Syrian leadership did in the early 1990s, when the fate of Iraq awakened their obsession with food security.[36] In order to prevail over domestic insurgents, the military also tends to adopt radical practices such as the destruction of villages and infrastructures, as the Turkish army did in South Eastern Anatolia in the 1990s, and mass massacres, as the Algerian army is accused of having committed during the civil war. Such actions clearly undermine the process of modernization.

State Building and the Institutionalization of Authoritarianism

Plagued by weak domestic and international legitimacy, most regional states chose authoritarianism in order to impose their rule on the society and launch ambitious development programs. This choice meant that they placed the military at the core of their new national institutions and secured a top-down control of their societies.

Compared to previous decades, today the militaries are less prone to come out of the barracks, and their direct participation in government has significantly decreased, albeit to different degrees. Egypt stands out in terms of the military's retrenchment from politics.[37] However, they continue to intervene in politics in more informal, yet powerful, ways, through their patronage network, as in Syria, or by negotiating with the civilian government from a position of power, as in Algeria. Not all military high commands are able to dictate their rule to a civilian government, as does the Turkish Milli Güvenlik Kurulu (MGK, national security council). Nevertheless, the generals in Algeria, Egypt, and Pakistan are tempted to emulate the "Kemalist model." In Pakistan a national security council was set up after Pervez Musharraf's coup in October 1999. Although President Musharraf said that the armed forces would restore democracy, several electoral operations culminating in rigged legislative elections in October 2002 made clear that in Pakistan, as in the rest of the Muslim world, the military fears democratization.[38] Military establishments have their own understanding of "vital" national interest, which they intend to realize even if it requires the suspension of the electoral process, as happened in Algeria in January 1992, or when, in the wake of Ceauşescu's fall, Hafez al-Assad declined to implement political reform, explaining that Syria had already accomplished democratization.[39] Moreover, the military are uncomfortable with the uncertainties of democratic transition and distrustful of its outcome because they fear that *infitâh* (opening) could bring to power contenders who might use the same authoritarian methods and show the same disrespect for the rule of law.[40]

It is too early to draw firm conclusions about the impact of the recent upgrading of security priorities in the international community on the prospects for democratization in the Muslim world. Nevertheless, the terrorist attacks of September 11, 2001, the removal of the Taliban regime in Afghanistan, and the occupation of Iraq illustrate the gradual shift in the militaries' mission in the Muslim world from defending state boundaries against external enemies to protecting the state against domestic foes and transnational terrorism. Today, military establishments are indirectly assigned a subordinate role under the leadership of the super-power that trains and equips them (post–Camp David Egypt), supports them financially (Pakistan), and sometimes threatens them (Syria). On the domestic scene, they are increasingly involved in police operations, such as fighting terrorism, drug trafficking, and insurrection. This shift has two consequences for the character of relations between the military establishments and national politics. First, the military is directly concerned with the redefinition of the national community and the stigmatization and exclusion of its enemies. This privilege prejudices a bottom-up socially constructed process of national integration and political participation. At the social level, it exacerbates social and ethnic cleavages and encourages mobilization among excluded segments of the nation. Second, the military subordinates all civilian rules and practices to security priorities to the point of depoliticizing the society, privatizing all expression of dissent, and inducing the emigration of intellectuals as a way to exit from an authoritarian system, as illustrated by the Syrian case.[41]

Military Order versus Public Space

The existence of numerous intercommunal tensions, the frequent occurrence of interstate conflicts, and the struggle against terrorism in the Middle East justify the adoption and upholding of restrictive state measures such as states of emergency, martial laws, exceptional military courts, censorship, and so forth. As control of information has become a major factor in modern wars, military establishments restrict access to public space and prevent the creation of free and pluralistic media by strict censorship and by labeling a large variety of areas "sensitive" and "related to state security." They monopolize public media and use them as their mouthpiece because they know that pluralism in the media facilitates public debate and democratization. Therefore, they rarely free the local media on their own initiative, and although laws are relaxed they continue arresting journalists and exercising censorship. For example, because the vibrant written press that blossomed in Algeria in the late 1980s challenged the military's hold on power, since 1992 a large number of journalists have become victims of assassination and others have been forced into political exile. In Syria and Egypt, intellectuals and newsmen cannot write on domestic political subjects. As witnessed in Latin America in the 1970s and 1980s and in Southeast Asia until the present time, there is a fundamental incompatibility between public debate, accountability, and transparency on the one hand, and military rule on the other. Meanwhile, information on international and domestic issues circulates within local societies through illegal access to satellite channels and challenges the tradition of secrecy of military leaders and the immunity of top officers involved in parastatal or illegal activities.[42]

In those countries, where the military has arrogated to itself the role of guarantor of national unity, minority groups such as the Kurds in Turkey and the Kabyle social movement in Algeria are treated harshly.[43] Similarly the so-called deviant individuals are victimized by police forces in the name of national security or the struggle against terrorism. The most positive factor of democratization, namely, the rapidly expanding and vibrant NGOs forming the basis of a growing civil society, is also subject to repression. In this context the linkage between the militaries and the security apparatus, including military intelligence services such as the Pakistani ISI (Inter-Services Intelligence Agency), enhances their coercive capacities.[44]

ECONOMIC REFORM UNDER MILITARY CONTROL

Considering the role of the military in the economic liberalization in the Middle East, one might agree with John Voll's suggestion in this volume (see Chapter 6) that modernization can be "a barrier" to democratization. This is not only because modernization has historically been the prerogative of the elite, who never succeeded in bridging the gap between their own modernizing aspirations and popular cultures.[45] It also has been because modernization has often been initiated and pursued *at the expense of* democratization. This proposition may seem anathema to the "transitologists" and "consolidologists" who expected economic reforms to empower local societies and give a positive impulse to democratization.

At first sight, economic reforms should challenge and reduce the role of the military in national economies, which has been growing over the last several decades. In the early period of development and state building, the economic success of military establishments was due to their ability to obtain exorbitant economic and financial privileges, including advanced information, exemption from taxes and other duties, cheap or even free manpower, and guarantee of monopoly of imports, as well as priority access to raw material and state credit, in the name of national security.[46] The Middle East's military institutions have also shown a great ability to adapt to economic liberalization measures and a great capacity to protect their vested interests by (1) resorting to neo-corporatism and (2) entering the world of business.

First, new international security and trade trends have led to the development of neocorporatist values and practices among the Middle Eastern militaries.[47] The militaries have entered the private sector, individually or collectively, and have adopted the most "modern" financial ethos, thus participating in the rapid transformation of their national economies and resisting the social turmoil of transition to economic liberalism.[48] The social crisis resulting from this liberalization cannot but deepen the gap between the civilians and the militaries, as the latter remain exempted from austerity measures.[49] But there is also a divide within the military, separating officer corps from the enlisted men, who are often ill-treated and reduced to living on family support or parallel civilian activities. Officers can be considered privileged even if not all military institutions have been as successful as the Turkish Ordu Yardimlasma Kurumu/Armed Forces Pension Fund (OYAK)[50] and the Pakistani Army Welfare Trust.[51] This situation often means that officers above the rank of captain live in a world apart from the rest of the society, protected from and possibly ignorant of the trials of ordinary life. Military establishments also manage to maintain their unproductive economic structures and escape International Monetary Fund (IMF)–imposed structural reforms.[52]

However, the corporatism developed among military top brass and middle-range officers might be both a component and a means of the modernization of the military in the Middle East. The well-trained and disciplined armies of Turkey, Pakistan, and Jordan have become more efficient because of their ability to improve the living conditions and educational level of their ranks. But such success has a price. Armed forces of the Middle East no longer tend to see themselves as representing the people as national armies. Rather, they have returned to their previous praetorian status. As illustrated by the example of Pakistan, modern armed forces organized along corporatist bonds often consider themselves a state aristocracy, psychologically superior to the rest of the society.[53] They also see themselves (and are considered by many Western observers) as depoliticized. Therefore, their rule is viewed as more legitimate, especially in response to the lack of accountability of the polity. Too often, however, they identify the defense of their corporate interests with the survival of the regime and, thus, they become more patronage-oriented according to enduring ethnic, tribal, or sectarian identities, rather than concerned with national development. Meanwhile, their lack of accountability to civilian authorities impedes progress toward democratization.

Second, since the initiation of economic reforms in the 1990s, the interplay between private businessmen and military officers has increased throughout the Middle East. Often, officers in Turkey, Egypt, and Syria take on roles as private businesspersons, both while in office and after retirement, thus blurring the distinction between private and public spheres and creating a dichotomy between private interests and public duties.[54] In Syria, low- and middle-rank officers have acquired implicit rights to smuggling and other illicit profits derived from the Syrian military and intelligence presence in Lebanon.[55] In Egypt, senior officers are involved in ventures related to the procurement business.[56] In Algeria, they play a strategic role in perpetuating the economy of scarcity[57] by running networks of legal and illegal imports.[58] In Turkey and Pakistan, they have taken advantage of deregulation to expand their engagement in private business and banking, initiate joint ventures with domestic and foreign companies, and increase their autonomy from the civilian government.[59]

The positive and negative impacts of this new engagement of the militaries on the process of modernization and democratization have been different in the cases of various countries. In Turkey, the military has interacted with the domestic private sector and foreign corporations with relative success, OYAK showing its ability to move with and even lead the country's transition to free-market economy. By contrast, in Pakistan and Iran, where the military pose a great burden on an ailing economy, the military's involvement in business has not yielded any positive results.[60]

CONCLUSIONS

The foregoing analysis has illustrated that the roots of the Middle East's present militaries and their underlying characteristics must be sought in the region's history of colonial rule, its struggle for independence, and the postindependence pattern of state and nation building. Similarly, the analysis has shown that changes in the character of regional and international systems have affected the political and socioeconomic functions of the militaries in the Middle East.

The record of the Middle Eastern militaries in modernization, notably in the development of a broad-based national identity, has been mixed. While initially aiming at consolidating state-based national identities, they have been unable to accommodate the age-old ethnic and sectarian cleavages. Consequently, in several Middle Eastern states, Islamism has been replacing a failed nationalism within the armed forces, a process also aided by a degree of affinity between military ethics and Islamic values.

In the economic field, the policies of many military-ruled countries have had negative results. Moreover, large military expenditures have diverted resources from social and economic development, including education, thus hampering modernization.

The militaries have adapted well to a more liberalized economy, but their growing participation in the liberalized sector of the economy reflects an incomplete and often distorted market liberalization, and sometimes opens the way to parallel and illegal economic activities. Military officers often enter into joint ventures with private foreign or domestic businessmen on a noncompetitive basis. While contributing to a limited modernization of civilian industrial production, they prevent further deregulation so as to protect their corporate interests, to the point of inducing deliberalization.[61]

In terms of democratization, the excessive influence of the military in the politics and the economies of the Middle East has had a limiting impact. Indeed, political institutionalization has come at the price of reinforcing authoritarian values and practices. Authoritarian regimes have placed not only the army but security agencies and sometimes paramilitaries at the core of the political decision making, especially with regard to the definition of the political community. For local societies, which bear the brunt of economic liberalization, inclusion in or exclusion from the nation depends on security criteria set by military institutions.

The continuing factionalism within Middle Eastern armies, meanwhile, is unlikely to lead to democratic bargains with the civilian population. Rather, new internal and international security requirements are likely to provide new opportunities for the militaries to maintain their political and economic influence. In fact, the political economies of the region are evolving toward a scenario that has little to do with Islam or long-standing historical stereotypes, namely, the Taiwanese scenario.[62] In this scenario, a coalition of military and businessmen make up the main support base of the regime and impose their rule on the rest of the society. At best, such a scenario implies fast economic growth capable of providing some benefits to a segmented and alienated society to appease its frustration because of authoritarianism. At worst, it might lead to the spread of extremist ideas, popular protest, and even civil strife. In short, despite the militaries' short-term success, the weakening of civilian elites and the absence of the rule of law do not augur well for the democratization of the Middle East.

NOTES

1. Manfred Halpern, *The Politics of Social Change in the Middle East and North Africa* (Princeton, NJ: Princeton University Press, 1962); Samuel P. Huntington, *The Soldier and the State: The Theory and Politics of Civil-Military Relations* (Cambridge, MA: Belknap Press, 1957); Vernon J. Parry and M. E. Yapp, *War, Technology, and Society in the Middle East* (London: Oxford University Press, 1975).

2. Guillermo O'Donnell and Philippe Schmitter, *Transitions from Authoritarian Rule: Tentative Conclusions About Uncertain Democracies* (Baltimore: Johns Hopkins University Press, 1986).

3. Morris Janowitz, *The Professional Soldier: A Social and Political Portrait* (New York: Free Press, 1971); Volker Berghahn, *Militarism: The History of an International Debate, 1861–1979* (Cambridge: Cambridge University Press, 1981).

4. However, Turkeys desire to join the European Union is beginning to shift the military-civilian balance. Mehmet A. Birand, *Thirty Hot Days* (Nicosia, Cyprus: K. Rustem & Bros., 1985).

5. Parry and Yapp, *War, Technology, and Society.*

6. United Nations Development Programme, "Creating Opportunities for Future Generations," *Arab Human Development Report 2002* (New York: United Nations Development Programme, 2002), http://www.undp.org/rbas/ahdr/english2002.html.

7. Preface to the reissue of Albert Hourani, *Arabic Thought in the Liberal Age, 1798–1939* (Cambridge: Cambridge University Press, 1983).

8. International Crisis Group, "Pakistan: Transition to Democracy?" ICG Asia Report 40 (Islamabad: International Crisis Group, October 3, 2002).

9. Alain Chouet, "L'espace tribal Alaouite à l'épreuve du pouvoir: la désintégration par le politique," *Maghreb-Machrek* 147 (Winter 1995): 109–11.

10. John P. Entelis, "Algeria: Technocratic Rule, Military Power," in I. William Zartman, ed., *Political Elites in Arab North Africa* (New York: Longman, 1982), 108–9.

11. Richard Tapper, introduction to Richard Tapper, ed., *The Conflict of Tribe and State in Afghanistan* (London: Croom Helm, 1983).

12. Adeed Dawisha, *Syria and the Lebanese Crisis* (New York: St. Martin's Press, 1980), 58–62; Fred Lawson, *Why Syria Goes to War* (Ithaca, NY: Cornell University Press, 1996).

13. Nikolaos Van Dam, *The Struggle for Power in Syria: Politics and Society under Asad and the Ba'th Party* (1979; repr., London: I. B. Tauris, 1996), 118–36.

14. Luis Martinez, *The Algerian Civil War, 1990–1998* (New York: Columbia University Press, 2000).

15. Svante Cornell, "The Military in Turkish Politics," in Bertil Duner, ed., *Turkey: The Road Ahead* (Stockholm: Swedish Institute of International Affairs, 2002), 30.

16. Isabelle Cordonnier, *The Military and Political Order in Pakistan* (Geneva: Programme for Strategic and International Security Studies, 1999).

17. The Bouyali group was the precursor to the armed Islamist groups of the 1990s. Abderrahmane Moussaoui, "De la violence au Djihad," *Annales HSS* 6 (November–December 1994), 1315–33.

18. Hans Günter Lobmeyer, *Opposition und Widerstand in Syrien* (Hamburg: Deutsches Orient-Institut, 1995), 294–336.

19. Annabelle Böttcher, *Syrische Religionspolitk unter Asad* (Freiburg: Arnold-Bergstrasser-Institut, 1998).

20. Christophe Jaffrelot, *Pakistan: Nationalism Without a Nation?* (London: Zed Books, 2002), 143.

21. Garassimos Karabelias, "The Evolution of Civil-Military Relations in Post-War Turkey, 1980–95," *Middle Eastern Studies* 35, no. 4 (1999): 130–51.

22. Ahmed Abdalla, ed., *The Army and Democracy in Egypt* (in Arabic) (Cairo: Sinai Publishers, 1990).

23. Panayiotis J. Vatikiotis, *The Egyptian Army in Politics: Pattern for New Nation* (Bloomington: Indiana University Press, 1961).

24. Gilles Kepel, *The Prophet and Pharaoh: Muslim Extremism in Egypt* (London: Al Saqi Books, 1985).

25. Rémy Leveau, *Le sabre et le turban* (Paris: François Bourin, 1993), 224.

26. Jacob Landau, *Radical Politics in Modern Turkey* (Leiden: Brill Academic Publishers, 1974).

27. Kenneth Katzman, *Warriors of Islam: Iran's Revolutionary Guards* (Boulder, CO: Westview Press, 1993); Michael Eisenstadt, "The Armed Forces of the Islamic Republic of Iran: An Assessment," *Middle East Review of International Affairs* 5, no. 1 (March 2001).

28. Elizabeth Picard, "Authoritarianism and Liberalism in the Reconstruction of the Lebanese Armed Forces" paper presented at the Fourth Mediterranean Social and Political Research Meeting, Montecatini Terme, March 19–23, 2003; A. Nizar Hamzeh, "Lebanon's Hizbullah: From Islamic Revolution to Parliamentary Accommodation," *Third World Quarterly* 14, no. 2 (1993).

29. Five hundred officers have been excluded from the Turkish army in the past decade for their alleged support or adhesion to Islamism. *Le Monde,* July 30, 2003. The army also used its influence to bring down Erbakan's government in 1997.

30. Martin Van Creveld, *The Transformation of War* (New York: Free Press, 1991); Mary Kaldor, *New and Old Wars: Organized Violence in a Global Era* (Stanford, CA: Stanford University Press, 1999).

31. Ali E. Hillal Dessouki, "Dilemmas of Security and Development in the Arab World: Aspects of the Linkage," in Bahgat Korany, Rex Brynen, and Paul Noble, eds., *The Many Faces of National Security in the Arab World* (Montreal: Macmillan, 1993), 76–90.

32. Jaffrelot, *Pakistan,* 161; Stephen P. Cohen, "The Nation and the State of Pakistan," *Washington Quarterly* 25, no. 3 (2002): 109–22.

33. Yahya Sadowski, *Scuds or Butter? The Political Economy of Arms Control in the Middle East* (Washington, DC: Brookings Institution, 1993); Miriam Lowi, "Algérie 1992–2002: une nouvelle économie politique de la violence," *Maghreb-Machrek* 175 (Spring 2003): 63–66.

34. Roger Owen, "The Political Environment for Development," in Ibrahim Ibrahim, ed., *Arab Resources* (Washington, DC: Georgetown University, 1983), 139–46; Yezid Sayigh, "Arab Military Industrialization: Security Incentives and Economic Impact," in Korany, Brynen, and Noble, *Many Faces,* 214–38.

35. Anthony Giddens, *The Nation-State and Violence* (Cambridge: Polity Press, 1985).

36. Karen Pfeifer, "Does Food Security Make a Difference? Algeria, Egypt, and Turkey in Comparative Perspective," in Korany, Brynen, and Noble, *Many Faces,* 127–44.

37. Ahmed Abdalla, "Military-Political Interactions in Egypt: An Historical Perspective," in May Chartouni-Dubarry, ed., *Armée et nation en Égypte: Pouvoir civil, pouvoir militaire* (Paris: Institut Français des Relations Internationales, 2001), 43–56.

38. Quoted in Ishtiaq Ahmad, "Turkish Model in Pakistani Politics," *The Nation* (Lahore), December 3, 1999.

39. Middle East Watch, *Syria Unmasked: The Suppression of Human Rights by the Asad Regime* (New Haven, CT: Yale University Press, 1991), viii.

40. Guillermo O'Donnell, Philippe Schmitter, and Laurence Whitehead, *Transitions from Authoritarian Rule: Prospects for Democracy* (Baltimore: Johns Hopkins University Press, 1986).

41. Albert Hirschman, *Exit, Voice, and Loyalty: Responses to Decline in Firms, Organizations, and States* (Cambridge, MA: Harvard University Press, 1970). For a discussion of a Middle Eastern case, see Lisa Wedeen, *Ambiguities of Domination: Politics, Rhetoric, and Symbols in Contemporary Syria* (Chicago: University of Chicago Press, 1999).

42. A good example is the wide coverage by the Turkish media of the "incident of Susurlik." On November 3, 1996, a member of parliament, a director of the national police, and a drug mafia boss recently escaped from prison were traveling together in an arms-loaded car. See Jean-François Bayart, "La combinatoire des forces nationalistes en Turquie: 'Démocratie islamique' ou criminalisation du communautarisme?" *Cahiers d'études sur la Méditerranée orientale et le monde Turco-Iranien* 24 (July–December 1997): 97–108.

43. Hamit Bozarslan, "The Kurdish Question in Turkish Political Life: The Situation as of 1990," in Turaj Atabaki and Margreet Dorleijn, eds., *Kurdistan in Search of Ethnic Identity* (Utrecht, Netherlands: Houtsma Foundation, 1990), 1–23. The Kurdish population of Turkey is generally estimated at 20 percent of the total population (67,800,000, according to the national census of 2000). A study commissioned by the MGK and published in *Milliyet*, December 18, 1996, indicated that in 2010 the Kurdish population of Turkey might amount to 40 percent of the total population.

44. David Chazan, "Profile: Pakistan's Military Intelligence Agency," BBC News Online, January 9, 2002, http://news.bbc.co.uk/2/hi/south_asia/1750265.stm.

45. Sami Zubaida, *Islam, the People and the State: Essays on Political Ideas and Movements in the Middle East* (London: I. B. Tauris, 1993).

46. Yezid Sayigh, "Security and Cooperation in the Middle East: A Proposal," *Middle East International* 429 (1992): 16–17.

47. Nazih Ayubi, *Over-Stating the Arab State: Politics and Society in the Middle East* (1995; repr., London: I. B. Tauris, 1999), 187–89.

48. Henry Barkey, "Why Military Regimes Fail: The Perils of Transition," *Armed Forces and Society* 16, no. 2 (Winter 1990).

49. John Sfakianakis and Robet Springborg, "Civil-Military Relations in Egypt," *Journal of Arabic, Islamic, and Middle Eastern Studies* 5, no. 2 (1999): 44–46.

50. Taha Parla, "Mercantile Militarism in Turkey," *New Perspectives on Turkey* 19 (1998): 29–52.

51. Owen Bennet Jones, *Pakistan: Eye of the Storm* (New Haven, CT: Yale University Press, 2002), 277.

52. Ismet Akça, "Peripheral Type of Military-Industrial Complex: Military Capital in Turkey," paper presented at the Fourth Mediterranean Social and Political Research Meeting, Montecatini Terme, March 19–23, 2003.

53. Stephen P. Cohen, *The Pakistan Army* (1984; repr., London: Oxford University Press, 1998), 120.

54. James Bill and Robert Springborg, *Politics in the Middle East* (London: Little, Brown Higher Education, 1990), 268–74.

55. Yahya Sadowski, "Cadres, Guns, and Money: The Eighth Regional Congress of the Syrian Ba'th," *Middle East Report* 134 (July–August 1985): 3–9.

56. Robert Springborg, "The President and the Field Marshal: Civil-Military Relations in Egypt Today," *Middle East Report* 147 (July–August 1987): 10–15.

57. More precisely of the "dictatorship over needs" as used by Loulouwa Al Rashid in her analysis of the Iraqi polity under Saddam, with reference to Ferenc Fehér, Agnes Heller, and Gyorgy Markus, *Dictatorship Over Needs: An Analysis of Soviet Societies* (Oxford, UK: Basil Blackwell, 1983).

58. Martinez, *Algerian Civil War*, 228–31.

59. "Empire-Building That Began with the Military Exercise," *Financial Times,* October 9, 2001; "Forces in Business," *Jane's Defense Weekly,* February 14, 2001.

60. Ayesha Siddiqa-Agha, "Power, Perks, Prestige, and Privileges: Military's Economic Activities in Pakistan," paper presented at the international conference Soldiers in Business: Military as an Economic Actor, Institute for Policy and Community Development Studies, Jakarta, October 16–19, 2000.

61. Fehér, Heller, and Markus, *Dictatorship Over Needs*.

62. Cal Clark and Steve Chan, "China and Taiwan: A Security Paradox," *Journal of East Asian Affairs* 5, no. 2 (1991): 466–97.

9

Lessons from Latin America for the Muslim World

Bruce W. Farcau

The fact that the military establishments have played a central role in the political development of third world countries over the past half century should not be surprising. This is so because, as Samuel Huntington noted, the armed forces of newly independent states were often the most modern, disciplined, coherent, and nationally aware element of society.[1] Consequently, they believed that they should have a strong and even dominant voice in the national political debate, even if this were to be achieved at the expense of democratic development. This attitude of the military establishments accounts for the prevalence of praetorian regimes, or of civilian governments existing at the sufferance of the military, throughout the third world. Huntington and other scholars have sometimes looked upon the military as a "rationalizing" force in the politics of developing nations.

However, such rationalization often has taken place at the cost of depriving civilian regimes of the opportunity to establish their legitimacy.[2] This has been particularly true in the Muslim countries extending from North Africa to South and Southeast Asia, albeit to different degrees. The thesis of this chapter, however, is that the factionalism that is a characteristic of the armed forces of all countries and that can partly explain military intervention in politics can also be a mechanism for transition to a more stable democratic system. This has been the case in Latin America and, despite some significant differences, can happen in some Muslim countries, including those in the Middle East.

PESSIMISM REGARDING DEMOCRACY IN THE MIDDLE EAST

In the days immediately before and after the 2003 Iraq war, many analysts expressed doubt whether democracy can be established and survive in the Middle

East; the dominant opinion was that it cannot. The empirical evidence upon which this assessment was based was that, with the possible exception of Turkey, there are no functioning stable democracies either in the Middle East or in other Muslim states. Rather, postindependence governments sporting at least some semblance of democratic practices either have been short-lived or have been mere facades for essentially authoritarian regimes.

Various explanations, ranging from cultural to historical and from internal to external, have been suggested for this phenomenon. None of these arguments is very satisfying intellectually. However, the fact of the absence of viable democracies in the region remains. Therefore, it is only human to assume that there must be a rational explanation for this phenomenon based on one or a combination of different factors and arguments. However, a scientifically rigorous explanation should take account of the fact that substantially differing variables throughout the Middle East have produced similar results while similar variables in other parts of the world have produced different results. Pakistan, for example, had the influence of the same British system as did India. Similarly, Algeria has ended up with an authoritarian, military-based regime after a long colonial history and bloody war of independence, but so have Syria and Iraq after only relatively brief "trusteeships" and a generally peaceful transition to self-rule. Could the failure of democracy in Pakistan be attributed solely to its Islamic character? If so, how can one explain the fact that a largely indigenous form of democracy, albeit with certain authoritarian aspects and an element of instability, has survived in Muslim Turkey?

More to the point is the following question: Why have so many other countries in Africa, Asia, and Latin America experienced nondemocratic regimes largely indistinguishable from those of the Middle East when none of them share any of the religious, ethnic, historical, or economic characteristics of the Middle East which supposedly have contributed to democracy's failure in this region? The failure of democracy to develop in oil-rich and grindingly poor countries and in nations that barely experienced colonial domination and those that were long ruled by European powers and had to fight for their independence presents some intriguing paradoxes.

The basic premise of this chapter is that Samuel Huntington is correct in his statement that the proper question is not "Why has democracy failed in some areas?" but "How has it ever managed to survive anywhere?"[3] Given the historical record, it is little short of miraculous that multiparty, representative democracy developed from the near anarchy and regionalism of postrevolutionary America or from various forms of absolute monarchy in Western Europe. Democracy has spread, very recently in historical terms, partly through imposition by military force as in Japan, Germany, and Italy, and partly through the influence of the established democracies using diplomatic, political, economic, and even military pressure in ways sometimes hardly distinguishable from outright coercion.

THE LATIN AMERICAN EXPERIENCE— PREVAILING THEORIES

As late as the 1980s, in discussions about failure and success of democracy in Latin America, explanations similar to those offered for the case of the Muslim world were current. Many expressed the opinion that it was Latin America's cultural peculiarities that hindered the development of stable democratic regimes. Historically, all Latin American nations initially established democratic governments and adopted constitutions similar to that of the United States. However, until the late 1980s these efforts had largely failed. After passing through the turbulent era of the *caudillos* (military leaders who emerged from the revolutionary–independence period) in the nineteenth century following independence, liberal democratic governments alternated with stultified oligarchies, single-party systems, and the occasional autarchic regimes. One constant feature was that the military remained posed to intervene and oust the incumbents, either to retain power only briefly before selecting a successor, or to rule for years.

Some countries fared better than others in this game of chance, but none seemed totally immune to the threat of military takeover. Chile and Uruguay, which had survived the wave of coups d'état of the 1960s, succumbed in a most brutal fashion to military rule in the 1970s. Even in the early 2000s the longest-surviving Latin democracies—Venezuela and Colombia—were threatened by radical populist policies. In Haiti, the reinstalled civilian government of President Aristide degenerated into a thoroughly corrupt and oppressive regime that has now been overthrown by a popular uprising, and rumblings in the barracks in Peru, Ecuador, Bolivia, Paraguay, and even Argentina and Brazil clearly indicate the fragility of Latin democracies.

The causes noted for the failure of democratic consolidation to take root in Latin America have been largely different from those mentioned in the case of the Middle East. However, some similarities exist. For example, one theory, paralleling the one that blames Islam for the lack of democracy, holds that Latin America's failure has been due to the hierarchical structure of the Catholic Church because it predisposes Latin American nations to authoritarian regimes. However, the fact that other Catholic or partially Catholic countries such as Ireland, Poland, Spain, Italy, Portugal, the Czech Republic, and Germany have thriving democracies weakens this argument.[4] Another theory holds that the Spanish colonial experience, and the almost feudal distribution of state lands and the population to work them, made Latin Americans susceptible to the centralization of power and the establishment of the state as the primary source of wealth and influence. This is in sharp contrast to the British colonies in North America in which the predominance of small landholders among the colonists and the absence of an easily superseded native social structure led to the rise of a grass-roots form of democracy from the outset. This theory is rather more valid than the one based on religion, as shown by the case of those Latin countries where small landholders tended to predominate over *latifundistas* (large estate owners), as in Costa Rica, and where democracy has had a much better track of being consolidated. It is also noteworthy that in the American South, where large plantation owners had gained their position because of political connections, there was slavery and political intolerance, and the concepts of universal suffrage and open political debate were suppressed.

However, even this theory has limited validity, because until the 1970s, Latin American countries had shown more affinity for democratic experimentation than the Spanish mother country. Another common explanation for the frequency of military intervention in Latin America has been that of the "middle class coup."[5] According to this view, the middle class turns to the military to "veto" populist programs sponsored by democratic regimes. Yet another theory is the bureaucratic authoritarian explanation, according to which civilian technocrats add their organizational skill and inherent desire for order and stability to that of the military to protect the economic interests of the bourgeoisie.[6] This theory explained the overthrow of populist regimes in Argentina and Brazil, among other places, in the 1960s and in Chile and Uruguay in the 1970s. The problem with this neo-Marxist approach is that it assumes too much commonality of interest between the "middle class" (or more properly the capitalist bourgeoisie) and the military, implying that the latter has been the willing tool of the former without any institutional interests of its own. This theory ignores the fact that, in Latin America and many other regions, the military officer corps is largely drawn from the working and lower middle classes and would likely share their overall values.

Furthermore, the military as an institution has a vested interest in a strong, well-funded central government, which conflicts with the bourgeoisie's laissez-faire philosophy. In some cases, military intervention has led to an infiltration of the economic structure by the military, either in the form of military direction of certain "strategic" or military-related industries as in Brazil in the 1960s and 1970s, or in the form of a kind of kleptocracy as in Bolivia in the 1980s.[7] However, this theory fails to explain the emergence of reformist, even radical populist, military governments as happened in Peru in the 1960s. These governments worked for unionization and socialization at the expense of the propertied classes.[8]

The "national security doctrine" attributes the rise of military governments in Latin America to the impact of the cold war. This theory is supported by largely anecdotal evidence of American complicity in the overthrow of populist, left-leaning regimes such as that of Jacobo Arbenz in Guatemala in 1954 and Salvador Allende in Chile in 1973, and American support for corrupt and military regimes such as that of Fulgencio Batista in Cuba or Rafael Trujillo in the Dominican Republic. The collapse of virtually all military regimes in Latin America in the waning years of the cold war, or in its immediate aftermath, validates the existence of some linkage between cold war politics and military rule in Latin America.

However, there are several problems with this theory: First, it does little to explain military interventions in Latin America prior to the start of the cold war. Furthermore, there is little correlation between American influence and involvement in a country and that country's propensity for military intervention in politics, as seen in the frequent and violent military coups in Argentina (with virtually no American influence) and the relatively moderate role of the military in Brazilian politics and the virtual absence of such intervention in Colombia and Venezuela despite close ties to the American military.[9] Second, American policy generally has been far more consistent in its support and encouragement of stable democratic regimes than of even the most fervently anti-Communist military dictatorships, despite occasional instances of opportunistic American support of nondemocratic regimes. Indeed, Washington has traditionally seen stable democratic regimes as less problematic, better trading partners, and more reliable allies than illegitimate military governments.

MILITARY FACTIONALISM AS A FACTOR

Notwithstanding the above, the question still remains: If all cultural, ethnic, socioeconomic, and external political factors do not explain the poor record of democracy in Latin America, what does? My view is that the answer lies, to a greater or lesser extent, within the nature of the military institutions themselves, namely a propensity that transcends geographic and cultural boundaries and affects all armed forces everywhere.

The primary shortcoming of most analyses of Latin American political evolution has been a tendency to look at the armed forces as a monolithic entity, acting in concert and with unanimity of purpose. The most noted scholars of political development in Latin America and the third world, including Samuel Huntington, Juan Linz, Alfred Stepan, and others, have been primarily concerned with the militaries' objectives and motivations in their quest for power. The idea that there are significant differences of opinion within the armed forces, even diametrically opposed opinions, is generally only found in more specialized studies, such as those of S. E. Finer or Edward Luttwak. These studies focus primarily on the military as an institution and only secondarily on its role in politics. It is the melding of these two approaches that brings into truer perspective the actions of the leaders of the armed forces in the political arena.

This tendency to see the armed forces as a solid mass is hardly surprising, since this is exactly the image that all military institutions endeavor to project. However, whether consciously or unconsciously, all military institutions ultimately recognize Clausewitz's dictum that their field of activity is simply the extension of politics. It is this inevitable connection with politics that forces the military, or at least its most prominent leaders, to become involved in politics.

The main traits of the military that endow it with a tendency to get involved in political affairs are factionalism and competition for resources within different cliques that tend to form around charismatic leaders. Such factionalism can be found in every military institution in every nation. The competition among factions can frequently become intense and even violent. It is only in societies with very strong traditions of legitimate, democratic government (or in those where democratic structure has been imposed and is enforced by some outside power) that this competition is kept within bounds and is limited to debates over allocation of the defense budget or future force structure. However, *most* societies have historically lacked this unassailable supremacy of the civilian government over the military, and competition for resources within the military institution can easily spill over into the political arena, posing a threat to democratic government.[10] Conversely, this same factionalism can, on occasion, serve the cause of democratization by destabilizing authoritarian regimes and providing allies within the armed forces for groups attempting to moderate the political system.

Given the heroic, warrior tradition in the military, it is hardly surprising that charismatic leaders gather around themselves a loyal group of followers. Military factions generally tend to form along a number of sometimes competing lines, such as family, school, clan, region, or branch of service.[11] However, it is the leader who is the most important link because he can use his position of authority to ensure promotion and favorable assignments for his supporters. In return, the followers lend their support to the leader, making their combined power greater than the power of individual parts. This is often the key to a leader's success in forming a cohesive clique and is also the military's main motivation for involvement in politics. It is unlikely that a senior leader unable to obtain promotions and choice assignments for his supporters will be able to count on their support for very long. If the leader is of sufficiently high rank, his success may also be measured in his ability to obtain government resources for the military or for the projects sponsored by his clique.

The existence of one faction within a military institution almost by definition engenders the creation of one or more competitors, although a considerable percentage of the officer corps may not be formally committed to any allegiance. Such a group constitutes a swing vote, awaiting some crisis to cast their lot with one side or the other. In any event, it is the competition among factions that often drives the charismatic military leaders to ensure their dominance of the institution, often at the expense of rival factions within the context of a zero-sum game. Ultimately, a military leader may see taking control of the entire machinery of government as the only means of ensuring the domination of his faction, or perhaps of preventing its destruction at the hands of its rivals. Even in countries where coups d'état are extremely rare, the "power" of one faction over another can often be measured in the utility of a given military unit and its commander in a hypothetical coup situation. Consequently, combat units (infantry and army mainly) located conveniently close to the capital city would be of greater value than engineering units or infantry units stationed away on some isolated border.

The same is true of naval and air force units, whose considerable firepower would hardly be usable against one's fellow citizens in urban areas. An elaborate calculation thus takes place in which rival leaders tote up the regiments and battalions they command to determine who "wins" the battle for influence. Sometimes, actual changes of government can occur, bloodlessly and with a minimum of trouble, through the same process.[12] When the competition becomes intense enough, rival military leaders may reach out to potential allies beyond the armed forces, seeking support from civilian bureaucrats, politicians, labor leaders, and the media. If such connections are pursued with sufficient vigor and are successfully established, they may result in a situation wherein electoral success for one political party may be taken as defeat for a particular military faction. It is at this point that the competition for dominance of the military institution can become an outright military interventionism. Likewise, the weaker of two military factions will find additional motivation in seeking out civilian allies, possibly on the fringes of the political spectrum, to enhance its own position, posing a separate threat to the system.

None of the foregoing is intended to suggest that military leaders do not have core values and ideologies that they would not be willing to compromise for short-term factional gains. There are some fundamental interests that military men tend to share and that take precedence over short-term gains. The most common of these shared values is a desire for the military to maintain its monopoly over the means of armed coercion. Thus, after numerous failed attempts to construct a consensus within the military for the ouster of an objectionable civilian regime, it has often been an effort by that regime to create some kind of armed force as a counterweight to the regular military that has prompted direct military intervention. This could be seen in Guatemala in 1954, Bolivia in 1964, and Chile in 1973. Beyond this, however, while an individual military leader may, indeed, have fervently held political beliefs, alliances between a military leader and civilian political groups more often represent an effort by that leader to seek additional allies in the struggle for dominance of the military rather than an expression of ideological commitment. One is often presented with a "chicken and egg" scenario. In this context, one must ask whether Argentina's Juan Perón really espoused the cause of unionized workers or whether he sought their support to offset his own unpopularity with the elitist navy and air force within the armed forces, thus further polarizing portions of the military against him and forcing him to rely more on his civilian supporters.

THE GLOBAL NATURE OF MILITARY FACTIONALISM

For the purposes of this chapter, the key point is that factionalism of some sort exists in the armed forces of every nation to a greater or lesser extent. The question thus becomes, What is it about a society that allows the competition between military factions to run its course more or less benignly and not carry over into the overall competition for political power in the society as a whole?

It is not coincidental that the countries that have the best record of civilian control over the military have been those that traditionally have had the smallest military institutions in relation to other powers. These countries have also enjoyed relative immunity from foreign invasion, which has allowed them to survive without large standing armies. Good examples are the United States and Great Britain.

This is not to say that even the small armed forces of Britain and the United States could not have seized power against an unarmed opposition had the situation required. But the odds against one part of a factionalized military succeeding in a coup attempt would have been very long indeed, thus making it all the more difficult for any potential coup leader to solidify a base of support for extreme action. However, this weakness of the military in relation to the civilian government has allowed the civilian political establishment the time to create a tradition of legitimacy for democratic procedures and the rule of law that would be difficult for any potential coup leader to overcome.

Even during the most politically turbulent time in American history—the Civil War—this sense of legitimacy had a palpable effect, although the existence of factionalism within the military could also be clearly seen. Abraham Lincoln's rivalry with General George B. McClellan boiled over during 1862, and McClellan seriously considered a "march on Washington" at the urging of some of his colleagues in the Army of the Potomac. McClellan was ultimately dissuaded, however, not by his consideration of constitutional obligations but because of the opposition provided by a powerful faction of generals under the leadership of Joseph Hooker and the likely hostility of the commanders of the western armies.[13] When a similar clash, between a sitting president, Harry Truman, and a field commander, Douglas MacArthur, occurred nearly a century later, in the Korean War, no serious consideration was given to physically opposing Truman's sacking of the general because of a consensus that "we just do not do that sort of thing in America."

Conversely, France has enjoyed a far less stable military–political tradition, partly due to the necessity of maintaining a large standing army for defense against its neighbors, and partly because factionalism within the military has played a key role in determining the success or failure of military intervention in politics. In the post–World War II era, the French military was divided between the metropolitan army, on the one hand, and the colonial army, dominated by the "paratroop mafia" of General Jacques Massu, on the other. It was pressure from the colonialists that raised Charles de Gaulle to power with the neutral stance of the metropolitan force. The massive firepower and convenient placement of the metropolitan army ensured de Gaulle's survival in the face of the colonial mutiny when he decided to abandon the struggle in Algeria.[14] Was it true commitment to the survival of French Algeria that drove the colonial generals into a bloody resistance to de Gaulle, or was it the realization that an end to France's last colonial conflict would permanently rob them of any claim to resources for their faction members in the future?

The armed forces have often also been created for the suppression of internal dissent. This is an unfortunate situation in terms of the survivability of democracy, as internal security duties invariably give the armed forces a say in determining, not just foreign policy, but also aspects of domestic policies that might give rise to civil unrest. This situation, in turn, blurs the barrier between strictly military activities and political activism. Since international wars in Latin America have been relatively rare, compared to the European experience, and since Latin American armies are the descendants of colonial armies of occupation designed to keep both native populations and transplanted European colonists in line, this has been the historical role for the armed forces there.

THE BOLIVIAN CASE

A classic case of factionalism in Latin America, resulting in coups and countercoups, is the conflict between the "institutionalists" and the "generationalists" in the Bolivian military, resulting from chronic Bolivian political instability. This instability had prevented the development of any kind of legitimacy for any regime since independence in 1825. The former faction was composed of officers of the regular army from before the Bolivian Revolution of 1952. Many of these officers had opposed the revolution and had been forced to retire after victory. However, some of them were called back to service because the government of President Victor Paz Estenssoro needed them to suppress the overly revolutionary miners. The generationalists were formed of younger officers who graduated from the military academy after the revolution. Both factions had become well established and in diametrical opposition to one another by the late 1950s.

The coup that ousted Paz and his National Revolutionary Movement Party (MNR) in 1964 was led by the institutionalists under General René Barrientos, who had recruited a body of younger officers who had entered the service since the revolution but who owed their careers to Barrientos and other institutionalist leaders. The generationalists were too weak to offer much resistance and suffered years of subservience until Barrientos' death in 1969. After his death, they briefly seized power under Generals Alfredo Ovando Candia and Juan José Torres but were quickly and bloodily suppressed, along with their allies among the miners and factory workers, by a new institutionalist wave under General Hugo Banzer Suárez in 1971. Banzer ruled for six years and then withdrew voluntarily from power because of a collapsing economy and after having arranged for relatively free elections. But General David Padilla Arancibia, who was dissatisfied with the election results, seized power in his turn in 1978.

World public opinion and the U.S. government during the Carter administration pressured Bolivia to return to civilian rule, and an interim government was established under Walter Guevara Arce. However, as the Guevara government proved totally inept the generationalists under Colonel Alberto Natusch Busch seized the presidency in late 1979, enjoying what appeared to be nearly universal support within the armed forces. This support proved to be illusory, however, and the commanders of key regiments (all of them institutionalists) engaged in a bloody repression of any resistance, in full view of the world media. Facing massive criticism on the international front and an immediate cutoff of all foreign aid, the Natusch government lasted barely two weeks, and a number of generationalist officers were forced into retirement, exile, or dead-end assignments. Another caretaker government took office, but in July of 1980 a new coup was launched, this time a brilliantly executed one by the institutionalists under Luis García Meza, which seemed to mark a victorious end to this decades-long rivalry.

However, factionalism within the military can actually work in favor of democratization of societies that have been plagued by military interventionism. Just as a military faction can seek to overthrow a civilian government in the hope of gaining control of the state's resources for the benefit of faction members, so can a rival faction see its interests best served by a return to civilian rule. This faction can undermine an existing military regime dominated by a hostile faction in exchange for a promise of promotion and favor from the newly installed and grateful civilians.

This was precisely what happened in Bolivia in 1981, when the García Meza regime came under pressure because of hyperinflation and a total collapse of the economy. The García Meza government had also become an international pariah because of severe internal repression and allegations of close ties between senior regime officials, including García Meza and the narcotics mafia. In short order, there were several unsuccessful coup attempts, prompted by the near total collapse of the Bolivian economy, including hyperinflation.[15] Finally, in August of 1981 the surviving generationalists ousted García Meza, but instead of seizing power they sought American and other international support by endorsing a return to civilian rule, which, despite occasional stumbles, has survived as of this writing.[16] A similar situation occurred in Brazil and Argentina in the 1980s and serves as a reminder that the ultimate goal of the leader of a military faction is the welfare and advancement of his followers, and not primarily the defense of any particular ideology or the interests of an economic class. If this goal can be met without the bother and responsibility of taking over the reins of government itself, so much the better.

SOME DISTINCTIONS IN THE MUSLIM WORLD

The Muslim world, notably the Middle East, has, unfortunately, suffered simultaneously from both conditions discussed here. The military there has often had a primary role of suppressing internal dissent, on behalf of either a colonial or imperial power or an authoritarian regime. Moreover, the potential for foreign invasion has also frequently been manifested, at least in frontline countries facing Israel or elsewhere on the frontiers of Islam, as in the case of Turkey, Pakistan, and Iran. This has given rise to the establishment of relatively large armed forces that have also been largely oriented inward and sensitized to domestic political events, with the inherent tendency to want to dictate government policies that they might be called upon to enforce. It is hardly surprising, therefore, that there has been little chance for the development of solid, legitimate civilian governments during the relatively brief period since the independence of most Middle Eastern and other Muslim countries.

It should be noted that military regimes in the Middle East have shown a tendency for far greater longevity than have their counterparts in Latin America. While occasional Latin American military leaders have shown substantial staying power, such as Alfredo Stroessner in Paraguay and Fidel Castro in Cuba, the most common scenario in Latin America over the past century has been that of revolving-door governments, alternating between civilian and military regimes or simply between competing military cliques. The Muslim world, on the other hand, has seen the establishment of some very long-lived regimes, such as that of Muammar Qaddafi in Libya, and of virtual dynasties, as in Syria, where the presidency of Hafez al Assad was passed on to his son, or as in Iraq, where a similar situation would very likely have developed had it not been for the American-led invasion of 2003. Even in Egypt, while no such familial dynasty has emerged, there is a clearly defined genealogy running from the Free Officers' Movement that overthrew King Farouk, through their figurehead leader General Muhammad Naguib, to Gamal Abdel Nasser, to his lieutenant Anwar el-Sadat, to Hosni Mubarak, a line spanning more than half a century. When one adds the apparent survivability of some of the monarchies in the region, as in Jordan, Morocco, and Saudi Arabia, the implication is that factionalism within the military might not be as strong a factor in the politics of the region as it has been in Latin America, and hence the chances for a democratic bargain between one or more military factions and civilians are remote.

However, some Muslim nations, notably Turkey and Pakistan, have experienced just the sort of revolving-door phenomena common in Latin America. Therefore, perhaps it is not a coincidence that Turkey is probably the closest thing to a functioning democracy in the region. In Indonesia, while the regimes have achieved considerable longevity, there has also been a constant turbulence within the military institution, a battling between factions that has only occasionally overflowed to the point of forcing actual regime change.[17]

Another distinction between the Muslim world and Latin America is the addition of religious and ethnic divisions, which do not generally exist in the latter area. The existence of minorities such as Kurds, Druze, and Berbers, and religious affiliations, not just Muslim versus Christian or Sunni versus Shi'a, but all the various subtle flavors within each, adds a new layer of competing loyalties to the equation required for the creation of military factions. While this poses a challenge for the charismatic military leader, it is not necessarily an insurmountable one. Saddam Hussein's inner circle may have been dominated by Sunni Muslims from his native town of Tikrit, but it also included Shi'as, Kurds, and at least one Christian (Foreign Minister Tariq Aziz). Consequently, even these apparently inflexible divisions can be overcome by a leader in forming his faction if other elements of attraction, such as the possibility of promotion, are present.

It is my contention, however, that a thorough study of the military institutions of key Muslim countries would show the existence of competing factions, based on branch of service, regional origin, or other ties, under the guidance of charismatic military leaders. This characteristic has, in the past, contributed greatly to political instability in the region and to the demise of democratic regimes, whenever they were attempted. Nevertheless, the Latin American example holds out hope that this same factionalism could ultimately serve to provide a route toward democratization. While a divided military poses a threat to civilian regimes without sufficient legitimacy to keep their competition in check, this also means that the military is not a monolithic organism that must be confronted directly, rather that it can be fragmented and undermined from within.

CONCLUSION

It is clear that the development of stable democratic regimes throughout the Muslim world, not just in the Middle East, will be a project of years, if not decades, of effort. However, the Latin American experience implies that, rather than being an implacable obstacle to this goal, under the right conditions the armed forces can serve as a mechanism toward this end. The same factionalism that tends to give rise to revolving-door coups can also create the environment necessary for the rise of democratic forces and can provide them with the physical strength necessary to protect them during the formative years. This is, in fact, what has occurred in Latin America during the past two decades, and, while democracy is hardly guaranteed survival there in the long term, all the authoritarian regimes in power in the 1980s, except Cuba, have fallen, and no new ones have risen. While the Muslim world possesses some notable differences from Latin America, the examples of Turkey and Pakistan give some hope that the status quo is not immutable.

NOTES

1. Samuel P. Huntington, *Political Order in Changing Societies* (New Haven, CT: Yale University Press, 1968), 219.

2. Juan Linz, "Crisis, Breakdown, and Reequilibration," in Juan Linz and Alfred Stepan, eds., *The Breakdown of Democratic Regimes* (Baltimore: Johns Hopkins University Press, 1978), 18.

3. Samuel P. Huntington, *The Third Wave: Democratization in the Late 20th Century* (Norman: University of Oklahoma Press, 1993), 28.

4. George Philip, *The Military in South American Politics* (London: Croom Helm, 1985), 182.

5. José Nun, "The Middle Class Coup Revisited," in Abraham Lowenthal, ed., *Armies and Politics in Latin America* (New York: Holmes and Meier, 1976), 58.

6. Guillermo O'Donnell, *Modernization and Bureaucratic Authoritarianism—Studies in South American Politics* (Berkeley: Institute of International Studies, University of California Press, 1973), 6.

7. Thomas E. Skidmore, *The Politics of Military Rule in Brazil, 1964–1985* (New York: Oxford University Press, 1988), 215.

8. Julio Cotler, "A Structural-Historical Approach to the Breakdown of Democratic Institutions: Peru," in Linz and Stepan, *Breakdown of Democratic Regimes,* 185.

9. Alain Rouquie, *L'etat militaire en Amerique Latine* (Paris: Seuil, 1982), 148.

10. Juan Linz, "Crisis, Breakdown, and Reequilibration," in Linz and Stepan, *Breakdown of Democratic Regimes,* 52.

11. This theme is discussed in much greater detail in Chapter 3 of my work *The Transition to Democracy in Latin America: The Role of the Military* (Westport, CT: Praeger, 1996).

12. This concept is discussed in depth in Chapter 3 of my work *The Coup: Tactics in the Seizure of Power* (Westport, CT: Praeger, 1994).

13. Allan Nevins, *The War for the Union: War Becomes Revolution 1862–1863* (New York: Charles Scribner's Sons, 1960), 6: 323.

14. Yves Courriére, *Les feux du désespoir: 1960–1962—des barricades á l'abime* (Paris: Marabout, 1971), 447.

15. Bruce W. Farcau, *The Transition to Democracy in Latin America* (Westport, CT: Praeger, 1997), 178.

16. For more details on the Bolivian experience, see Chapter 5 of my *Transition to Democracy.*

17. Harold Maynard, "Indonesian Military Elite Role Perceptions," in Amos Perlmutter, ed., *The Political Influence of the Military* (New Haven, CT: Yale University Press, 1980), 426.

10

The Political Geography of the Arab Private Sector

Giacomo Luciani

The question of the relationship between the economic foundations of societies and states and the nature of their political systems, notably democracy and dictatorship, has long been debated. Also, a connection has often been made between economic and political liberalism, on the one hand, and direct state intervention in the economy and authoritarianism, on the other. However, historical experience has often contradicted such direct linkage, as several democratic states have pursued economically interventionist policies, while many authoritarian regimes have adopted economic liberalism.

A connection has also been established between the prevailing mode of production and the political order, ranging from Wittfogel's hydraulic societies to the role of *latifundia* or other land ownership patterns to the impact of information and communication technology (ICT).[1] Following this tradition, some authors, using the concept of petro-states or petro-monarchies, have linked the nature of political order to the role of oil in the national economy.[2]

This chapter, however, will not focus on either of these linkages; rather, it will emphasize the fiscal foundations of the state, namely, who pays for the state and how, and how the state obtains the means to cover its budget. The hypothesis here is that the political order is closely connected to the relative size and structure of the state budget. In other words, the existence of a certain type of political order is a prerequisite for a certain budget size and structure. Similarly, the latter may validate and consolidate the political order with which it is most compatible. This connection is particularly clear in the case of the rentier states. Within this broad context, this chapter will address three additional points, namely, (1) the new political geography of the Arab private sector in parts of the Arab world; (2) emerging shifts in the equilibria that existed between the state and the private sector and supported authoritarianism; and (3) how these shifts may, over time, prompt greater political participation on the part of the business and intellectual elite and generate demands for governmental accountability, eventually leading to democratization.

THE CASE OF RENTIER STATES

The rentier state paradigm was first proposed by Hossein Mahdavy in 1970[3] and was further developed by Hazem Beblawi and Giacomo Luciani.[4] Over the past three decades, it has been used to explain the political dynamics of oil-producing countries.[5]

The rentier state differs fundamentally from the petro-state because it is not necessarily linked to oil production. Under contemporary conditions, oil production and exports generate the largest international rent payments accruing directly to some states. However, there are other examples of rent, such as those provided by diamonds and other precious raw materials, as well as drugs and other illicit traffic. These rents may support rentier states, if the state manages to control them, or they can support anarchy and rebellion whenever appropriated by nonstate actors, or they may even support both, if both have access to a portion of the rent. During the Angolan civil war (1975–2002), the central government was supported by oil and the armed opposition by diamond rent. Drug trafficking may be primarily controlled by the state, as in some Central Asian countries, or may be a factor limiting state authority, as is the case in Colombia and Yemen. Rents may also be connected to the control of logistical bottlenecks (e.g., the Suez Canal or international pipelines) or religious or strategic assets. Foreign aid is another form of rent. However, the concept of the rentier state is mostly applied to the case of oil-producing countries.

PRINCIPAL CHARACTERISTICS OF RENTIER STATES

The essence of the rentier state is that it is financed by the oil rent rather than supported by the society through taxation. This rent accrues directly to the state from the rest of the world and enables it to support the society. This fundamental trait distinguishes "production" states from "rentier" states.

The details of this definition are essential.[6] First, the source of the rent should be the rest of the world. States relying on the control of a specific source of domestic rent have always existed. A contemporary example is state lotteries. But these states do not qualify as rentier states, because different mechanisms through which the surplus is extracted from society have varying political impact.[7] Nevertheless, in all cases of domestic rent, the direction of the aggregate financial flows is negative for the society and positive for the state. In short, the society supports the state.

In rentier states, because the rent accrues from abroad and is spent, at least in part, domestically, the balance of the relationship is positive for the society and negative for the state. This means that the society is at least partly supported by the state and that the state is financially independent from the society.

Second, the rent should accrue directly to the state. The distinction between a rentier state and the presence of important private rents in the society is of fundamental importance. The rentier state is neither necessarily at the origin of, nor the product of, the rent-seeking society. In all societies, economic players seek to establish a rent position for themselves. In short, rent-seeking sectors and rentier mentality in a society are a more common phenomenon than rentier states.

Some rentier states may spend more domestically by paying higher salaries or by allowing for larger profits on government contracts. Historically, this was a passing phenomenon connected with the surge in oil rents in the 1970s and the early 1980s, which now have mostly disappeared. The increased oil rent from 1973 to 1981 flooded the Arab, South Asian, and, to some extent, Southeast Asian countries, thus engulfing everybody in the process of rent circulation. The increased oil rent also led to the categorization of the earnings of expatriate workers as containing an element of rent, and the inflow of remittances by immigrant workers as a potential base for a rentier state in the receiving country.[8] This assumption contains a double fallacy because (1) expatriate earnings, if they initially contained an element of rent, do not do so any longer, and (2) remittances are private income flows, and the state must resort to taxation to appropriate all or part of them.

But this was a limited experience: oil-exporting states had been rentier before 1973, and they still are. The commonly held hypothesis that rent circulation creates entitlements because it prevents people from being productive and turns them into rentiers is correct for only a very short period of time in history.[9] The assumption that the decline in the available rent creates a crisis for the rentier state because it can no longer deliver benefits on a level that people have become accustomed to is also based on a complete misunderstanding of the dynamics of relations between the rentier state and the society. The fact is that benefits may have decreased progressively since 1985, but still very few extractive mechanisms—proper taxation—exist, and it is still the state that supports the society. Even states with access to very limited rent, such as Dubai, are and behave as rentier.[10]

POLITICAL ORDER IN THE RENTIER STATE

The rentier state, being financially independent of the society, is politically autonomous. Therefore, it does not need to obtain political legitimacy through democratic representation. Historically, demands for democratic representation and government accountability rose out of the attempt of the ruler to impose new taxes. In the rentier state, the paradigm of "no taxation without representation" has been transformed into "no representation without taxation."

Nevertheless, rentier states inherit a political order from history; they do not create their own. Rentier states such as Norway or Venezuela were democracies when they gained access to external rent, and they have remained democracies.[11] The major Middle Eastern oil producers were authoritarian before the advent of the rent. The new rent only consolidated their authoritarian foundations. It has been argued that patrimonial states ruling tribal societies are especially suited to the rentier state because the state is viewed as the ruler's property, and the distributive function, necessary to maintain a desired balance in the segmented society, is considered the government's essential function.

It is natural, therefore, that rentier states are not subjected to significant popular pressure to democratize. Even a democratically elected ruler would be tempted to turn authoritarian once he acquires the control of the oil rent and the accompanying power over the society. Nonrentier states, because of their reliance on taxation, are subjected to popular pressure for democratic representation.[12] However, evidence shows that even nonrentier states are frequently unresponsive to popular demands and avoid democratization by (1) resorting to violent repression, (2) utilizing the available outside rent to divide society and consolidate a supporting minority, and (3) developing forms of taxation that are politically less risky.

The rentier state paradigm, therefore, implies continuing authoritarianism in rentier states and a demand for political participation in nonrentier states. Yet, in the early twenty-first century, these trends pointed in a different direction. Rentier states such as Bahrain, Kuwait, Oman, Qatar, and even Saudi Arabia have been moving toward wider political participation, although not full-scale democracy, while nonrentier states have resisted such moves.[13] This paradox can best be explained by the varying strength of the private sector in the rentier and nonrentier states.

THE RENTIER STATE AND THE PRIVATE SECTOR IN THE GULF ARAB STATES

Over time, major changes have taken place in the economic realities of the Gulf states, creating conditions for a gradual evolution of their rentier foundations. These changes include an increase in the relative strength of the private sector vis-à-vis the government, which has happened because of the following reasons: (1) although thanks to the oil rent the government remains strong, it is unable to deliver on its original promises of economic and social well-being; and (2) the private sector has become much stronger and independent of the government.

The Private Sector: Domestic and International Investment

In the absence of attractive domestic investment opportunities, the private sector has placed large financial resources internationally, which have grown significantly. These investors claim that they would like to invest in their own countries but cannot do so because of the lack of opportunities due to administrative and legal barriers, which reserve promising sectors for state-owned companies and government agencies.

There are significant differences among the member countries of the Gulf Cooperation Council (GCC) regarding the degree of autonomy of the private sector and its relative strength vis-à-vis the state—a situation rooted in their different economic, demographic, and geographic characteristics. The Kuwaiti and Saudi Arabian private sectors have been pushed abroad in massive proportions. In both countries, the large dimension of the domestic circulation of the rent and its long duration have led to the accumulation of immense private fortunes by leading individuals and families, and smaller ones by a larger number of medium-sized and small businesspeople. Consequently, wealth available for investment is very great, while investment opportunities are limited. The latter is due to the low rate of economic growth, the crisis of confidence caused by the Iraq invasion of 1990, and political stagnation, which have delayed necessary reforms. The removal of the Iraqi threat following the fall of Saddam Hussein's regime in March 2003 created opportunities for effective change, but realizing the changes would require energetic leadership.

In Saudi Arabia, the tension between the state and the private sector is of a different kind. There, the private sector is still very optimistic about the future of the country and the opportunities it offers. However, the private sector is kept at bay by regulations that limit their role in all of the most promising activities, ranging from those directly linked to oil production and transformation (refining and petrochemicals), to infrastructure and telecommunications, and various types of advanced services (notably financial—although the situation is changing rapidly). The question of succession to King Fahd, which has not yet been resolved, and may not be for years, has created a climate of uncertainty since the early 1990s, which the private sector has found especially frustrating. The complex regional events following the September 11, 2001, attacks have set in motion a debate on domestic political reform that has polarized Saudi society, including the business community. In this context, political instability has become a factor in evaluating the prospects of the Saudi economy, but this does not seem to have reduced the desire to invest in the country. For the Saudi private sector the problem is not how to protect itself against domestic instability by investing abroad, but rather the opposite—that is how to rebalance their portfolio and increase the weight of domestic investment.

A new public–private relationship is required in Saudi Arabia to accelerate economic growth, arrest declining per capita gross domestic product (GDP), and stem the rise in unemployment. Thus, although the state remains rentier, this new phase of ebbing rent tides creates new investment opportunities for the private sector, which complement the state's objectives. This is not true of those rentier states in which the private sector remains weak, or those where the private sector has lost or never had any attachment to the home country. Qatar and Dubai present a different picture.[14] Both are city-states with small populations, a relatively small group of merchant and business families, and a very entrepreneurial and business-oriented political leadership. Both of these states have been promoting big investment schemes. In Dubai, the focus has been on the Internet and media cities, large real estate and tourism development schemes, shopping festivals, Emirates Airline, and the industrial and transshipment facilities in Jebel Ali and Port Rashid. In Qatar, the focus has been on liquefied natural gas (LNG) and petrochemicals, the Aljazeera satellite television station, and the Udaid base. Consequently, the private sectors of Dubai and Qatar have not been pushed out of the country. Rather, they have been constantly engaged and challenged by the entrepreneurialism of the political leadership, which is also young and confident. This climate has also attracted a number of Kuwaiti and Saudi business people.

Qatar and Dubai are also exceptions because enough rent is available and the national population is small enough that the government can still play a developmental role. Elsewhere in the GCC, the ratio of available rent to population is less favorable, and the leadership is either old or divided and fearful.

International Investment and Private Sector Autonomy

Private investors from the Gulf Arab countries have been skillful and prudent in their international investments. As a result, according to some estimates, the total wealth accumulated internationally by Gulf Arab investors in 2000 stood at $1.3 trillion. This figure, although questionable, is not unreasonable. On the basis of this figure, the annual income on this accumulated wealth must be approximately $65–$70 billion. Most probably it was higher during the 1990s.[15]

In short, the income gained by the Gulf Arab private sector from international investments is several times more than the income it could have obtained from domestic operations. This situation means that domestic investment may be undertaken even if the initial rate of return is low, provided that a clear strategic motivation exists, such as positioning oneself for better future opportunities.

Domestically, the Gulf Arab merchant families tend to invest in different sectors and in multiple ventures, including small and uneconomic ones, thus avoiding negative effects of downturns. But this strategy limits these investment opportunities and prevents the formation of larger companies capable of facing international competition and possibly expanding internationally.

The excessive fragmentation of the Saudi corporate structure seriously limits investment opportunities and the repatriation of private wealth. In Dubai, the problem is openly discussed and the political leadership urges the reorganization and consolidation of family businesses. Some observers believe that a process of corporatization of family businesses is also well under way in Saudi Arabia, stimulated primarily by the old age of the businesses' original founders and the danger that disagreement among the heirs will cause the demise of the family business.[16] Therefore, clear corporate structures are created that insulate management from possible family infighting. Over time, the separation between companies and families is likely to become clearer, leading to the adoption of modern management styles and culminating in the regrouping of private interests and the emergence of a number of larger corporations.

Meanwhile, the private sector is increasingly attracted by equity investment in the stock exchange, thus facilitating privatization and the emergence of large "private" Arab corporations. The list of the Global 500 largest corporations includes one United Arab Emirates and five Saudi Arabian firms. Three of the Saudi corporations (the Saudi Telecommunications Company [STC], the Saudi Arabian Basic Industries Corporation [SABIC], and the Saudi Electricity Company [SEC]) are majority owned by the government, and two banks, Al Rajhi and SAMBA (Saudi American Bank, a joint venture with Citicorp), are privately held. Private investors also seem interested in acquiring significant equity positions in the large corporations, which are being privatized. Therefore, a convergence between the process of corporatization and professionalization of the family businesses, and privatization of some government-owned enterprises, could lead to the creation of a large corporate sector.

EROSION OF THE STATE'S DEVELOPMENTAL ROLE

While the private sector grows stronger in the Gulf region, the developmental role of the state is in crisis, as government expenditure becomes less and less closely tied to the rate of GDP growth.[17] Indeed, because of the constantly growing share of current over capital expenditure, government expenditure has become less effective as a stimulus to growth; by contrast, private investment is essentially financed by partial repatriation of the income from wealth accumulated abroad and is independent of domestic cash flow. Consequently, the private sector will not curtail domestic investment in a downturn, notably in real estate, which is where it is concentrated. Therefore, even if the economy is slack because prices of land and cost of building are lower, construction continues and promotes economic growth independently from government expenditure and oil revenue.

The inability of governments in Saudi Arabia, Kuwait, Abu Dhabi, and even Bahrain to launch any large-scale projects that could serve as catalysts for private investment is notable. This was not the case in the past, and it need not be so at present if government finances are better managed, which requires the reduction of current expenditures, the introduction of a sales or value-added tax, or the mobilization of private finance. This record contrasts starkly with the hyper-activism of Dubai and Qatar.

Presently, most of the net investment in Saudi Arabia is done by the private sector and is concentrated in real estate and retail trade. It is believed that the private investors will not risk their money in other ventures. But this is an untested proposition, contradicted by the progressive multiplication of manufacturing activities and the eagerness of private investors to pick up prime equity offerings under privatization schemes. So far, private entrepreneurs have been invited to invest in other sectors in minority positions, leaving in control the government or its appointee. The private sector has not been seduced by these offers. Private entrepreneurs are still keen to receive advantageous government contracts, but these are increasingly rare and are mostly offered to those entrepreneurs who either belong to or have a close association with the ruling families. It is hard to predict how the private sector would react in the event of a very serious recession in the Gulf Arab countries.

POLITICAL IMPLICATIONS OF PRIVATE SECTOR STRENGTH

The Gulf's private sector, or at least its leading entrepreneurs, wants to expand its autonomous role. The Saudi private sector, in particular, wants to redeploy some of its assets to the kingdom, partly because the international investment arena has its share of pitfalls, and partly because social recognition and influence come with investment at home. Internationally, the Gulf Arab entrepreneurs and financiers are regarded as good clients, but rarely as partners, and certainly not as leaders of industry. Some invest significantly in other Arab countries, but they are aware that they are not necessarily appreciated and remain vulnerable. In short, it is only investment at home that will enable them to play a role internationally and be seen as entrepreneurs and not rentiers.

The attachment of the Gulf's private sector elements to their respective home bases is a trait that distinguishes them from the private sectors of other countries, such as Venezuela and Argentina, which have an opportunistic and predatory attitude toward their home countries and which want to become integrated in the business environment of the United States or Europe. A key weakness of the Washington Consensus is that it does not factor in the strength of the attachment of private sectors to their home countries. Yet, depending on the level of the private sector's long-term commitment to its home country, the same policies can lead to entirely different outcomes, as illustrated by Argentina's and Venezuela's problems and the success of Southeast Asia and China.

To achieve its goal of investing in its home country, the private sector, including that of the Gulf, is interested in the establishment of competent government, an efficient economic system, economic liberalization, openness to private investment, transparency, and a level playing field. The message of the private sector is not immediately and intrinsically political; however, it becomes so out of frustration with the persistent immobilism of power holders and the stubborn resistance of bureaucracies to reform. Various Gulf players have different, sometimes contrasting, interests and increasingly tend to coalesce in informal interest groups. They are attached to their countries, and they pursue their future agendas through their investment decisions and increasingly through open political discourse.

The private sector plays different political games with its investment decisions. Who can miss the political symbolism of the prince turned private investor who calls his group "Kingdom" and builds the tallest tower in town?[18] Why are so many, for example, Dar al Maal al Islami and Dallah al Baraka, investing in the media—printed press, television, and Internet portals? Is there not a political undertone to establishing global networks of Islamic banks that are not allowed to operate in Saudi Arabia?[19] All these activities are indicative of private investors' competition for political and social consensus, and not just profit.

Private investment in education also indicates the private sector's political agenda. There has always been private investment in education in the Arab world, but as governments devoted increasing amounts of money to education, the private sector did not see much point in becoming involved. It is therefore remarkable that in recent years several private schools catering to nationals, in competition with public schools, have been established, reflecting the private sector's dissatisfaction with the products of public education.

The political undertones of some of these initiatives are accentuated by the fact that some of the private investors in education are members of the ruling families. The private sector cannot be considered a force opposed to the existing systems. Their attitude can, at best, be characterized as one of criticism and stimulus. The engagement of members of the ruling families in business is resented whenever it brings additional competition—especially if it is unfair. But this is not very important compared to the sanction that business activity and the profit motive receive from the involvement of members of ruling families. This involvement creates a continuum of common interests and language, which facilitates a progressive evolution of the political system through wider and increasingly institutionalized channels of consultation. Initially, greater space for private investment may be sought for the benefit of members of the ruling family. But in the process, regulatory changes become consolidated to the benefit of the entire business community.

POLITICAL TRENDS WITHIN THE BUSINESS COMMUNITY

The Gulf Arab business community is a very large universe within which different political positions are represented. Osama bin Laden is not the offspring of a destitute nomad family; he may have deviated from the right path, but he must have found some inspiration for his thoughts in his immediate environment. However, for the time being most members of this community are primarily interested in playing their role as entrepreneurs and in improving business conditions and investment opportunities. Their way of expressing their political views is, in some cases, indirect, through charity and financial support given to groups and causes abroad, some of which would not be allowed to operate at home. In the climate prevailing after September 11, 2001, private Gulf donors may be expected to be more cautious in their granting of charity donations, but this will undoubtedly remain a key mode of expressing political priorities, as it always has been.

In the past, the private sector used to plead for contracts, cheap loans, and protection from international competition.[20] Today, it is increasingly demanding a redefinition of its role vis-à-vis the government in order to undertake some of the investment burden, which the government is no longer able to carry and will gradually yield, albeit cautiously. The immediate battle is not with the ruling families but with the entrenched bureaucracies. Once this battle is won, a much greater space will open for competition, and the issue of transparency and a level playing field—primarily regarding princely entrepreneurs—will become even more important.

This does not mean that the Gulf Arab "bourgeoisie" will turn Jacobin. But greater attention will be paid to open debate, the formalization of the decision-making process, the neutrality of government, and administration in private interests. The size and diversity of the business community are such that it would appear to be impossible for the ruler to rely on a small clique of clients and ignore the rest. The playing field will never be perfectly level, but favoritism must not exceed the limit beyond which it would engender protest, although protest is occasionally expressed, albeit in subdued form.

PRIVATE SECTOR AS THE PROMOTER OF DEMOCRACY

The private sector is unlikely to demand greater democracy, the only exception being a few individuals who may do so out of personal conviction.[21] Yet the private sector may be expected to seize the opportunity for greater participation that may be offered in a process of gradual liberalization and retrenchment of the state. The private investors—largely coinciding with those capable of taking advantage of the ICT revolution—will avoid any adventurism and will support a limited franchise for the uneducated majority. They will continue to alternate their domestic and international residences, so as to maintain their personal freedoms, and will not mind a degree of Big Brotherhood, provided that it keeps the house in order.

The twin goals of recognizing the increased strength and autonomy of the private sector and incorporating it in the political process, while keeping the uneducated majority at bay, can be achieved provided a degree of institutional inventiveness is displayed.

OTHER ARAB COUNTRIES

The private sector is much weaker outside the Gulf region. In many Arab countries, the business community was destroyed either during the struggle for independence or by successive "socialist" regimes. These regimes have generated their own "new bourgeoisie," but it remains financially and professionally weak. Even in Morocco and Jordan, which have always favored a market economy and openness to international trade and investment, the national private sector remains small. No private non-Gulf Arab enterprise or entrepreneur has a recognized global standing.

By international standards, the non-Gulf Arab entrepreneurs and companies are small or medium-sized enterprises, and their ability to withstand international competition is limited. They therefore oppose trade and investment liberalization. Because their financial means are limited, their participation in privatization is possible only within the context of lack of transparency and collusion with the government. Private entrepreneurs emerge and prosper only if they are close to the government. Corruption is endemic to the system. The private sector in other Arab countries is, thus, less autonomous vis-à-vis the government.

The problem of political evolution in other Arab countries is thus more serious than it is in the Gulf Arab countries. The only way to resolve this is to change the regional political environment, thus creating conditions for a return of the diaspora entrepreneurs and undermining the stability of the current power holders.

The issue of democratization is closely connected to the question of economic reform. The Middle East countries must reform their economies to keep pace with the process of globalization. Yet so far they have resisted fundamental reforms. Moreover, the few countries that have followed the precepts of the Washington Consensus[22] over the past twenty years, for example, Jordan, Morocco, and Tunisia, have not benefited from their efforts. Thus, the region has no economic success story, no "cub tiger" that can be used to galvanize support for reform and participation in the process of globalization.[23]

The reasons for this economic failure are closely related to the reasons for the lack of democracy. Just as democratization is hindered by the lack of democrats,[24] the establishment of an open and competitive market economy is hindered by the weakness of the private sector.

Some of the best-established entrepreneurs from non-Gulf Arab states such as Egypt, Jordan, and Syria are expatriates that have the center of their interests either in the Gulf or in the United States and Europe. They might someday return to their home countries, but so far very few have done so. The Lebanese and Palestinian entrepreneurs in the diaspora have larger international means but have so far found conditions at home unacceptable for serious investment and have consequently remained largely outside the political debate. The potential impact of a "repatriation" of this entrepreneurial diaspora is not to be overlooked, as the personal trajectory of Rafiq Hariri, the prime minister of Lebanon, indicates.

The dissatisfaction of the resident entrepreneurs, who are often marginalized and sometimes effectively pushed into exile, and the reluctance of the diaspora entrepreneurs to return and become economically and politically engaged in the life of their countries demonstrate the existence of an unsatisfied demand for political accountability throughout the Arab world. The implication of the weak private sector is that economic reform is bound to result in the domination of all major productive assets by foreign interests—mostly multinational corporations. The prospect of selling all major economic assets to foreign owners runs against residual nationalist feelings, which are manipulated by the authoritarian incumbents to justify maintaining control over those economic levers most necessary to their political survival.

One of the major weaknesses of the Washington Consensus is that it offers no tools to attract expatriate national capital in preference to the large multinational corporations. Incumbent regimes sometimes prefer multinational corporations because they do not enjoy political legitimacy and cannot have a political agenda. National entrepreneurs, by contrast, must be offered political guarantees and a say in the system. Multinational companies are also used to justify a nationalist discourse to slow down the process of liberalization and to adopt nontransparent procedures.

It is very difficult to establish a process of selective opening to international investment that will attract and mobilize the diaspora entrepreneurs. However, to the extent that the Gulf countries, where many of the Arab diaspora entrepreneurs have the center of their interests, succeed in establishing a broader political base for their regimes with the active participation of their private sectors, it is likely that their influence will be felt in other Arab countries.

Another key "private sector" component in these countries is immigrant workers, with their substantial savings. This group is also cautious and wary of giving up its opportunity to work and keep its savings abroad. In a sense, immigrants choose exit over voice, and, by leaving the country, reduce their political relevance. In this way, the system manages to prevent those who are left behind from pursuing a political agenda and encourages them to seek a visa.

IMPACT ON INTRA-ARAB RELATIONS

An important question to consider is how the new geography of the Gulf Arab private sector will affect the character of intra-Arab relations. The Arab private sector and the business elite, who are supposedly the main drivers of economic development and democratization, are primarily Gulf Arabs either by nationality or by "residence," because many non-Gulf Arabs have made their fortunes in the Gulf. This means that in business, the Gulf is becoming hegemonic in the Arab context, and to the extent that an entrepreneurial business sector is the key to development, the Gulf will increasingly be the Arab world's economic leader. Moreover, should the growing role of the Gulf private sector be translated into increased participation and some democratization, the gap in business culture between the Gulf and other Arab countries can eventually lead to a gap in political development.

The new post–September 2001 regional and international context will also influence this process. Since September 11, a fundamental process of revision of alliances has been under way. The wars for regime change in Afghanistan and in Iraq, coupled with the spread of terrorism to Saudi Arabia, unmasked the complacency and immobilism that has prevailed in the region for twenty-five years. It also led the United States and the European Union to revive their prodemocracy agenda and pursue it more forcefully than before. Some of the key tools to push this agenda are economic: trade liberalization, openness to international investment, and a better investment climate through greater transparency and good governance.

This new democracy drive will threaten all regional regimes, forcing them to adapt to new conditions. It is not certain that they will succeed in this effort, and therefore crises are possible. Moreover, regional regimes arrive at this critical juncture in widely different positions.

The patrimonial Gulf monarchies still have an advantage because of their continuing access to the oil rent. They will need to introduce taxes so that they can use the oil rent for investment rather than current expenditure. Nevertheless, the oil rent will allow them crucially important flexibility regarding public finances. Even if all of the oil rent is used for investment, it would benefit the private sector and the population. Part of the drive to reduce current expenditure will translate into privatization and other policies aimed at transferring to the private sector some of the tasks currently carried out by the government. The fact that the private sector is strong and keen to invest at home implies that such policies stand a good chance of succeeding.

The situation is different for non-oil-producing countries. Their authoritarian governments have no fiscal flexibility and will be forced to progressively surrender their residual instruments of control over the economy. Therefore, their only available tool would be repression, which will make them the target of U.S. and European criticism. They can speed up reform by relying on private and international investment. But their domestic private sectors are weak and often antagonized: they have neither the tools nor the will to be the protagonists of the next phase in their countries' political and economic development. Hence, implementing economic reforms inevitably means surrendering the control of the national economy to foreign investors: either multinational corporations or Arab investors from the Gulf countries. Will the latter alternative be preferred to the former? It is difficult to predict accurately which option the Arab countries will choose. If they were to choose the latter, this could lead to the regionalization of the Gulf Arab private sector, providing a basis for regional integration founded on private economic ties rather than nationalism.

This development would also allow the Gulf Arab private sector to pursue its political agenda regionally and thus contribute to greater economic and political openings in non-Gulf Arab states. Presently, however, the Arab region does not favor this kind of Gulf Arab economic and political hegemony and prefers multinational investment and strengthening direct and vertical ties with the European Union and the United States.

NON-ARAB STATES

Non-Arab Islamic states belong to both the rentier and nonrentier categories. The Central Asian states are—and increasingly will be—rentier. Thus, not surprisingly, they have resisted both democratization and economic reform. They are likely to maintain their "Soviet" heritage for as long as they enjoy access to an oil and gas rent, the peak of which time is yet to come. Moreover, these states have rediscovered tribalism, partly because it never truly disappeared, and partly because it is a convenient way to rule a rentier state. Over time, all of the former Soviet bureaucrats may attempt to turn themselves into patrimonial monarchs; some are already quite advanced along this road.

Iran, too, is a rentier state, though a much more complex one. The state has maintained direct control over most economic levers, directly or indirectly through the Bonyads "foundations" inherited from the Shah's time and expanded by the Islamic regime. The latter are one of the pillars of the power of the conservative wing of the Islamic government. The nascent prerevolutionary private sector has effectively been nationalized at home, and many of the professional and entrepreneurial families have left the country. Consequently, Iranian private entrepreneurs do not have tools comparable to those of the Saudi and Kuwaiti business families. Yet the successive postrevolutionary governments have not taken an ideological stance against the private sector. In this respect, Iran may be said to occupy a position between that of the Gulf Arab states and that of the "socialist" rentier states, such as Algeria and Libya, which have moved against their own private sectors.

Iran has also made more progress than any other country in the region toward better popular representation. The majority of Iranians have demonstrated support for economic and political reform, despite the fact that the efforts of the reformists have been frustrated by conservative forces occupying key nonelected positions in the state. This situation results in an unstable equilibrium leading to the frequent use of repressive tools. However, given the popular constituency for reform, Iran may yet manage to advance a reformist agenda. Under better political conditions, diaspora capital, which is not negligible, can return to the country. Should this happen, the diaspora entrepreneurship will further push for a reformist agenda.

Turkey is a nonrentier state with an increasingly strong private sector, including the industrial sector. Domestic investors actively participate in the privatization of the large state-owned industrial holdings, frequently in alliance with multinational corporations. For Turkey, the consolidation of democratic institutions is closely tied to membership in the European Union (EU). Most entrepreneurs, including a new breed of Islamically oriented business class, support Turkey's EU membership.

Islamic countries in South Asia have rather weak private sectors, while the contrary is true in Southeast Asia. Malaysia, in particular, has very successfully changed from an essentially rentier state to a diversified economy with a strong private sector. Malaysia's democracy preexisted the rentier state and has survived the experience; it may be less than perfect, but is not out of step with other Asian representative governments. Malaysia is indeed viewed as a model to be emulated by the Gulf Arab countries.

CONCLUSIONS

The foregoing discussion has illustrated that the availability of substantial external rent to governments, by making them independent from society, retards the development of a civil and political sphere and demands for representation. But in places where the rent circulation is high in volume and continues for a long period of time, individuals accumulate wealth, which renders them independent from the state. This financial wealth also generates demands for economic reform and integration in the global economy. In fact, successful economic reform and integration in a globalized world economy require a strong national private sector that is capable of assuming those tasks that the state should relinquish and that is internationally competitive. International investors should not be excluded from opportunities created by reform. But their involvement should be in the form of balanced and mutually rewarding alliances, not a sellout of national assets.

Today, only the private sectors of the Gulf rentier states have the financial and managerial capabilities and commitment to their home countries necessary to benefit from economic liberalization. The rentier states, because of their financial resources, face fewer obstacles in pursuing economic reform but have been slow to reform because of weak and complacent leaderships.

The connections among the rentier nature of the state, economic reform, and democratization are very complex. Meanwhile, the nonrentier states are loath to embrace economic reform because it might weaken their grip on power and because appropriate conditions do not exist to make reforms successful, as illustrated by the experience of the few countries that have implemented reforms. Since the late 1990s, the rentier states have become conscious of the need to reform, and since then they have enjoyed favorable conditions to make reform successful. They have been considering opening the political space to greater popular participation to facilitate the development of a broad-based consensus about reform. This opening of the political space, however, is not necessarily a precursor to democracy. The state remains rentier, and all that it truly needs is the consensus of an elite, consisting essentially of private entrepreneurs and remaining essentially loyal to the political status quo, to define a new public-private relationship. Nevertheless, should this happen, it will, over time, create more propitious conditions for democratization.

NOTES

1. Karl A. Wittfogel, *Oriental Despotism: A Comparative Study of Total Power* (New Haven, CT: Yale University Press, 1957).

2. Terry L. Karl, *The Paradox of Plenty: Oil Booms and Petro-States* (Berkeley: University of California Press, 1997).

3. Hussain Mahdavy, "The Patterns and Problems of Economic Development in Rentier States: The Case of Iran," in Michael Cook, ed., *Studies in the Economic History of the Middle East* (Oxford: Oxford University Press, 1970).

4. Hazem Beblawi and Giacomo Luciani, eds., *The Rentier State* (London: Croom Helm, 1987).

5. Rex Brynen, "Economic Crisis and Post-Rentier Democratization in the Arab World: The Case of Jordan," *Canadian Journal of Political Science* 25, no. 1 (March 1992); Gregory F. Gause III, *Oil Monarchies: Domestic and Security Challenges in the Arab Gulf States* (New York: Council on Foreign Relations, 1994); Dirk Vandewalle, *Libya since Independence* (Ithaca, NY: Cornell University Press, 1998); Clement M. Henry and Robert Springborg, *Globalization and the Politics of Development in the Middle East*

(Cambridge: Cambridge University Press, 2001); Kiren A. Chaudhry, *The Price of Wealth* (Ithaca, NY: Cornell University Press, 1997); Michael Herb, *All in the Family: Absolutism, Revolution, and Democracy in the Middle Eastern Monarchies* (Albany: State University of New York Press, 1999).

6. Some authors tend to expand the definition of rentier states in such a way that all Arab states are considered rentier.

7. Giacomo Luciani, "The Oil Rent, the Fiscal Crisis of the State, and Democratization," in Ghassan Salamé, ed., *Democracy without Democrats? The Renewal of Politics in the Muslim World* (London: I. B. Tauris, 1994).

8. Mahmoud Abdel-Fadil, "The Macro-Behaviour of Oil-Rentier States in the Arab Region," in Beblawi and Luciani, *Rentier State.*

9. It is crucial here to distinguish between entitlements and expectations. People have expectations, based on recent experience, but they understand the difference between such expectations and entitlements, which are rights based on some explicit or implicit pact.

10. Bernard El Ghoul, "De la cité-marchande à la cité-globale—Pouvoir et société à Doubai" (PhD diss., Institut d'Etudes Politiques de Paris, 2003).

11. Venezuela became a democracy well after oil production started there but initially received very little fiscal benefit from it.

12. Giacomo Luciani, "Economic Foundations of Democracy and Authoritarianism: The Arab World in Comparative Perspective," *Arab Studies Quarterly* 10, no. 6 (1988): 457–75.

13. Eberhard Kienle, "More than a Response to Islamism: The Political Deliberalization of Egypt in the 1990s," *Middle East Journal* 52 (Spring 1998): 219–35, and *A Grand Delusion: Democracy and Economic Reform in Egypt* (London: I. B. Tauris, 2000).

14. El Ghoul, "De la cité-marchande à la Cité-Globale."

15. This is based on a very low rate of return of 5 percent.

16. This point was made to me by the head of one of the leading law firms in Riyadh.

17. Ugo Fasano and Quing Wang, "Fiscal Expenditure Policy and non-Oil Economic Growth: Evidence from GCC Countries" (IMF Working Paper WP/01/195, December 2001).

18. I refer to Prince Waleed bin Talaal bin Abdalaziz al Saud.

19. Dar al Maal al Islami is a group chaired by Prince Mohammed al Faisal, a son of the late King Faisal. Dallah al Baraka is the business group of Sheikh Salah Abdallah Kamel.

20. On the tension between old and new, see Gulf Research Center (GRC), *Reform in Saudi Arabia: Current Challenges and Feasible Solutions*, September 2003, http://www.grc.to/grc_publications/. The GRC is a nonprofit research center established in Dubai by a Saudi business entrepreneur, Sheikh Abdalaziz al Sager.

21. GRC, *Reform in Saudi Arabia,* 31–32.

22. The Washington Consensus is the standard one-size-fits-all recipe for structural readjustment, liberalization, privatization, and so on that the International Monetary Fund (IMF) and the World Bank have imposed on a number of developing countries since the beginning of the 1990s. For a critique of the Washington Consensus, see Joseph E. Stiglitz, *Globalization and Its Discontents* (New York: W. W. Norton, 2002).

23. The Economic Research Forum for the Arab Countries, Iran, and Turkey (ERF), *Economic Trends in the MENA Region 2002* (Cairo: American University in Cairo Press, 2002).

24. Salamé, *Democracy without Democrats?*

11

Systemic Factors and Economic Development in Islamic Countries

Peter Nunnenkamp

For decades, development economists have tried to assess the role of the international economic system in the underdevelopment of many third world countries. This question comes to the fore especially at times of financial crisis, such as the Latin American debt crisis of the 1980s and the emerging markets' currency crises since the mid-1990s.

In the 1970s, the predominant view in the third world was that attempts to catch up economically with the industrialized countries were doomed unless a new world economic order was agreed upon.[1] The spectacular economic success of some developing countries has altered this fatalistic view, but because most developing countries, including Muslim states, still lag behind in development and per capita income, the role of systemic factors is still debated.

This chapter discusses the role of systemic factors by (1) identifying those characteristics of the international economic system that may have hindered the third world's development, (2) assessing the empirical relevance of these characteristics for a broad set of developing countries, and (3) evaluating the impact of these characteristics on Islamic countries.

The following analysis has clear limitations: The discussion of systemic factors is limited only to the most important aspects. Moreover, it does not attempt to assess the relative impact of these determinants on economic performance. It is based on data for as many countries as possible, but because of limited data, the sample of Islamic countries as well as the control group of all developing countries is fairly small in some instances.

For the purposes of this chapter, the members of the Organization of the Islamic Conference (OIC) are viewed as Islamic countries. This chapter is divided into four sections: (1) profile of economic development of Muslim states; (2) summary of earlier thinking on the role of systemic factors in hindering economic development in the third world; (3) discussion of continued relevance of the notions of economic distance and colonial legacy; this section will also portray the external environment in which developing countries have to act because the trading system limits their gains from participation in the international division of labor, and international capital markets are plagued by inefficiencies affecting the developing countries; and (4) suggestions on how to remove systemic impediments to development.

ECONOMIC DEVELOPMENT OF ISLAMIC COUNTRIES IN A COMPARATIVE PERSPECTIVE

The relatively poor economic performance of Islamic countries is reflected in the fact that in 2001 their average per capita income (in purchasing power parity) was substantially below the corresponding average for all developing countries. Moreover, the growth in per capita income of Islamic countries in 1975–2001 fell considerably short of average income growth in all developing countries (Figure 11.1).

In 2001, the average per capita income of all OIC member countries amounted to about 11 percent of U.S. per capita income. The relative income position of non-oil OIC members was even lower. By contrast, the relative income position of major oil exporters among OIC members continued to be more favorable, despite their poor growth performance. Growth performance is measured by the ratio of per capita income in 2001 to that in 1975, both relative to the per capita income in the United States. Hence, countries with a ratio below 1 failed to catch up economically with industrialized countries. While the income gap between the United States and the average of all developing countries widened by 12 percent, OIC member countries fell back by about twice as much since 1975,[2] hence the question, Has the international economic system been particularly hostile to Muslim countries?

BLAMING THE SYSTEM: EARLIER THEORIES

As a result of growing disenchantment with previous models of economic development, during the 1970s the dependency theory gained considerable support, especially among third world intellectuals.[3] Particularly in international-dependence models based on Marxist thinking, labeled "neocolonial dependence models" by Todaro, underdevelopment in the third world is considered an *externally* induced phenomenon. Dos Santos defines dependence as "a conditioning situation in which the economies of one group of countries are conditioned by the development and expansion of others."[4] Since dependent countries cannot expand through self-impulsion, "the basic situation of dependence causes these countries to be both backward and exploited."[5]

Underdevelopment of third world economies is attributed to the historical evolution of a highly unequal international system, with various dimensions of de-

Figure 11.1
Economic Development: Islamic Countries Compared to All Developing Countries

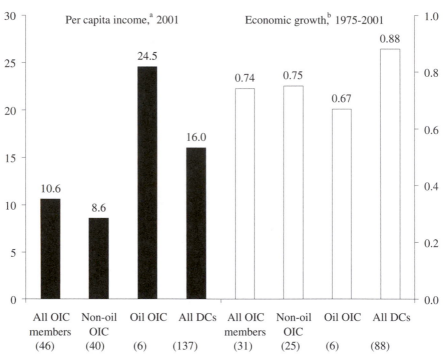

Source: World Bank Group, *World Development Indicators 2003* (Washington, DC: World Bank, 2003).

[a]Gross national income (GNI) per capita (PPP) as a percentage of GNI per capita in the United States; unweighted average for all countries for which the data are available (number of countries in parentheses).
[b]Ratio of GNI per capita in 2001, as defined in note a, to GNI per capita in 1975.

pendence and exploitation characterizing the relationships between the *center,* made of rich developed countries, and the *periphery,* made of poor developing countries.[6] In this context, free trade is considered a convenient vehicle of exploitation.[7] Trade relations between the developed and developing worlds are an "unequal exchange" because developing countries produce and export mainly primary commodities, the demand for which is income inelastic, while importing manufactured goods, which they hardly produce.[8] Consequently, developed countries reap the benefits of trade, while developing countries suffer welfare losses because of a decrease in export relative to import prices.[9]

Multinational enterprises (MNEs) are also viewed as part of the mechanism to dominate the periphery. MNEs strangle local producers and deprive the periphery of investment resources by transferring profits to the center. With profit remittances exceeding the initial investment in the long run, MNEs contribute to "the development of underdevelopment."[10] Whatever economic development takes place is considered inappropriate because it is imposed by the center.[11]

Other capital flows to developing countries are criticized for adding to economic dependency. Over time, debt-related inflows may induce much higher capital outflows in the form of amortization and interest payments. Moreover, debt financing of developing countries depends on the permanent rollover of short-term loans, and the debtors bear the exchange-rate risk, as loans are typically denominated in hard currency. International financial institutions, particularly the International Monetary Fund (IMF), are blamed for representing the interests of the financial center and for having contributed to the third world's debt problems.

Foreign aid is seen as a means of opening up the periphery to foreign capital; it "oils the mechanisms of surplus transfer."[12] Infrastructural projects, benefiting foreign companies, are said to absorb a large proportion of aid. Meanwhile, local elites prevent aid from being used for the benefit of the poor in order to improve their own living standards.[13] Generally, the corrupt local elites at the periphery are viewed as the center's accomplices in the exploitation of the developing countries and in the perpetuation of neocolonial structures. Indeed, their privileged economic and power status largely depends on this system of inequality and dualism, which are seen as permanent phenomena with an inherent tendency to increase.[14]

Many of these arguments were dismissed as irrelevant during the "neoclassical free market counter-revolution."[15] The mainstream theorists of the 1980s maintained that the notions of dependency, center-periphery relations, and unequal exchange rested on vague analytical foundations; many of the hypotheses of the dependency theory could hardly be subjected to rigorous empirical tests;[16] and the proponents of this theory were—rightly—criticized for stressing the negative effects of the international economic system and ignoring its positive impact.[17] Thus, dependency theory fell victim to the new economic mainstream, which was increasingly oriented to precise mathematical modeling and up-to-date econometrical testing of concrete hypotheses.[18] According to Krugman, the neoclassical counterrevolution went too far by simply leaving behind the earlier discursive, nonmathematical development theories. In fact, some discarded insights of the 1970s were rediscovered recently, with new analytical and empirical advances allowing a more rigorous treatment of systemic factors. This applies, in particular, to the concept of economic distance implicit in the center-periphery framework and to the colonial origins of institutions and economic development.

ECONOMIC DISTANCE AND COLONIAL LEGACIES: STILL RELEVANT?

Earlier critics of the international economic system portrayed center-periphery relations in terms of intentional exploitation. The notion of distance differs from this view in that distance is viewed as a structural impediment to economic development at the periphery. Distance has become a standard argument in mainstream economics, especially regarding international trade relations. Gravity models, considering distance to be a determinant of the intensity of bilateral trade flows, reveal that it is more difficult for remote economies to benefit from international trade.

Distance is usually measured in geographical terms, that is, how far away are remote economies from the world's economic centers, but is not limited to geography. According to new economic geography models, economic transactions between the center and the periphery involve higher costs related to information, communication, monitoring, and transportation.[19] Additionally, trade policy (e.g., tariffs) may put the periphery at a competitive disadvantage in trading with the center. Consequently, firms in remote locations tend to be systematically constrained by higher transaction costs on both their exports and their intermediate imports, thus reducing the amount of value added left to remunerate the factors of production at the periphery.[20] Moreover, it is argued that distance-related transaction costs may lead to a downward spiral, with "peripheral countries . . . becoming more economically remote over time."[21]

The data in Figure 11.2 indicate that distance has had a negative impact on the economic development of developing countries since 1975. However, the correlation between distance and economic growth performance is fairly weak. This is so, mainly, because China, Korea, Singapore, and Chile performed significantly better than their distance to economic centers would have suggested, as did a few Islamic countries, notably Malaysia and Indonesia. In sum, although relevant, distance is not a determining impediment to the economic development of Muslim and other third world countries.

Moreover, because on average, the location of Islamic countries is slightly less remote than that of other developing countries, distance cannot explain their inferior growth performance. With the exception of Bangladesh, Egypt, Indonesia, Malaysia, and Tunisia, Muslim countries have performed worse than their distance to economic centers suggests.

Another aspect of current thinking on economic development relates to colonial foundations of current institutional deficiencies. According to conventional wisdom, the persistent divergence in economic development is largely due to institutional deficiencies of peripheral economies.[22] The institutional framework comprises political stability, effective government, the rule of law, and control of corruption.[23] Most of these elements, as well as their average, are strongly correlated with economic growth in developing countries.[24] Meanwhile, there is a wide variation in institutional development across developing countries. In Islamic countries, institutional development ranges from fairly advanced in Jordan (0.35), Kuwait (0.40), United Arab Emirates (0.47), Oman (0.57), Qatar (0.60), and Tunisia (0.66) to highly deficient in Sierra Leone (−1.04), Libya (−1.05), Turkmenistan (−1.07), Sudan (−1.26), Tajikistan (−1.26), Somalia (−1.55), Iraq (−1.75), and Afghanistan (−1.92).[25]

Figure 11.2
Distance and Economic Development across Developing Countries[a]

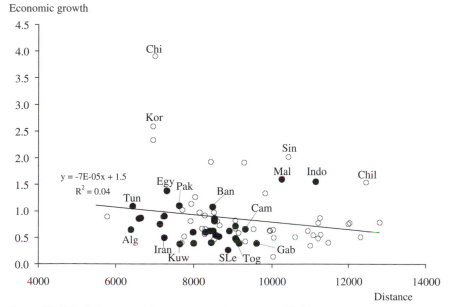

Source: World Bank Group, *World Development Indicators 2003* (Washington, DC: World Bank, 2003);
http://www.macalester.edu/research/economics/PAGE/HAVEMAN/Trade.Resources/Data/
Gravity/dist.txt.

[a]Black dots represent Islamic countries. Economic growth measured as stated in text.

Institutional deficiencies are relevant to the discussion of systemic impediments to development because recent research has shown that current institutional deficiencies can be traced to the colonial past of many developing countries. The World Bank maintains that many business regulations in developing countries are the legacy of European legal systems.[26] Acemoglu et al. have found that (1) Former colonial powers pursued different strategies depending on whether colonizers settled in the colonies. In colonies with high settler mortality, settlements remained insignificant and colonial powers set up "extractive states" without introducing development-friendly institutions. By contrast, domestic institutions tended to be replicated in colonies where settlements were feasible because of low mortality rates. (2) Extractive states and the lack of institutional development persisted after political independence of non-settler colonies. A main reason for the persistence of institutional deficiencies was the desire of postcolonial local elites to use the existing extractive states to their own benefit. (3) Institutional development, or its lack, affects current economic per-

Figure 11.3
**Current Institutions and Colonial Legacies: Islamic Countries Compared to All
Developing Countries**

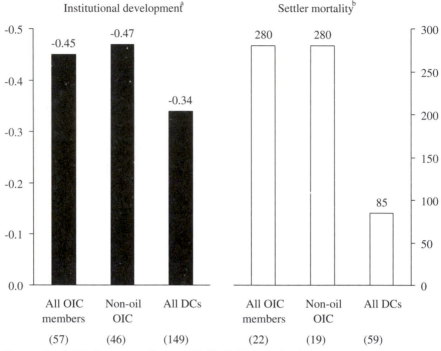

Institutional development[a]   Settler mortality[b]

	All OIC members	Non-oil OIC	All DCs	All OIC members	Non-oil OIC	All DCs
	(57)	(46)	(149)	(22)	(19)	(59)

Sources: Daniel Kaufmann, Aart Kraay, and Pablo Zoido-Lobatón, *Governance Matters, II: Updated
Indicators for 2000–01* (Washington, DC: World Bank, 2002); Daron Acemoglu, Simon Johnson, and James A. Robinson, "The Colonial Origins of Comparative Development: An Empirical Investigation," *American Economic Review* 91, no. 5 (2001).

[a]Median of institutional development; index values range from –2.5 to 2.5, with higher bars corresponding to more serious institutional deficiencies.
[b]Median of potential mortality rates (deaths per annum per 1000 settlers).
Number of countries in parentheses.

formance. These authors also provide convincing empirical evidence on these
links for a large number of former colonies.

The data in Figure 11.3 show that Muslim countries, on average, suffer from
more serious institutional deficiencies compared to the overall sample of developing countries. But the difference is rather small when considering the wide
variation of institutional development within country groups. Meanwhile, settler
mortality during colonial times was considerably higher in Islamic countries.
Nevertheless, there is no clear evidence that colonial legacies bear major responsibility for the relatively poor economic performance of Islamic countries

Table 11.1
Colonial Legacies, Current Institutions, and Economic Performance:
Correlation Results for Islamic Countries[a]

	All OIC Members		Non-Oil OIC Members	
	Institutional Development	Economic Growth	Institutional Development	Economic Growth
Settler Mortality	−0.31	−0.64*	−0.34	−0.65*
	(22)	(20)	(19)	(17)
Institutional Development		0.29		0.57*
		(31)		(25)

Sources: World Bank Group, *World Development Indicators 2003* (Washington, DC: World Bank, 2003); Daniel Kaufmann, Aart Kraay, and Pablo Zoido-Lobatón, *Governance Matters, II: Updated Indicators for 2000–01* (Washington, DC: World Bank, 2002); Daron Acemoglu, Simon Johnson, and James A. Robinson, "The Colonial Origins of Comparative Development: An Empirical Investigation," *American Economic Review* 91, no. 5 (2001).

[a]Spearman rank correlations.
*Denotes statistical significance at the 10 percent level (two-tailed test).
Number of observations in parentheses.
See text for definition of variables.

(Table 11.1). The link between the colonial past, reflected in settler mortality, and current institutions remains statistically insignificant, suggesting that institutions in Islamic countries have developed independently from colonial legacies. This underscores Acemoglu et al.'s statement that "our findings do not imply that institutions today are predetermined by colonial policies and cannot be changed."[27]

International Trade:
Limited Gains in an Unfavorable Environment?

Current international trade patterns contradict notions of dependency and unequal exchange prevalent in various theories critical of the international economic system. In contrast to the formerly prevailing view that the developing countries' exports are largely confined to primary commodities, manufactured exports accounted for two-thirds of their total exports in 2001; the share of manufactured exports has more than tripled since 1980.[28] Manufactured exports of developing countries are not restricted to labor-intensive or technologically inferior goods; rather, chemicals, machinery, and transport equipment contributed

60 percent to manufactured exports of all developing countries in 2001, up from 38 percent in 1980.

The share of all developing countries in world trade of manufactured goods increased from 11 percent in 1980 to 29 percent in 2001 (Figure 11.4). Industrialized countries were the target of about 60 percent of the manufactured exports of developing countries.[29]

However, it should be stressed that developing countries differ greatly in making use of international trading opportunities. Successful penetration of world markets for manufactured goods is largely limited to Asian countries, including Muslim Malaysia, while poor African countries, including Muslim ones, have not become competitive suppliers of manufactured goods. Figure 11.5, presenting the change in the share of overall exports in the exporting countries' gross domestic product (GDP) between the second half of the 1970s and 1997–2001, underscores significant differences among regions and developing country groups. The export orientation of non-oil OIC member countries, on average, increased more strongly than the export orientation of all developing countries, but only half as much as that of Asian developing countries.

Furthermore, the differences in export performance were associated with varying developments in the terms of trade. In the 1960s, it was argued that the terms of trade of developing countries were bound to deteriorate in the long run because, as argued by Prebisch and Singer, their exports, largely restricted to primary commodities, were characterized by low income elasticity. This view was contested on conceptual and empirical grounds,[30] and the significant shift from primary commodity to manufactured exports should have further eroded its relevance. However, recent evidence suggests that the terms of trade between the manufactured goods exported by developing countries and those imported by them are deteriorating together with the terms of trade between primary commodities and manufactured goods.[31] Lutz finds that, despite the change in the structure of their exports, developing countries are still experiencing declining terms of trade as a problem.[32] According to Lutz, the poorest countries have suffered a particularly serious decline in their terms of trade.

Figure 11.6 supports the reasoning of Sapsford and Chen and Lutz for the past twenty years. The OIC members' terms of trade developed more unfavorably compared to the overall sample of developing countries. This should be attributed to the overriding importance of oil prices for oil-exporting OIC members. On average, non-oil OIC members suffered less severe terms-of-trade losses than all developing countries. However, the averages for OIC (and non-OIC) developing countries conceal huge variations in country-specific terms of trade. The terms of trade of some Latin American and OIC member countries, such as Brazil, Costa Rica, Paraguay, Jordan, Morocco, Burkina Faso, and Mauritania, improved considerably compared to the terms of trade in the early 1980s.

The foregoing analysis challenges the validity of the view that the prevailing international trading system prevents trade-related benefits for developing coun-

Figure 11.4
Share of Developing Countries in World Trade of Manufactured Goods, 1980 and 2001 (in percent)

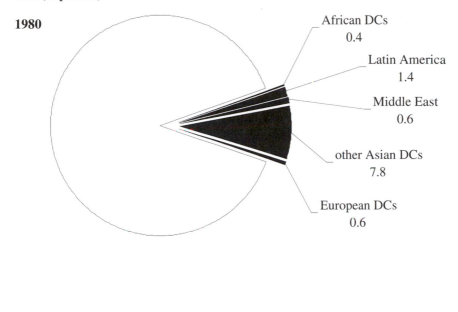

1980

African DCs
0.4

Latin America
1.4

Middle East
0.6

other Asian DCs
7.8

European DCs
0.6

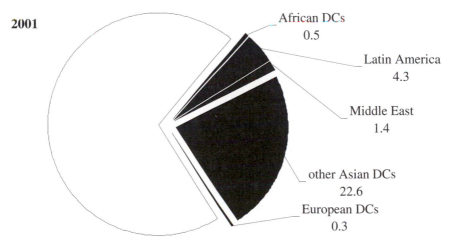

2001

African DCs
0.5

Latin America
4.3

Middle East
1.4

other Asian DCs
22.6

European DCs
0.3

Source: UN *Monthly Bulletin of Statistics* (New York: United Nations, 2003).

Figure 11.5
Change of the Export-to-GDP Ratio for Selected Developing Country Groups, 1997–2001 versus 1975–1979 (in percentage points)

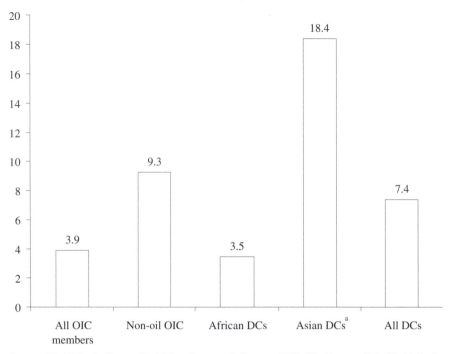

Source: World Bank Group, *World Development Indicators 2003* (Washington, DC: World Bank, 2003).

ªExcluding the Middle East.

tries, although trade practices of major players limit the developing countries' gains from participation in the international division of labor.[33]

Agriculture

Industrialized countries spend more than US$300 billion annually on farm subsidies—about six times the amount they spend on foreign aid. Direct subsidies and border protection provided by the European Union to European farmers is estimated at more than half of farm output at world prices in recent years. Tariff rate quotas apply to 28 percent of agricultural output, on average, in Organization for Economic Cooperation and Development (OECD) countries (39 percent in the European Union), and protection increases with each stage of processing.

Cotton provides a telling example of how subsidies impair market access for poor countries. U.S. cotton growers receive US$4 billion in subsidies for pro-

Figure 11.6
Terms of Trade for Selected Developing Country Groups, 1980–2000 (1980 = 100)

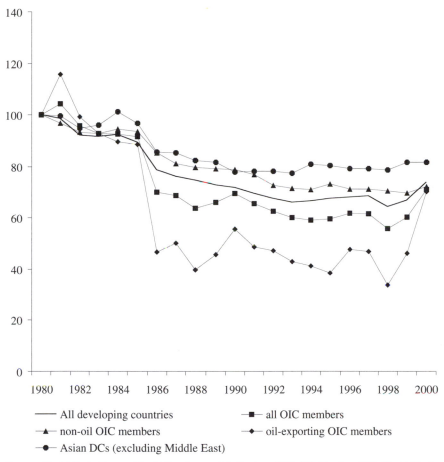

— All developing countries   —■— all OIC members
—▲— non-oil OIC members   —♦— oil-exporting OIC members
—●— Asian DCs (excluding Middle East)

Source: World Bank Group, *World Development Indicators 2003* (Washington, DC: World Bank, 2003).

ducing US$3 billion worth of cotton.[34] American cotton costs 50 percent more to produce than African cotton from Benin, Burkina Faso, Chad, and Mali. Nevertheless, the African countries' request for fair trading opportunities was rebuffed at the World Trade Organization's (WTO) ministerial meeting in Cancún in September 2003.

Major players apply double standards to agriculture trade. Influential WTO members made the WTO accession of Cambodia conditional on its commitment not to subsidize agriculture and to adopt a maximum agricultural tariff of less than a quarter of tariff peaks in the European Union.[35]

MANUFACTURED GOODS

Developing countries face discrimination in trade of manufactured goods. OECD countries are reluctant to phase out restrictive import quotas for textiles and clothing. Other labor-intensive manufactures, in which developing countries are competitive, are subject to high tariff barriers. The United States collects tariff revenues on imported shoes in the order of tariff revenues on imported automobiles, although the import value of shoes is only about 14 percent of that of automobiles.

On average, tariffs levied by OECD countries on imports from developing countries are four to five times higher than tariffs levied on imports from other OECD countries.[36] In some instances, including those relevant to OIC members, this discrepancy is even wider. Imports from Bangladesh face an average tariff rate of 14 percent in the United States, compared to 1 percent for imports from France.

Tariffs on manufactures escalate with value added in developing countries, thereby discouraging the processing of goods, and antidumping measures by OECD countries are disproportionally targeted against competitive suppliers from developing countries. In 1995–2002, about three-quarters of antidumping actions initiated by industrialized countries were targeted against developing countries.

The foregoing discussion indicates that the global trading system is still characterized by many inequities. However, developing countries themselves are partly responsible for this situation by demanding, and to some extent receiving, special and differential treatment. This approach has proved self-defeating because,[37] first, it ignores the political economy of WTO negotiations, which is based on quid pro quo considerations, and second, the developing countries' reluctance to remove their own trade barriers ignores a widely held insight that the gains from trade depend as much on domestic liberalization as on better access to foreign markets.[38]

In sum, developing countries would benefit more from international trade if industrialized countries did not discriminate against their products. However, compared to trade barriers that developing countries erect against one another, the barriers of industrialized countries are rather low. Furthermore, although developing countries face the same unfavorable external environment, their individual trade performance varies greatly, suggesting that the way developing countries adjust to exogenous factors is crucially important. Active participation in multilateral trade negotiations is one of the ingredients of successful world-market orientation.

Exposure to Foreign Capital:
Uncertain Benefits at Considerable Costs?

The critics of globalization view international capital markets as harmful to developing countries. Unlike trade liberalization, capital account liberalization, except for opening up to foreign direct investment (FDI), is not an ingredient of the Washington Consensus.[39] Yet globalization critics rightly point out that the IMF advised, or rather pressed, developing countries to open up to capital inflows.[40] This pressure was justified on the grounds that free capital inflows would prove as beneficial to developing countries as free trade did. By attracting foreign savings, free capital inflows would enable them to complement their own limited investment resources. In contrast to proponents of free trade, however, the proponents of unrestricted capital flows have "offered more 'banner-waving' than hard quantitative evidence on the benefits of financial globalization."[41]

The IMF's reasoning that economies that open up to capital inflows have better prospects for development has been challenged by empirical studies; Rodrik, analyzing the link between capital controls and economic growth in about 100 countries, concludes that "the data provide no evidence that countries without capital controls have grown faster."[42] Many globalization critics accuse the IMF of having acted in the interest of globally engaged banks and international speculators rather than that of developing countries, which are subjected to its rules of conditionality. Chile and Malaysia are often referred to as models showing that the IMF's preoccupation with capital account liberalization was counterproductive. Chile discouraged short-term capital inflows by a nonremunerated reserve requirement in the 1990s, which may have insulated the country from speculation. Malaysia refused IMF financial support and imposed controls on capital outflows in September 1998, which according to its government enabled it to recover rapidly from the Asian crisis.

Although the effectiveness of capital controls in Chile and Malaysia remains heavily disputed,[43] it is now widely accepted that given the vagaries of international capital markets, developing countries should pursue a cautious and gradual approach to capital account liberalization. Different types of capital inflows may have varying effects on the development of third world economies, and the risks are higher regarding debt-related capital as compared to FDI flows.

Debt Problems

International bond and loan markets may cause more harm than good to developing countries because international debt contracts shift maturity and currency risks to the borrower. A maturity mismatch results when developing countries have access only to short-term loans, while foreign borrowing finances long-term investment projects. A currency mismatch exists because foreign loans are denominated in hard currency, while the borrower's revenues are often in local currency. Poor borrowers will find it particularly difficult to manage maturity and currency risks; debt-related capital flows are characterized by high volatility.[44] In recent financial crises, various emerging market economies suffered sudden reversals from excessive debt inflows to massive outflows. Even if international speculation did not cause these crises, it exacerbated them by deepening recession in the afflicted countries, for example, in Asia in the late 1990s. According to various critics, the IMF and its major shareholders were accom-

Figure 11.7
Foreign Debt Burden of Developing Countries (Median)[a]

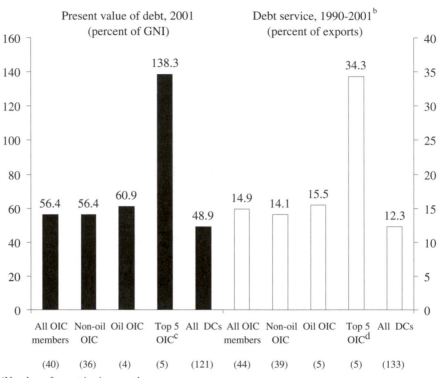

| | Present value of debt, 2001 (percent of GNI) | | | | Debt service, 1990-2001[b] (percent of exports) | | | | |

[a]Number of countries in parentheses.
[b]Period average.
[c]In ascending order: Côte d'Ivoire, Sierra Leone, Guyana, Mauritania, and Guinea-Bissau.
[d]In ascending order: Indonesia, Guinea-Bissau, Uganda, Sierra Leone, and Algeria.

Source: World Bank Group, *World Development Indicators 2003* (Washington, DC: World Bank, 2003).

plices of foreign banks and investors that were engaged in the countries affected by the crisis because

- the IMF did not prevent the banks and investors from fleeing the afflicted countries and remained opposed to capital outflow controls; and
- the IMF enforced an unfair distribution of crisis-related costs as shown by Sachs in the case of Korea: "Under the IMF deal, the creditor governments forced Korea to guarantee the repayment of bad debts owed by private Korean banks to private U.S., European, and Japanese banks."[45]

Foreign debt constitutes a considerable burden for some developing countries (Figure 11.7). The foreign debt trap may stifle economic development by discouraging local investment and thus economic growth if local investors antici-pate that their profits will be taxed to service foreign debt. Major creditor coun-tries acknowledged that the foreign debt burden of at least some developing countries was unmanageable when they launched the heavily indebted poor coun-tries (HIPCs) initiative in 1996. The aim was to reduce the debt to sustainable levels provided that the beneficiaries of debt relief embarked on strategies to al-leviate poverty. However, the poverty-alleviating effects of the HIPC initiative are questionable, not least because effective relief tends to be substantially less than the writing off of nonperforming debt on the books would suggest.[46]

Foreign Direct Investment

Heavily indebted developing countries might have fared better had they relied on FDI. According to current conventional wisdom, FDI is superior because it offers access to technology and management know-how in addition to capital.[47] The risk properties of FDI are more favorable to developing countries since ma-turity- and exchange-rate risks remain with foreign direct investors. In sharp con-trast to the earlier critique of multinational enterprises as one of the mechanisms of exploitation of peripheral economies, FDI is today regarded by many as a panacea. Yet this euphoria about FDI neglects several shortcomings in terms of access to FDI, the economic effects of FDI, and the bargaining position of de-veloping countries competing for FDI.

FDI inflows are distributed unevenly across developing countries, although nearly all countries have opened up to FDI. The data in Figure 11.8 indicate that multinational enterprises are strongly engaged in various third world locations considered attractive, while being virtually absent from others. The median of FDI inflows in 1990–2001 (in percent of the host countries' GDP) is consider-ably lower for the OIC member countries (1.3 percent compared to 2.5 percent for other developing countries). Almost half of OIC members, compared to 20 percent of all other developing countries, attracted FDI inflows in the order of less than 1 percent of GDP, and FDI inflows to Bangladesh and Cameroon re-mained below 0.2 percent of their GDP.

The developmental impact of FDI remains questionable, especially in those countries where multinational enterprises operate in foreign-dominated enclaves, for example, in resource extraction, and where a poor endowment of comple-mentary factors of production hinders FDI-induced spillovers to the local econ-omy.[48]

Uncertain growth effects of FDI notwithstanding, FDI projects often involve subsidies amounting to hundreds of thousands of dollars per job to be created, including in developing countries such as Brazil and India.[49] An international agreement to prevent incentives-based competition for FDI may help host coun-tries to escape the prisoner's dilemma when multinational enterprises play ju-risdictions off against each other to increase incentives. However, the investment rules proposed by industrialized countries are regarded by many developing countries as seriously biased against their interests. Industrialized countries are

Figure 11.8
FDI Flows to Developing Countries, 1990–2001:ª Distribution of the FDI/GDP Ratio

Percent of subsample

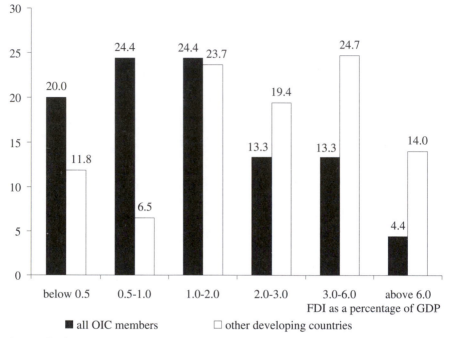

Source: World Bank Group, *World Development Indicators 2003* (Washington, DC: World Bank, 2003).

ªPeriod average.

not prepared to tie their own hands with regard to FDI subsidies and refuse to agree on binding corporate obligations that developing countries deem necessary to improve the developmental impact of FDI. Moreover, industrialized countries, notably those in the European Union, pressed for a multilateral investment agreement (within the WTO) which, according to critics, would have prevented developing countries from pursuing selective and flexible FDI policies.[50]

Development Aid

Many poor developing countries still depend on foreign aid. Yet OECD countries have failed to meet the internationally agreed target of 0.7 percent of GNP to be allocated to official development assistance (ODA). In fact, ODA declined from 0.33 percent of the donors' GNP in 1990–91 to 0.22 percent in 2000–2002.[51] Insufficient fund-raising by the donor community also hinders the fight against global "public bads" such as AIDS, malaria, and tuberculosis. Jeffrey Sachs criticizes the miserly response of donors to global emergencies.[52]

Figure 11.9
Distribution of Aid According to per Capita Income of Recipient Countries

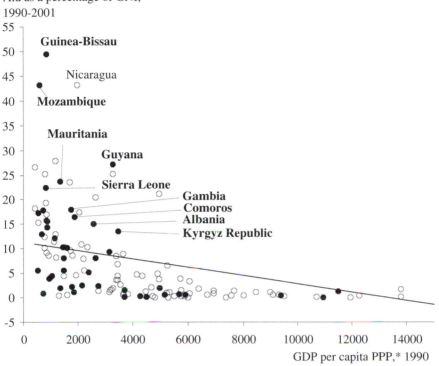

*Purchasing Power Parity

Source: World Bank Group, *World Development Indicators 2003* (Washington, DC: World Bank, 2003).

The donors' aid fatigue derives largely from the disappointing developmental effects of aid. According to Burnside and Dollar, aid had no measurable impact on the recipients' per capita income growth in 1970–93.[53] The recipients' failure to use foreign aid productively is mostly responsible for this outcome, but the donor community is also to blame. The effectiveness of aid could have been improved if the focus were on those developing countries with particularly low per capita incomes and reasonable local policy conditions.[54] In practice, the allocation of aid is not based on these requirements.[55]

Lower-income developing countries, on average, receive more aid, but the aid-to-GNI ratio of some countries, which, according to World Bank definitions, belong to the middle-income group, is significantly above the trend line (Figure 11.9). OIC members Guyana and Albania are in this category. For some poor recipients with extremely high aid-to-GNI ratios, including OIC members Guinea-Bissau and Mozambique, the effective absorption of aid is questionable.

Figure 11.10
Distribution of Aid According to Local Policy Conditions

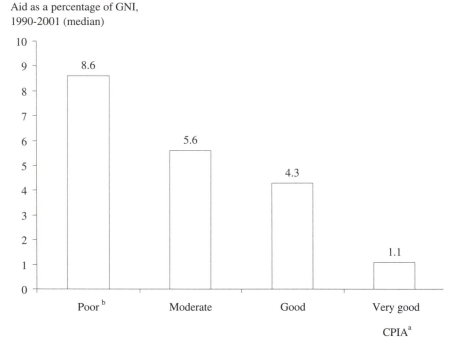

Aid as a percentage of GNI,
1990-2001 (median)

CPIA[a]

[a]CPIA refers to the World Bank's Country Policy and Institutional Assessment as a measure of policy conditions.
[b]Including very poor.

Sources: World Bank Group, *World Development Indicators 2003* (Washington, DC: World Bank, 2003); Paul Collier and David Dollar, "Can the World Cut Poverty in Half? How Policy Reform and Effective Aid Can Meet International Development Goals," *World Development* 29, no. 11 (2001), table 3.

Developing countries with unfavorable policy conditions, on average, received considerably more aid than countries where the World Bank regarded policy conditions as good or very good (Figure 11.10). Some OIC member countries, such as Chad, the Comoros, Niger, and Sierra Leone received aid in the order of 14–22 percent of their GDP, although policy conditions were rated poor in these countries.[56]

Political and strategic considerations have determined the amount and conditions of aid, as shown by Alesina and Dollar. U.S. aid to Egypt, Israel, Pakistan, and Turkey and French aid to its former African colonies exemplify this type of aid.[57]

In sum, even if the major donors substantially increase their aid budgets without better allocation, the effort will be insufficient to promote economic development in recipient countries.

HOW TO REMOVE SYSTEMIC IMPEDIMENTS TO ECONOMIC DEVELOPMENT

The foregoing discussion has shown that many aspects of the international economic system are prejudicial to developing countries, including large parts of the Islamic world. However, systemic factors alone do not explain persisting underdevelopment. Systemic factors cannot explain why Argentina, which belonged to the world's relatively rich economies, has fallen back dramatically, while Asian tigers have narrowed the income gap to the advanced economies considerably. Nor do they explain differences in the economic performance of OIC member countries. Rather, the extent to which the developing countries can benefit from a more favorable external environment depends on their ability to remove domestic impediments to development. Domestic challenges include implementing various aspects of the Washington Consensus, notably macroeconomic stability and openness to trade, plus institutional reforms. The colonial legacies must not be used as excuses for not fighting corruption, enforcing the rule of law, and enhancing governmental effectiveness.

Nevertheless, a number of measures can be taken to improve the external environment for developing countries. In this regard, the removal of agricultural subsidies and other discriminatory trade practices in both agricultural and manufactured goods is very important. For WTO negotiations to result in a successful development round, industrialized countries, notably those of the European Union, should not insist on broadening the agenda to include investment rules. It is hypocritical of industrialized countries to sell the idea of a multilateral investment agreement by arguing that it would result in substantially more FDI flows to developing countries.[58]

In other areas, too, industrialized countries and multilateral institutions, such as the IMF, should not impose their policy agenda on developing countries. The criticism that the application of the Washington Consensus does more harm than good to developing countries is not justified. The real problem is that the traditional approach of pressing for policy reform in developing countries by combining financial support with economic policy conditions has failed because local "ownership" of the reform agenda is often insufficient. This applies both to adjustment programs designed by multilateral institutions, notably IMF programs,[59] and to conditional foreign aid.[60] Therefore, externally imposed conditionality should be replaced by more effective means to encourage reforms.

Regarding IMF lending, it has been suggested that both sides agree *ex ante* on prequalification criteria related to the terms of access to financial support, rather than relying on *ex post* conditionality.[61]

Distribution of foreign aid should increasingly be based on self-defined development strategies of potential recipient countries and on the selective granting of aid to those countries whose development strategies are most promising.[62]

Finally, the major global economic players should devote more attention and resources to fighting global "public bads." Global financial instability and the high incidence of major crises in emerging market economies require that the IMF focus on crisis prevention. If the crises cannot be prevented, reforms of the international financial architecture should ensure that the ensuing economic costs are shared fairly between developing-country debtors and private foreign creditors. Furthermore, sufficient financial resources should be harnessed to fight global pandemics such as AIDS, tuberculosis and malaria. To conclude, systemic impediments alone do not explain the persistence of underdevelopment, but the reform of the system would certainly help the progress of the developing countries.

NOTES

1. See, for example, Resolution 3281 in United Nations, Resolutions of the General Assembly at Its Twenty-ninth Regular Session, New York, September 17–December 18, 1974; see also the references given in the next section.

2. These averages conceal wide variations in country-specific growth trends.

3. Michael P. Todaro, Economic Development in the Third World, 4th ed. (New York: Longman, 1989), 78–82.

4. Theotonio Dos Santos, "The Crisis of Development Theory and the Problem of Dependence in Latin America," in Henry Bernstein, ed., Underdevelopment and Development: The Third World Today (Harmondsworth: Penguin Books, 1973), 57–80.

5. Ibid.

6. Keith Griffin and John Gurley, "Radical Analyses of Imperialism, the Third World, and the Transition to Socialism: A Survey Article," Journal of Economic Literature 23, no. 3 (1985): 1089–1143.

7. Subrata Ghatak, Introduction to Development Economics, 3rd ed. (London: Routledge, 1995), 65.

8. Arghiri Emmanuel, Unequal Exchange (London: New Left Books, 1972).

9. Raul Prebisch, Towards a New Trade Policy for Development (New York: United Nations, 1964).

10. André Gunder Frank, "The Development of Underdevelopment," in Robert I. Rhodes, Imperialism and Underdevelopment: A Reader (New York: Monthly Review Press, 1970), 4–17.

11. Samir Amin, Unequal Development: An Essay on the Social Formations of Peripheral Capitalism (New York: Monthly Review Press, 1976).

12. Todaro, Economic Development, 105.

13. This criticism of foreign aid is not restricted to proponents of dependency theory. See Peter T. Bauer, Dissent on Development: Studies and Debates in Development Economics (Cambridge, MA: Harvard University Press, 1972), who was among the most forceful critics of external aid.

14. Hans W. Singer, "Dualism Revisited: A New Approach to the Problems of Dual Society in Developing Countries," Journal of Development Studies 7, no. 1 (1979): 60–75.

15. Todaro, Economic Development, 82.

16. Ghatak, Introduction to Development Economics, 66.

17. Todaro, Economic Development, 104.

18. Paul Krugman, "Toward a Counter-Counterrevolution in Development Theory," in Lawrence H. Summers and Shekhar Shah, eds., Proceedings of the World Bank Annual

Conference on Development Economics 1992 (Washington, DC: World Bank, 1993), 15–38.

19. Masahisa Fujita, Paul R. Krugman, and Anthony J. Venables, *The Spatial Economy: Cities, Regions, and International Trade* (Cambridge, MA: MIT Press, 1999).

20. Stephen Redding and Peter K. Schott, "Distance, Skill Deepening, and Development: Will Peripheral Countries Ever Get Rich?" *Journal of Development Economics* 72, no. 2 (2003): 515–41.

21. Ibid., 531.

22. William Easterly and Ross Levine, "Tropics, Germs, and Crops: How Endowments Influence Economic Development" (NBER Working Paper 9106, National Bureau of Economic Research, Cambridge, MA, 2002).

23. Daniel Kaufmann, Aart Kraay, and Pablo Zoido-Lobatón, *Governance Matters, II: Updated Indicators for 2000–01* (Washington, DC: World Bank, 2002), http://www.worldbank.org/wbi/governance/govdata2001.htm.

24. Peter Nunnenkamp, "Wachstumsdivergenz zwischen Entwicklungsländern: Hat die Entwicklungsökonomie versagt?" *Zeitschrift für Wirtschaftspolitik* 52, no. 2 (2003): 227–53.

25. The index, based on data in Kaufmann, Kraay, and Zoido-Lobatón, *Governance Matters*, ranges from −2.5 to 2.5, with higher values corresponding to better institutions.

26. Daron Acemoglu, Simon Johnson, and James A. Robinson, "The Colonial Origins of Comparative Development: An Empirical Investigation," *American Economic Review* 91, no. 5 (2001): 1369–1401; World Bank Group, *Doing Business in 2004: Understanding Regulation* (Washington, DC: World Bank, 2003).

27. Ibid., 1395.

28. United Nations, *Monthly Bulletin of Statistics* (New York: United Nations, 2003).

29. Ibid.

30. Ghatak, *Introduction to Development Economics*, 340–42; David Sapsford and John-Ren Chen, "Introduction. The Prebisch-Singer Thesis: A Thesis for the New Millennium?" *Journal of International Development* 11, no. 6 (1999): 843–49.

31. Sapsford and Chen, "Introduction," 845.

32. Matthias G. Lutz, "Commodity Terms of Trade and Individual Countries' Net Barter Terms of Trade: Is There an Empirical Relationship?" *Journal of International Development* 11, no. 6 (1999): 859–70.

33. The selective evidence is largely from Carlos A. Primo Braga, *The Doha Agenda: Opportunities and Challenges for Developing Countries* (mimeo, World Bank, Washington, DC, 2003).

34. "Special Report World Trade Talks: Cancún Challenge," *Economist*, September 6, 2003, 61–63.

35. "Cambodia and the WTO: Welcome to the Club," *Economist*, September 13, 2003, 55.

36. "Special Report World Trade Talks."

37. Trade preferences, embodied in the Generalized System of Preferences (GSP) since 1971, "did little for the poor countries." Jagdish Bhagwati, "The Poor's Best Hope," *Economist*, June 22, 2002, 25–27; Rolf J. Langhammer, "The WTO and the Millennium Round: Between Standstill and Leapfrog" (Kiel Discussion Papers 253, Institute for World Economics, Kiel, Germany, 1999).

38. Braga, *Doha Agenda*.

39. John Williamson, "What Washington Means by Policy Reform," in John

Williamson, ed., *Latin American Adjustment: How Much Has Happened?* (Washington, DC: Institute for International Economics, 1990).

40. Martin Khor, *The IMF's Role and Policy Conditionality: The Relationship Between Ownership, Conditionality, Appropriateness of Policy and Governance, and the Way Forward* (Berlin: Deutsche Stiftung für Internationale Entwicklung, 2003), http://www.dse.de/ef/cond/khor2/htm.

41. Helmut Reisen, "After the Great Asian Slump: Towards a Coherent Approach to Global Capital Flows" (Policy Brief 16, OECD Development Centre, Paris, 1999), 7; Jagdish Bhagwati, "The Capital Myth: The Difference between Trade in Widgets and Dollars," *Foreign Affairs* 77, no. 3 (1998): 7–12.

42. Dani Rodrik, "Who Needs Capital-Account Convertibility?" in Stanley Fischer et al., "Should the IMF Pursue Capital-Account Convertibility?" Essays in International Finance 207 (Princeton, NJ: Princeton University, 1998).

43. Peter Nunnenkamp, "Liberalization and Regulation of International Capital Flows: Where the Opposites Meet" (Kiel Working Papers 1029, Institute for World Economics, Kiel, Germany, 2001).

44. Peter Nunnenkamp, "To What Extent Can Foreign Direct Investment Help Achieve International Development Goals?" (Kiel Working Papers 1128, Institute for World Economics, Kiel, Germany, 2002), figure 5.

45. Jeffrey Sachs, "The Charade of Debt Sustainability," *Financial Times*, September 25, 2000.

46. Romilly Greenhill, Ann Pettifor, Henry Northover, and Ashok Sinha, *Did the G8 Drop the Debt?* (London: Jubilee Debt Campaign, 2003).

47. Peter Nunnenkamp, "Foreign Direct Investment?"

48. Ibid.

49. Charles P. Oman, "The Perils of Competition for Foreign Direct Investment," in Jorge Braga de Macedo and Enrique V. Iglesias, eds., *Foreign Direct Investment versus Other Flows to Latin America* (Paris: Organization for Economic Cooperation and Development, 2001).

50. Peter Nunnenkamp and Manoj Pant, "Why the Case for a Multilateral Agreement on Investment Is Weak" (Kiel Discussion Papers 400, Institute for World Economics, Kiel, Germany, 2003).

51. Organization for Economic Cooperation and Development, *Aid from DAC Members, Statistics, Data, and Indicators*, http://www.oecd.org/statisticsdata/0,2643,en_2649_34485_1_119656_1_1_1,00.html (accessed February 17, 2004).

52. Jeffrey Sachs, "A Miserly Response to a Global Emergency," *Financial Times*, July 17, 2003.

53. Craig Burnside and David Dollar, "Aid, Policies, and Growth," *American Economic Review* 90, no. 4 (2000): 847–68.

54. Paul Collier and David Dollar, "Can the World Cut Poverty in Half? How Policy Reform and Effective Aid Can Meet International Development Goals," *World Development* 29, no. 11 (2001): 1787–1802.

55. Peter Nunnenkamp, "Shooting the Messenger of Good News: A Critical Look at the World Bank's Success Story of Effective Aid" (Kiel Working Papers 1103, Institute for World Economics, Kiel, Germany, 2002).

56. Collier and Dollar, "Can the World Cut Poverty in Half?" table 3.

57. Alberto Alesina and David Dollar, "Who Gives Foreign Aid to Whom and Why?" *Journal of Economic Growth* 5 (March 2000): 33–63.

58. Peter Nunnenkamp and Manoj Pant, "Multilateral Agreement on Investment."

59. Graham Bird, "IMF Programs: Do They Work? Can They Be Made to Work Better?" *World Development* 29, no. 11 (2001): 1849–65.

60. Jakob Svensson, "Why Conditional Aid Does Not Work and What Can Be Done About It?" *Journal of Development Economics* 70, no. 2 (2003): 381–402.

61. John Williamson, "The Role of the IMF: A Guide to the Reports" (International Economics Policy Briefs 00–5, Institute for International Economics, Washington, DC, 2000).

62. Ravi Kanbur, Kevin M. Morrison, and Todd Sandler, "The Future of Development Assistance: Common Pools and International Public Goods" (Policy Essay 25, Overseas Development Council, Baltimore, 1999).

12

The Muslim World's Poor Record of Modernization and Democratization: The Interplay of External and Internal Factors

Mohammed Ayoob

Over the past decade, it has become conventional wisdom to assert that Muslim countries, especially those inhabiting the Greater Middle East, are incapable of successful modernization and transition to democracy. Moreover, Muslim inability is attributed to Islam's specific characteristics as a religion and culture. Yet this culturalist and essentialist argument does not explain the slow pace of the Muslim world's modernization and the uneven, intermittent, and unsatisfactory development of its democratization, especially in the Greater Middle East, which is the focus of this chapter. Rather, an objective analysis of the multiple factors responsible for the Middle East's poor record of modernization and democratization yields totally different conclusions. It shows that Islam, as religion or culture, plays a far less determining role in either modernization or democratization of the Muslim world than assumed by the cultural determinists.

The impact of various internal and external factors that have affected the character and pace of the Muslim countries' modernization is fully discussed in different chapters of this volume, including various case studies. Here, the focus will be on an analysis of the question of democratization and those external factors that, in a dynamic interaction with internal forces, have so far hindered the establishment and consolidation of democratic forms of government in the Muslim world, most notably in the Middle East. Among these factors, the following are particularly important.

First, the legacies of colonial rule have determined to a great extent the trajectory of democratization in the Middle East. Second, the early stage of state making and nation building in third world countries that is shared by the countries of the Middle East has further exacerbated the problems they inherited from colonial rule. In addition, certain unique features in the process of state formation in the Middle East have made the problem more acute for them. Third, the elevated level of conflict and insecurity in the Middle Eastern region derived largely but not exclusively from the Arab-Israeli dispute has had major deleterious effects on the democratization process in these countries. Fourth, the high degrees of great-power involvement and intrusion in the region both during and after the cold war have held the political evolution of these countries hostage to the policies of the major powers.

UNRAVELING THE PROBLEM

The development of democracy, while commonly assumed to be the product of internal social, economic, and cultural variables, is greatly influenced by external factors. This is particularly true of postcolonial countries that are relatively new entrants into the system of states. Such polities usually lack societal cohesion, economic maturity, and political legitimacy. This situation makes the democracy project difficult to implement domestically and renders such states highly vulnerable to penetration by stronger external actors. Consequently, their political life becomes subject to outside influences to such a degree that it is virtually impossible to disentangle the internal from the external variables. Historically, key external actors—major powers—have often used their intrusive capabilities in a way that has retarded these societies' democratic development.

Indeed, it is regrettable that the majority of the literature on democratization produced in the past two decades has concentrated almost exclusively on internal dynamics, and the causes for the reversal of the democratization process have also been sought in the domestic sphere, to the near total exclusion of external influences.[1] This attitude is a carryover from the assumptions of the now largely discredited modernization theory, popular in the 1960s, which attempted to explain third world underdevelopment by focusing exclusively on domestic factors.[2] Its critics made the compelling case that modernization theory was an ahistorical exercise that also failed to appreciate the connection between the domestic situation in the third world and systemic conditions—economic, political, and military—that to a significant degree determined the domestic context.

In fact, dependency and world system theorists pointed out that there was nothing "traditional" left in third world societies because their economies and polities were crafted by the colonial powers. The relations of dependence and subordination that were instituted in the colonial period were carried over in the postcolonial era, which contributed to keeping the third world underdeveloped. Andre Gunder Frank referred to this phenomenon as the "development of underdevelopment."[3] Superpower military and political intervention in the third world provided the political counterpart of the economic stratification that was perpetuated in the postcolonial era. In short, there has been nothing purely "domestic" in the domestic politics and economies of third world countries.[4] This debate demonstrates that one-dimensional explanations including the culturalist thesis provide an incomplete picture of the obstacles to democratization in the third world, notably its Muslim parts.

Western countries developed their political and economic systems over long periods of time through a largely autonomous process and within a neutral or favorable external environment. Even latecomers, such as those in southern and eastern Europe, have operated in a relatively favorable environment. For example, both the European Community, later European Union, and NATO facilitated the modernization and democratization of southern European countries and since the 1990s have been helping the East European countries. The U.S. security shield helped Japan, Taiwan, and South Korea's modernization and democratization. By contrast, most third world countries, especially those situated in the predominantly Muslim Middle East, have been operating in an intrusive and largely unfavorable external environment.

THE LEGACY OF COLONIALISM

The interests and calculations of the European colonial powers largely determined the political geography of third world states and the nature of their economies,[5] thus laying the foundations of their economic vulnerabilities and the distortions of their political development. It is true that the colonial experience did provide many third world countries with proto-states that could be used as jumping-off points for the creation of a postcolonial political order. Further, without the colonial interlude, non-European elites might not have become familiar with the notion of the modern state to the extent they are now.

However, the discontinuities introduced by the colonial process were equally, if not more, important to the future political and economic evolution of third world countries and peoples. The first of these discontinuities was the creation of colonial administrative units by the imperial powers in total disregard for the population's precolonial affinities and loyalties. Political boundaries drawn for purposes of administrative convenience or as a result of territorial trade-offs among imperial powers arbitrarily cut across ethnic, tribal, religious, and linguistic ties; dismembered established political units; and linked more than one precolonial entity in uneasy administrative unions. The partition of Africa in the late nineteenth century was the example, par excellence, of the totally arbitrary division of colonized lands and populations.[6] The division of the Arab portions of the Ottoman Empire after World War I and their assignment to Britain and France ranks almost on par with the carving up of the African continent.

As a result of such cavalier construction of colonial borders, imperial powers bequeathed to the successor states territorial entities that were composed of distinct, sometimes hostile, ethnic groups or that divided previously homogenous communities into two or more states. Most new third world states, therefore, found themselves facing challenges of either a secessionist or irredentist character soon after independence. In some cases, postcolonial states got the worst of both worlds when they were left facing problems created by both these predilections of their former rulers simultaneously. The problems of Kurdish secessionism and Pan-Arab irredentism in the Middle East can both be traced to the boundaries drawn by the colonial powers in the aftermath of World War I.

The general problems associated with secessionism, irredentism, and ethnic conflict in the third world were greatly aggravated in the Middle East because of the contradictory promises made to Arabs and Jews by the British during World War I and the secret Anglo-French agreement that divided up the Arab parts of the Ottoman Empire. The Arabs were given to understand, through the Sharif-MacMahon correspondence, that the Arab territories of the Ottoman Empire—consisting of today's Syria, Lebanon, Iraq, Jordan, Palestine-Israel, and the western portions of Saudi Arabia—would be united into one independent state if the Arabs rose in revolt against the Ottomans and supported the Allies in the war. Simultaneously, the World Zionist Organization was promised, through the Balfour Declaration, a "homeland" for the Jews in Palestine. To top it all, the British and the French agreed secretly, under the Sykes-Picot Agreement, on the division of the Fertile Crescent between themselves.

The Allied victory in World War I saw the implementation of the Sykes-Picot Agreement as modified by the Balfour Declaration. This caused Arab anger to boil over, especially since Arab nationalism that espoused a Pan-Arab state, at least in the Fertile Crescent, had taken hold among intellectual circles, as well as the politically conscious strata of Arab society. The legacy of colonialism, therefore, did not merely bequeath artificial borders to the Arab world; it laid the foundations of a Jewish state in the Arab heartland, as well as betrayed Arab aspirations for political unity in the Fertile Crescent. Postcolonial Arab states had, therefore, to struggle to define their national identities in a very adverse context, faced as they were by a militarily superior and Western-supported Israel on the one hand and the ideological challenge of Pan-Arab nationalism on the other.[7] As will be discussed later, such a milieu was far from conducive to the promotion of democracy in the Middle East in general and the Arab world in particular.

Colonial rule also delayed the transformation of several major colonies from backward to modern economies through what should have been natural processes of economic development. It therefore stunted the growth of the social classes—especially the commercial and industrial bourgeoisie—whose commitment to a centralized state as well as representative government helped fashion the modern effective and democratic states in the Western world. Colonial powers were not interested in the healthy, autonomous development of subject economies. They were primarily concerned with extracting maximum benefit from these societies' resources for the metropolitan economies and turning them into captive markets. Colonial rule disrupted or destroyed flourishing agricultural economies by switching them from food to cash crops meant for export. It also decimated traditional handicraft industries that were seen as competitors to the factories producing manufactured goods in the metropolitan countries as well as native traders and financiers that had dominated the monetized sector of the more sophisticated precolonial economies.[8]

The negative impact of the unequal terms on which third world countries were integrated into the global capitalist economy, and the international military power structure during the colonial era, became more acute as the aspirations of newly established states for independent action collided with the reality of economic dependence and military subordination vis-à-vis the great powers.[9] The proclivity of using multiple "traditional" structures of authority in the colonies as instruments of rule that mediated between the colonial power and the colonized populace not only checked but even reversed the normal process of political development in most colonial territories. It did so because it established major impediments to the creation of modern authority structures based on rational principles of legitimacy. Ali Mazrui has noted that this form of "indirect rule . . . aggravated the problems of creating a modern nation-state after independence. The different groups in the country maintained their separate ethnic identities by being ruled in part through their own native institutions . . . different sections of the population perceived each other as strangers, sometimes as aliens, increasingly as rivals, and ominously as potential enemies."[10]

Moreover, many of these so-called traditional authority structures that were used to mediate between the colonizers and the colonized were themselves the products of colonial rule, either through the revival and augmentation of precolonial political institutions that often had lost their authority and fallen into near disuse or through the creation of what were essentially new institutions that were given traditional nomenclatures to provide them with a semblance of traditional legitimacy.[11]

Furthermore, new ethnic solidarities were formed during colonial rule largely as a result of the workings of the colonial process, which introduced new definitions of communal identity. These solidarities were determined by various factors, including migration from rural to urban areas, links between Western education and upward social mobility, a change from subsistence farming to cashcrop production, and increasing concentration of populations around areas of labor-intensive extractive and manufacturing enterprises. These new ethnic solidarities were also crucially influenced by the piecemeal introduction of representative government based on colonially devised formulas of communal representation that tended to consolidate tribal, religious, and linguistic solidarities and to sharpen ethnic divisions.

This situation has been particularly true in the case of Africa.[12] However, even in India, where religious-communal identities (but not antagonisms) at the local level had crystallized before the advent of the British Raj, it was during the colonial period that these identities were augmented, consolidated, and pitted against one another—often as a result of deliberate colonial policy of "divide and rule"—at the "national" level, finally leading to the partition of the country in 1947. In short, these countries' lack of political and economic autonomy made their political and economic development largely hostage to the vicissitudes of international politics and shifting interests and policies of major international actors.

This does not mean that internal obstacles to democratization do not exist in these countries. They do; however, such internal obstacles cannot be treated in isolation from external impediments to the democratization of postcolonial societies. Muslim countries share the characteristics, conditions, vulnerabilities, and impediments common to their non-Muslim counterparts in the third world. Additionally, there are certain specific factors that are applicable to the Middle East and that make these societies more prone to authoritarian governance. A discussion of these specific factors may help explain why Muslim countries, especially those of the Greater Middle East, have not been affected by the wave of democratization of the 1980s and 1990s, itself largely confined to electoral democracy. This chapter's thesis is that these specific factors bear little relation to Islam but are products of other conditions and policies, partly internal and partly external to these societies.

These obstacles to democracy assume significance in certain regions of the world, such as the Middle East, not because they are predominantly Muslim but because they are more prone to external intrusion and intervention for a variety of reasons. This applies to the post-Soviet space in Central Asia and the Caucasus as well, which since the early 1990s have become of major interest to Western powers while remaining of vital interest to Russia. Again, the fact that Muslims are in the majority in Central Asia and the South Caucasus does not explain their regimes' antidemocratic proclivities (see chapter 18 in this volume by Mehrdad Haghayeghi).

DEMOCRACY AND STATE AND NATION BUILDING

Recognizing that external factors are important in hindering democratization should not lead to underestimating internal factors. Domestic conditions are important not only in their own right; they also lay third world societies open to external intervention.

Democracy is a variable that is dependent for its existence and success on a number of prior factors, notably, territorial satiation (completed state making), societal cohesion (completed nation building), and shared affluence (a relatively equitable, although not equal, distribution of income and wealth). These conditions make internal conflict irrational and counterproductive in terms of most groups' cost-benefit calculations. Where state boundaries are contested, state institutions do not possess unconditional legitimacy, multiple definitions of national identity compete for predominance, and immense disparities of wealth and income exist, democratic governance even if initially established is likely to exhibit extreme fragility. In many cases, such formal democracies descend into illiberal populism, paving the way for the emergence of charismatic dictators who routinize authoritarian regimes by building alliances with the armed forces and with state bureaucracies.

This is not to argue against attempting to establish democratic governance in postcolonial societies, nor is it a justification for authoritarian rule à la Huntington.[13] It is simply an attempt to provide an explanation as to why genuinely democratic governments have been such a rare commodity in the third world.

Where representative institutions have functioned they have usually taken on the character of electoral or procedural democracies lacking the liberal content of mature—that is, satiated, cohesive, and affluent—democracies. The existence of a procedural democracy consisting of periodic elections and political parties is a necessary, but not sufficient, condition for the existence of liberal democracy. What is essential is the existence of a political culture in which the values of democracy are so thoroughly infused that no government or majority can dare to tinker with the unhindered operation of the rule of law, the exercise of fundamental rights, and the equality of opportunity for ethnic and religious minorities. In postcolonial societies, conditions accompanying early stages of state making and nation building have militated against such a democratic political culture from taking root for the following reasons.

First, the early stage of state making is almost always accompanied by violence, as recalcitrant segments of the population resist the imposition of a particular political order and state elites use force to impose that order. In the process, human rights of groups and individuals are almost invariably violated. Whether one likes it or not, state making is to a substantial extent the "violent creation of order."[14] Only when order has been imposed, made secure, and accepted as legitimate by the overwhelming majority of the population do states begin to liberalize and allow political dissent. They do so because state structures and institutions are no longer faced with existential challenges. As long as postcolonial state elites, whether predominantly Muslim or not, feel that there is a possibility that such existential challenges may emerge, they will curb dissent and prevent the emergence of a genuinely democratic political culture. This is evidenced by the history of state making in Europe and the lack of any convincing arguments that the trajectory of state making in the third world is or will be in its essence different from that of its European precursor.[15]

Second, nation building in multiethnic and multireligious societies (which most third world societies are) is often accompanied by violence and suppression. It is rare that national identities in early stages of nation formation are determined primarily by civic criteria. Normally, dominant groups—ethnic or religious or both—define national identities in their own image and impose their version of the "nation" on entire populations, thereby excluding and alienating minority groups.[16] The latter, especially if they are concentrated in certain geographic locales that they consider to be their homelands, usually resist this process of nation formation, often by force.[17] The Kurds form the preeminent example of this phenomenon in the Middle East; the Sri Lankan Tamils do so in South Asia; and the Moro of the southern Philippines in Southeast Asia. Such resistance leads to violent repression on the part of dominant groups in control of the state. Democratic functioning becomes the first casualty of this contestation.

Even where formal procedures of democratic governance survive, they often provide a veneer for majoritarian rule that is by definition illiberal in character. For decades, Buddhist-dominated Sri Lanka formed an outstanding example of "majoritarian democracy" that eventually propelled the country into a long and bloody civil war. The Hindu nationalists' increasingly bold attempts to create and consolidate a Hindu religious majority at the expense of India's diverse population, including its Muslim minority, numbering 130 million, could be leading India in the same direction.[18] As these examples demonstrate, there is nothing unique about Muslims that predisposes them to dominate religious or ethnic minorities. This is a shared phenomenon across much of the third world.

Third, early stages of state and nation building, because they entail conflict and violence, are conducive to the emergence of authoritarian regimes because the latter are better able to project an image, usually false, of centralized control, efficient decision making, and speedy action. Once such regimes gain power they come to possess a vested interest in prolonging their rule and reproducing themselves. They do so by creating structures of power within the larger society that do their best to help perpetuate their existence. Furthermore, such regimes are quite adept at establishing linkages with major powers whose economic and military support form essential ingredients of the regimes' survival strategy. Such linkages also reduce their dependence on internal sources of revenue, thus rendering a social compact with their populations redundant.

Fourth, for a number of reasons the twentieth century witnessed unprecedented political mobilization, including in the third world. This changed the normative climate in which states function, subjected new states to system overload as societal demands outran the capacity of states to respond to them, and ruled out the strategy of gradual co-optation of segments of society that had worked so well in Europe during earlier centuries. Paradoxically, the increased demand for voice and participation in the third world led in most cases not to the institutionalization of democratic governance but to a combination of populism and authoritarianism. The establishment of democratic institutions and democratic culture takes time; populist slogans meanwhile act as surrogates, helping authoritarian rulers to consolidate power and acquire a certain amount of legitimacy. This happened across the board in the third world but probably nowhere in as dramatic a fashion as in the Middle East, for reasons connected to its colonial legacy as well as to the regional and global environments in which Middle Eastern states operated.

CONTIGUOUS STATE MAKING AND REGIONAL CONFLICTS

The fact that third world states are geographically clustered together has meant that state making and nation building have been undertaken by proximate and contiguous states within more or less the same time span. Concurrent state building in countries with shared and often disputed borders and with overlapping populations has meant that internal conflicts have spilled over state boundaries, causing interstate tensions and sometimes war.[19] Consequently, entire regions have suffered from instability and insecurity, conditions that have militated against democratic governance and worked to the advantage of populist regimes and military dictators.

Predominantly Muslim countries inhabit some of the most insecure regions in the world, above all the Middle East, where tension and conflict are endemic. This may partly explain the Muslim world's, and especially the Middle East's, lack of democracy. As stated above, the rudiments of most conflicts in the Middle East were put in place during the period between the two world wars, when the British and the French divided the Arab parts of the Ottoman Empire, creating artificial states in defiance both of Arab nationalist aspirations and of assurances given to Arab leaders during World War I. This frustration of Arab nationalist aspirations may have contributed to the emergence of a more chauvinistic and expansionist version in the form of Nasserism and Ba'thism. The British also promoted the migration of European Jews into Palestine, thus changing the demography of the mandated territory, creating a massive backlash from the indigenous population as witnessed in the Arab revolt of 1936–39, and laying the foundations of the Arab-Israeli conflict that has bedeviled the region for decades. Not surprisingly, the peace agreement that was imposed on the Middle East at the end of World War I has been termed "a peace to end all peace."[20]

If a counterfactual history of the Middle East could be written that would depict the region without the Arab-Israeli conflict and the Palestinian exile, it would be possible to come up with a considerably more democratic and liberal scenario. Egypt, Syria, Iraq, and Lebanon were all in the process of undertaking fledgling experiments in democratic governance. These experiences were aborted partly because of the disastrous outcome of the first Palestine war, the subsequent continuing conflict with Israel in which Arab states suffered humiliating reverses, the impact of the Palestinian diasporas on delicate domestic political balances in countries surrounding Palestine, and the consequent radicalization of Arab politics (see chapter 13 in this volume by Saad Eddin Ibrahim).[21]

This pattern was not limited to the predominantly Muslim Middle East. Concurrent state building created and exacerbated tensions in Africa, South Asia, and Southeast Asia as well. The conflict over Kashmir between India and Pakistan and the confrontation between Malaysia and Indonesia over the creation of Malaysia in 1963 by the incorporation of northern Borneo, to which Indonesia also laid claim, represented major instances of interstate tensions created by concurrent state building. The latest examples of conflict, emanating from concurrent state building efforts of contiguous states, occurred in the Balkans, the Caucasus, and Central Asia. Several of the states in these regions demonstrate the same antidemocratic traits that are common to states in the early stages of state and nation building, whose attempt to control territories and populations is disputed both by segments of the domestic populations and by neighboring states.

The problems of early state building become compounded when the departing colonial power leaves behind extremely negative political and economic legacies.

These are exacerbated when empires and/or multiethnic federations break apart precipitately, as they did in the Soviet Union and Yugoslavia. Such rapid disintegration unleashes political elites that appeal to segmented solidarities in order to retain or attain power. In the process they not merely tear apart successor states but launch interstate conflicts that make entire regions highly insecure. The intertwining of the regional and the domestic factors that promote violence and conflict becomes most clear in such cases as both sets of variables feed off each other.[22]

GLOBAL FACTORS AND THE PROSPECTS
FOR DEMOCRATIZATION

The intertwining is not merely between the regional and the domestic; it is also among the global, the regional, and the domestic. The global structures of power and great-power policies have had a profound effect on the process of and prospect for democratization in the third world. This has been particularly true of the predominantly Muslim Middle East. During the cold war, not only did the two superpowers export their rivalries to the periphery, the third world became the major arena where competition for global supremacy was played out, since it was too dangerous in the nuclear age to tinker with the cold war boundaries drawn in Europe. The logic of mutual assured destruction (MAD) provided precarious peace in Europe, but it did so at the expense of instability and insecurity in the third world. Much of the third world was not considered to be vital to superpower concerns, and therefore conflict and competition were not only permitted but also often actively promoted in the global periphery. Interstate and intrastate wars were encouraged, gains were made and losses suffered, and new weapons and the political will of the adversary were tested without incurring the danger of direct confrontation and nuclear escalation.

Moreover, a tacit understanding emerged between Washington and Moscow after the Cuban missile crisis of 1962, that at the slightest threat of such escalation they would act to ensure that their strategic relationship was delinked from regional conflicts that demonstrated a propensity to embroil them directly. They would simultaneously force the regional protagonists to de-escalate as well.[23] The superpowers came closest to violating this rule in the October 1973 war in the Middle East. However, in the final analysis, that episode augmented this principle by bringing home to the superpowers that any miscalculation could end in nuclear catastrophe. Another unwritten rule of the cold war game related to those instances where one superpower was directly involved militarily, as in Vietnam and Afghanistan. In such cases, the other superpower desisted from direct military confrontation and conducted the competition through proxies, denying any direct responsibility for their actions.

All this worked very well for the superpowers, but it wreaked havoc on the third world. Interstate and intrastate conflicts were exacerbated; sophisticated weapons supplied by the major powers added tremendously both to the intensity of conflicts and to the scale of destruction.[24] The exacerbation of internal and interstate conflicts immensely complicated the state-building project in the third world as well. Regional conflict, as in the case of the Middle East, became linked to cold war rivalries and "spurred the militarization of the *mukhabarat* state, diverted resources away from social priorities, and justified domestic repression in the name of national unity against an external enemy."[25]

All in all, superpower involvement had deleterious consequences for regional as well as domestic systems and made the third world more Hobbesian than it would have been otherwise. In terms of democratization, superpower intervention was often an inhibiting factor as the superpowers covertly and overtly supported regimes that suited their own geopolitical ends, while acting against democratically elected governments, as illustrated by the examples of Mohammad Mossadegh in Iran in 1953, Jacobo Arbenz in Guatemala in 1954, and Salvador Allende in Chile in 1973.

External support, in some cases quite massive, reduced the need for regimes receiving such support to enter into social compacts with their populations in order to extract resources necessary to rule over the country. Such compacts, as the earlier European experience had shown, are essential for the promotion of democratic ethos since they entail quid pro quo on the part of the rulers, usually in the form of increased participation by the ruled in state affairs. In the absence of such a compact, regimes become insulated from their populations and increasingly predatory in their behavior toward their citizens.

The habit and culture of dependence on external patrons accompanied by predatory behavior domestically paved the way for eventual state failure by delegitimizing regimes that had not invested in building solid bases of social support. State failure usually led to civil war that pitted ethnic groups and political factions against each other. This process was accelerated after the cold war and the withdrawal of superpower support from many client regimes no longer strategically relevant. This led to the sudden collapse of a number of regimes, such as those of Afghanistan, Somalia, Liberia, and Zaire-Congo, taking their fragile state structures with them. The war of all against all became the rule in such societies. Democracy was the last thing on the minds of conflict entrepreneurs, who benefited immensely from state collapse and did their best to prevent state regeneration.[26]

Finally, those regimes supported by superpowers that had succeeded in establishing relatively strong authoritarian structures continued to exist despite the end of the cold war and the withdrawal of external support. Some regimes, such as those of Egypt and Jordan, continue to receive substantial external economic and military support from the United States for strategic reasons unconnected to the cold war. In North Africa, Tunisia, Morocco, and Algeria receive substantial help from Europe without any pressure to democratize. In other cases, such as the Arab Gulf states, these regimes continue to receive military support because they control strategically important energy resources.

DEMOCRACY IN THE MIDDLE EAST AFTER THE COLD WAR

These generalizations apply both to predominantly Muslim and principally non-Muslim countries. However, as the cases of Egypt, Jordan, the Gulf Arab states, and now the Central Asian states demonstrate, the strategic and resource importance of the Greater Middle East has made the extended region an exceptional one in the post–cold war era. It has also meant that the authoritarian regimes presiding over the overwhelmingly Muslim countries located in the Greater Middle East have received a further lease on life, frustrating prospects for democracy in the region. External pressures, U.S.-led in many cases, for democratization that helped move many countries in other regions down the democratic path, at least in the procedural sense, have not operated on most regimes in the Greater Middle Eastern region. Therefore, the positive impact of external forces that was demonstrated in parts of Latin America, Asia, and Africa has remained marginal if not irrelevant as far as this extended region is concerned. In this sense, the Middle East stands out as unique among regions of the third world. Its exceptional experience is related to the fact that its strategic importance to the West, especially the United States, is closely tied to the operation of two factors—energy resources and the Arab-Israeli conflict—that do not have a major bearing on the politics and economics of other regions.

The Gulf subregion of the Middle East has two-thirds of the world's proven oil reserves. The export capacity of the Gulf oil producers is even higher, amounting to probably well over three-quarters of the world's exportable oil reserves. Moreover, "oil currently accounts for 40 percent of global energy consumption and is not anticipated to fall much below this share in the next twenty years."[27] Proven oil reserves in Central Asia, the Caucasus, and Russia are not likely to undermine the Gulf's preeminence in the long term as a producer and exporter of oil. This concentration of oil reserves guarantees that while "outside oil production may continue to rise over the next decade . . . all major production increases from 2010 to 2020 are projected to come, once again, from the Persian Gulf."[28] Moreover, production and transportation costs of the Gulf are far below those of other regions.

Given the crucial importance of these oil-producing countries to the international economy, the West's vital strategic and economic interests will continue to be engaged in the Persian Gulf. The Gulf, in turn, is inextricably intertwined with the larger Middle Eastern region for reasons ranging from geopolitics to ethnic, linguistic, and religious affinity. The still-authoritarian kingdoms of the Arab littoral of the Gulf form an integral part of the Western security network. But they are also part of the Arab regional system and thus subject to the pull of their Arab and Muslim identities, so they cannot remain immune to currents prevailing in the Arab and Muslim worlds, especially if these currents can affect the legitimacy of their regimes.

Consequently, the Gulf monarchies remain in a constant state of tension between their dependence upon the United States and the pressures emanating from Arab and Muslim disenchantment with U.S. policies in the Middle East. By and large, so far they have been able to manage this tension and continue to be dependable suppliers of oil and important military assets for the United States. Consequently, the United States and its Western allies are reluctant to pressure them, except gently, to liberalize politically because of the uncertainties that may accompany democratization. Above all, they are afraid that it could set off a chain of uncontrollable events that may end up in genuine regime change and the coming to power of groups hostile to Western interests.

The other major factor that determines the United States' and other Western countries' post–cold war approach toward regimes of the region is the latter's attitude toward the state of Israel. The United States has a special relationship with Israel, deriving from a sense of moral responsibility rooted in the genocide committed against the Jews by Nazi Germany, perceived common strategic interests, and the influence of the pro-Israeli lobby in Washington. This makes Israel a "domestic politics" as well as a "foreign policy" issue in the United States and gives it far greater importance in America's foreign policy calculations. Several of the authoritarian or semiauthoritarian Arab regimes are considered by the West to be "moderates" vis-à-vis Israel. The West, especially the United States, therefore has a major interest in preserving these regimes, especially since there appears to be a fair chance that their replacements would have a less accommodating attitude toward Israel and, by extension, the United States. This could well turn out to be true since political liberalization in the Middle East, including the Persian Gulf, is likely to unleash political forces, including radical Islam, that can be expected to be hostile to Israel and the United States.

It should be noted that Islamists have become important players in the struggle for democracy in the Greater Middle Eastern region as vocal proponents of human rights and political liberalization in countries suffering under oppressive authoritarian rule.[29] This has partly resulted from authoritarian regimes' decimation of secular opposition and the gravitation of democratic and oppositional forces toward Islamist political formations as the only viable alternatives to the corrupt ruling oligarchies. Consequently, Islamist groups have gained major political advantage that is likely to help them come to power in several countries of the Greater Middle East, if free and fair elections are held. This is a scenario that the United States and its allies would like to avert or to abort, as in the case of Algeria in 1992. Authoritarian regimes across the Greater Middle East have played upon these Western fears by representing themselves as the West's last best hope in this extended volatile region. Democracy in the Middle East has, among other things, become a casualty of the West's strategic and energy interests.

In sum, there is a fundamental contradiction in the West's position vis-à-vis the Middle East. In theory, Western policy makers accept that a democratic Middle East will in the long run be in the interest of the West. But they cannot escape the dilemma that in the short to medium term, democratization of Middle Eastern countries is likely not merely to unleash anti-Western sentiments but also bring to power groups that are inimical toward the West. The American decision to hold elections in Iraq in early 2005 has made this dilemma very acute for Washington. Early elections are likely to bring to power elements, especially Shi'a Islamist groups, that may not be acceptable to the United States. However, postponing elections into the indefinite future is no longer an option because it will detract from the credibility of the U.S. argument that Washington is committed to the democratization not only of Iraq but of the rest of the Middle East. It will also give a tremendous fillip to what seems to be turning into an Iraqi national resistance to American occupation. Western, especially U.S., policy makers are bound to face this sort of conundrum continuously if and when the democratization of the Middle East picks up speed.

Several Middle Eastern regimes, such as Egypt, Morocco, Jordan, and Kuwait, had begun a process of controlled liberalization even before the war against Iraq in anticipation of American and European pressure on them to democratize. These largely cosmetic moves, when combined with Western reluctance to pile too much pressure on fragile, yet friendly regimes, have led to the emergence of a form of governance in the Middle East that has been aptly termed "liberalized autocracy." However, as Brumberg has convincingly argued, such liberalized autocracies that "guarantee freedom of speech, but not freedom *after* speech" engage in controlled liberalization in order to extend their lives rather than to usher in genuine democratization.[30] In the long run, they are likely to thwart the transition to democracy in the Middle East rather than aide the process. Popular disenchantment with the "liberalized autocracy" model is likely to increase the attraction of anti-Western Islamist options for disenfranchised populations aggrieved at continued Western support for autocratic and semiautocratic regimes in the Middle East.

CONCLUSION

The above analysis makes clear that variables other than that of Islamic exceptionality explain the resistance to democratization in the Greater Middle East. These variables are domestic, regional, and global in character. Negative colonial legacies, early stages of state making and nation building, a very high degree of regional insecurity and conflict, the concentration of energy reserves in the Gulf and Central Asian subregions of the Greater Middle East, the United States' and other major powers' support for authoritarian regimes, and the Arab-Israeli conflict and the policies that flow from it, when taken together, provide a much more satisfactory explanation for the Middle East's democratic shortcomings. Indeed, poring over sacred Islamic texts is unlikely to shed much light on this problem.

The contrast between the predominantly Muslim Greater Middle East and other parts of the developing world on the progress of democratization in the post–cold war era demonstrates one thing very clearly. Great-power interests and policies matter a great deal in promoting or retarding democracy in various parts of the world. They can have both a positive and a negative impact. This has been particularly true in the past decade and a half, when the Western powers in general, and the United States in particular, have adopted policies that have put pressure on regimes in Latin America, Africa, and Asia to liberalize politically and institute some variant of democratic governance. Despite certain reversals, this pressure has worked in great part in terms of promoting at least procedural democracy in the non-Western world. However, the Middle East has largely remained immune from this pressure. This has been the case not because there is something inherently undemocratic about the peoples of this particular region but because the sustained application of such pressure does not suit the strategic and economic interests of the major powers in relation to the Middle East. A change of heart in the major capitals, especially Washington, on this issue is likely to make a substantial difference to the fortunes of democracy in the Greater Middle Eastern region.

NOTES

1. Samuel P. Huntington, *The Third Wave: Democratization in the Late Twentieth Century* (Norman: University of Oklahoma Press, 1993); Stephan Haggard and Robert R. Kaufman, *The Political Economy of Democratic Transitions* (Princeton, NJ: Princeton University Press, 1995); Larry Diamond, *Developing Democracy: Towards Consolidation* (Baltimore: Johns Hopkins University Press, 1999).

2. Walt Rostow, *The Stages of Economic Growth: A Non-Communist Manifesto* (Cambridge: Cambridge University Press, 1962); Almond lays out the "structural functional" framework in Gabriel Almond, "Introduction: A Functional Approach to Comparative Politics," in Gabriel A. Almond and James S. Coleman, eds., *The Politics of the Developing Area* (Princeton, NJ: Princeton University Press, 1960); Vicky Randall and Robin Theobald, *Political Change and Underdevelopment: A Critical Introduction to Third World Politics,* 2nd ed. (Durham, NC: Duke University Press, 1998).

3. Andre Gunder Frank, *Capitalism and Underdevelopment in Latin America* (New York: Monthly Review Press, 1969).

4. Fernando Henrique Cardoso and Enzo Faletto, *Dependency and Development in Latin America* (Berkeley: University of California Press, 1979); Immanuel Wallerstein, *The Modern World System: Capitalist Agriculture and the Origins of the European World Economy in the Sixteenth Century* (London: Academic Press, 1974).

5. Christopher Clapham, *Third World Politics* (Madison: University of Wisconsin Press, 1985), chap. 2.

6. Crawford Young, "The African Colonial State and Its Political Legacy," in Donald Rothchild and Naomi Chazan, eds., *The Precarious Balance: State and Society in Africa* (Boulder, CO: Westview Press, 1988), 25–66.

7. Elizabeth Monroe, *Britain's Moment in the Middle East* (Baltimore: Johns Hopkins University Press, 1963).

8. Amiya Kumar Bagchi, *The Political Economy of Underdevelopment* (Cambridge: Cambridge University Press, 1982).

9. Mohammed Ayoob, "The Third World in the System of States: Acute Schizophrenia or Growing Pains?" *International Studies Quarterly* 33, no. 1 (March 1989): 67–79.

10. Ali A. Mazrui, "The Triple Heritage of the State in Africa," in Ali Kazancigil, ed., *The State in Global Perspective* (London: Gower/UNESCO, 1986), 112.

11. Joel S. Migdal, *Strong Societies and Weak States: State-Society Relations and State Capabilities in the Third World* (Princeton, NJ: Princeton University Press, 1988).

12. Jeffrey Herbst, "The Creation and Maintenance of National Boundaries in Africa," *International Organizations* 23, no. 4 (Autumn 1989).

13. Samuel P. Huntington, *Political Order in Changing Societies* (New Haven, CT: Yale University Press, 1968).

14. Youssef Cohen, Brian R. Brown, and Abramo Fimo Kenneth Organski, "The Paradoxical Nature of State Making: The Violent Creation of Order," *American Political Science Review* 75, no. 4 (1981): 901–10.

15. Charles Tilly, ed., *The Formation of National States in Western Europe* (Princeton, NJ: Princeton University Press, 1975).

16. Anthony W. Marx, *Faith in Nation: Exclusionary Origins of Nationalism* (New York: Oxford University Press, 2003).

17. Walker Connor, "Homelands in a World of States," in Montserrat Guibernau and John Hutchinson, eds., *Understanding Nationalism* (Cambridge: Polity Press, 2001), 53–73.

18. It can be argued that attempts at creating a majoritarian polity in India may have received a setback by the electoral defeat of the Hindu nationalist government in the parliamentary elections held in the spring of 2004. However, one cannot be sanguine about it because the Hindu nationalists have been able to build a significant base in the country with a committed voter support of between 20 and 25 percent of the electorate, they continue to control several state governments, their rhetoric has become even more shrill after the electoral defeat, and they have successfully infiltrated the bureaucracy especially in the educational and policing spheres. Above all, they have been able to change the political discourse in the country to such an extent during the past two decades that it is no longer politically incorrect to publicly indulge in the most virulent form of anti-Muslim rhetoric. All this does not bode well for the future of a secular India. Fareed Zakaria, *The Future of Freedom: Illiberal Democracy at Home and Abroad* (New York: W. W. Norton, 2003), 106–13.

19. Mohammed Ayoob, *The Third World Security Predicament: State Making, Regional Conflict, and the International System* (Boulder, CO: Lynne Rienner, 1995), chap. 3.

20. David Fromkin, *A Peace to End All Peace: The Fall of the Ottoman Empire and the Creation of the Modern Middle East* (New York: Henry Holt, 1989).

21. Gregory F. Gause III, "Regional Influences on Experiments in Political Liberalization in the Arab World," in Bahgat Korany, Rex Brynen, and Paul Noble, eds., *Political Liberalization and Democratization in the Arab World*, vol. 1, *Theoretical Perspective* (Boulder, CO: Lynne Rienner, 1995), 283–306.

22. Michael E. Brown, "The Causes and Regional Dimensions of Internal Conflict," in Michael E. Brown, ed., *The International Dimensions of Internal Conflict* (Cambridge, MA: MIT Press, 1996), 571–601.

23. Roger E. Kanet and Edward A. Kolodziej, eds., *The Cold War as Cooperation* (Baltimore: Johns Hopkins University Press, 1991).

24. Ayoob, *Third World Security Predicament,* chap. 5.

25. Bahgat Korany, Rex Brynen, and Paul Noble, "Introduction: Theoretical Perspectives on Arab Liberalization and Democratization," in Korany, Brynen, and Noble, *Political Liberalization*, 1: 19.

26. According to Charles King, "There is a political economy of [ethnic] warfare that produces positive externalities for its perpetrators." Charles King, "The Benefits of Ethnic War: Understanding Eurasia's Unrecognized States," *World Politics* 53, no. 4 (July 2001). For the role of "conflict entrepreneurs" in the perpetuation of civil wars, see David Keen, *The Economic Functions of Violence in Civil Wars,* Adelphi Paper 320 (Oxford: Oxford University Press for International Institute of Strategic Studies, 1998); Mats Berdal and David M. Malone, eds., *Greed and Grievance: Economic Agendas and Civil Wars* (Boulder, CO: Lynne Rienner, 2000).

27. Shibley Telhami and Fiona Hill, "Does Saudi Arabia Still Matter?" *Foreign Affairs* 81, no. 6 (November–December 2002): 167.

28. Ibid., 168.

29. Carrie Rosefsky Wickham, *Mobilizing Islam: Religion, Activism, and Political Change in Egypt* (New York: Columbia University Press, 2002). This study holds important lessons that go beyond the Egyptian case.

30. Daniel Brumberg, "The Trap of Liberalized Autocracy," in Larry Diamond, Marc F. Plattner, and Daniel Brumberg, eds., *Islam and Democracy in the Middle East* (Baltimore: Johns Hopkins University Press, 2003), 35–47. The quote, with emphasis in the original, is from page 43 of the article.

III

Case Studies

13

Arab Liberal Legacies Full Circle

Saad Eddin Ibrahim

Since the events of September 11, 2001, the Arab world has become a battlefield for armed conflicts of all kinds: civil strife, interstate wars, and the war on terrorism. The United States and, to a lesser extent, other Western coalition partners added spreading "democracy" to the list of objectives of their military intervention in Afghanistan and Iraq. This, in turn, has triggered a heated debate among social scientists, politicians, and laymen in the Arab world, revolving around the question, can democracy be imposed by force from the outside? The examples of post–World War II Japan and Germany are often cited by those who favor the introduction of democratic governance by all means to countries long ruled by autocratic regimes. Others have argued that there is an Arab or Middle East "exceptionalism"; in other words, methods applied elsewhere do not necessarily work in this region. A multitude of historical, cultural, religious, and structural factors are believed to underline such exceptionalism. Leading U.S. policy makers have recently challenged this exceptionalism. In a November 6, 2003, speech, President George W. Bush stated:

Our commitment to democracy is also tested in the Middle East, which is my focus today, and must be a focus of American policy for decades to come. In many nations of the Middle East—countries of great strategic importance—democracy has not yet taken root. And the questions arise: are the peoples of the Middle East somehow beyond the reach of liberty. . . . Some skeptics of democracy assert that the traditions of Islam are inhospitable to the representative government. This "cultural condescension," as Ronald Reagan termed it, has a long history. After the Japanese surrender in 1945, a so called Japan expert asserted that democracy in that former empire would "never work." Another observer declared the prospects for democracy in post-Hitler Germany are, and I quote, "most uncertain at best"—he made that claim in 1957. . . . It should be clear to all that Islam—the faith of one-fifth of humanity—is consistent with democratic rule. . . . More

than half of all the Muslims in the world live in freedom under democratically constituted governments. They succeed in democratic societies, not in spite of their faith, but
because of it. A religion that demands individual moral accountability, and encourages
the encounter of the individual with God, is fully compatible with the rights and respon-
sibilities of self-government.[1]

Missing from the current debate on democratization of the Arab world are the
region's own modern legacies, one of which was a "liberal age," extending from
the mid-nineteenth to the mid-twentieth century. This liberal age provides a test
of the competing hypotheses over democratization, a collective memory and a
potential basis upon which to build future democracies. Fareed Zakaria has cor-
rectly argued that "liberalism" is a precondition for a sound democracy. He uses
the term "liberal" in the nineteenth-century sense, meaning concern with individual economic, political, and religious liberty, which is sometimes called "classical liberalism," not in the modern, American sense, which associates it with the
welfare state, affirmative action, and other policies.[2] He warned U.S. policy makers against the rush to electoral politics in Iraq after the April 9, 2003, fall of
Saddam Hussein. By liberalism, Zakaria and others mean a sociocultural framework and a way of life in which an open society for trade, free media, competent legal institutions, rule of law, and ethno-religious tolerance prevail, at least
on the normative level. The proponents of this prerequisite contend that the above
elements of liberalism make individuals receptive to the spirit, roles, and actual
behaviors of "citizenship." They also predispose groups, communities, and other
collectivities to the rules of fair play. This, in turn, makes people receptive to and
tolerant of the unpleasant outcomes of electoral politics. For example, this attitude ensures that "losers" would not always contest the outcome of elections nor
resort to violent means to overturn them and that "winners" would not totally
disregard the legitimate interests of the losers or take advantage of their own pro-
visional majority to change the rules of the political game. Such restraints cannot always be "legislated." They have to be learned and internalized by citizens.
A period of liberalism is, therefore, needed for this type of civic culture to take
root before electoral politics are introduced into a country. It is also argued that
the spread of civil society organizations (CSOs) in a country could facilitate its
transition to a full-fledged democracy because it is within such organizations that
people learn the skills of organizing, mobilizing, debating, and compromising.
No doubt, CSOs help the consolidation of democracy. Alexis de Tocqueville
noted this strong correlation in the case of America some 160 years ago. However, observers have noted that in the third wave of democracy, starting with Portugal in 1977 and sweeping across more than sixty countries in the following
quarter of a century, there are several cases of countries' successfully transition-
ing to democracy without having passed through a liberal phase.

During the past two centuries, the Arab world has gone through several successive and overlapping phases, each with its own legacy: an early liberal, a colonial, a middle liberal, a populist radical, an Islamic, and a new liberal. Not every

Arab country experienced all six phases, and there are those that have not done so in exactly the same sequence or with the same intensity. But key Arab countries, notably Egypt, Syria, Iraq, Jordan, Libya, and Tunisia, have gone through enough of these successive experiences in approximately the same time that both the overall flavor and the discourse of their experiences warrant a number of generalizations.

Whatever the mounting internal pressures, it was an external factor that triggered the commencement of each of these six legacies, namely the encroachment of foreign powers, such as the French, British, Italian, Israeli, and American, on Arab countries. These encroachments both sowed the seeds of modernity and unleashed forces of resistance to foreign powers. With the fading of one legacy and the onset of another, certain social formations (e.g., classes, professions, and ethnic groups) declined and new ones arose. Thus, each legacy was associated with a particular social formation both as a propeller and as a beneficiary. The landed bourgeoisie championed the first liberal age; the middle class manned the second; the lower-middle class dominated the populist radical legacy; and a mix of the lower and lowest urban formations have sustained the Islamic legacy. A coalition of Western-educated professionals and businessmen is the force that is presently advocating a return of liberalism.

The articulation of various legacies into ideological isms is mainly a function of the twentieth century. As the Moroccan historian Abdulla Laroui noted, there was a 50- to 100-year lag between the appearance of such isms in the West and their adoption by Arab advocates.[3] The thesis of this chapter is that many of the elements of liberalism had existed in the Arab world and helped create Western-type democracies, first in Egypt during the last quarter of the nineteenth century, and then in a score of other Arab countries during the interwar period (1920s–1950s). The seeds of liberalism were laid as early as the turn of the 1800s.[4]

SEEDS OF AN ARAB LIBERALISM

When Napoleon Bonaparte's navy anchored in Alexandria in July 1798, it was the first massive encounter of the Arab Middle East with the West since the last Crusade in the thirteenth century. Like other eastern provinces of the Ottoman Empire, Egypt was stagnating in its medieval traditional Islamic ways, while Europe was advancing on a path of science, knowledge, technology, and religious and political reformation. When Napoleon's navy and army set foot in Egypt, it was the French Revolution that was present on the banks of the Nile. According to the Egyptian historian al-Jabarti, the French may as well have been creatures from another planet for the sense of amazement they produced. But, it was their openness that impressed him the most:

If any of the Muslims came to them in order to look around they did not prevent him from entering their most cherished places, and if they found in him any appetite or desire for knowledge they showed their friendship and love for him, and will bring out all kinds of pictures and maps, and animals and birds and plants, and the histories of the ancients and of nations and tales of the prophets. I went to them often, and they showed me all that.[5]

Among the many things that the French expedition brought to Egypt were the printing press and new vocabulary—including terms such as "liberty," "fraternity," "equality," "human rights," and "municipal councils." As it turned out, the Egyptians revolted against the French and with the help of the British and the Ottomans expelled them after three years. The French left Egypt, taking with them the guns but leaving behind the printing press and the revolutionary slogans. These would prove to be of a more lasting impact on the emergence of a modern state and society in Egypt than did the brief French presence. That is why many historians consider the arrival of the French expedition in 1798 as a marker in Egypt's and the Arab world's modern history.

One of the young Ottoman officers stationed in Egypt at the time, Muhammad Ali, closely observed Napoleon and the French with great admiration. Shortly after their departure and with the help of the native *ulama,* Muhammad Ali became Egypt's ruler and succeeded where Napoleon had failed. Unlike Napoleon's short tenure, Muhammad Ali's reign lasted forty-four years (1805–1848). While Napoleon was unable to pacify the *ulama* or control the Mamluks, Muhammad Ali manipulated the former and eliminated the latter. While Napoleon was unable to conquer all of Greater Syria, Muhammad Ali did, and went far beyond— into Arabia, the Sudan, and southern Anatolia. It was Muhammad Ali's ambitious modern state building that would unintentionally lead to the gradual emergence of Egypt's modern civil society and its first liberal experience.

To begin with, Muhammad Ali sent 311 of Egypt's youngest and brightest to study in France, Italy, Austria, and Britain and brought to Egypt tens of European officers, engineers, and doctors to train more Egyptians at home.[6] It is estimated that more than 2,000 native sons benefited from this at-home training. Thus, between 1818 and 1849, these modern educated Egyptians became the backbone of a new middle class (NMC). From their ranks emerged proponents of liberal values and practices. By the early 1860s elements of this NMC began to establish modern CSO newspapers and theaters and to advocate liberal politics. The presence of growing Syrian and other foreign communities (mostly Greek, Italian, and French) enhanced these liberal, social, and political practices.

By 1866, Kedive Isma'il, a fairly enlightened viceroy of Egypt, responded favorably to these liberal aspirations. He decreed a constitution that allowed Egypt's first parliamentary elections. Isma'il proudly wrote to a fellow Egyptian, Nubar Pasha, living in Paris at the time:

At long last, elections were held all over the country, and the date of November 18 has been set to inaugurate the Council. You will be interested to know that the election turn out was tremendous, despite the fact that the general standard of the people is still below that of Europe. But people seem to fully comprehend the benefits and advantages which will occur to them from the Council. The commoners say that from now on higher and lower officials alike will have to give up their arrogance and to observe a straight proper path in all their conduct. The elections, my dear Nubar, were conducted in full freedom, with all participating—Muslims and Copts with no religious discrimination whatsoever. Copts say that the government will no longer be biased against them. It will cease treating them as minors.[7]

In his letter, Kedive Isma'il could not hide his glee or sarcasm vis-à-vis his rival in Istanbul, the Ottoman sultan, for being "so pathetically lazy in carrying out similar reform, that the future of the entire Sultanate will be hanging in the balance."[8]

That first parliamentary council was made of seventy-five members elected by an assembly of rural and urban notables who were top salaried government employees or taxpayers.[9] Limited in its representation and legislative powers, that council was the crowning of the first cycle of Egypt's liberal quest. As the case often is, that first council, which was quite timid in its early years, gained so much self-confidence that it challenged the kedive and was at the forefront of what came to be known as the Urabi Revolt of 1881. The deputies simply refused to rubber-stamp a new tax bill without their own proper auditing of the state budget.[10] One of the more outspoken deputies invoked a slogan of the American Revolution: "No taxation without representation." To quell this unexpected parliamentary defiance, Kedive Tawfiq (Isma'il's son) issued a decree dissolving the council. To his surprise, the deputies refused to disband and barricaded themselves in the council building. Another outspoken deputy invoked the French revolutionary leader Mirabeau's phrase in a similar situation: "On our dead bodies."[11] This act of parliamentary defiance triggered a similar rebellion in the army and a popular uprising demanding "a proper constitution," with complete separation of the branches of the government and full accountability of the executive to the legislature. This chain of events prompted Kedive Tawfiq to resort to external help to put down what was becoming a full-fledged revolution. It ultimately led to the British occupation of Egypt in 1882, bringing the first sixteen-year democratic experiment to an end. However, many of Egypt's other sociocultural liberal elements endured under the British. Liberalism in Egypt may have been even more enhanced under the British because of the instituting of full measures protecting private property, free trade, and the market economy—all of which would further empower both the landed bourgeoisie and the NMC. In due course, these social formations demanded political independence from Britain and a constitutional democracy. Thanks to a famous popular uprising, known by the Egyptians as the 1919 Revolution, both goals were achieved. In February 1922, Britain granted Egypt independence, and King Fu'ad (son of Tawfiq and grandson of Isma'il) agreed to a liberal constitution in 1923, thus ushering in the second cycle of Egypt's liberalism.

Egypt's long liberal march, a few decades later, was paralleled in a score of Arab countries. Although nominally parts of the Ottoman Empire, Iraq, Lebanon, and Tunisia at different points in the nineteenth century gained substantial autonomy and under the leadership of ambitious modernizers instituted large-scale socioeconomic and educational reforms that within one generation created NMCs. With liberal values but initially apolitical, these NMCs, in due time, became politically assertive, first against the Ottomans (from the mid-nineteenth century to World War I), then against Western occupying powers (e.g., Britain, France, and Italy) during the interwar period (1918–1939).

The liberal march for Iraq started with Dawood Pasha (1830) and continued under his successor, Midhat Pasha (1869). Besides sending young Iraqis to study abroad, he brought in foreign trainers to newly created modern institutions. Midhat Pasha was in a hurry to emulate his Egyptian counterpart (Kedive Isma'il). He proposed a constitution for Iraq in 1869—just three years after that of Egypt. Though it did not materialize due to his untimely death, it was a clear indication of a prevailing trend among several rulers of the Arab provinces of the Ottoman Empire. Obviously, they were taking advantage of a declining center while trying to ward off encroaching Western colonial designs.[12]

In Tunisia, an energetic reformer, Khyr al-Din (d. 1889), and in Mount Lebanon a local ruler, Bashir al-Shihabi, initiated similar reforms in the first half of the nineteenth century. Al-Shihaby was so impressed by the Egyptian model that he closely allied himself with Muhammad Ali and his son Ibrahim Pasha against the Ottoman sultan. His fortunes ran out with the demise of the Egyptian rule in Greater Syria. Though never matured to the same political level of Egypt, whatever sociocultural elements introduced by these reformers in Iraq, Tunisia, and Syria outlived their originators.

PRINCIPAL CHARACTERISTICS

Among the most salient features of the first cycle of the Arab liberal age was the proliferation of a variety of civil society organizations. Students of the subject mark the beginning of modern Western-style Arab CSOs from the time the Greek expatriates living in Egypt established the Hellenistic Philanthropic Association in Alexandria in 1821; native upper- and middle-class Egyptians soon followed suit. Active pioneers in this regard were the Egyptians who had studied in Europe and were familiar with the role of these organizations in complementing state institutions or filling in where such institutions were nonexistent or ineffective. By the end of the nineteenth century, some 65 CSOs had been established. By 1925, the number had increased nearly fivefold to 300, and by 1950 to over 3,000.[13]

Most of these early CSOs were welfare associations. Later, some were established to perform developmental tasks and over time became known as community development associations (CDAs). Still a third type took on advocacy functions—that is, promotion and propagation of specific causes or enhancement of certain interests. Some of these were public and registered—like cooperatives, clubs, and trade unions. What made these CSOs effective was their voluntary membership.[14] They reactivated older native traditions of *awkaf* (religious endowments), Sufi orders, and guilds in modern secular forms.

There were also politically motivated secret societies. Initially manned by Arab students abroad, from the mid-nineteenth century to World War I they were devoted to resisting Ottoman rule and later (1920s–1950s) that of Western colonial powers. There were often public "legitimate CSOs" that functioned as cover for these underground secret societies. Their significance lies in the fact that they were incubators for many of the leaders of the independence movements who actually became the rulers in the postindependence era.[15]

The press also played a significant role in the flowering of the first and second cycles of Arab liberalism. Newspapers sprouted very rapidly, and in Egypt the number of newspapers grew from one in 1800 to twenty-three in 1900. In Lebanon, the number grew from three to forty-six during the same century. These papers were less news-oriented and more engaged in polemics and expressions of opinions. The media entrepreneurs in Egypt and the rest of the Arab world consisted disproportionately of Lebanese Christians who had suffered from Ottoman discriminatory practices through the nineteenth century. The ones who took refuge in Egypt started publishing houses, some of which still exist today and are known worldwide—Al-Ahram and Al-Hilal, for example. Publications from these houses preached liberal values and practices. The fact that much of the content was polemical triggered protracted debates among prominent thinkers, politicians, and lay readers.[16] Among the topics of such heated debates were Darwinism, Marxism, secularism, Arab nationalism, Islamic reformation, and women's emancipation and unveiling. One such debate, about the earth revolving around the sun, was triggered as late as 1876. Both Muslim and Christian clerics coalesced in refuting this claim, "which goes against indisputable divine text—verses of the Holy Qur'an and Bible."[17] To their credit, passionate as they were, the contenders in these debates maintained a climate of tolerance. Moreover, the period also witnessed the rise of reformist Islam as exemplified by Muhammad Abduh's views.

Thus, many of the values and practices associated with liberalism did in fact exist in the Arab world as early as the second half of the nineteenth century. To be sure, these liberal beliefs and practices were prevalent among a limited stratum of society—that is, the modern educated Arabs. Strategically located at the time, this stratum had manned the newly established institutions during the reign of early indigenous reformers in the nineteenth century. It was also this stratum that led the resistance against Western colonial occupation in their respective countries during the first half of the twentieth century, and from their ranks rose the early postindependence rulers and state builders.

THE END OF LIBERAL EXPERIENCE

The form of governance chosen partly by the new native rulers and partly by the colonial or mandatory authorities was a pluralistic, multiparty constitutional democracy. It was not surprising that Egypt, Iraq, and Jordan modeled theirs along a British-type constitutional monarchy, while Syria and Lebanon modeled theirs after that of France.[18] Naturally, these were models adapted to the specificities of each country. Thus, the questions of religion and identity were debated and handled somewhat differently in each case, as reflected in their respective constitutions. The 1923 Egyptian constitution, for example, skirted the question of "national identity" but not that of religion. Though one of the articles asserted full equality of all Egyptian citizens before the law, regardless of their race, religion, or creed, another article stipulated that the "religion of the state is Islam." The first Syrian constitution (1942), on the other hand, did the opposite, that is, ignored the religion of the state but not the national identity. An early article asserted that "Syria is an integral part of the Arab Homeland; and its people is an integral part of the Arab Nation." Lebanon and Iraq ignored both issues. Other than these country-specific features, all Arab constitutions were quite on par with their European counterparts in terms of guaranteeing basic freedoms and human rights. The governance dimension of the Arab liberal age came to an end in most of the countries that had it during the 1950s and 1960s, at the young ages of thirty to forty years. Its early mortality was caused by several factors. The most immediate of these was the 1948 Arab defeat in Palestine at the hands of the newly established Jewish state of Israel. The Arab public opinion was primed by the demagogic press that the mission would amount to no more than "a one or two weeks picnic."[19] It turned out to be a real war that lingered for several months and ended in a humiliating defeat. The returning armies blamed the defeat on their liberal governments. Allegations of corruption and treason were flown in all directions. This paved the way for a series of military coups d'état: Syria (1949), Egypt (1952), Iraq (1958), Sudan (1958), and Libya (1969).

But the 1948 defeat in Palestine was not the only cause of the discreditation of the liberal regimes. One important cause was widespread discontent resulting from the neglect of what was termed the "social question." From the 1930s on, Arab critics and foreign observers noted growing imbalances in the distribution of wealth and power among various social classes. Such imbalances worsened in the 1940s as a result of higher rates of population growth, urbanization, and the stresses and strains of World War II, of which the Arab world was one of the two major theaters. With the postwar demobilization, the rates of unemployment skyrocketed in Arab urban centers. Fascist, socialist, and Islamic movements exploited this state of affairs by fomenting anger among the growing disenfranchised new urban proletariat. The burning of Cairo, on January 26, 1952, was the most dramatic manifestation of this growing popular anger.[20]

The Arab countries with civilian liberal governments were not able to act independently, because they were tied by practices, defense agreements, or aid to their former colonial masters. One of these ties was in the form of foreign military bases on their soil. Four of these countries, Egypt, Iraq, Jordan, and Libya, were constitutional monarchies. On paper, the monarch was to reign, not rule. However, in all four countries, each king meddled substantially in politics. Consequently, elected governments hardly acted independently from the throne. In the rare cases when they did, the elected government and its parliament were dissolved and a minority or transitional cabinet was appointed until new elections were held. The nonelected minority and the transitional governments ruled in Egypt and Iraq longer than the majority elected parties did during the so-called Arab liberal age because of the persistent machination of the throne and foreign powers. This state of affairs crippled elected governments and cast doubt on the viability of the multiparty democratic system. Hence, when military regimes took over, dissolved political parties, and did away with democracy, hardly any tears were shed.

ARAB POPULISM

The first military coup d'état in reaction to the Arab defeat in Palestine occurred in Syria in 1949, but it was Egypt that provided the archetype of a military regime, not only for the Arab world, but also for Africa, Asia, and Latin America. Gamal Abdel Nasser disliked being the leader of a military coup d'état. In 1954, he authored a book titled *The Philosophy of the Revolution*, in which he asserted that what the Free Officers did on the night of July 23, 1952, was, in fact, a revolutionary action. Its intention was not only to change the ruling regime but also to transform the entire society. The new Egyptian rulers undertook far-reaching distributive measures that dramatically affected the country's class structure and educational system and reoriented its economic life.[21] These measures were meant to address the "social question" for the benefit of the less privileged in society, who were neglected by governments during the liberal age (1920s–1950s). The targeted constituencies initially showed support and enthusiasm. The new regime addressed deep-seated national political sentiments and aspirations, and declared its anticolonialist, anti-Zionist, and anti-Communist orientations. The nationalization of the Suez Canal and the gallant resistance to the Anglo-French-Israeli invasion (1956) enhanced Nasser's charisma as a Pan-Arab leader. When Syria and Egypt were joined in what was called the United Arab Republic in 1958, the credibility of Nasser's vision was enhanced. This vision came to be known by students of the Arab and third world as a populist social contract (PSC). It promised the fulfillment of all the desirable popular demands—for example, social justice, free education, full employment, free health care, the liberation of Palestine, and Arab unification.[22]

The PSC tantalized the Arab masses for much of the 1950s and 1960s. Enough of the promises were fulfilled to keep people's expectations alive if not soaring. More sober observers at the time questioned the price that was being asked of the masses in return, namely, a suspension of basic political rights, democracy, and other public freedoms. Obviously, there was an implicit mass endorsement of the PSC, and clearly only members of the upper-middle and upper classes, in other words, no more than 25 percent of the population, agitated for democracy and basic freedoms.

However, this situation changed substantially with the 1967 Arab defeat by Israel in the Six-Day War. The shock of the swift defeat paralyzed the Arab masses for several weeks. Investigating the causes of the defeat and putting the responsible military commanders on trial took several months. But as the public sensed attempts at cover-ups, because of the lenient sentences dealt to the responsible parties, massive demonstrations broke out in all major urban centers, protesting and demanding democracy. Nasser responded to the public anger by issuing the February 28 Declaration (1968), in which he reiterated his regime's responsibility for the defeat and stated that "a major reason behind it was the absence of accountability, which could only be assured through democracy."[23] He promised to return to a full democratic system as soon as "the traces of aggression are removed." But Nasser died two years later, and it took his successor, President Anwar el-Sadat, several more years to wage another war (1973) to remove those "traces of aggression" (i.e., the Israeli occupation of Egyptian Sinai) and to begin the process of restoring democracy (1976).

Thus, it was the 1948 defeat in the first Arab-Israeli war that expedited the demise of the first Arab liberal regimes, and it was the second defeat, in the 1967 Arab-Israeli war, that ushered in the beginning of the end of the Arab radical populist regimes. However, while it took only a decade (1949–1958) for the liberal regimes to disintegrate, it is taking much longer for radical populist regimens to fall, or to change substantially from within. Equally, it is taking much longer than previously anticipated, and more than is the case elsewhere in the world, for democratic systems to be reinstituted in the Arab countries. One possible explanation for this protracted transition is the unfolding role of another radicalism, that is, political Islam.

AN ISLAMIC LEGACY

In the aftermath of the 1967 defeat, it was not only liberal democratic forces that emerged to reclaim the mantle of societal leadership but others as well— ranging from Arab radical left, à la George Habash's Popular Front for the Liberation of Palestine, to a variety of Islamic movements. The Arab radical left had brief moments of capturing headlines in the late 1960s and early 1970s, mainly through the sensational hijacking of passenger airplanes or fomenting civil strife, as in Jordan (1970) and Lebanon (1972–1975). But in terms of regime change, this radical left had only one modest success in South Yemen (1968).

It was radical political Islam that seemed to have more staying power, both in the Arab world and in neighboring Muslim countries. Islamic groups challenged the Sadat regime in Egypt as early as April 1974, till one of them assassinated Sadat in October 1981. The challenge continued to his successor, Hosni Mubarak, violently in the 1990s and peacefully as represented by the Muslim Brotherhood afterward. Similar violent confrontations with militant Islamists took place in Saudi Arabia (seizure of the Grand Mosque at Mecca) and Tunisia (at the town of Jafsa) at the end of 1978. But what made the Islamic alternative more credible was the success of the Islamic Revolution in Iran in 1979.

The success of the Iranian revolution gave a tremendous moral boost to advocates of the Islamic vision in several Arab countries. Its proponents posed a serious challenge to the entrenched populist regimes in Egypt, Sudan, Algeria, and Yemen. Only in Sudan did they manage to seize power through a military coup d'état in 1989. However, the bloodshed entailed in the Islamists' challenge to regimes in Algeria and Egypt, the harsh and backward implementation of *Shari'a* by the Iranian revolution, and later the rise of the Taliban in Afghanistan in the 1990s caused a disillusionment with the Islamic alternative. Even the Iranian revolution lost its vigor. Its "reign of terror" at home and adventurism abroad discredited its version of the Islamic vision.[24] By the beginning of the twenty-first century, the promising Islamic legacy in practice looked, after two decades, to be no better than secular populist autocracies in the region. In some ways, it proved even worse by justifying its practices on sacred religious grounds.

THE POST–SEPTEMBER 11 PICTURE

The events of September 11, 2001, have had many far-reaching consequences in the United States and abroad. One of these consequences may turn out to be the beginning of the end of militant political Islam. Should this occur, it will not be so much because of the devastating American military reaction, but rather due to a painful collective reassessment of the entire Islamic legacy as projected in the last quarter of the twentieth century. It also means that the Islamic legacy will be cut down to human size and move toward moderation.

In fact, this has been happening to some degree in Turkey, Morocco, and Bahrain. All three countries held parliamentary elections at the end of 2002 and the beginning of 2003. In all three, Islamic political parties ran a campaign of moderation, tolerance, and affirmation of utmost respect for the rules of democratic governance. Such expressions should not be taken at face value, because in politics what matters is actual behavior as perceived by the respective constituencies. Nevertheless, the fact that the Islamic Justice and Development Party obtained the biggest bloc of votes in Turkey and the third biggest in Morocco and Bahrain is indicative of its credibility. Should this moderate trend continue and expand to other Arab and Middle Eastern countries, the prospects of liberal democracies in the region will become brighter. An eminent Islamic thinker, Sheikh Gamal al-Banna, has been advocating that the current Islamic movements evolve into Muslim democratic parties, akin to the Christian democratic parties in Western Europe.[25] His writings on this issue and on Islamic reformation in general have resonated with wider circles since September 11. His credibility is partly due to the fact that he is the only surviving brother of the famous Hasan al-Banna, the founder of the Muslim Brotherhood (1928).

RETREAT OF ARAB RADICALISM

Over the past thirty years, namely since the 1967 Arab defeat, one radical ideology after another has displayed varying but definite signs of retreat. The first was Nasser's quasi-socialist populist Pan-Arabism, plus those modeled after Nasser in Iraq, Syria, Libya, Algeria, Yemen, and Sudan, albeit not simultaneously. For some, it took nearly three decades. Nor did the retreat necessarily mean regime change or even its collapse. It simply meant a toning down of rhetorical aggressive policies abroad and loss of appeal at home. In some cases, a radical Arab regime was replaced or succeeded by another radical regime. This was the case in Iraq, where the radical regime of Abdul Karim Qassim was replaced by a Ba'thist radical regime in 1963, then by Abdulsalam Aref's regime in 1963, and again by another Ba'thist, Hassan al-Bakr, and his associate Saddam Hussein, from 1968 to 2003. Something similar occurred in Syria, Sudan, and Yemen.

The most significant radical retreat is one in the regime's own policies and practices. A case in point is that of the de-Nasserization of Egypt by Anwar el-Sadat (1970–1981). Another example is that of Ja'afar Numairy in Sudan, in which the same regime and the same leader's policies shifted from socialist to capitalist to Islamic radicalism in sixteen years (1969–1975). Libya's Muammar Qaddafi, since 1969, has shifted from extreme Pan-Arabism to extreme Pan-Islamism to extreme Pan-Africanism. His sharpest turn is his capitulation in 2003 to his former Western foes (the United States, the United Kingdom, and France) over previously contested issues of terrorism and weapons of mass destruction.

The fall of Iraq's Ba'thist regime following the war with a U.S.-led coalition (April 9, 2003) was so dramatic that many observers predicted the further retreat, if not the total demise, of other radical regimes in Syria, Libya, Sudan, and neighboring non-Arab Iran.

THE RETURN OF LIBERALISM

With every defeat or retreat of Arab radicalism, whether secular or religious, the door opens for the return of liberalism. It is almost a zero-sum game. This occurred first in the economic sphere in Egypt and Tunisia in the 1970s, following the October war and the skyrocketing of Arab oil revenues.[26] Many of the poor Arab command economies began to liberalize, partly to attract deposits, remittances, and investments from oil-rich Arab countries. The rulers who undertook economic liberalization measures may have not intended to go beyond that. But there are always unintended consequences of human actions.

Certainly, no significant democratization took place simultaneously with, or following, economic liberalization, but there were greater freedoms of expression and travel. Three years after the October war, Egypt reinstituted a limited multiparty system to replace the one-party system that had been in effect for more than thirty years. Each new party was allowed to have its own publications. The number of Egyptian newspapers jumped from four to fourteen between 1976 and 1986 and to sixty-two by 1996.

Two other wars also contributed to greater fluidity in the region—the Lebanese civil war (1975–90) and the Iraq-Iran War (1980–88). Both contributed in peculiar ways to the mushrooming of Arab media in diasporas, which enjoyed much greater freedom than their counterparts at home. Notably among these were the *Al-Hayat* and *Al-Sharq Al-Awsat* Arab dailies. Though published in London, Paris, or Cyprus, these newspapers found their way back to the home readership. With the Internet, in the 1990s such readership jumped to tens of millions.

The first Gulf War (1990–91), to liberate Kuwait from Iraqi occupation, ushered in yet one more avenue of freedom of expression—that is, Arab satellite television networks. The most well known of these is Aljazeera, which transmits from the small Gulf state of Qatar. But there were others before (e.g., Orbit, Middle East Broadcasting Centre) and many after (e.g., Arabiya, Mustakila, Abu Dhabi, Lebanese Broadcasting Corporation, and Al-Huriya). The new media has opened up the Arab public space as never before. The competition for an ever-growing viewership has improved the professional quality and expanded the margins of freedom even in countries still controlled by the more repressive authoritarian regimes.

Arab monarchies have been, on the whole, more responsive than their republican counterparts to domestic demands for change and to regional and global developments. Despite rough starts in the 1950s and 1960s, King Hussein of Jordan and King Hassan of Morocco earned their tenure in the 1990s with significant political reforms. Both presided over steady democratization, which allowed at least three successive parliamentary elections.[27] Their successors to the throne, Abdullah II and Muhammad VI, respectively, continued the practice of relatively fair and honest elections into the twenty-first century. Opposition groups, including leftists and Islamists, have participated, won seats in those elections, and occasionally occupied cabinet positions. This seems to have contributed to a marked political stability in both countries, despite the ups and downs of economic conditions. The young king of Morocco is equally leading a social revolution. In November 2003, he urged the Moroccan parliament to approve a radical family bill that gives Moroccan women equal rights with men in all matters of marriage, divorce, child custody, and the like. The bill was approved in December 2003. On January 7, 2004, the king went an extra mile toward the accommodation of victims of human rights violations during the reign of his father, Hassan II. He announced the establishment of the National Commission for Fairness and Reconciliation—an organization similar to that established by Nelson Mandela in South Africa upon the fall of the white racist regime in 1994.

Virtually evolving into constitutional monarchies, Morocco and Jordan have become role models for other Arab monarchies in Bahrain, Qatar, and Oman. All three have moved in the same direction. Bahrain was the swiftest, not only in democratization but also in establishing political gender equality. Even the staunchly conservative Saudi Arabia has moved more forcefully toward more representative governance. A Saudi *shura* (consultative) council was established shortly after the first Gulf War (1991) but has limited, symbolic powers. Shortly after the Iraq war (2003), Saudi Arabia announced plans for municipal and local elections. Along with this greater opening of the Saudi system, several new civil society organizations have formed and engaged Crown Prince Abdullah in an active dialogue over sociopolitical-educational reform.[28]

Thus, it is the monarchies that are currently leading the newest cycle of Arab liberalization, while the weighty republics of Egypt, Syria, Tunisia, Algeria, and Libya are reluctant and falling behind. It must be noted that this impulse for liberalization is not merely a function of the good hearts of these kings. It is as much in response to growing domestic and external pressures. In the case of Morocco, for example, the number of NGOs has mushroomed from less than 20,000 in 1980 to more than 80,000 in 2003, many of which are human rights and women's advocacy pressure groups, networking with European counterparts, especially in France. In the case of the Gulf Arab states, the events of September 11 and their aftermath focused Western, especially U.S., attention on the need for overall sociopolitical reform, which converged with long-standing domestic demands. This benign convergence tipped the balance against the old conservative forces long using narrow interpretations of Islam to resist such changes. The battle is far from over and occasional reversals are to be expected. But thanks to the steady and rapid growth of the NMCs, the pressure for sustainable reform now has substantial indigenous support. Since the 1970s, oil revenues have helped build modern institutions, which expanded the NMC in all the Gulf states, including Iraq and Iran. The fall of the despotic regime of Saddam Hussein in Iraq (April 2003) has unleashed many suppressed forces and sent many signals to rulers and people in the region. In many respects, these forces would enhance liberalization and democratization—closing the deficits that the 2002 United Nations Arab Human Development Report dramatically highlighted.

However, the fact that regime change was brought about with the help of a coalition of Western powers, thus symbolizing "foreign occupation," is unleashing another set of patriotic-nationalist forces. The danger for the reformists is to be viewed by the conservative forces as agents, not of change, but of foreign occupation. Thus, the fate of this latest cycle of Arab liberalization is contingent on, among other factors, how rapidly the visible symbols of foreign occupation can be removed. By the same token, because liberalization and democracy have been closely associated with the West, local detractors will continue to resist them so long as other outstanding accounts from the colonial legacy have not yet been settled. The most potent and complicated of these is the Palestinian question.

CONCLUSION

It is often said that for Middle Easterners, history never dies, but merely fades away temporarily, to come back full circle. At least this seems to be the case with liberalism in the Arab world. This time around, at least four things are new and different. New countries that did not even exist as states during earlier cycles are zealously joining the latest wave of liberalism. Sociopolitical formations that had previously flirted with radical populism or militant Islamism are either reacting to or seriously revising their beliefs and practices to join or come closer to other liberal forces. Though somewhat impoverished in some Arab countries, the

NMCs are growing and steadily reclaiming liberal values and democratic ideas. Finally, with the cold war over, Western powers seem more committed to advancing a democratic system in the Arab world—at least in the hope that more inclusionary governance would serve as an antidote to both religious extremism and terrorism. In short, there are more chances at this time for sustainable liberal democracies in the Arab world than ever before.

NOTES

1. "President Bush Discusses Freedom in Iraq and Middle East" (remarks by the president at the twentieth anniversary of the National Endowment for Democracy, United States Chamber of Commerce, Washington, DC, November 6, 2003), http://www.white house.gov/news/releases/2003/11/20031106-2.html.

2. Fareed Zakaria, *The Future of Freedom: Illiberal Democracy at Home and Abroad* (New York: W. W. Norton, 2003), 19.

3. Abdulla Laroui, *Azmat al-Muthakafin al-Arab* [Crisis of Arab Intellectuals] (Beirut: Dar al Talia'a, 1970), 11–28.

4. Albert Hourani, *Arabic Thought in the Liberal Age,* rev. ed. (Cambridge: Cambridge University Press, 1983), 1–60.

5. Abdul Rahman al-Jabarti, *Ajaib al-Athar fi-Tarajim wa al-Akhbar* (Cairo: Bulaq, 1880), 4:266.

6. Khaled Fahmy, *All the Pasha's Men* (Cairo: American University in Cairo Press, 2002), 76–111.

7. Saad Eddin Ibrahim, *Egypt, Islam, and Democracy* (Cairo: American University in Cairo Press, 2002), 21.

8. Ibid., 22.

9. Mohammed Ouda, *al-Demokratiya al-Urabiya* [Urabi Democracy] (Cairo: Al-Ahali, 1982), 5.

10. Ibid., 55.

11. Ibid.

12. Hourani, *Arabic Thought,* 305–6.

13. Ibrahim, *Egypt, Islam, and Democracy,* 234.

14. Ibid., 240.

15. Ibid., 13–20.

16. Hourani, *Arabic Thought,* 110–50.

17. Rifaat El Said, *Alliberaliya al Misriyya* [Egyptian Liberalism] (Cairo: Al-Ahli, 2003), 67.

18. Michael Hudson, *Arab Politics: The Search for Legitimacy* (New Haven, CT: Yale University Press, 1977).

19. Ibrahim, *Egypt, Islam, and Democracy,* 13.

20. Nazih N. Ayubi, *Over-Stating the Arab State: Politics and Society in the Middle East* (London: I. B. Tauris, 1995), 106–8.

21. Ibid., 135–38.

22. Ibid., 196–224.

23. Ibrahim, *Egypt, Islam, and Democracy,* 112.

24. Abdulaziz Sachedina, *The Islamic Roots of Democratic Pluralism* (Oxford: Oxford University Press, 2001), 58–60.

25. Gamal al-Banna, *Demokratiya Jadida* [New Democracy], 2nd ed. (Cairo: Dar al-Fikr al-Islami, 2000), 79–122.

26. Ibrahim, *Egypt, Islam, and Democracy*, 10–73.

27. Ibid.

28. *Al-Sharq Al Awsat Daily,* July 16, 2003; January 8, 2004.

14

Hindrances to Democracy and Modernization in Indonesia

Fred R. von der Mehden

Indonesia is not only the most populous Muslim country, but also one of the biggest and newest democracies striving to modernize its economy. However, it has attained this position only after experiencing decades of political and economic difficulties. To understand why Indonesia faced such a rocky road, it is necessary to analyze the country's development in the light of its colonial and postcolonial history and the fundamentals of the republic's economic and political infrastructure. It is the contention of this chapter that democracy and modernization can best be achieved with an educated population, a well-trained bureaucracy, a sense of national identity rather than ethnic and religious fragmentation, and elite and mass support for democratic values. Hindrances to these desirable foundations are analyzed, followed by an assessment of the impact of Islam on contemporary efforts to attain modernization and democracy.

IMPACT OF COLONIALISM

Three centuries of Dutch colonial rule provided Indonesia with experience with a money economy, developed the archipelago's natural resources, and established a rudimentary representative political system. However, twentieth-century colonial policies resulted in a number of conditions that had negative implications for independent Indonesia's efforts to achieve democracy and modernization. This was particularly true with regard to education, bureaucratic, economic, and political experience, and the development of a sense of national identity.

Education

The Dutch did not develop a well-educated population at the mass or elite level. The 1930 census, the last complete accurate count during the colonial period, showed that only 6.4 percent of all Indonesians were literate.[1] Of that group, only 5 percent could write in Dutch, the language of modern commerce and science at that time in the Indies. Unfortunately, the depression forced a decrease in government expenditure on education in the 1930s, declining by approximately 40 percent during the decade. Not only was there mass illiteracy, but only a small percentage of Indonesians received upper-level schooling. The 1930 census reported that only 10,021 Indonesian pupils were enrolled in Western advanced elementary and secondary schools, and only 637 were participating in university education (plus another small number in universities in the Netherlands). In sum, the educational foundation for democracy and modernization was weak at the end of the colonial era. These conditions declined even further during the Japanese occupation and years of nationalist conflict following World War II.

Bureaucracy

A well-trained bureaucracy is essential to implement government programs. The Dutch maintained a relatively large European element in their bureaucracy, particularly at the upper levels. Among middle-level government personnel in 1938, more than 60 percent were European, but among the 3,029 at the upper level, only 7.3 percent were Indonesian.[2] In part, this paucity of Indonesians in upper levels of the bureaucracy was due to the unwillingness of many educated nationalists to join the colonial government. However, making the postindependence bureaucracy even less experienced was the fact that many Indonesian upper civil servants were Christians, who later often did not keep their positions because of questions of loyalty.

National Identity

If there is little sense of national identity and if religious, ethnic, or regional fragmentation is present, it is difficult to successfully implement democracy or modernization. The Dutch colonial system divided the colony into areas, one of which was Java, with some two-thirds of the colony's population, where the administration was directly run by the Dutch. In other parts of the archipelago the system of indirect rule placed governance under the nominal leadership of local traditional leaders. In the first instance, nationalism flourished and there was a greater sense among the population of being Indonesian. Where traditional rulers were the symbolic powers, loyalty tended to be more local and nationalism weaker. In addition, many indigenous Christians felt loyalty to the Dutch and joined them in opposition to the nationalists. During the postwar nationalist conflict the Dutch reinforced this division by forming a quasi-federal system led by local pro-Dutch leaders. The result was postindependence conflicts, as groups in various parts of the islands sought to maintain their autonomy, become independent, or even become part of the Netherlands.

Economic Power

Under the colonial system, economic power in the Indies was in the hands of either the Europeans or the Chinese minority. The Europeans tended to be in control of larger financial, mining, and plantation activities, while the Chinese dominated smaller commercial operations that were used by the indigenous population. Disparities in ownership and income were obvious. In 1939, there were 33,165 Europeans with over 1 million guilders in property and only 1,500 Indonesians with the same amount, although the former was less than 1 percent of the population and Indonesians approximately 97 percent. This not only resulted in an Indonesian population with little commercial experience, but also led to strong anticapitalist views within the nationalist elite. The prewar Communists defined this situation in terms of Marxist class warfare while the leader of the largest Muslim nationalist party stated that there were two classes, the rich Dutch Christians and the poor Indonesian Muslims.[3]

Political Fragmentation

Although it was not the fault of the colonial system per se, the prewar era produced a fragmented political party pattern that has plagued Indonesian politics to this day. Not only were there divisions on the left between Socialists and Communists, but the Islamic parties were also not able to establish a consistent consensus. Sarekat Islam, the first mass nationalist party, initially dominated the political scene, but what followed was political fragmentation on religious, economic, and personality bases. This reflected fundamental differences among the politically aware elements in the Indies, as no party or leader was capable of coalescing the disparate forces.

Weak Representative Institutions

Experience with democratic institutions is important for the development of a strong democracy. The Dutch began to establish representative government at the national level early in the twentieth century with the formation of the Volksraad (people's council). There were also provincial, regency, and local councils with Indonesian elected members. However, the Volksraad never developed into a truly representative legislature, and in the last elections prior to World War II, less than a third of the members elected were Indonesians (there were also appointed Indonesians).[4] In addition, many nationalists either would not participate in these activities or were not allowed to because of their illegal political activities. Leaders such as Indonesia's first president, Ahmad Sukarno, were exiled to isolated areas and had no political experience in governing prior to the war.

In sum, the colonial experience sowed the seeds of postindependence problems, although not all the ensuing problems in modernizing and democratizing can be laid at the door of Dutch colonization. The remainder of this chapter will explore hindrances to these goals during the three postindependence periods: the Sukarno years, from 1945 to 1967; Suharto and the New Order, from 1967 to 1998; and the present experiment with democracy. Finally, consideration will be given the role of Islam in this process.

THE SUKARNO YEARS: THE FIRST DEMOCRATIC EXPERIMENT

Indonesia declared its official independence on August 14, 1945, and Ahmad Sukarno, leader under the Japanese instigated puppet regime inaugurated in 1943, became the first president of the republic. The first four years after the 1945 declaration were not auspicious for either democracy or modernization because of a colonial-nationalist conflict. During this period, there was little postwar reconstruction, and by 1949 much of the leadership of the republic was incarcerated. Meanwhile, the Dutch established a federal system with many of the states with relatively little public support. The conflict also divided Christian and other minorities from the nationalists, and many educated Indonesians became persona non grata to republican supporters.

The republic was finally reestablished in 1950, but it faced several conditions that made democracy and modernization difficult to achieve. First, modernization was hindered by the lack of a well-trained bureaucracy, as many bureaucrats of the colonial regime were either rejected by the republic or decided to enter politics. The lack of a strong bureaucracy was particularly apparent outside Java, where most of the country's export economy was based. There was also a high level of corruption widespread at all levels. This situation was exacerbated by the socialist orientation of the political leadership, which put demands on the bureaucracy that it could not meet, thus weakening the government's legitimacy.

Second, there was considerable suspicion regarding Western political and economic intentions, and anticapitalism was strong. It grew more virulent during the latter years of the Sukarno regime (1958 to 1965). The largest Communist party in a non-Communist state existed in Indonesia by the early 1960s. Prewar plantations, factories, and mining interests found it difficult to reestablish themselves as government regulations and labor unrest hindered their efforts.[5] Beginning in 1957, first Dutch and later British interests were nationalized. In 1958, the remaining Dutch were expelled from Indonesia. Exports steadily declined after 1959, particularly in the nonpetroleum sectors. Most foreign investment dried up by the early 1960s. Inept development planning and implementation meant that the physical infrastructure was not repaired and, in fact, deteriorated. Inflation became hyperinflation by the early 1960s, and foreign imports became a trickle. As the economy declined, semifeudal military units took control of the economy in export-oriented sections of the archipelago, further depriving the central government of much-needed funds. This extremely difficult situation was further exacerbated by military expenditures rising from successful efforts to obtain West Irian from the Dutch and by the unsuccessful armed confrontation with Malaysia over the formation of that country in 1963. The result of these factors was that Indonesian recovery from the devastations of World War II was significantly later than that of other Southeast Asian states, such as Malaya (Malaysia) and Thailand.

Finally, Sukarno became increasingly disenchanted with Western concepts of development, commenting that Indonesian greatness did not need economic development and that the country could successfully incorporate any size population. At the end of his era, financial assistance from abroad was almost nonexistent. By the mid-1960s the Indonesian economy was in shambles and economic development had come to a standstill or had even deteriorated.

Indonesia did attempt to establish a pluralist democracy in the decade after independence and held its first national elections in 1955. These were free and generally untainted by fraud or coercion. However, the political fragmentation that had been a hallmark of prewar politics returned, and the elections resulted in a parliament with four parties with approximately 20 percent of the seats each and more than two dozen smaller parties. The result was an inability to reach consensus on policies, further exacerbated by increasing tensions between the rising Communist party and the military and Muslim organizations.

By 1957, Sukarno ended liberal democracy and declared "guided democracy," based on a view that the competitive nature of politics of the West did not suit Indonesian culture.[6] The constitution was abrogated, parliament disbanded, and an appointed legislature formed. Sukarno condemned "50 per cent plus one democracy" and posited that consensus through discussion was the traditional Indonesian way. Opponents argued that this was simply a rationale for dictatorship. Thus, at the end of the Sukarno era neither democracy nor modernization had progressed.

SUHARTO AND THE NEW ORDER

In 1965, there was an attempted coup that led to the death of a number of high military officers and ultimately implicated both the Communists and Sukarno. The military, led by General (later President) Suharto, used this as the rationale for moving against both. Over the next months the military, aided by Muslim youth groups, killed several hundred thousand Communists and alleged Communists and imprisoned many others, thereby eliminating the Communist party.[7] In the years following the attempted coup, Sukarno was gradually eased out, dying in house arrest in 1970. This ushered in three decades of military-dominated rule, called the New Order. An end to the political and economic problems of the latter Sukarno years became the foundation for the new regime's policies with regard to democracy and modernization. In the name of stability and national unity, a facade democracy was established that had all the accoutrements of democracy, including elections and democratic institutions. In reality, political party activity was prohibited, elections were controlled, allegiance to the national ideology, the Pancasila, was demanded of all public organizations, and dissent was discouraged. This facade was considered useful domestically to ease pressure on the regime and internationally to legitimize the New Order for investors and donors.

In contrast to the government of Sukarno, the New Order set out on a path of modernization based on a market economy and foreign investment. As with the facade democracy institutions, this was also seen as a means of legitimizing the regime and gaining popular support. Suharto liked to be known as the Father of Development, and his regime used Western-trained technocrats to foster the new economic system. Under their leadership, most barriers to foreign investment were dropped after an initial hesitancy based on protectionist interests. There is little doubt that the economy grew rapidly during the initial decades of the Suharto years. Gross domestic product (GDP) rose at an annual average of over 8 percent in the 1970s, dropped to 4 percent in the first half of the 1980s, and then grew again to 7 percent through much of the 1990s.[8] From 1970 to 1996, the Indonesian economy grew on the average of 7.2 percent per year. Inflation dropped from its dramatic highs of the 1960s with some minor resurgence in the mid-1970s, oil production more than doubled in the decade after 1967, and major liquefied natural gas (LNG) export projects were developed. Manufacturing also rose by 15 percent a year in the 1970s and overtook oil as a source of export revenue by 1990. Domestic land, sea, and air services were modernized, thus improving communications among various islands. A national television system was established, and television became available to most of the population. Between 1976 and 1990, per capita incomes rose approximately four times and Indonesia experienced the largest reduction of poverty in the world during this period.[9] Life expectancy rose from forty-nine to sixty-five years, adult literacy increased from 57 percent to 84 percent, and infant mortality decreased by more than half.

Despite these developments, many problems, deriving from inefficiencies and disparities within the system, persisted and came to a head in the late 1990s. Today, they pose difficulties for the new democratic leaders. These problems include the lack of financial transparency and corruption. The Suharto family alone was reported to be worth some $16 billion by the late 1990s.[10] Particularly disturbing to many Indonesians were the family's close ties with wealthy members of Indonesia's Chinese community. The banking system had little oversight, and during the 1990s, in particular, there was a rapid increase in borrowing, often for projects without sufficient economic viability or with poor investments of capital. Increased foreign capital inflows could not be readily absorbed, and by the late 1990s commercial debt amounted to approximately $58 billion.

While the growing economy did "raise all boats," there were major disparities. The political and economic elite received undue profits from the system. Rural areas tended to be less advantaged and growth rates varied markedly among the provinces. Export earnings and taxation patterns aided the central government rather than the profit centers in regions where the commodity-based export economy was to be found. There was a growing sense of disillusionment, which came to a head when the economic crisis of the late 1990s hit Indonesia particularly hard.

THE NEW DEMOCRATIC EXPERIMENT

The present democratic system was born out of the economic debacle that caused Suharto's fall in 1998. The new leadership faced a significant increase in the number of Indonesians falling below the poverty line, a major drop in the value of the rupiah, the closing of more than sixty banks, high corporate debt, interest on public-sector foreign liabilities that was 30–40 percent of export incomes, an increase in the budget deficit, and declining domestic tax revenues. The International Monetary Fund (IMF) agreed to provide $43 billion in aid with severe conditions—which were not universally supported—as the way to aid the republic most efficiently.[11] How have modernization and democracy fared under these new conditions?

Modernization

The process of modernization in today's Indonesia is proceeding, but with significant obstacles. Many of the financial problems left by the former regime remain. Indonesia has been slower than other Southeast Asian countries in coming out of the 1990s financial crisis. A weak, undercapitalized banking system is reforming all too slowly. Unemployment remains very high, inflation has not been conquered, and domestic consumption is weak. Foreign investment approvals dropped significantly, particularly after the Bali bombings instigated by Muslim radicals. Tourism was badly hurt by a series of events, including the Asian economic decline, the Bali bombings, the severe acute respiratory syndrome (SARS) epidemic, and the Marriott Hotel bombing. These events, combined with various foreign governments' warnings to their citizens regarding travel to Indonesia, had a serious impact on the economy. On the positive side, gross domestic product growth has been slow but steady in recent years, down from the 7–8 percent average of the 1990s to about 3–4 percent. The rupiah has stabilized at a rate far below its highs of the late 1990s, and high oil and other commodity prices, particularly after the Iraq war, have aided the balance of payments and reduced the budget deficit. However, perceptions of political instability remain a primary obstacle to both tourism and foreign investment.

Democratization

Indonesia is no longer the facade democracy of the New Order. It is now a fragile pluralist democracy, albeit with competitive elections and freedom of speech and press. In 1999, the republic held the first free elections for the national legislature since 1955, and the April 2004 elections produced an even more fractured legislature. Again, the secular parties dominated the voting and the Islamic parties remained in the minority. The old system of indirect elections for president has been eliminated, and the first direct elections for that office in mid-2004 saw the election of Susilo Bambang Yudhoyono on a platform calling for reform and the elimination of corruption. There have been no significant criticisms regarding the democratic process by which these elections have taken place. However, Indonesia's democracy remains fragile and is vulnerable in a number of significant ways.

1. Indonesia has entered this new democratic effort with little contemporary experience with competitive politics. As previously noted, there were almost forty-five years between the first and second democratic elections, and more than forty years have passed since a freely elected legislature and executive have governed the country. At the same time, these elected officials have had to deal with the old civil and military bureaucracies with all their corruption and inefficiencies. In fact, these officials have done remarkably well, despite their inexperience.

2. Historic political fragmentation has continued, and the 1999 elections presented the Indonesian people with a parliament severely divided along party lines. The 462 elected members (38 were chosen by the military) of the People's Representative Council (DPR) divided into six parties with at least thirty members, plus seventeen minor parties. No party has held even a third of the membership. This has made it difficult to pass some legislation.

3. Political leadership in Indonesia has been accused of personal aggrandizement, a lack of party loyalty, and weak organizational abilities. An unwillingness to take difficult decisions has all too often characterized party leaders. There have been charges of corruption at the highest levels. In 2004, expatriate businessmen in Asia listed Indonesia as the most corrupt country in Asia.[12]

4. Limitations on political and religious freedom that were part of the old Suharto regime remain, although they are being revised. Some religious groups were banned under the New Order. Bans have been lifted for organizations such as the Jehovah's Witnesses and those practicing Chinese religions, but they remain officially in force for others, and "deviant" Islamic sects have been especially targeted. Identity cards still require religious identification, and atheism is not an option. All political and religious organizations are still supposed to follow the national ideology, the Pancasila. It is illegal to teach communism or to attempt to undermine the Pancasila. However, these regulations are not always implemented in practice.

5. The government's methods of containing regional autonomy movements in places like Aceh and Papua have resulted in numerous complaints by human rights groups. There have been charges that the military has been involved in killings, torture, kidnappings, and a wide range of violent actions, particularly in Aceh.[13] The post-independence Indonesian armed forces have frequently been described as weak in discipline at the lower levels and their actions against dissidents and civilians have been widely condemned in Indonesia and abroad.

6. Significant ethnic and religious divisions imperil political stability. The economic problems of the late 1990s brought attacks on minority scapegoats. The Chinese were identified with the Suharto regime and thus have been objects of retaliation. Mob actions

against the Chinese in Indonesia brought criticism from other Chinese populated states in Asia, including China, Taiwan, and Singapore. The government has been accused of being unable or unwilling to provide the necessary protection to targeted groups.

7. The judicial system remains weak, and fair trials, legal imprisonment, appropriate police activities and other elements of the rule of law are not always practiced. Additional legal pressures on the press and other media have been employed to silence criticism,[14] and the use of corruption to circumvent the law is present. This is a long-standing pattern, and the new government is attempting to address these problems.

8. The armed forces remain a threat, albeit diminishing, to democracy. In times of crisis, speculation about the possible return to power of the military increases. There has been pressure by elements of the armed forces on the civilian administration to forcibly move against autonomy movements, and occasionally military officers make statements that appear to challenge civil authority. The armed forces are also regularly accused of human rights violations across the archipelago. Yet, the old idea of *dwi-fungsi,* the view that the armed forces had both military and civil functions, is no longer promulgated. The old nonelected military representation in the DPR is gone, and the present command in principle publicly accepts civilian leadership.

9. There are those in Indonesia who argue that international donors and organizations such as the IMF make demands on the elected government that are equivalent to economic blackmail. They charge that these demands limit the ability of the people's representatives to make democratic choices.

Despite these problems, most observers do not expect to see the immediate collapse of Indonesia's fledgling democracy and a return to authoritarian rule. The fact that, for the first time, the republic is experiencing a regularized free electoral cycle is encouraging. Commissions have been established to investigate violations by authorities, and the press does complain about government activities.

THE ISLAMIC FACTOR

The final question addressed in this chapter is, What impact has Islam had on the processes of modernization and democracy?

Modernization

I have argued elsewhere that the relationship between religion and modernization in Southeast Asia is very complex and that Islam is not intrinsically against modernization.[15] In Indonesia, it is particularly difficult to interpret the Islamic factor in isolation because of the synthesis between Islam and other religious elements and because of the melding of religion and ethnicity. In the first instance, pre-Islamic traditions, whether Hindu, Buddhist, or animist, frame the beliefs of many Muslims, especially in Java. Indonesians have historically differentiated between religious and ethnic identity. For example, one prewar Sundanese, when asked why he did not become a Christian, replied, "Because I am a Sundanese."[16] Finally, deciding what can be attributed to Islam and what to traditional cultural values can be difficult. This problem with identification of causality remains an issue in many areas, such as in the analysis of forces framing women's rights in the islands.

It is possible to make the case that elements of Islamic practice could be a hindrance to modernization. It can be argued that funds and time given to any religious activity could better be employed for modernizing agents such as education. Thus, the secular modernist might consider that Islamic practices of giving alms (*zakat*) or spending on the *hajj* do not foster material development, or that fasting during Ramadan (holy month of fasting) undermines efficiency. Meanwhile, those who practice Islam can point to the discipline and strengthening of mind fostered by fasting and other religious acts. A detailed analysis is beyond the scope of this chapter. What can be said is that the process of modernization at the national level has apparently not been affected by these factors in either a positive or negative sense.

However, it can be argued that in Indonesia most religious leaders and organizations in the past century have not consciously fought modernization. Although historically there have been religious individuals who have rejected material development in the name of religious purity, this has not been the norm in the past century. At the same time, many Indonesian Muslims have rejected what they see as perverse Western values or the dominance of foreign capitalism that accompanies the modernization process and have sought security in religious identity. Traditional Indonesians confronting what they see as undesirable Western values have positively reinforced the Islamic revival in Indonesia.

The largest Muslim organization in Indonesia has been the modernist-oriented Muhammadiyah, founded in 1912.[17] From its earliest years the Muhammadiyah sought to promulgate modern education and social services for Indonesian Muslims. Nahdatul Ulama (NU), a traditionalist organization with some 30 million members, has actively engaged in rural development activities in *pesantren* (Islamic boarding schools) run by the NU.[18] During the Suharto regime, Abdurrahman Wahid, leader of the NU, argued the need to carry out rural development to meet the paucity of such programs in these areas and to lay the foundation for future democracy.[19] Other development programs through *pesantren* have included the Center for the Development of Pesantren, focusing on rural development, the Pondok Pesantren An-Nawawi, treating mental illness, and Pesantren Surialaya, treating drug addicts. It has been interesting to note the number of students from the "MIT of Indonesia," the Bandung Technological Institute, taking part in Islam-oriented development projects.

In recent years, the actions of a small element of radical Muslims, such as bombings and threats against foreigners, have adversely affected the Indonesian economy. At the local level these acts have deterred normal economic development in east Indonesia, where the Christian-Muslim conflict has been prevalent, and in Aceh, where autonomy efforts driven by historic Islamic-ethnic considerations have caused the suspension of profitable LNG operations. The economy as a whole has been adversely affected by the Bali and Marriott Hotel bombings by Islamic radicals and by warnings from foreign governments regarding the dangers of travel to Indonesia. Tourism and Western investment have suffered in particular. In sum, together with other forces of instability, these attacks have slowed Indonesia's economic recovery.

Democracy

All parties in the DPR, including those in the Islamic bloc and major nonpolitical Muslim associations, support the principles of competitive democracy. The first president after the 1999 elections and longtime leader of the Islamic NU was Abdurrahman Wahid. He has been a vocal proponent of liberal democracy and of the protection of the rights of minorities and an ardent advocate of religious tolerance. A significant number of Muslim intellectuals have presented similar positions, including Nurcholish Madjid, presidential candidate and former leader of the Muslim Students Association, and Syafi'i Ma'arif, president of Muhammadiyah. Dr. Syafi'i has argued that the idea of democracy is implicit in the Qur'anic doctrine of *shura* (consultation).

Yet Islamic elements have made statements and committed acts that can be seen as antithetical to pluralist competitive democracy. These fall into three categories:

1. statements by Muslims that Islam is not compatible with democracy;
2. violent actions against non-Muslims in the name of Islam; and
3. efforts to implement policies that are perceived to limit religious rights.

A number of Islamists have expressed negative views of democracy. The influence of Salafi Wahabis has been important in many of these cases. The leadership of the Wahabi-influenced Laskar Jihad rejected pluralist democracy as "sinful."[20] Others have argued against pluralist elements of democracy, rejecting full participation in the public sphere by religious minorities. Ahmad Sumargono, member of the Crescent Star Party and presidential candidate in 1999, has given only qualified support to democratic principles and believes that only a Muslim should be president. This position was also posited by the manifesto of the first Congress of Mujahidin in 2000, which called for prohibiting non-Muslims from holding public office if Muslims would serve.[21] While the congress purported to be a meeting of 1,500 conservative and radical individuals, its manifesto was later supported by two Islamic factions of the DPR. Elements of organizations such as the Islamic Dakwah Council and the Indonesian Committee for Solidarity with the Islamic World have expressed anti-Christian and anti-Chinese views in Islam's name. Even some members of major moderate organizations such as the Muhammadiyah have warned of the dangers arising from what they see as undue Christian influence.

Some radical Islamic groups have been willing to bypass the democratic process and employ violence against their opponents. The U.S. government has named more than a half dozen violent extremist Muslim groups.[22] In the early postindependence era there have been other small radical elements employing violence, such as Kommando Jihad in the 1970s, but they generally lacked widespread public support. The best example of a contemporary radical group expressing antipluralist views and taking violent actions against opponents has been Laskar Jihad. It was responsible for many deaths in its anti-Christian campaign in east Indonesia prior to its officially closing down in 2002. It did not receive public support from major Islamic parties but was allegedly aided by elements of the Indonesian armed forces and had the sympathy of some conservative Muslim politicians.

At this point these violent radical groups do not endanger the viability or legitimacy of the government, in spite of support by some elements in the Muslim community. Sympathy for antipluralist activists does not generally translate into support for violence. Nor has this backing translated into electoral success at the polls. Many Indonesians believe that acts such as the Bali bombings have been propagated by outside Western organizations, such as the CIA,[23] but these actions are generally seen as counter to traditional Indonesian views of tolerance.

Perhaps a more subtle danger to a pluralist democracy in Indonesia has been the effort to promulgate legislation limiting religious equality. The Islamic parties generally do not call for the present establishment of an Islamic state. However, there are calls for greater acceptance of the *Shari'a*. This issue is one of long-standing debate. At the time of the formation of the new independent state there were abortive efforts to incorporate the *Shari'a*, and various Islamic groups have since seen this as a goal. A provincial *Shari'a* court was formed in Aceh in an effort to meet autonomy demands, and some have seen this as only the beginning.

There have also been efforts by Muslim politicians to promulgate laws regarding extramarital sex and other social legislation. In the education field, in 2003, a bill was passed to require non-Muslim schools to hire Islamic teachers to teach Islam to their Muslim students. Non-Muslims fear encroachment on their rights from this and future legislation. These efforts at Islamically oriented laws have resonance within a sizable section of the population that wants Islam to play more of a role in their lives. One scholar on Islam in Indonesia has questioned whether Muslims in the country are prepared for the give-and-take of democracy or are ready to accept a nonreligious basis for policy.[24]

CONCLUSIONS

Throughout the postindependence era, decision making at the national level has not been in the hands of those with an Islamic agenda. Sukarno was a secularist. Although he had an interest in Islam early in his life and once was married to the daughter of the leader of Sarekat Islam, he did not believe that Islam should have a special place in the new republic. If we look at the composition of the parliament after the 1955 elections, only 19 of 234 surveyed had received any formal Islamic education.[25] The Suharto regime attempted to keep Islam out of politics and economic policy making until the 1990s, and the religious orientation of the officer corps and upper civil service tended toward the Javanese mystical interpretation of Islam. Although the first president after the 1999 elections was a leader in the Islamic community, the majority of the DPR did not belong to Islamic parties, and his successor, Megawati Sukarnoputri, daughter of Sukarno, tended to follow her father's path of secularism. Thus, for good or bad, the decisions that have challenged democracy and modernization at the national level have generally not been controlled by Islamic political organizations or politicians. That does not mean that they have not had an influence, but their influence has tended to be peripheral. There has been an increased sense of religious identity in Indonesia in recent years. This means that Islam may come to play a more important role in Indonesia's future evolution for good or ill. However, it is not yet possible to discern the patterns of this potentially major role of Islam.

NOTES

1. Dutch East Indies Department of Economic Affairs, Central Bureau of Statistics, *Statistical Pocket Book of Indonesia, 1941* (Batavia: G. Kolff, 1941), 26.

2. *Ibid.,* 59–63.

3. *Volksraad Debates* (Batavia: Dutch East Indies, 1920), 213–14.

4. Amry Vandenbosch, *Dutch East Indies* (Berkeley: University of California Press, 1944), 114–19.

5. Jusuf Panglaykim and Kenneth D. Thomas, "Indonesian Exports: Performance and Projects," in Theodore Morgan and Nyle Spoelstra, eds., *Economic Interdependence in Southeast Asia* (Madison: University of Wisconsin Press, 1969), 337–70.

6. President Sukarno, *Toward Freedom and the Dignity of Man* (Jakarta: Department of Foreign Affairs, 1961).

7. Arnold Brackman, *The Communist Collapse in Indonesia* (New York: W. W. Norton, 1969).

8. Hal Hill, *Indonesian Economy Since 1996: Southeast Asia's Emerging Giant* (Cambridge: Cambridge University Press, 1996), 16; Huib Poot, Arie Kuyvenhoven, and Jaap Jansen, *Industrialization and Trade in Indonesia* (Yogyakarta: Gadjah Mada University Press, 1990), 42–46.

9. Steven Radelet, "Indonesia: Long Road to Recovery" (Development Discussion Paper 722, Harvard Institute for International Development, Cambridge, MA, 1999), 1.

10. George Aditjondro, "Suharto and Sons," *Washington Post,* January 25, 1998.

11. Radelet, "Indonesia: Long Road to Recovery."

12. *Jakarta Post*, March 3, 2004.

13. U.S. State Department, "Indonesia," in *Country Reports on Human Rights Practices 2002,* released by the Bureau of Democracy, Human Rights, and Labor, Washington, DC, March 31, 2003.

14. Human Rights Watch, *World Report 2004*, http://www.hrw.org/wr2k4/.

15. Fred von der Mehden, *Religion and Modernization in Southeast Asia* (Syracuse, NY: Syracuse University Press, 1986).

16. "Insulinde," World Dominion Survey Series (London: World Dominion Press, n.d.), 6.

17. M. Alfian Darmawam, *Mumammadiyah* (Yogyakarta: Gadja Mada University Press, 1989).

18. Peter Riddell, "The Diverse Voices of Political Islam in Post-Suharto Indonesia," *Islam and Christian-Muslim Relations* 13, no. 1 (2002): 71.

19. Abdurrahman Wahid, interview by the author, Jakarta, 1993.

20. Martin van Bruinessen, "Genealogies of Islamic Radicalism in Post-Suharto Indonesia," *South East Asia Research* 10, no. 2 (July 1, 2002).

21. Mark Woodward, "Indonesia, Islam and the Prospect for Democracy" (SMU Asian Symposium, Dallas, TX, 2001).

22. U.S. State Department, "Indonesia," in *International Religious Freedom Report 2003,* released by the Bureau of Democracy, Human Rights, and Labor, Washington, DC, December 18, 2003, 13.

23. Greg Fealy, "Another Mindset," *Courier-Mail,* October 20, 2003.

24. Woodward, "Indonesia, Islam," 17–18.

25. Soelaeman Soemardi, "Some Aspects of the Social Origin of Indonesian Political Decision Makers," transactions of the Third World Conference of Sociology, 1956.

15

Malaysia's Path to Modernization and Democratization

Osman Bakar

On August 31, 2003, Malaysia celebrated forty-six years of political independence. A nation of 22 million, with Muslims forming slightly more than half the population, Malaysia is precariously multiethnic, multireligious, and multicultural. Yet it is unique among Muslim nations as a politically stable, modernized, and prosperous country enjoying relatively peaceful interethnic and interreligious relations. Malaysia's success in maintaining a Westminster-style parliamentary democracy, with only a yearlong interruption of the democratic process because of the May 13, 1969, racial riots in Kuala Lumpur, is equally remarkable. The election of five prime ministers in fifty years, through democratic means, testifies to Malaysia's political stability.

Internationally, Malaysia is known for its independent foreign policy and its leadership in regional and multilateral organizations, including the Association of Southeast Asian Nations (ASEAN), the Organization of the Islamic Conference (OIC), and the Non-Aligned Movement (NAM).

This chapter analyzes the major factors that have contributed to Malaysia's success and the remaining obstacles to further progress.

MALAYSIA'S MODERNIZATION: ENABLING FACTORS

Modernization and democratization, although distinct, are interrelated societal phenomena. Modernization can take place without democratization, but democratization requires a degree of modernization. Malaysia had embarked on the process of modernization and on the introduction of parliamentary democracy before independence. But later, democracy accelerated the pace of Malaysia's modernization.

Malaysia's modernization has encompassed all sectors of national life, including the religious.[1] For example, the tradition of *hajj* (pilgrimage) has led to the creation of the Tabung Haji (Pilgrimage Fund), a modern religious-economic institution that has developed into a successful multipurpose corporation.[2] In its intensity, Malaysia's economic modernization approximates that of Western countries, making Malaysia a serious competitor to the West in such sectors as information technology, manufacturing, and international trade.

Malaysia's success has led political scientists, development experts, and scholars of the Islamic world to discover the factors behind its achievement. The thesis of this chapter is that societal forces generated by six major factors have played determining roles in the success of Malaysia's modernization. These factors are:

1. colonial modernization and the reformation of the Malay monarchy;
2. promodernization political and religious leadership;
3. singular emphasis on modern education;
4. a professional and functioning civil service;
5. the predominance of politics of development in electoral contests (the intertwining of modernization and democracy); and
6. Malay Islam and interethnic rivalry and competition.

COLONIAL MODERNIZATION: THE REFORMATION OF THE MONARCHY AND ITS IMPLICATIONS FOR MALAYSIA'S MODERNIZATION

The Malay experience of modernity is often traced to the formation of the first Malay-Muslim city-state, Pasai, in the thirteenth century C.E.[3] With the spread of Islam in the Malay Archipelago, other Malay-Muslim nation-states or sultanates were established. Thus, since the thirteenth century, the Malays have been engaged in the process of state formation inspired and informed by Islam's societal values. According to T. N. Harper: "The early modern state reached its apogee in Melaka: a state based on trade, whose hegemony reached over much of the Western archipelago; a richly cosmopolitan world, and the center of the *darul Islam* in the east."[4]

A fundamental underpinning of the traditional Malay statehood was the monarchy.[5] European colonial rule, beginning with the Portuguese military conquest of Malacca in 1511, had a destructive impact on the Malay monarchy. Nevertheless, unlike the cases of Indonesia in the seventeenth century and the Philippines in the eighteenth century, which came, respectively, under Dutch and Spanish colonial rule, the Malay monarchy survived under British rule and underwent reforms.

These reforms played a significant role in reinvigorating the institution of the monarchy, which contributed to Malaysia's modernization.[6] The reforms were particularly significant because of the fractured and decadent state of the Malay

political world prior to the advent of British rule in 1824. In the Malay Peninsula following the fall of Malacca, Malay political unity was lost. Although the
Malacca monarchy survived in the form of several successor states, because of
persistent conflicts among them none grew very strong. The British exploited
local conflicts to their own ends. Nevertheless, their strong and "permanent" presence in Malaysia, achieved through "treaties of protection" with the Malays,
strengthened and stabilized the Malay monarchy. It created conditions for the
forging of new relationships among the rulers and promoted Malay unity.

Despite a degree of transformation of the Malay rulers into constitutional monarchs under British rule, the monarchy remained powerful and the Malay rulers
commanded great loyalty and respect from their subjects. The British were fully
aware of this fact, but they chose to "reinvent" the Malay monarchy, tame the
Malay sultans, and neutralize their opposition to colonial rule. Despite occasional
violent uprisings against the British, led by chieftains linked to the royal courts,
the British achieved their objectives.

By the beginning of the twentieth century the monarch's power and jurisdiction had become limited to the domain of Malay religion and *adat* (customs), including the administration of Islamic personal, family, and inheritance laws, and
religious education. As official heads of Islam in their respective states, the sultans retained their influence on the Muslim masses and helped shape a mainstream Islam that is largely traditionalist, conformist, moderate, and loyal to the
monarchy. This situation suited the British, who were always concerned about
religiously inspired uprisings.

Education

As part of the British taming of the monarchy and satisfying the needs of the
colonial administration,[7] modern education was offered to the sons of the rulers
and Malay aristocrats. The first and most important British educational institution established for the Malay elites was the Malay College, built in 1905, in
Kuala Kangsar in the state of Perak. The college produced native agents of modernization and formed the nation's postindependence leaders in politics, business,
public administration, economics, and the military.[8] For many decades, the best
Malay minds were the products of this college, and the college helped modernize the thinking of the Malay elites.[9] The success of the college in opening up
modern educational space for Malays was noticed by the Malay community and
raised their expectations, leading Malay intellectuals to demand similar schools
that would admit students from all social backgrounds.[10] However, because of
opposition from the Malay rulers and the limited objectives of the colonial educational policy, a more liberal policy of student admission to the college was not
adopted until after World War II.[11] General democratization of English-medium
education also did not take place until after the war.

The modernization of the Malay monarchy, including through education, was
important in the future development of modern education in Malaysia. Given

their stature and influence among the Malays in preindependence days, especially in the rural areas, the Malay rulers helped remove psychological barriers to modernization among the majority of the people who equated modernization with Westernization. Their position as protectors of Islam backed by a religious administrative service that was being modernized[12] provided them with the necessary religious and moral legitimacy to serve as institutional supporters of modernization. The state of Kelantan, situated in the northeast of peninsular Malaysia and ruled by PAS (the Islamic Party) currently and during the greater part of the postindependence years, provided an early example of collaborative efforts in modernization among the monarchy, the religious establishment, and the colonial administration.[13]

Civil Administration

The British also created an efficient civil administration by attracting the best Malay brains. The service also achieved great prestige.

The Beginning of Democracy

The Malays traditionally prefer slow, evolutionary, and peaceful change over rapid and revolutionary alteration. The British colonialists understood this and therefore in the post–World War II period adopted a plan to groom Malaya for self-government. As part of this plan the British tried to establish a system of multiracial politics as a precondition for self-rule. In 1952, the country had its first taste of democracy when the British experimented with multiparty elections in the Kuala Lumpur municipality. An alliance formed by United Malays National Organization (UMNO) and Malayan Chinese Association (MCA) won the election. This was a victory for multiracial politics and interethnic cooperation in the quest for self-governance. Further progress was made with the first national election, held in 1955, in which the Alliance Party, a coalition of UMNO, MCA, and the Malayan Indian Congress, led by Tunku Abdul Rahman, won fifty-one out of fifty-two seats in the Federal Legislative Council. After that victory Tunku became chief minister.

The path to democracy was thus charted before independence. The emerging paradigm of that democracy was ethnic sharing of power as represented by the Alliance. Undoubtedly, progress made in democratization and multiracial politics helped to hasten independence. An Islamic opposition had also emerged as part of that democracy in the form of the Pan Malayan Islamic Party, which won only one seat. Indeed, elements of democratic ideas and practices were not entirely absent in the community prior to the British introduction of parliamentary democracy. With the federal elections the colonial government made its contribution to the birth of Malaysian democracy.[14] These elections demonstrated the predominance of the interethnic Alliance, heralded political stability, and helped settle the question of who would be the legitimate parties to lead independent

Malay, since the Tunku-led Alliance had earned the mandate to pursue negotiations for independence, set up a transitional administration, and draw up a federal constitution for the new nation.

Continuity of Colonial and Postcolonial Modernization

The fact that there was continuity between colonial and postindependence modernization greatly contributed to Malaysia's success in practically every field. The British legacy of modernization and democratization, especially the efforts initiated in the postwar years as "decolonization experiments," have endured in postindependence Malaysia.[15] Especially important were Malaysia's adoption of a constitutional monarchy and parliamentary democracy, thus blending tradition with modernity.

The colonial educational system was also retained after independence and served as a foundation for the expansion of the postindependence educational system. The traditions of the British-era civil service were also upheld. In the economic sector, where because of colonial interests in Malaysia's natural resources, modernization was most extensive, however, aspects of colonial policy had certain disadvantages.[16] The most significant was the pattern of development along ethnic lines that favored the Chinese. Yet even the development and modernization pattern of the colonial economy was not changed until the second decade of independence, when ethnic violence involving the Malays and the Chinese erupted in May 1969.[17] The main cause of the conflict was not disagreement over development and modernization but rather was caused by the crystallization of economic activities along ethnic lines during the colonial era. These clashes sent a clear message, namely, that in a multiethnic nation the identification of race with economic vocation is dangerous and socially unacceptable and that economic prosperity and justice must cut across ethnic boundaries.

PROMODERNIZATION POLITICAL AND
RELIGIOUS LEADERSHIP

In all Muslim societies, religious scholars (*ulama*) and intellectuals are highly esteemed and play a very influential role in shaping and articulating the values of their respective societies. Therefore, an important factor in the shaping of Malay Muslim opinion on the issue of modernization before and after independence has been the religious establishment.[18]

Since the fall of the Ottoman caliphate, which significantly impacted Malay religious thought, the Malay-Muslim intelligentsia has been divided into three main groups:[19] First is the religious establishment, headed by the monarchy in various states and the conservative and mainly rural *ulama*. Except for the monarchy, members of this group are all products of religious education. Second are those intellectuals and the urban middle class who have a religious inclination but are reform-minded. They are the product of either a formal religious or a Western-oriented educational system. The membership of this group, known in the colonial period as the Kaum Muda (the Young Party)—as distinguished from the first group, the Kaum Tua (the Old Party)—represents intellectuals with a broad spectrum of views on religion and the modern world. However, they share a number of fundamental beliefs: Islam must serve as the foundation and the guiding principle of Malay-Muslim life and thought; contemporary Malay religious thought needs reform; and societal modernization is necessary. Third are the secular minded liberals with a Western-oriented education. This group believes that religion is a private matter and advocates a strict separation of religion and the state. Za'ba, a noted twentieth-century Malay-Muslim literary figure and philosopher who belongs to the second group, described his contemporaries in the third group as being "indifferent to systematic religion" like "the average European."[20] In the wake of Islamic resurgence in the country in the 1970s, this group has been identified by its religious opponents as staunch secularists.

These groups have demonstrated different degrees of enthusiasm and support for modernization. While the first group is not opposed to selective modernization, the last two groups have had the greatest impact on postindependence modernization, largely because the secular-minded, pro-Western, and pro-modernization Malay nationalists were entrusted with political power by the British to manage self-rule. This new political leadership pursued economic development and modernization in all sectors of national life relatively unhindered and vigorously along the lines of colonial rule. The first three prime ministers—Tunku Abdul Rahman (1957–69), Tun Abdul Razak (1970–76), and Tun Hussein Onn (1976–81)—who among them ruled Malaysia for almost a quarter of a century, were all promodernization. Razak, known as the "father of development," was devoted to the economic development of rural areas where most Malay-Muslims live and which were neglected during colonial rule.[21]

Rahman, Razak, and Hussein were also secularists and modernists. However, because of the following political and religious conditions they were unable to pursue a totally secular modernization strategy. First, every five years Malaysia's parliamentary democracy requires British-style general elections for a new mandate from the electorate. These leaders knew that their political survival required sensitivity to the concerns of many Malay-Muslims that modernization not undermine Islamic values and practices. The political party they headed, UMNO, which dominated the ruling coalition of ethnically based political parties, faced a formidable challenge from its traditional enemy, PAS, known for its more religious stance.[22] This political reality helped turn those leaders into pragmatic secularists and modernists. Second, the intellectuals in the second group became more vocal after independence as their numbers increased. They did not have political power, but their significant contributions to the national struggle for independence had raised their moral standing in the community. Leading reformists such as Syed Sheikh al-Hadi, Sheikh Tahir Jalaluddin, and Za'ba—later called Pendeta ("the thinker-intellectual")—all played important roles in the independence movement.[23] They also provided intellectual and religious leadership that inspired pre-independence modernization of the Malays, mainly in education. Za'ba greatly contributed to the development of postindependence Malay-Islamic thought and culture. His balanced views on Islam and modernization and his insistence on the Malay pursuit of modernization within the framework of Islamic values and ethics left a lasting impact on later generations.[24] His ideas, once a minority view, have entered the mainstream.

Increasing numbers of Malay-Muslim intellectuals emerging from the ranks of educationists, writers, and civil servants, echoing Za'ba's modernization and voicing Islamic-nationalist critique of government policies on development and modernization, forced national political leaders to listen to them. Thus, Islamic political opposition and Islamic intellectual and cultural opposition moderated the force of secular modernization. The Islamic resurgence of the 1970s unleashed and consolidated a new and more comprehensive and enlightened Islamic opposition,[25] which turned the tide in an Islamic-centered direction. An important force within this movement was the Muslim Youth Movement of Malaysia (ABIM), founded in 1971 and led by Anwar Ibrahim, who later joined Mahathir Mohammad's cabinet and rose in the ruling party, UMNO, to become his deputy and designated successor. He was sacked in 1998 over political differences.

The real turning point in Malaysia's history of modernization occurred in 1981, when Mahathir Mohammad became its fourth prime minister. The distinguishing feature of Mahathir's modernization program is that it was done in the name of Islam.[26] Intellectually transformed from a Malay nationalist to a Muslim globalist when he became Malaysia's leader, Mahathir wanted to turn Malaysia into the "Japan of the Muslim world" and the first Muslim country to join the advanced nations. In his own words, Mahathir's political ambition was "to make Islam in Malaysia synonymous with economic progress and modernization."[27] It is arguable whether he can be included in the second group of Malay-Muslim reformers and revivalists, but his frequent identification with Islam and the interests of the global *ummah* suggests that more than political opportunism had been his main motivation. He appeared totally convinced not only that Islam and modernization are compatible but that Islam can only reclaim its rightful place in the contemporary world through modernization.[28] His political leadership transformed Malaysia into one of the most modernized and economically prosperous Muslim countries in the world.

EMPHASIS ON MODERN EDUCATION

A strong emphasis on education has greatly contributed to the success of Malaysia's modernization. This commitment to education and its critical role in modernization is reflected in the fact that since independence education has accounted for the largest share of Malaysia's national expenditure. The result is that in 2003 Malaysia's literacy rate was 93 percent, with a target date of 2010 to eliminate illiteracy completely. Building on the colonial infrastructure, Malaysia's educational system, including colonial-era institutions such as the

Malay College, was democratized and universalized with special emphasis on rural areas and with a view to provide equal opportunity to all Malaysians without regard to ethnicity, religion, or gender. Today in practically all of Malaysia's public and private universities female students outnumber males.

In multiethnic Malaysia, education and language have been interrelated and volatile issues. Existing parallel school systems using the languages of major ethnic groups as mediums of instruction—Malay, Chinese, and Tamil—are a colonial legacy. They operate despite fierce opposition from Malay nationalists, who favor Malay as the sole medium of instruction in schools. The main consideration here is the nation's politics of multiculturalism. Successive national governments—based on interethnic political cooperation—have renewed their commitment to the preservation of minority languages through preuniversity education, while staying committed to the goal of national integration and unity. Consequently, while minority languages are taught in Chinese and Tamil schools, Malay—Bahasa Malaysia—is the official medium of education in all schools.

The role of English language in the educational system is controversial and became a national problem with many political implications after Mahathir, in 2002, ordered science and mathematics to be taught in English.

Malay-Muslims can send their children to Islamic religious schools supported by the government or to community religious schools run by religiously minded individuals or organizations. The former are better equipped and are more oriented toward modern education. There has been a steady increase in the number of students of both kinds of religious schools. With both UMNO and PAS drawn into a polemical war on the future of religious schools, the issue of religious education may have far-reaching consequences for Islam's character and position in Malaysia.

Despite frequent tensions over sensitive educational issues that tend to strain the fabric of Malaysia's multiethnic cultures, the country has managed to maintain interethnic peace, a necessary condition for successful modernization. Malaysia's educational system has been geared toward meeting the needs of its modern economy, emphasizing scientific and technical education and thus contributing to its modernization. Those Malaysians educated abroad have also been important agents of Malaysian modernization.

A PROFESSIONAL CIVIL SERVICE

Malaysia inherited a well-functioning and disciplined colonial administrative service with a strong reputation. In the postindependence period that prestige increased, as the best brains continued to be drawn into the service, attracted by the government's provision of new incentives and privileges. A vastly improved higher educational system provided a growing pool of talent for the civil service, making it the most important machinery of Malaysia's modernization.

For historical and political reasons the civil service has always been Malay-dominated. The Malay middle class primarily consists of members of the service in the officers' ranks, especially in the upper echelon,[29] and has contributed to the strengthening of a multiethnic middle class, which many believe has become an important factor of political stability in Malaysia.

The Malaysian civil administrative service has evolved in response to the nation's changing needs and developmental strategies and has adapted to global, economic, and technological changes. Major reforms of the civil service occurred in the early 1970s under Abdul Razak, who turned it into a more efficient, development-oriented public agency sensitive to the needs of the rural population.

The next major reform took place under Mahathir. He launched several controversial policies including the following: (1) the Look East Policy recommended, among other things, that Malaysians emulate the Japanese in their work ethic.[30] Mahathir justified this policy by arguing that the Western work ethic was declining and could no longer be emulated and that in the contemporary Muslim world there was no country worth emulating. (2) The Islamization policy aimed to bring government policies in line with Islamic values. (3) Electronic government policy involved the use of high technology within the administrative service. Consequently, Malaysia today is perhaps the most electronically wired of Muslim countries.[31] Putra Jaya, Malaysia's new administrative and political capital, testifies to Mahathir's commitment to the creation of a modern world-class public administrative service.

THE IMPACT OF DEMOCRATIC SYSTEMS ON MALAYSIA'S MODERNIZATION: POLITICS OF DEVELOPMENT AND RELIGIOUS SALVATION

The following discussion of the politics of development and religious salvation as factors in the modernization in Malaysia shows how a democratic system can positively impact modernization in developing countries. The Malay Muslim community, which dominates Malaysian democracy, has chosen a two-party system to represent its political interests.[32] UMNO and PAS have competed for the Malay-Muslim vote since the first general elections in 1955. Over the years, new Malay parties such as the Malaysian Islamic Collective Front known as BERJASA (an offshoot of PAS) and Semangat 46 (a breakaway faction from UMNO) have emerged, but none has survived beyond two general elections, as the Malays continue to vote for either UMNO or PAS. In the general elections of 1999 many supporters of UMNO voted for PAS's candidates primarily because of their disapproval of Mahathir's treatment of Deputy Prime Minister Anwar Ibrahim,[33] thus causing UMNO to lose many parliamentary and state assembly seats to PAS.

Ideologies of UMNO and PAS: Perspective on Modernization

Although both Malay and Muslim, UMNO and PAS have markedly different political ideologies. UMNO is secular-minded, promodernization, pragmatic, and open to sharing of power with non-Malays; it has, in fact, shared power with non-Malays since independence while remaining the dominant partner in the ruling coalition. PAS is religiously minded, conservative, doctrinaire, and dogmatic in its religious orientation. It has never shared power with non-Malays, except for the brief period 1974–77, when it joined the ruling coalition, which was headed by UMNO and included the National Front. Disagreement on the politics of development has been central in the fierce electoral contests between UMNO and PAS. PAS has largely campaigned on the platform of spiritual development, by which it means development based on the five pillars of Islam.

UMNO knows that these issues are dear to the Malays, especially the rural segment, whose political support is decisive in the outcome of electoral contests. Consequently, UMNO has responded to PAS's politics of spiritual development by seeking to convince the Malays that it has a better policy on the development of Islam and the Muslim community. The term for that policy in the pre-Mahathir era was "balanced development." Spiritual development, "good life, or salvation in the next world," is to be balanced with material development, necessary for "good life and salvation in this world." UMNO has quite successfully delivered this message to the Malays, thus thwarting PAS's religious challenge.

The history of electoral battles between UMNO and PAS for the Malay-Muslim vote exhibits an evolutionary pattern that points to an increasingly visible role for Islam in public affairs. As PAS continuously intensifies its Islamic brand of opposition to the ruling coalition, UMNO is pressured to deliver its own Islamic development package. Not to appear less Islamic than PAS, UMNO usually initiates new religious and development programs or strengthens old ones in the name of Islam. The Malay-Muslim appreciation of Islam has grown as a result of this interplay of two brands of political Islam and of Islamic resurgence spearheaded by Muslim nongovernmental organizations (NGOs), and it has made Malaysian Islam more politicized and divisive, causing fear among many non-Muslims.

In terms of development and modernization, Malaysian Islam has gained from the Islamic politics of UMNO and PAS. Malaysia has the best nationwide network of modern mosques and religious schools. The aforementioned Tabung Haji has become Malaysia's richest investment mechanism for Muslims. The *zakat* system has been modernized and now includes religious tax collection from large Muslim corporations.

The political battle for Muslim votes has also led to the eradication of poverty and illiteracy among the Malay-Muslims, elevation of their socioeconomic status, and expansion of the Malay middle class. In short, democracy and party politics have helped Malaysia's modernization. With Mahathir's commitment to make Islam in Malaysia synonymous with economic development and modernization, and his frequent attacks on the kind of Islam propagated by PAS as detrimental to the Muslims' quest for progress and contrary to Islamic teachings, development and modernization have ceased to be the dominant issue in the two-party rivalry. PAS's new political strategy now calls for the implementation of Islamic law and the establishment of an Islamic state in the context of which it has also increased criticism of Mahathir's excesses of modernization. To counteract PAS's challenge, in September 2001 Mahathir proclaimed Malaysia an Islamic state before PAS could unveil its model.[34]

MALAY-ISLAM, INTERETHNIC RIVALRY AND COMPETITION BEFORE IMPACT OF MODERNIZATION

Ethnic and religious diversity can contribute either to unity, progress, and greatness or to sectarian conflicts, anarchy, and backwardness.[35] Malaysia's path to modernization cannot be fully understood unless the factor of simultaneous interethnic cooperation and competition is taken into account.

The large presence of the commercially minded ethnic Chinese and Indians, who were more open to modernization, has positively impacted the indigenous Malays, by forcing them to modernize in order to compete with other ethnic groups in the acquisition of wealth. For example, in order to create a common modern Malay writing system for all Malaysians, the Malays had to change their traditional Jawi (Malay-Arabic) script to Latin. In the economic sector, Malay-Muslims have made significant gains and there has been growth, albeit slow, in the number of joint Malay-Chinese and Malay-Indian business ventures.

Although the Malays still lag behind the Chinese in terms of higher education and wealth, it is doubtful that they would have reached the current level of socioeconomic development without interethnic competition.

MALAYSIAN DEMOCRACY: ITS SHAPING FACTORS

Malaysia is one of very few democratic Muslim countries. However, when compared with Western democracies, Malaysia has been labeled by some of its local and foreign critics as a "semi-democracy."[36] What is of major interest here is not to compare Malaysia's performance with that of the West, but rather to understand why unlike other Muslim countries, Malaysia has tried to develop Western-inspired democracy. Many of the factors that have helped Malaysia's modernization have also contributed to the building of its democracy. These include the colonial legacy, the monarchy, strong emphasis on modern education, and the role of Islamic opposition.

Colonial Legacy

As noted earlier, the British policy of preparing Malaysia for self-rule, which included the introduction of a system of multiracial and multiparty political systems, facilitated postindependence consolidation of democracy.

The Role of Monarchy

In the postindependence period, the monarchy lost most of its traditional power and prestige, and many Malaysians questioned its usefulness and favored its abolishment. Although the popularity of the complex Malay constitutional monarchy has fluctuated, by and large most Malaysians, especially the Malay-Muslims, favor the monarchy because it provides checks and balances to other branches of government, thus strengthening Malaysia's democracy.

Indeed, the new constitutional monarchy's role as a factor of political stability, and hence an enabling factor of Malaysian's democracy, cannot be overemphasized. For the Malays, the constitutional monarchy represented continuity of their postindependence political institutions with their traditional past. At a time when the Malays were anxious about democracy within the context of the new interethnic political partnership and about the survival of their ethnic, cultural, and religious identity, the monarchy provided a symbol for the Malay nationhood, served as a guardian of Malay interests, and helped the people of Malaysia to deal confidently with these uncertainties. The monarchy has also served as a symbol of national identity for the multiethnic and multireligious Malaysia. Without the monarchy, it is doubtful that Malaysia could have successfully dealt with the challenge of ethnic, religious, and cultural pluralism. Subsequent developments confirmed the continued relevancy of the monarchy.

The constitution calls upon the monarchy to play a special role in relation to both Islam and democracy.[37] The monarchy's role regarding Islam was noted earlier. Regarding democracy, its role is to ensure the smooth functioning of the nation's political democracy at the federal and state levels. There have been instances when a sultan or ruler was directly involved in controversial political matters or unilaterally engaged in resolving political crises, which called into question his faithfulness to his constitutional role. But these cases have been infrequent, and it is widely realized that only by adhering to its constitutional role can the monarchy contribute to the growth of a healthier democracy.

Early Leaders as Malay Muslim Democrats

Malaysia's early leaders were not only promodernization, they were also committed to democracy and cultural pluralism. Tunku and Razak are widely regarded as far more democratic and tolerant of public criticism than is Mahathir, although they firmly rejected any legitimate political role for the outlawed Malayan Communist Party. They were also supportive of interethnic cooperation.

Tunku was perhaps the Malaysian leader most liked by the non-Malays, especially the Chinese, although later in his rule he was seen by his fellow Malays as neglecting their economic and business interests. Non-Malays saw Razak as a pro-Malay leader and even anti-Chinese, at least when he was deputy prime minister. This negative perception evaporated when he became prime minister and adopted fairly balanced policies toward all ethnic groups. Although the worst racial riots occurred during Tunku's rule, at issue was neither the principle of democracy nor that of ethnic pluralism, but rather the fair distribution of national wealth. It was important for the survival of democracy that Tunku resigned when he lost the confidence of his own party (UMNO) following the riots. Similarly, although the parliament was suspended in response to the riots, and the country was ruled by decree by the National Operation Council, chaired by Razak, within a year Razak restored the parliament and initiated the New Economic Policy to address the legitimate needs of all ethnic groups. In short, the democratic character and leadership style of these early leaders stabilized Malaysian politics during the first two decades of independence and consolidated Malaysia's democracy.

UMNO's Democratic Tradition

The democratic culture of UMNO has also helped in building Malaysia's democracy. Indeed, many claim that UMNO has always been far more democratic than the nation, a view with which I agree. Tunku and Razak strengthened the democratic tradition within UMNO. However, some believe that under Mahathir that tradition declined. Be that as it may, what many people object to is that the same kind of intraparty democracy has not been extended to the entire nation.

The Role of Islamic Opposition

The positive response of the Islamic opposition to democracy has contributed to its consolidation. Leaders such as Burhanuddin El-Helmy, a Malay Muslim intellectual and political philosopher, who believed in Islam's compatibility with democracy, contributed to the success of Malaysian democracy.[38] As a PAS leader, El-Helmy led the party in 1959 in the first postindependence national election, in which it performed better than it did in 1955. El-Helmy organized an Islamic political opposition along democratic lines and strengthened democracy within PAS. Consequently, although the democratic space within the party needs expansion, PAS is one of the very few Muslim political parties in the world that have been both in government and in opposition within a democratic system. In 2003, PAS ruled two of fourteen states.

TRADITION OF REPRESENTATIVE GOVERNMENTS

The representative character of governments has been a major enabling factor in Malaysian democracy. Malaysian governments since 1957 have basically been coalition governments made up of representatives of all ethnic groups. The distribution of seats in the parliament and in state assemblies is based on a formula that takes into account the demographic strength of each ethnic group and the ethnic makeup of voters in constituencies. In determining representation in the cabinet, in addition to electoral performance other factors are considered. Attempts are made to give the losing parties some role in the government, thus making the coalition government as representative as possible. Beginning with a ruling coalition of three political parties under Tunku, the coalition was broadened under Razak to fourteen members. Then, in his attempt to consolidate national unity in the aftermath of the racial riots, Razak worked toward the formation of a truly national government. He took the bold step of broadening the ruling coalition, and later, in 1974, he included the opposition, PAS, which was then led by Asri Mohammad, in the coalition.

FAVORABLE EXTERNAL ENVIRONMENT

The fact that Malaysia was not a principal arena of East-West rivalry and was not bedeviled by protracted regional or other interstate conflicts contributed to the success of its modernization and democratization. This favorable external environment saved Malaysia from militarization and diversion of economic resources from development. The lack of a significant external threat also allowed it to focus on modernization and to consolidate its democracy. All these benefits to Malaysia are partly due to its progressive foreign policy, charted since the Razak administration, which seeks to have friendly relations with all the great powers and especially to promote regional economic cooperation.

CRITIQUES OF MALAYSIAN MODERNIZATION

There are many domestic and foreign critics of Malaysian modernization, especially under Mahathir's rule.[39] These criticisms cover a wide spectrum—political, economic, sociocultural, and religious. Mahathir's modernization has been the most severely criticized because it has produced the most sweeping changes in Malaysia. A frequent criticism of Mahathir's modernization is that, although it has provided a world-class infrastructure for socioeconomic development, it has done so at the expense of human development, democratic reforms, socioeconomic justice, environmental health, and a better quality of life. I tend to agree with these criticisms. Consequently, it is certain that in the coming years there will be numerous assessments of Mahathir's era. Malaysia's civil society and other critics of Mahathir's rule will pressure the Badawi government to shift the focus of national development to those aspects neglected during Mahathir's rule.

OBSTACLES TO DEMOCRACY

Critics have identified the following obstacles to the further growth and progress of Malaysia's democracy, and they have proposed reforms to overcome them. First, the present ethnic-based politics promotes sectarianism and constrains the pursuit of a universal discourse in Malaysian politics. Indeed, some believe interethnic and interreligious peace has been achieved at the cost of limiting civil and political liberties and hindering debate on vitally important national issues. This ethnic-based politics needs to be gradually replaced by a genuine multiracial politics. Second, the Internal Security Act inherited from the colonial period allows detention without a trial. Many demand its abolishment, while others seek its reform. Third, government controls the media. Critics would like to see a freer yet responsible media to promote democratic values and practices. Fourth, Mahathir has been accused of destroying the independence of the judiciary, the constitutional role of the monarchy, and the checks and balances between the legislative, the executive, and the judiciary. It remains to be seen whether Abdullah Ahmad Badawi can deliver his promise to help in the restoration of the proper roles of these governmental branches.

CONCLUSION

A number of factors have contributed to Malaysia's success in modernization and democratization, notably the following: the existence of a Malay tradition of statehood, albeit weakened at the dawn of the colonial period; the institution of monarchy; the relatively more enlightened handling of Malaysia by the British colonial administration, including the process of transition to independence; an ethnically pluralist society; the existence of progressive and liberal-minded Muslim leaders and intellectuals; and democratically minded modernizing political leaders.

The relatively benign regional environment and the fact that Malaysia was not an arena of East-West rivalry have also helped in this regard. Nevertheless, in the last few years of former prime minister Mahathir's rule, criticism was voiced that he neglected democratization. Consequently, his successor, Abdullah Ahmad Badawi, will find it easier to expand and modernize Malaysia's economy, but he may find it difficult to satisfy Malaysians' demand for human development and the promotion of a democratic culture.

NOTES

1. Abdul Rahman Embong, *State-Led Modernization and the New Middle Class in Malaysia* (New York: Palgrave Macmillan, 2002).

2. Norhashimah Mohd Yasin, *Islamization/Malaynization: A Study on the Role of Economic Development of Malaysia, 1963–1993* (Kuala Lumpur: A. S. Noordeen, 1996).

3. Anthony H. Johns, "Islam in Southeast Asia: Problems of Perspective," in C. D. Cowan and O. W. Wolters, eds., *Southeast Asian History and Historiography: Essays Presented to D. G. E. Hall* (Ithaca, NY: Cornell University Press, 1976), 304–20.

4. Timothy N. Harper, *The End of Empire and the Making of Malaya* (Cambridge: Cambridge University Press, 1999), 15.

5. Anthony C. Milner, "Islam and Malay Kingship," *Journal of the Royal Asiatic Society of Great Britain and Ireland* 1 (1981): 46–70. On the Malacca sultanate as the apogee of Malay statecraft, see Muhammad Yusoff Hashim, *The Malay Sultanate of Malacca: A Study of Various Aspects of Malacca in the Fifteenth and Sixteenth Centuries in Malaysian History* (Kuala Lumpur: Dewan Bahasa dan Pustaka, 1992).

6. On the British "reinvention" of the Malay monarchy, see Harper, *End of Empire,* 18–21.

7. For discussion of specific examples, see Heather Sutherland, "The Taming of the Trengganu Elite," in Ruth T. McVey, ed., *Southeast Asian Transition: Approaches through Social History* (New Haven, CT: Yale University Press, 1978), 50–52; J. M. Gullick, *Rulers and Residents: Influence and Power in the Malay States, 1870–1920,* South-East Asian Historical Monographs (Singapore: Oxford University Press, 1992).

8. Khasnor Johan, *The Emergence of the Modern Malay Administrative Elite* (Singapore: Oxford University Press, 1984).

9. Yeo Kim Wah, "The Grooming of an Elite: Malay Administrators in the Federated Malay States, 1903–1941," *Journal of Southeast Asian Studies* 11, no. 2 (1980): 287–319; Harper, *End of Empire,* 19.

10. Adnan Hj. Nawang, *Za'ba and the Malays* (in Malay) (Kuala Lumpur: Berita Publishing Sdn. Bhd., 1998), 102.

11. Philip Loh Fook Seng, *Seeds of Separatism: Educational Policy in Malaya, 1874–1940* (Kuala Lumpur: Oxford University Press, 1974), 118.

12. Early modernization of religious administration and schools in Malaysia appeared to have been inspired by *ulama* identified with Muhammad Abduh's reformist school of thought. See Anthony H. Johns, "From Coastal Settlement to Islamic School and City: Islamization in Sumatra, the Malay Peninsula and Java," *Hamdard Islamicus* 4, no. 4 (1981): 25.

13. Nawang, *Za'ba and the Malays,* 101; Abdullah Alwi Hj. Hassan, "The Development of Islamic Education in Kelantan," in Khoo Kay Kim and Mohd Fadzil Othman, eds., *Tamadun Islam di Malaysia* (Kuala Lumpur: Persatuan Sejarah Malaysia, 1980), 196–98.

14. Ariffin Omar, *Bangsa Melayu: Malay Concepts of Democracy and Community, 1945–50* (Kuala Lumpur: Oxford University Press, 1993).

15. Harper, *End of Empire,* chap. 9, which discusses the colonial inheritance of independent Malaysia.

16. Ibid., 18–19.

17. After the riots, the New Economic Policy (NEP), whose dual aims were "to achieve national unity through the two-pronged objectives of eradiating poverty irrespective of race, and restructuring society to eliminate the identification of race with economic function," was introduced.

18. Ibrahim bin Abu Bakar, *Islamic Modernism in Malaya: The Life and Thought of Sayid Sheikh Al-Hadi, 1867–1934* (Kuala Lumpur: University of Malaya Press, 1994); Nawang, *Za'ba and the Malays,* chaps. 2 and 7.

19. Za'ba, the pen name of Zainal Abidin bin Ahmad, himself a leading Malay-Muslim intellectual of the twentieth century, has discussed this threefold division in his writing *The Malays and Religion.* See Nawang, *Za'ba and the Malays,* 67–71.

20. Ibid., 70.

21. Harper, *End of Empire,* 366–67.

22. Ramlah Adam, *UMNO: Organisasi dan Kegiatan* (Kota Bahru: Mohd Nawi Book Store, 1978); Safie bin Ibrahim, *The Islamic Party of Malaysia: Its Formative Stages and Ideology* (Kuala Lumpur: Nawi Ismail, 1981); Alias Mohamed, *PAS Platform: Development and Change, 1951–1986* (Petaling Jaya: Gateway Publishing House, 1994). On the traditional rivalry between these two parties, see John Funston, *Malay Politics in Malaysia: A Study of the United Malays National Organization and Party Islam* (Kuala Lumpur: Heinemann Educational Books [Asia], 1980).

23. Shaharuddin Maaruf, *Malay Ideas on Development, from Feudal Lord to Capital-*

ist (Singapore: Times Books International, 1988); Abu Bakar, *Islamic Modernism in Malaya*; Nawang, *Za'ba and the Malays*.

24. Nawang, *Za'ba and the Malays*.

25. John L. Esposito and John O. Voll, *Makers of Contemporary Islam* (New York: Oxford University Press, 2002).

26. For a good analytical account of Mahathir's modernization, industrialization, and Islamization, see Seyyed Vali Reza Nasr, *Islamic Leviathan: Islam and the Making of State Power* (New York: Oxford University Press, 2001), esp. chap. 5.

27. *International Herald Tribune*, May 6, 1991; Osman Bakar, "Islam and Political Legitimacy in Malaysia," in Shahram Akbarzadeh and Abdullah Saeed, eds., *Islam and Political Legitimacy* (London: RoutledgeCurzon, 2003), 133–34. For a critique of Mahathir's economic policies, see Jomo K. Sundaram, *Mahathir's Economic Policies* (Kuala Lumpur: INSAN, 1988).

28. Hashim Makaruddin, ed., *Islam and the Muslim Ummah: Selected Speeches of Dr Mahathir Mohamad* (Subang Jaya: Pelanduk Publications, 2001).

29. Nordin Selat, *Kelas Menengah Melayu* (Kuala Lumpur: Utusan Melayu Bhd., 1976); Embong, *State-Led Modernization*.

30. Diane K. Mauzy and R. S. Milne, "The Mahathir Administration in Malaysia: Discipline through Islam," *Pacific Affairs* 56, no. 4 (Winter 1983): 628–30; Gordon P. Means, *Malaysian Politics: The Second Generation* (Singapore: Oxford University Press, 1991), 91–98.

31. The Multimedia Super Corridor launched in 1997 symbolizes Malaysia's entry into and commitment to the digital age.

32. Funston, *Malay Politics in Malaysia*. On the PAS challenge to UMNO during Mahathir's rule, see John Hilley, *Malaysia: Mahathir, Hegemony, and the New Opposition* (London: Zed Books, 2001).

33. On what has come to be known as Mahathir's "Anwar crisis," see Hilley, *Malaysia,* chap. 5; on their differing visions, see Claudia Derichs, "Competing Politicians, Competing Visions: Mahathir Mohamad's *Wawasan 2020* and Anwar Ibrahim's Asian Renaissance," in Ho Khai Leong and James Chin, eds., *Mahathir's Administration: Performance and Crisis in Governance* (Singapore: Times Books International, 2001), 188–214.

34. Osman Bakar, "Islam and the State in Malaysia," *Journal of Institute of Diplomacy* (forthcoming); Patricia Martinez, "The Islamic State or the State of Islam in Malaysia," *Contemporary Southeast Asia* 23, no. 3 (December 2001): 474–503.

35. International Studies and Programming, Macalester College, "Malaysia: Crossroads of Diversity in Southeast Asia," *Macalester International* 12 (Autumn 2002).

36. On different terms used to describe Malaysian democracy, see William Case, *Politics in Southeast Asia: Democracy or Less* (London: RoutledgeCurzon, 2002); Zakaria Hj. Ahmad, "Malaysia: Quasi Democracy in a Divided Society," in Larry Diamond, Juan J. Linz, and Martin Seymour Lipset, eds., *Democracy in Developing Countries: Asia* (Boulder: Lynne Rienner/Adamantine Press, 1989), 3:347–82; James Jesudason, "Statist Democracy and the Limits to Civil Society in Malaysia," *Journal of Commonwealth and Comparative Politics* 33, no. 3 (1995).

37. On the monarchy's role regarding Islam, see Ahmad Ibrahim, "The Position of Islam in the Constitution of Malaysia," in Ahmad Ibrahim, Sharon Siddique, and Yasmin Hussain, eds., *Readings on Islam in Southeast Asia* (Singapore: Institute of Southeast Asian Studies, 1985), 213–20.

38. Kamarudin Jaffar, *Dr. Burhanuddin Al Helmy: Pemikiran dan Perjuangan* (Kuala Lumpur: IKDAS SDN BHD, 2000).

39. Jomo K. Sundaram, *A Question of Class: Capital, the State, and Uneven Development in Malaysia* (Singapore: Oxford University Press, 1986). Ahmad Ibrahim has emerged as the most important critic of what he calls Mahathir's extravagant practices and mega projects.

16

Islam, Modernization, and Democratization: The Case of Iran

Shireen T. Hunter

Within the context of modernization and democratization, Iran occupies a special place among Muslim countries. The following factors account for this situation. First, Iran has achieved a certain degree of modernization without, however, actualizing its potential and while still suffering from many ills afflicting developing countries. Second, Iran had a popular constitutional revolution in 1905–6 and has since intermittently experienced parliamentary politics, though it has been highly flawed. Third, Iran has had a strong socialist intellectual and political tradition dating back to the late nineteenth century without ever having gone through a revolution and never having been ruled by a socialist government. Fourth, Iran has had an Islamic revolution and has tried to create an Islamic republic by combining elements of a *Shari'a*-based polity and society with concepts of republicanism and popular sovereignty. Fifth, since the early 1990s Iran has been undergoing profound cultural and intellectual changes reflected in a broad-based and spirited debate that encompasses issues such as Iran's national identity and its underpinnings, Iran's future political system, and the role of religion in politics, civil society, and democratization. An important aspect of this debate has been the emergence of a reformist and liberal Islamic discourse involving both clerical and lay figures.

Iran has not yet resolved the contradictions inherent in its dualistic form of government—Islamic and republican. Similarly, differences between the conservatives and the more reform-minded and liberal elements within its leadership and polity still remain, and it is not yet clear when and how these contradictions will be resolved.

Yet, irrespective of its outcome, Iran's experience has relevance and implications for other Muslim countries. Iran's history of modernization and efforts at democratization are also instructive as examples of the enabling or hindering consequences of external factors in these processes; Iran is a prime example of the hindering impact of these forces.

The following are the most important factors that have affected the process of Iran's modernization and democratization: (1) a long and turbulent history and its demographic, economic, social, and cultural consequences; (2) geographic isolation; (3) Shi'a faith and the character of the religious establishment; (4) personality-based politics and a fragmented elite; and (5) a sensitive geostrategic situation.

A TURBULENT HISTORY AND ITS CONSEQUENCES

According to E. C. Black, nations and countries that undergo traumatic experiences or are colonized have more difficulty in modernizing.[1] Iran's history is replete with such traumatic experiences. Because of the vagaries of its long history, even Iran's name is a subject of controversy. Indeed, there is a widespread misunderstanding that the country's name was changed from Persia to Iran in 1937 by Reza Shah Pahlavi as part of his modernization project.[2]

Historically, Iran has experienced several waves of invasion, each with far-reaching demographic, social, economic, political, and cultural consequences. The first was the destruction of the Achemenid Empire by Alexander of Macedonia in 330 BCE.[3] Despite some superficial Hellenization among the elite, Iran did not become Hellenized, and by 222 CE the rise of the Sassanian Empire heralded a Persian political and cultural renaissance that lasted for four centuries.[4]

The second was the Arab defeat of the Sassanian Empire in 642 CE and Iran's eventual Islamization. Iran did not become Arabized, but the cultural and territorial cohesion of "Eranshahr" was lost forever. The Arab conquest caused a major ethnic and cultural divide in Iran, namely, that between the indigenous Iranians and the newly settled Arabs and between the cultural Arabizers and those loyal to the Iranian culture.

Islamization, meanwhile, caused a bifurcation in Iran's national identity and created a cultural duality, as many Iranians became torn between the Iranian and Islamic poles of their identity. The Arab conquest further increased nomadism in Iran and opened it to recurring attacks by Turkic tribes.

The third—and the most damaging—events were the Mongol invasions of the thirteenth and fourteenth centuries CE. While suffering much damage from the Arab conquest, Iran had succeeded in recovering culturally, physically, and economically and had even made some advances.[5] All these were lost because "as a result of Mongol invasions several millions were massacred or died from famine or epidemics, and many towns were either obliterated (e.g., Ray) or remained in ruins for decades or even centuries."[6] Meanwhile, the large increase in the nomadic population, following the migration of Turkic and Mongol tribes, disrupted agriculture, and the fiscal policy of the Ilkhans reduced the peasants to destitution.[7] It also further eroded Iran's ethnic and linguistic homogeneity by adding to the Arab-Iranian divide that is between the Turks and Iranians.[8] Even after a considerable degree of economic recovery under the Safavids, Iran never reached the pre-Mongol-invasion level of economic prosperity.

The fourth traumatic and destructive event was the Afghan invasion, which led to the collapse of the Safavid state and the Turkish and Russian attacks on Iran. During the period between the Afghan attack in 1722 and the coming to power of Nadir Shah in 1736 the country suffered heavy human and economic losses.[9] Nadir's assassination in 1749 led to another period of turmoil until the consolidation of the Qajar dynasty in 1796.

Thus, at the dawn of the nineteenth century, when Iran simultaneously faced the challenge of modernization and the superior European powers on its borders, it was a country "suffering from depopulation, poverty, and economic exhaustion and largely isolated from the mainstream of world politics, trade, science, and culture."[10] Additionally, the lack of a trained and well-organized military and an effective state leadership invited insubordination of the tribes, generated an atmosphere of insecurity, and negatively impacted the economy and trade. In the twentieth century, the violation of Iran's neutrality in 1914–18 and 1939–45, during the world wars, adversely affected the course of its modernization and democratization. In more recent times, the eight-year war with Iraq (1980–88) had similar effects.

GEOGRAPHIC CONSTRAINTS: IMPACT ON STATE POWER

Iran's large size, aridity, combination of mountains and lowlands, lack of major navigable rivers, and location near the heart of the Eurasian land mass have adversely affected its economic and political structures and hence the trajectory of its modernization.

According to Charles Issavi, these characteristics historically have prevented large-scale centralization and the development of strong governments with large standing armies and complex bureaucracies.[11] They have also rendered Iran politically and economically more loosely knit than other Middle Eastern countries. In fact, except for certain periods, comparatively Iran has been more feudal and tribal and less bureaucratic than other countries in the Middle East. However, Iranian feudalism was not of the European type, where certain feudal privileges limited the absolute power of the king and provided the basis for future development of constitutionalism and democracy. Rather, in theory the king's power was absolute, although in reality its writ did not extend far, thus giving all power relationships in Iran an arbitrary and unpredictable nature. This weakness of the state was a major hindrance to Iran's early modernization. In addition, the society's equally weak state plus the lack of law and order prevented it from embarking on modernization. This situation also meant that despite Iran's long history of nationhood and statehood, the process of state and nation building in Iran resembled that of other postcolonial states.

Iran's remoteness from Europe, exacerbated by the barrier of the Ottoman Empire, was another disabling influence in terms of its modernization because it "left

[Iran] outside the influence of currents of trade and ideas that were flowing over the other parts of the Middle East."[12] Geographical factors also determined the approach of European states toward Iran, which was purely derivative of other interests, notably containing the Ottoman state. Thus, in 1551 and 1601 Spain and England instigated Iran to engage in costly and unproductive wars against the Ottomans.[13]

GEOSTRATEGIC LOCATION: A FATE WORSE THAN A COLONY

As noted by Hamid Algar, "It was Iran's misfortune, in the classical age of imperialism to lie athwart the path on which two expansionist powers threatened to collide."[14] These two imperial powers were tsarist Russia and Britain. Indeed, since the signing of the Treaty of Turkmenchai in 1828 with Russia, which deprived Iran of all its Transcaucasian provinces and gave Russia extraterritorial privileges, trade concessions, and a veto power over the successorship to the throne, for a century "at least the political affairs of Iran were seldom free of the imprint of real or imagined European influence. Superimposed on the rivalries and intrigues constituting the Iranian political process was a weightier and greater contest, that between Britain and Russia."[15] Iran's greatest misfortune, however, was that neither of these two competing powers considered it vital to their interests and hence worthy of any investment. According to Sir Dennis Wright, the British ambassador to Iran in the early 1960s, "Britain never considered Iran a place worth colonizing."[16] On the contrary, the British saw Iran "as a glacier to be kept denuded of any facilities which might make it easier for the Russians to advance through it to the [Indian] subcontinent."[17] Britain also saw a revitalized Iran as a potential economic rival, especially to India. This concern is evident in the comments by the British envoy to Iran, Scheal, to Lord Palmerston, the British foreign secretary, opposing the building of a rail system in Iran:

The building of the railroad would awaken Iran's talents which, because of need and poverty have remained dormant. The movement of part of the European trade would increase Iran's importance and its dependence on Britain. However, this would also put the fate of Britain's enormous trade with the East all the way to China in the hands of this treacherous and hypocrite nation. *Thus there is no balance between the benefit that Iran would derive from the railroad and that which would incur to the British.* (emphasis added).[18]

The same was true of Russia.

Furthermore, unlike in the Ottoman empire or Egypt, where interests and the presence of a larger number of powers reduced the impact of great-power pressures, in Iran "the competition of Britain and Russia meant that each was determined to thwart any scheme proposed by the other, and was generally in a position to do so."[19]

Meanwhile, whenever it was convenient, Russia and Britain reached agreements at Iran's expense, as illustrated by the Anglo-Russian Agreement of 1907, which divided Iran into spheres of Russian and British influence.

THE SHI'A ESTABLISHMENT

Iran's large-scale Shi'aization under the Safavids helped unify its diverse peoples and imbued the new state with vitality. However, Safavid Shi'ism had certain dogmatic and superstitious dimensions, which became stronger toward the end of the dynasty. These characteristics adversely affected Iran's modernization. As noted by Rouhallah K. Ramazani, "Blind adherence to Shi'i dogma narrowed the intellectual horizons of the people. . . . At a time when European intellectuals were beginning to see how dogma had been overturned by scientific research and how the same method could be applied to politics and religion, the unquestioning acceptance of Shi'i dogma left little room for receptivity to new ideas in Iran."[20] There were, of course, enlightened clergy in Iran, but a large majority of them saw modernization, including modern forms of government, as threatening to Islam and to their interests and livelihood.

Some clergy supported the Constitutional Revolution of 1905, but with reservations. These reservations were eventually written into the text of the 1906 constitution and gave the clergy a supervisory role over all legislation to ensure that no legislation was in contravention of Islamic law. However, the number of clergy supporting the king was more numerous. The ideal type of government for the clergy was one based on the *Shari'a* or *Hokomut Mashru'ah*.

Iran's clerical establishment, which had become stronger during the Qajar period, was also financially independent from the government and acted as a countervailing center of power.[21] If Iran had a strong and well-functioning state, an independent and enlightened clergy would have been an important moderating force. But in Iran in the nineteenth and early twentieth centuries the state was extremely weak. Thus, the clerical power combined with the power of tribal chieftains and elements of the merchant class and landed aristocracy acted as obstacles to modernization and especially democratization. Indeed, provided that the monarchy did not go too far in challenging basic Muslim laws, the clergy preferred striking a bargain with the king rather than siding with nationalist and modernist forces. In this way, the clerical establishment contributed to the rise of modernizing dictators such as the Pahlavi kings by making the parliamentary road to reform difficult. The spread of leftist ideas with their atheistic connotations to Iran contributed to this tendency among the clergy as they saw these ideas as posing an even greater threat to Islam's and to their own interests than the monarchy.[22]

The situation only changed in the early 1960s because of the following factors: (1) the more aggressive modernizing policies of Muhammad Reza Pahlavi, including the granting of voting rights to women and land reform; (2) the official elimination of the Iranian Left (the Tudeh) and the Soviet Union's courting of Islam abroad while suppressing it within; and (3) the instrumentalization of the Islamic discourse by the Left as best illustrated by the work of Ali Shariati, which is a Marxist reading of Islam, and the ideology of the Mujahedin-e-Khalgh. The clerical establishment finally succeeded in acquiring political power with the Islamic Revolution of 1979.

CENTRALITY OF THE KING, FRAGMENTED ELITE, AND PERSONALITY-BASED POLITICS

Since pre-Islamic times and until the Islamic Revolution, the institution of kingship had been the centerpiece of political and judicial power in Iran. This situation did not change with Iran's Islamization, because the Islamic caliphate increasingly acquired the characteristic of a secular monarchy, a model that was also emulated by Iran's Turkic rulers. The centrality of the king meant that his personal character and qualities of statesmanship largely determined Iran's political and social destiny. It was Iran's misfortune that at a time when two major imperial powers were gradually dominating its immediate neighborhood it was ruled by kings of weak intellectual prowess and failing commitment to the improvement of Iran's conditions.

During the early nineteenth century, the long reign of Fathalishah Qajar (1798–1834), a self-indulgent and superstitious monarch, and the untimely death of Abbas Mirza, the crown prince, hampered Iran's progress and opened it to foreign intervention.

In practice, the power of Iranian monarchs in modern times has not been absolute, because often they have lacked the financial and military means to extend their power over powerful tribal khans, who were often supported by either Britain or Russia. Moreover, the king was bound by the rules of the *Shari'a* and later by the constitution. Nevertheless, the inescapable fact is that the concept of power in Iran was personal and arbitrary. Lord Curzon's view that "the government of Persia is little else than the arbitrary exercise of authority by a series of units in a descending scale from the sovereign to the headman of a petty village" is largely correct.[23]

The tradition of absolute monarchy in Iran had another long-term negative dimension, namely belief in personalities rather than institutions in determining the nation's fate, hence the pervasive view that a single individual, be it Reza Shah, Mossadegh, or Khomeini, can save Iran. This has meant that major political figures were by the force of circumstances transformed into absolute monarchs, though under different guise. The best example of a metamorphosis of absolutist monarchy into a religious garb is the institution of the Velayat-e-Faqih (Guardianship of Jurist Council) and the position of the *rahbar* (leader) in the Islamic Republic as the rahbar is the final arbiter on all domestic and foreign affairs. The Iranian elite, meanwhile, has lacked cohesion, and intra-elite relations have been highly competitive, thus providing opportunities for foreign powers to penetrate and dominate Iran.

EARLY EFFORTS AT MODERNIZATION: CAUSES OF FAILURE

The first impetus to modernization in Iran was its defeat in the first round of Russo-Iranian wars (1804–12). Abbas Mirza, the crown prince, "the only Qajar in the dynastic line devoted to self-strengthening reform,"[24] initiated reforms in the army, the bureaucracy, and education during his governorship of Azerbaijan; he also sent the first group of Iranian students abroad to study. He was aided in his efforts by two able and patriotic assistants, Mirza Issa and Mirza Abulqasem Farahani (Qaem Maqam). Abbas Mirza's untimely death in 1833 ended this first and modest phase of reforms.

Abbas Mirza's son, who succeeded to the throne as Muhammad Shah, was a religious man without much understanding of the need for reform. His chief adviser was the reformist Mirza Abulqasem Farahani. However, because of intrigues instigated by those whose interests were threatened by his reforms, and some British involvement, he was killed by the king's orders and replaced by Haj Mirza Agasi, who was not interested in reforms.

Meanwhile, as a result of various capitulatory treaties Iran was beginning to be flooded by European exports, which were undermining Iranian crafts. As noted by Nikkie Keddie, these privileges opened Asian countries "to European goods while prohibiting any protection of domestic industry. Free trade was thus imposed on Iran before it was even accepted in Great Britain,"[25] leading to "the first petitions from bazaris protesting unfair competition from Western imports."[26]

AMIR KABIR AND HIS REFORMS

When Nasser ed-Din Shah came to power in 1848 he was only eighteen years old and relied heavily on his reformist prime minister Mirza Taghi Khan Amir Kabir. Within less than three years Amir Kabir reorganized the military along Western lines; implemented financial reforms; reduced the financial perks of princes and courtiers; established Iran's first newspaper and first secular educational institution, Dar-ul-Fonoun, with European instructors; and built a number of industries. He also introduced reforms in the bureaucracy and initiated what could have become the beginnings of a more consultative form of government. To balance the British and Russian influence he tried to establish contact with the United States and other European countries and tried to build a navy to protect Iran's Persian Gulf shores, which were increasingly coming under the purview of the British navy.[27]

However, Amir Kabir had powerful enemies, including the king's mother. His economic measures and his educational reforms alienated the courtiers and the *ulama*, and his independent posture worried the British, all of whom conspired to poison the king's mind against him.[28] The king's youth and, according to some, Amir Kabir's "imperious and tutorial" tone toward him led the king to order his assassination in 1852.[29]

THE SPREAD OF REFORMIST IDEAS

With Amir Kabir's death the first serious effort at systematic modernization came to an end, not to be resumed—half-heartedly—until the 1870s. However, the ideas of reform, and especially the importance of the establishment of the rule of law, constitutionalism, a modern bureaucracy, and the spread of modern education, continued to gain strength in Iran, partly spurred by the return of Iranian students from abroad.

One of the most influential reformists was Mirza Malcom Khan. He was of Armenian origin and had studied in France at the Iranian government's expense.[30] His main goal was to modernize Iran along Western lines because he believed that if non-European countries could import the products of Europe's technology, such as the telegraph, they could also adopt their principles of government.[31] He further believed that any attempt to develop an indigenous model of progress would be a waste of time. However, being aware of Islam's influence among the people, Malcom argued that Islam, especially Persian Islamism, is fully compatible with Westernization. Malcom therefore concluded that the greatest obstacle to the progress in the Muslim East was not Islam but rather the presentation of principles of civilization "as essentially European, and by association Christian in origin." Consequently, in Malcom's view the only way to make them acceptable was "to divest them of their European aspect and to present them as the long forgotten achievement of the Muslims themselves."[32] In this attitude toward Islam, Malcom found himself in agreement with Sayyid Jamal ed-Din al-Afghani. For Malcom and other reformist thinkers, such as Mirza Yusuf Khan Mustashar ul Dawleh, the establishment of the rule of law and the curbing of the arbitrary powers of the king and other officials were essential. Indeed, these intellectuals and political leaders attributed Europe's progress to the rule of law.[33]

Malcom was also a believer in organizing the merchant community within a chamber of commerce so as to enable merchants to pool their resources for investment in the country. However, despite his brilliance and his contributions to Iran's intellectual revival, Malcom, like many other Iranian reformists, had serious weaknesses, namely greed and excessive ambition, and a naive belief in the power of legislation to set the society right in the absence of fundamental economic, social, and cultural changes.

RISE OF IRANIAN CONSCIOUSNESS AND NATIONALISM

The nineteenth century saw the awakening of Iranian ethnic and cultural consciousness and a growing interest in pre-Islamic Iran, largely as a result of the works of European archeologists and scholars, especially the reading of Darius' carvings in Bisitun.[34] This reawakening led to the emergence of a school of thought that blamed Iran's decline partly on Arab and Turkic invasions and partly on Islam—an Arab export. As a remedy, this school advocated a resurrection of the old Iranian culture and virtues and recommended ridding the Persian language of Arabic words. Among those representing these ideas in the nineteenth century, Mirza Agha Khan Kirmani, Fathali Akhundzadeh, and Jalaleddin Mirza Qajar stand out. In short, the reassertion of Iranian identity and later the popularity of a nationalist discourse attributed to Reza Shah and his son had earlier roots.

THE SPREAD OF SOCIALIST IDEAS

One of the factors that have deeply affected Iran's evolution in the past century has been the spread of socialist ideas and the emergence, transformation, and consolidation of a leftist discourse.[35]

Although the Left never achieved power in Iran, leftist ideas permeated and transformed nationalist and Islamist discourses. The intellectual interaction between the Islamists and the leftists since the early 1960s has been particularly interesting and has resulted in what can be called the lefticization of Islam and the Islamization of the Left. The best example of lefticized Islamists are Ali Shariati and the Mujahedin-e-Khalgh movement.[36] The lefticization of Islam is symbolized by Ayatollah Mahmud Taleghani, the current supreme leader Ayatollah Khamenei, and the old hardliners, such as the followers of the Khat-e-Imam.

The emergence of the Left added a new layer to Iran's other fissures, making the achievement of national consensus on many issues difficult. By excessive championing of the cause of ethnic and linguistic minorities, the Left increased centrifugal tendencies in Iran, thus justifying coercive measures against them to prevent territorial disintegration.[37] Also, the traditional Left behaved according to Moscow's directives and contrary to Iran's interests. At crucial junctures, such as the Mossadegh era, and between 1979 and 1981, the Left did not support the nationalists—liberal or Islamist—hoping that their failure would lead to a socialist revolution, thus contributing to the complete Islamist takeover.

In short, the Iranian Left did not help the cause of modernization or democratization in Iran. By posing an existential challenge to all-important institutions of the country and, in some cases, to the country as a whole, it justified repressive policies of various governments.

THE CONSTITUTIONAL REVOLUTION

Three factors were responsible for Iran's Constitutional Revolution of 1905–7, which is one of the few truly grassroots movements of the Muslim world. First, reforms had led to a greater political awakening of substantial segments of the Iranian people. Students coming back from Europe were spreading ideas of constitutionalism and the rule of law. Their activities and particularly those of Mirza Malcom Khan had also led to the creation of various and often secret societies.[38] During this time some of these societies were known as "Anjuman" and played an important role in garnering grassroots support for the constitutionalists. Second, there was growing anger at the extent of foreign economic and political penetration of Iran and the ensuing socioeconomic dislocation. Among these dislocations were the replacement of handmade products by industrial imports, resulting in unemployment. The merchants were also angry at the concessions granted to foreigners. Some of these merchants with enough capital were interested in investing in industry in Iran but could not do so because of the lack of order and foreign competition.[39] One of the most sweeping concessions was that granted to Baron Julius Reuter in 1872, which Lord Curzon called the most extraordinary surrender of the entire industrial resources of the country. This concession was finally revoked because of popular opposition and pressure from Russia.[40] But the concession that brought about a broad-based coalition involving the intellectual elite, the *ulama,* and the merchant community, and which was supported by the ordinary people, was the tobacco concession granted to a British subject, Major G. Talbot, in 1890 for fifty years. The terms of the concession were highly unfavorable to Iran.[41]

The excessively generous terms of this concession elicited Russia's opposition and, more important, popular outrage. Indeed, the tobacco revolt, as it came to be known, is considered the most important milestone in the history of the Iranian people's political awakening. The concession was revoked because of massive popular opposition led by three prominent religious leaders who issued a fatwa (religious edict) calling on the people to stop smoking until the concession was canceled.

Third, the uprising in Russia between 1905 and 1907, forcing the tsar to establish a parliament, had an influence in Iran, especially in Tabriz, which was a principal bastion of constitutionalism. An added factor was Russia's defeat in the Russo-Japanese War of 1905, which punctured the myth of its invincibility.

CONSTITUTION OF 1906 AND COUNTERREVOLUTION

Despite the tobacco revolt, no major change was made to satisfy public demands for a more fair and efficient government. Meanwhile, Muzaffar-ed Din Shah, who had succeeded to the throne, continued his father's tradition of foreign borrowing and foreign travel, which kept people's anger alive. Moreover, there was mounting dissatisfaction with the new government-imposed tariffs and the behavior of the Belgian customs adviser, Mr. Naus, on the part of the merchants.[42] These frustrations finally boiled over in December 1905, and a number of merchants took sanctuary in the Masjid-e-Shah mosque, where they were joined by some clerics. After promises given and broken by the king and some efforts at repression, finally the king issued a *Farman* (order) for the formation of an assembly. The Majlis (parliament or assembly), composed only of the representatives of Tehran, drafted a constitution, which finally received royal approval on December 7, 1906.

However, from the beginning Iran's fledgling attempts at constitutional democracy were threatened by internal and external opposition. Externally, Russia was extremely unhappy with Iranian developments, given the fact that Russia itself had suspended its reforms. Internally, Muhammad Ali Shah was against constitutionalism and, moreover, was completely under Russian influence.

Morgan Shuster, the American adviser the Iranian government had hired to reform its finances, noted that the shah "hated and despised his subjects . . . and from having a notorious scoundrel for his Russian tutor, he easily became the avowed tool and satrap of the Russian government."[43]

Muhammad Ali Shah quickly destroyed the first parliament by using force. He was assisted in this by the Russians. However, the people once aroused were not willing to submit to authoritarian rule. Resistance continued in Tabriz and was joined later by similar movements in other major cities and finally led to the dismissal and exile of Muhammad Ali Shah.

An important point to note here is that the British attitude to Iran's constitutional movement was purely self-serving. The British initially supported the constitutional movement largely because Russia was against it. But after the 1907 Russo-British agreement, Britain changed its attitude. Now it was important for Britain to maintain the agreement with Russia and secure its European interests. This attitude is best reflected in the statement of S. D. Sazonov, the Russian foreign minister at the time: "The English, engaged in the pursuit of political aims of vital interest in Europe, in case of necessity, will be prepared to sacrifice certain interests in Asia. . . . This is a circumstance which we can, of course, exploit for ourselves as, for instance, in Persian affairs."[44] In the remaining years until World War I and the emergence of Reza Shah, Russian and British intrigues and willing Iranian accomplices frustrated Iran's every effort at reform. The case of Morgan Shuster, the American adviser to the Iranian government who was let go because of Russian pressures, is the best example of these intrigues.

Iran's occupation by the British, Russian, and Ottoman troops during World War I and the devastation that they brought were additional blows to Iran's young democracy. Nevertheless, the period also saw the emergence of party politics and a lively press.

REZA SHAH: IRAN'S FIRST MODERNIZING DICTATOR

Reza Shah Pahlavi (1925–41) is a controversial figure in Iran. To some he is the man who saved Iran from chaos and disintegration, and to others he is a greedy tyrant that nipped in the bud Iran's nascent democracy and implemented what one author has called "pseudo modernization."[45]

There is no doubt that Reza Shah laid the foundation for Iran's modernization along the lines of a nationalist discourse. However, by neglecting the task of nurturing constitutional rule and by curbing free expression of ideas and forcing certain social changes without a broad-based popular consensus, he polarized Iranian society. Some of this polarization between the impatient modernizers and the lethargic traditionalists was inevitable, but other fissures were avoidable. According to some, Reza Shah's reforms were too fast-paced and created psychological dislocations.

Be that as it may, in a short period Reza Shah succeeded in subduing rebellious tribes, establishing a modern army and the first European-style university, and building the Trans-Iranian Railroad. He also purchased equipment for building a steel mill, but the outbreak of World War II, which led to the Allied occupation of Iran and Reza Shah's removal from power, prevented the realization of this goal. It was during Reza Shah's reign that relatively large numbers of students were sent to Europe to study.[46]

Initially, Reza Shah had wide popular support. Therefore, it is possible that he could have achieved his goals within the limits of the 1906 constitution—revised to accommodate his accession to the throne. This would have endowed his actions with greater legitimacy, making their reversal more difficult. Moreover, a constitutional approach to modernization would have helped Iran's institutional development and endowed it with viable institutions capable of channeling the newly unleashed forces of intellectuals, factory workers, and other societal groups. However, Reza Shah mishandled relations with the clergy. Arguably, Reza Shah could not have done what Ataturk did in Turkey, since unlike their Ottoman counterparts, members of the Iranian clergy were financially independent from the state. But he could have forged an alliance with the more progressive clergy and thereby gained support for his reforms. Similarly, by banning any activity by those accused of socialist leanings, he prevented the development of a more nationalist and independent Left in Iran. Perhaps most important, Reza Shah perpetuated the tradition of the centrality of the king in determining Iran's destiny. Thus, unlike in Turkey, no united elite dedicated to the cause of reform emerged in Iran.

However, without World War II and Iran's occupation by the Allied forces, Iran's modernization would have continued and perhaps in time would have led to a more open system.

THE ERA OF MUHAMMAD REZA PAHLAVI

Muhammad Reza Pahlavi ruled Iran for thirty-seven years, and during his reign Iran went through several stages, each with its special characteristics. During this time, Iran became a full-fledged rentier state, as oil production reached high levels and the price of oil began to increase by the late 1960s and rose dramatically between 1973 and 1976.

Iran underwent considerable transformation during this period. However, this transformation was not complete. In the area of political development, namely the building of independent institutions and practices conducive to democracy, very little was achieved. The reign of the Shah is best studied according to the following three phases.

Troubled Democracy: 1941–1953

The first part of this period, coinciding with the Allied occupation of Iran, resulted in a substantial opening of the political space. Consequently, it led both to the empowerment of the parliament and to the formation of different parties. This was partly because Allied powers, who had justified their intervention in Iran on the basis of a struggle against Nazism and getting rid of a "pro-German" regime, encouraged such political opening. However, it also introduced a degree of instability to Iranian politics, since the parliament abused its right of appointing and dismissing government. The political party to take full advantage of this was the Tudeh Party, the reorganized version of the early Communist Party of Persia. However, the Tudeh Party was rife with internal disputes, notably between those who wanted a democratic system and the hardcore Marxist elements, mostly subservient to Moscow.

The other groupings either were too disorganized to qualify as political parties or were essentially underground clandestine organizations. Among the first was the Iran Party, consisting mostly of European-educated technocrats with liberal and/or social-democratic leaning; the Pan-Iranist Party, an extreme nationalist party; the Fedayin-e-Islam, Islamists inspired by the Ikhvan ul Muslimin (Muslim Brotherhood); the conservative party Iradeh-e-Milli (Popular Will); and the Democratic Party.

On other fronts, the Allied occupation not only did not contribute to Iran's development but had significant negative fallouts, notably inflationary pressures, which continued to plague the country later.

The most problematic issue in occupied Iran was the emergence of separatist, socialistically oriented, and Moscow-supported republics in Azerbaijan and Kurdistan. The Azerbaijan crisis was the more important of the two and was finally resolved in 1946, when the Soviet troops withdrew from Iran under U.S. and international pressure. But the emergence of a hostile superpower on its doorstep would deeply impact Iran's future options and its internal and external evolution.

Other landmark events of this period were the nationalization of the Anglo-Iranian Oil Company (AIOC) in 1951 and the emergence of Mohammad Mossadegh as the foremost Iranian nationalist leader.

The nationalization of oil was a natural impulse for a country that had suffered so much from foreign economic penetration. However, from a purely pragmatic perspective it was not a wise move. The handling of the crisis by Mossadegh at the time left much to be desired. In particular, Mossadegh's hope that the United States would support Iran against the British was naive. The act of nationalization was viewed by the Americans as a breach of contract and thus could not be supported by the United States, which saw this as setting a disturbing precedent for other countries.[47]

The nationalization of the AIOC was also manipulated by various internal political forces and external powers to their own interests, thus creating an atmosphere of instability. The Tudeh Party played a negative role in this period. Initially, to weaken the monarchy, it supported Mossadegh, but later, when he came under pressure, the party and its patron the Soviet Union withdrew their support because both wanted an eventual socialist revolution in Iran rather than the strengthening of nationalist and democratic forces.

The rivalry and mutual distrust between the Shah and Mossadegh, themselves a reflection of the divided state of Iran's political leadership and elite, further contributed to Iran's instability. This instability was evidenced in the parliamentary life of the country, wherein various factions recklessly pursued their own parochial interests.

It is very difficult to determine exactly what contributed to the coup d'état of August 1953. What is certain is that the United States was afraid of a Communist takeover in Iran and had concluded that Mossadegh was incapable of preventing such an outcome.

During this period, Iran's lively political life deteriorated into chaos. This led the people to yearn for order and stability, a factor that enabled the Shah to consolidate his power and close the political sphere following the 1953 events.

The situation of turmoil and Iran's financial difficulties, partly the result of the British embargo on the export of Iranian oil, meant that not much attention was paid to development issues. Thus, in terms of modernization, this was a lost period.

Planned Development: 1953–1962

At the end of World War II, Iran had established a planning organization and had drawn up a seven-year development plan. However, the lack of funds and the oil nationalization and its fallout had rendered the plan's implementation impossible.

The focus of the second development plan, as that of the first, was the building of the country's infrastructure and the expansion of existing industries. However, the plan in reality was an amalgam of various projects and did not represent "a clearly-defined development policy."[48] Nevertheless, this period witnessed a good deal of modernization of Iran's physical infrastructure and the development of its human capital through the expansion of education and health care.

Politically, the facade of parliamentary constitutionalism was maintained but the political space had greatly narrowed. By 1960, however, a combination of internal economic and external political factors led to an effort at liberalization.

Among the external factors was the hostility of the Soviet Union and the different approach of the Kennedy administration toward developing countries in general and Iran in particular. The latter factor emboldened various opposition movements, such as the National Front (supporters of Mossadegh) and those personalities gathered around Ali Amini (former cabinet minister), to challenge the Shah. Finally, the shah appointed Amini as prime minister, and a period of relative political openness followed. Amini tried to co-opt the National Front leaders to his side, but the latter refused to cooperate and asked for Amini's dismissal. This was a serious miscalculation on the part of the Front because it was based on the assumption that Amini's failure would provide the Front with a chance to gain power. However, the Front was wrong and the shah managed to outwit both Amini and his collaborators and the Front. Meanwhile, the Kennedy administration, whose support of the Amini government had enhanced the Shah's fear for his own survival, did not provide it with the financial aid it needed to succeed.

From White Revolution to Islamic Government: 1962–1978

The Amini episode convinced the shah that if he wanted to stay in power he had to regain the confidence of the United States and champion reforms. It was this realization that led him to launch his so-called White Revolution or the Revolution of Shah and People. While most scholars of Iranian affairs have mocked the idea of the Shah as a revolutionary leader, many of the actions undertaken by the Shah in this period were indeed of a revolutionary character. Paramount among these were land reform and the granting of voting rights to women. Other reforms included the creation of health and literacy corps.

These reforms, coupled with other developments, such as the granting of extraterritorial rights to the American military mission in Iran, ignited the anger of the clerical establishment, the landowners, and the *bazaris* (merchant community). It was during this period that the Ayatollah Khomeini emerged as the leader of the opposition to the shah. There were riots and uprisings, which were suppressed, and the Ayatollah Khomeini was forced into exile in Najaf. Until the late 1960s, however, the Shah did not feel secure enough to do away with the outward trappings of parliamentary constitutionalism, although political parties such as the Melat, Mardom, and later Iran Novin had no grassroots support and lacked independence. Other civil society organizations, such as the trade unions and professional associations, also lacked real independence. But two events, namely the first wave of increases in the price of oil and the British decision to withdraw from the east of Suez, created conditions for the Shah to implement his vision of the future for Iran. The increase in oil prices gave the Shah the financial means and the British withdrawal meant that the West needed Iran more than ever, thus making the Shah a principal instrument of U.S. policy in the Persian Gulf. This meant that for some time the United States would not pressure Iran on democratization and other reforms.

During this period, Iran did achieve a certain level of modernization, including industrialization, urbanization, and improved gender equality, literacy, and health care. There was also a greater degree of social mobility, partly caused by sending students abroad at government expense or by granting them a favorable rate of foreign exchange, and partly due to the overall expansion of education and the needs of an expanding bureaucracy. Ironically, many of these students turned against the Shah and supported the Islamic Revolution. However, opportunities for upward mobility were not commensurate with the numbers of educated youth. Some observers have seen this imbalance as contributing to the revolution.

In terms of democratization, Iran regressed in this period. The shah dissolved political parties and replaced them with the single-party Rastakhis. More damaging still was that the Shah himself increasingly became the center of government and policy. Meanwhile, the increased tempo of modernization created new fissures in the society, especially in the cultural area.

The cultural policy of the Shah was a continuation and acceleration of his father's and was based on the resurrection of pre-Islamic Iranian symbols and traditions. This policy had always had its detractors within the *ulama* and other traditional classes, whereas the educated public basically supported it. However, during this period, the Shah went too far in terms of legitimizing his rule on the basis of the pre-Islamic traditions of Iran, while simultaneously undermining Islam and the material interests of the clergy and other traditional classes. The identification of the regime with pre-Islamic Iran and the subversion of Iranian nationalism into the cult of the monarchy turned many sectors of society, beyond those traditionally identified with Islam, away from Iranian nationalism and toward a more militant form of Islam.

The Islamists, in fact, attacked everything Iranian and characterized pre-Islamic Iran as the era of darkness and ignorance (*jahiliya*). However, the greatest failure of the Shah was his inability to absorb sufficient numbers of the new emerging middle classes and intelligensia into the state system and to create a vibrant and large private sector that could accommodate these groups' aspirations.

The result was the emergence of a coalition of forces with diverse interests and attitudes that opposed the Shah. When by the late 1970s the price of oil went down and the Carter administration in the United States changed its strategy, the Shah's regime could no longer hold and collapsed from within.[49]

THE ISLAMIC REPUBLIC

The mass movement that brought down the shah's regime in February 1979 consisted of groups with widely different ideological tendencies, interests, and visions of Iran's future. The first group consisted of various shades of the Left, from Islamists to traditional leftists and Maoists. The second group consisted of nationalists of either liberal or Islamic coloring. Finally, there were the Islamists who were divided into traditional and revolutionary subgroups.

All these groups were united in their opposition to the shah, but beyond that they shared few things in common. Moreover, the leftists and nationalist forces were internally divided. Consequently, the Islamists managed to manipulate these forces and reduce them to incompetence.[50]

The political system that finally emerged was a hybrid that combined elements of republicanism with notions of polity and government based on Islam. The fact that the Islamists had to bow in the direction of republicanism and to recognize the people as a basis, albeit secondary, of sovereignty and legitimacy shows that a century of modernizing and democratizing efforts had made an impact that could not be totally eradicated. An important indication of this is the fact that despite their earlier opposition to women's suffrage the Islamists did not take away women's voting rights.

The unstable and even chaotic state of Iran in the immediate postrevolution period, followed by the outbreak of the Iran-Iraq War in September 1980, adversely affected Iran's modernization and democratization. The chaotic conditions coupled with repressive measures on the part of the government led to a significant outflow of money and talent, including nearly all of Iran's newly emerging entrepreneurs, while industrial output plummeted. But most seriously the Iran-Iraq War incurred horrendous economic and human costs and also diverted funds from development to military efforts.

During the first decade of the revolution, the government pursued a statist economic policy, which further undermined whatever private sector had existed. Meanwhile, a variety of foundations emerged that were in fact economic fiefdoms for influential members of the ruling elite. The reshaping of the country's banking and financial system on the basis of Islamic principles further accelerated capital flight and discouraged savings and investment.[51]

When, after the signing of the August 1988 ceasefire with Iraq, the government tried to liberalize the economy, the structures it had created after the revolution proved extremely resistant to change. The government, however, did make some advances in rural development, education, and literacy.

Politically, despite some aspects of democratic governance, such as regular elections, the Islamic regime is no more democratic than its predecessor was. This is because the rights of elected bodies are severely limited by three factors: (1) sovereignty belongs to God and only secondarily to the people; (2) no legislation can be enacted (and the Guardian Council makes sure that it is not) if it is against the *Shari'a*; and (3) the supreme leader can veto legislation. Indeed, as Ayatollah Khomeini repeatedly said, the function of the parliament in the Islamic Republic is not legislation (*ghanoun ghozari*) but rather developing plans (*barnameh ghozari*). Similarly, nothing was done to create political parties. Again, according to Ayatollah Khomeini's vision, political parties have no place in Islamic societies. According to him, in Islam there are two parties: the Party of God (Hizbullah) and the Party of Satan. In reality, however, a number of factions have behaved as political parties. Individual freedoms, too, became more limited as anti-vice corps even inspected people's homes to ensure that no sinful activities were under way.

On the cultural front, initially there was an attack on Iran's pre-Islamic traditions. For example, at one time Ayatollah Khomeini expressed the hope that the Iranian people would not celebrate Norouz (the pre-Islamic Iranian new year) and would celebrate only the birthday of Islam's prophet. However, popular resistance and the outbreak of the Iran-Iraq War forced the government to relent and even use Iranian nationalism in its war efforts.

REACTION TO ISLAMIC RULE

The Islamic Revolution was in many ways a classic, albeit extreme, reaction to the dislocations caused by the process of modernization in a late-modernizing country. Yet, paradoxically, the revolution itself was a modern phenomenon in the sense that it ideologized Islam by using a revolutionary discourse and used religious symbols to mobilize the masses.[52]

Moreover, inadvertently, the Islamic Republic itself became an agent of modernization. The Islamic revolutionaries had accused the Shah of neglecting the less advantaged segments of society and ignoring democratic rights. They had promised that things would be different under Islamic rule. These factors led the government to encourage education among the rural and other traditional segments of society and set up military organizations such as the Revolutionary Guard and Basij to implement its plans. The result of these activities was the emergence of a more educated and politically conscious population, including large numbers within the clergy itself. As is often the case, however, these products of the revolution were no longer satisfied with the system as it was and demanded reform.

REFORMIST DISCOURSE IN THE ISLAMIC REPUBLIC

From the beginning, a number of senior religious leaders and considerable segments of the population were opposed to the direct involvement of the clergy in government and politics and the excessive sacralization of the sociopolitical sphere. However, initially, there was considerable support for the idea that a government and polity based on Islam could remedy Iran's many ills. Furthermore, Iraq's invasion of Iran in September 1980 rallied nearly all the people around the government.

However, by August 1988, when Iran was forced to accept a humiliating ceasefire, disenchantment with the government and the Islamic republic was widespread. The popular disenchantment was the result of the government's policy of casting the war against Iraq in absolute terms as that between truth and falsehood (*haq* versus *batil*) and its claims that God was on Iran's side. Iran's defeat consequently shattered the Iranians' belief in the rightness of their cause and in the validity of their ideology and their political system. An additional factor behind this questioning was Iran's international isolation and later the imposition of punitive measures, such as economic sanctions in the context of the United States' containment policy. One result of these developments was the emergence of a reformist discourse in Iran.

EVOLUTION OF REFORMIST DISCOURSE

The reformist discourse has evolved in the past fifteen years. Initially it had two aspects. One was a procedural aspect related to changing certain elements of the 1979 constitution, especially those parts pertaining to the relative role of the prime minister and president, in order to ensure a better functioning of the government. The second aspect was related to issues such as the institution of the Velayat-e-Faqih and whether after Khomeini's death this institution was necessary, plus democracy, civil society, and the role of religion in society and politics.

The first set of issues was quite easily resolved when the constitution of 1979 was reformed, but the more fundamental issues still remain unsettled and mark the division between the reformers, or what one author has called the "post-Islamist intellectuals,"[53] and the conservatives.[54]

The underlying principles of the reformist discourse, despite certain differences among its protagonists, are the following. The first principle is a more limited and restrained definition of the religious domain. A principal proponent of this view is Abdolkarim Soroush. He advocates a minimalistic definition of religion (*ghabz-e-din*) and limits the domain of religion to the inner self of individuals. In this way Soroush—and Ayatollah Mojtahed-e-Shabestari—put the social, political, and technical domains outside the realm of religion.

The second principle is a distinction between the divine and metaphysical or, in other words, between spiritual dimensions of religion and its more concrete actualization within society and polity, which is bound by time and space and affected by many factors. Soroush explains this in the following way:

When the divine inspiration [religion] acquires a concrete and external existence it also acquires a history, it builds societies and civilizations and attracts different peoples to itself. In the history of this actualized religion many wars and peaces, agreements and disagreements, and deviations take place; various sects are created and leaders and clergy emerge . . . later misinterpretations take place . . . religion acquires the imprint of different ethnic, intellectual, and philosophical trends. The religious order interacts with other orders [and] thus becomes influenced by them and exerts influence over them. . . . In short, religion becomes a human and earthly organization and order and it becomes an instrument of corrupt and self-serving interests.[55]

He further asserts that not all religious acts are triggered by religious motives. Moreover, Soroush maintains that external manifestations of religion are not always in keeping with its essence. According to Soroush, if the outward manifestations of religion are determined by their spatial and temporal context, then they are representative of relative and not absolute truth. Therefore, this aspect of religion should be subject to the same methods of analysis as applied in the case of other political and social philosophies. Moreover, everyone with sufficient knowledge and mastery of the methods of scientific inquiry can engage in this endeavor, and interpretations are conditioned by the interpreter's personal background, socioeconomic condition, and political preference. Therefore, members of the clergy who make their living out of religion are uniquely unqualified to interpret religious roles because they will interpret them in ways to serve their own parochial interests.[56] He maintains that religion does not offer a plan for government and that any efforts to derive such a plan are fruitless. In addition, dealing with social, economic, and political affairs requires special expertise and therefore must be entrusted to skilled professionals who are well versed in the modern social sciences of economics, sociology, and public administration. He states that religion cannot explain these dynamics or deal with questions raised and problems created by them: there can be no religious thermodynamics and, by the same token, there can be no religious politics and economics.[57]

Soroush does not prescribe a simple and total separation of religion and politics. Instead, believing that the politics of each society reflects—or should reflect—the beliefs of its members, he argues that in a religious society politics takes a religious form and this religious form should be the result of a system based on public opinion and participation, in other words, democracy. He also opposes the ideologization of religion because of the relationship of religious ideology—like secular ideologies—to power and the use of religion by the holders of power to reduce individual freedom and prevent rational inquiry about religion. Soroush believes that all human beings have rights that while compatible with religion are not defined by it.

The third principle is that the concept of the Velayat-e-Faqih is unnecessary. This is implicit in Soroush's writings. But other reformist thinkers have expressed this view more openly. One of these thinkers is Ayatollah Abdullah Nouri, the editor of the newspaper *Khordad*, who was imprisoned on the charge of insulting Islam and opposing Velayat-e-Faqih. Nouri in his extensive defense during his trial said that "although there were references to the concept of the Velayat-e-Faqih in religious texts (Kotob-e-Feqhi) the politico-governmental philosophy of this concept as embodied in the constitution derived from the society and not from the Imam [Khomeini]." He further adds that the Imam's leadership derived from the society and not from the concept of Velayat-e-Faqih.[58] What this statement and Soroush's views amount to is that ultimately popular will has the last word. Soroush's views and those of other reformists ultimately lead to pluralism and democracy. Indeed, the reformists believe that they have a blueprint for an "Islamic democracy" within which the place of Islam "will ultimately be determined by the will of the people."[59]

The emergence of this reformist discourse, plus the existence of more openly secularist intellectuals in Iran, is a natural by-product of the Islamic Revolution because, as put by D. E. Smith, "religion helps to produce mass mobilization and then declines politically as increasing numbers of participants come to perceive politics as a relatively autonomous area of human activity."[60]

Together with this reformist-Islamic discourse there has been a revival of Iranian nationalist discourse, and even the notion that Islam is an alien (Arab) export have gained new currency.[61] However, despite the emergence of Islamic reformist and nationalist discourses, plus burgeoning civil society organizations, the balance of power, notably coercive forces, remains in favor of the state and hence the status quo.

Consequently, despite the election of a reformist president in 1997 and 2001 and a reformist-dominated parliament in 2000, the pace of reform has been slow. Moreover, the antireform and conservative elements managed to exclude reformist candidates from the February 2004 elections, thus making the future of democratization in Iran uncertain. Ironically, however, the conservatives could encourage economic liberalization. Should they succeed in this by creating a viable private sector, in future they could tip the balance of state-society relations in favor of the latter and thus make the conservatives the unwitting promoters of democracy.

CONCLUSIONS

Iran's efforts at modernization over the past 150 years have been hampered by the country's geographic and geostrategic characteristics, its turbulent history, its heterogeneous population, the character of the Shi'a establishment, its divided elites, and peculiarities of its leadership, most notably the centrality of individuals instead of institutions. The traditionally conservative as well as the revolutionary readings of Islam have been hindering elements in Iran's modernization and, more important, its democratization. However, the new progressive and reformist reading of Islam can change this situation and make Islam an enabling factor of modernization and democratization. Because of its geostrategic condition and its power potential, external powers have tried to hinder Iran's modernization and democratization. Iran has also been particularly vulnerable to the vagaries of international politics. Historically, these external factors have had an inhibiting influence on Iran's modernization and democratization and often have undone some of its achievements in these areas.

In the future, Iran's success in modernization and democratization will depend on the ability of its political elite to develop a broad-based consensus on these issues and to find more effective ways of dealing with the dynamics of regional and international politics as they impact Iran.

NOTES

1. E. C. Black, *The Dynamics of Modernization* (New York: Harper & Row, 1966), 98–99, 124.

2. Iran means "the land of Aryans" and has always been called so. Avesta, the holy book of the Zoroastrians, refers to the mythical homeland of the Iranian peoples as "Iranovaj." The Sassanian divided the world into Eran and non-Eran. Even in the Qajar period Iran's official name was "Mamelek-e-Mahrusah-e-Iran."

3. For the Achemenid, Parthian, and Sassanid periods, see Ilya Gershevitch, ed., *The Cambridge History of Iran*, vol. 2, *The Median and Archaemenian Periods* (Cambridge: Cambridge University Press, 1985), and Ehsan Yarshater, ed., *The Cambridge History of Iran*, vol. 3, *The Seleucid, Parthian, and Sasanid Periods* (Cambridge: Cambridge University Press, 1983).

4. Sassanid culture deeply influenced Islamic civilization. Adda Bozeman has called this process Iran's conquest of Islam. Adda B. Bozeman, "Iran: US Foreign Policy and the Tradition of Persian Statecraft," *Orbis* 23 (Summer 1979).

5. In fact, in the tenth and eleventh centuries there was a remarkable Iranian cultural and political renaissance. Such Iranian dynasties as the Samanids and the Buyids achieved considerable power first in the east and later in north central and southern Iran. The Buyids even conquered Baghdad in 945 CE but kept the caliph in power.

6. Charles Issavi, ed., *The Economic History of Iran: 1800–1914* (Chicago: University of Chicago Press, 1971), 9.

7. Ibid.

8. According to British historian Sir Henry Rawlinson, the Turks and Persians for all practical purposes had "divided the kingdom." In fact, by the mid-nineteenth century it was feared that an internecine struggle between the two factions would lead to the dismemberment "of the empire." Quoted in Rouhallah K. Ramazani's *The Foreign Policy of Iran: A Developing Nation in World Affairs 1500–1941* (Charlottesville: University of Virginia Press, 1966), 35.

9. From 1722, however, Nadir was Iran's effective ruler since the last king, Tahmasseb II, was not yet of age.

10. Issavi, *Economic History of Iran*, 13.

11. Ibid., 1.

12. Ibid., 3.

13. Ramazani, *Foreign Policy of Iran*, 28.

14. Hamid Algar, *Mirza Malkum Khan: A Study in the History of Iranian Modernism* (Berkeley: University of California Press, 1969), 127.

15. Ibid.

16. Dennis Wright, *The English Amongst the Persians* (London: William Heinemann, 1977), 1–4.

17. Issavi, *Economic History of Iran*, 16.

18. Quoted in Fereydaun Adamiyat, *Amdisheh Taraghi va Hakoumat Ghanoun: asr-e-Sepahsalar*, trans. by the author (Tehran: Enesharat-e-Kharazmi, 1973), 338–39.

19. Issavi, *Economic History of Iran*, 15–16.

20. Ramazani, *Foreign Policy of Iran*, 28.

21. Hamid Algar, *Religion and State in Iran, 1785–1906: The Role of Ulema in the Qajar Period* (Berkeley: University of California Press, 1969); Shahrough Akhavi, *Religion and Politics in Contemporary Iran: Clergy-State Relations in the Pahlavi Period* (Albany: SUNY Press, 1980).

22. Akhavi, *Religion and Politics.*

23. George N. Curzon, *Persia and the Persian Question* (London: Longman, 1892), 2:391.

24. Nikkie R. Keddie, *Qajar Iran and the Rise of Reza Khan* (Costa Mesa, CA: Mazda Publishers, 1999), 24.

25. Ibid., 23.

26. Ibid.

27. Fereydoun Adamiyat, *Amir Kabir va Iran* (1323; repr., Tehran: Chapkhaneh-e-Payam, 1944–45).

28. To illustrate, when Amir Kabir eliminated the pension of a pro-British prince the British envoy strenuously protested. Ibid., 56.

29. Keddie, *Qajar Iran*, 29.

30. Algar, *Mirza Malcom Khan*, 1–6.

31. Ibid., 17.

32. Ibid., 14–15.

33. Mirza Yusuf Khan, who hailed from a prominent family in Tabriz, wrote a book called *Yek Kalameh* (*One Word*) advocating constitutionalism and the rule of law. He was imprisoned and beaten with his own book.

34. Adamiyat, *Amdisheh Taraghi*; Fereydoun Adamiyat, *Andishehay-e-Mirza Agha Khan Kirmani* (1346; repr., Tehran: Chapkhaneh-e-Piriuz, 1967–68).

35. Sepehr Zabih, *The Communist Movement in Iran* (Berkeley: University of California Press, 1966).

36. Ervand Abrahamian, *The Iranian Mujahedin* (New Haven, CT: Yale University Press, 1984).

37. Good examples of these types of activities are the Jangali Movement of Mirza Kuchek Khan Gilani during 1914–1921 and the Moscow-supported democratic republics of Azerbaijan and Kurdistan. See Zabih, *Communist Movement in Iran*, 13–29.

38. After his Faramoushkhaneh (a precursor of Freemasonry in Iran) was closed, Malcom created another society called Adamiyat, preaching essentially humanist ideas. See Algar, *Mirza Malcom Khan*, 248–58.

39. Haj Amin ul-Zarb was the most important merchant in the late nineteenth century and established some industries, many of which did not survive. See Issavi, *Economic History of Iran*. On the Anjumans, see Edward G. Brown, *The Persian Revolution* of 1905–1909 (Cambridge: Cambridge University Press, 1910).

40. On the history of concessions in Iran, see Ibrahim Teymouri, *Asr-e-Bikhabari Tarikh-e-Imtiazat Dar Iran* (1332; repr., Tehran: Chap-e-Eghbal, 1953–54).

41. Ramazani, *Foreign Policy of Iran*, 68–69.

42. Morgan Shuster recounts that Mr. Naus spent most of his time playing cards with members of other foreign delegations. W. Morgan Shuster, *The Strangling of Persia* (New York: Century, 1912; Westport, CT: Greenwood Press, 1968).

43. Ibid., 21.

44. Quoted in Ramazani, *Foreign Policy of Iran*, 94.

45. Homa Katouzian, *The Political Economy of Modern Iran: Despotism and Pseudo-modernism, 1926–1979* (New York: New York University Press, 1981), 275.

46. On Reza Shah's policies, see Amin Banani, *The Modernization of Iran, 1921–1941* (Stanford, CA: Stanford University Press, 1961).

47. For a discussion of this period, see Katouzian, *Political Economy of Modern Iran*, 171–82.

48. Robert E. Looney, *Economic Origins of the Iranian Revolution* (New York: Pergamon Press, 1982), 12.

49. Nikkie R. Keddie, *The Roots of the Revolution: An Interpretive History of Modern Iran* (New Haven, CT: Yale University Press, 1981).

50. Shaul Bakhash, *The Reign of the Ayatullahs: Iran and the Islamic Revolution*, rev. ed. (New York: Basic Books, 1990).

51. On Iran's economy, see Thiery Caville, *L'Economie de L'Iran Islamique l'entre ordre et desordres* (Paris: Hartman, 2002); also Houshang Amirahmadi, *The Revolution and Economic Transition: The Iranian Experience* (Albany: State University of New York Press, 1990).

52. Donald Eugene Smith, "Religion and Political Modernization in Comparative Perspectives," in Donald Eugene Smith, ed., *Religion and Political Modernization* (New Haven, CT: Yale University Press, 1974), 17.

53. Farhad Khosrokhavar and Olivier Roy, *Iran: Comment sortir d'une revolution religieuse* (Paris: Editions du Seuil, 1999).

54. Shireen T. Hunter, *Iran After Khomeini* (Washington, DC: Center for Strategic and International Studies, 1992).

55. Abdulkarim Soroush, "Shariati va Jameeshenasi-e-Din" (author's translation from the Persian original), *Kian* 3 third year, no. 13 (June–July 1994): 5.

56. Ibid.

57. Ibid.

58. Abdullah Nouri, *Shokhran-e-Islah: Defaiatal-e-Abdullah Nouri* (1378; repr., Tehran: Tarh-e-Naw, 1999).

59. Khosrokhavar and Roy, *Iran*, 92–93.

60. Smith, "Religion and Political Modernization," 18.

61. Khosrokhavar and Roy, *Iran*, 93.

17

A Secular Democracy in the Muslim World: The Turkish Model

Binnaz Toprak

The question is often asked whether Turkey as a secular democracy can be a model for other Muslim states. The Turkish example raises the question of why Turkey has partially succeeded in establishing a functioning democracy while other Muslim states have so far failed. The answers to these questions have policy relevance for all parties interested in modernization and democratization in the Muslim world.

The Turkish experience is of interest because it challenges the view that the structural changes and historical processes that contributed to modernity and democracy in the West and elsewhere are not relevant to Muslim countries, and that in the case of Muslims, these should be replaced by the "explanatory" variable of culture. The possibility that the Turkish experience can be repeated in other Muslim countries can be meaningfully analyzed only if one goes beyond reductionist theories, as exemplified by Samuel Huntington's thesis on the clash of civilizations.[1] Indeed, recent research contradicts Huntington's thesis that the dividing line between Islamic and Western publics is about attitudes toward democracy. Evidence from surveys covering more than 80 percent of the world's population shows that the majority of Muslims throughout the globe support democratic forms of government. Exceptions are found in attitudes toward gender equality and sexual liberalization,[2] topics of major importance. (See Chapter 7 by Valentine Moghadam in this volume.) Despite these findings, the culturalist thesis has dominated discussions on the resistance to democratization in Muslim societies.

The thesis of this chapter is that development and democratization depend on a combination of historical processes and the choices made by political actors. The Turkish road to modernity evolved from initial attempts at modernization also taken by other Muslim countries. However, Turkey later took a different course that eventually allowed for radical changes. The uniqueness of the Turkish case lies in the fact that the evolution of the political system from an Islamic empire into a secular democracy was a continuous process. Moreover, although checkered, this process did not suffer major reversals, and Turkey's incorporation into Western modernity was eventually internalized by the masses.

The early attempts to arrest the decline of the Ottoman Empire by emulating the West later became a political project to integrate Turkey within Western civilization. This project was relatively successful in Turkey because of its state tradition of self-rule, the multiethnic composition of its population, and its historical contacts with and proximity to Europe. Other Muslim countries faced greater difficulty because of colonial memories, or lack of a tradition of statecraft and self-rule, or distant geographies from Europe and hence less contacts with it. The radical secularization program of the Turkish Republic and its acceptance of a democratic form of government were also factors largely absent in the route followed by other Muslim states. Initially, Islamist opposition to the republican project was suppressed; then it was contained, and finally it was integrated into the system. Hence, Turkey escaped the fate of, for example, Iran, where Islamic ideology became the only channel around which the opposition to the Shah's repressive regime could be organized. Similarly, democracy in Turkey meant that it also escaped the fate of, for example, Algeria, where the Islamist opposition turned to terrorism as the only alternative means of gaining political power. As different social groups saw the benefits of a democratic form of government in defending and promoting their interests, the authoritarian route, through long periods of military dictatorship, single-party regimes, or monarchical governments, was also closed for Turkey. Turkey's geographic position and hence its strategic importance for the West led to its inclusion in the Western alliance, thus strengthening this evolution, as Turkey was forced first by the United States to make the transition from one-party rule to democracy and later by the European Union (EU) to consolidate it.

Most important, however, it was the vision of first the late Ottoman and later the republican statesmen and elite to integrate Turkey with the West, to keep a vigil over the realization of this project, and to keep it as an undercurrent of all attempts to change that determined Turkey's route. Undoubtedly, this was accomplished at first by force and later through restrictions on basic rights and freedoms. Nevertheless, it succeeded in the long run to convince the majority, indeed at times in opposition to the state elite's resistance to further change, that a secular democratic Turkey that is part of the European Union is better than alternative projects such as isolating Turkey from developments in global markets and networks of communication or entrapping it within an ideologically oriented state. This initial choice was internalized by the masses as the benefits that a secular democratic system brought to the majority of the population became tangible. Note that at present, around 80 percent of the population consistently support EU membership. The AKP-led government, which is an offshoot of the neo-Islamist movement of the 1970–90 period, is a strong supporter of Turkish membership in the European Union, and the party no longer defines its identity as Islamist. This identity shift in itself is indicative of Turkey's unique road among Muslim societies.

This chapter will focus on the analysis of those characteristics most important for understanding the Turkish case. These factors have important implications for policy analysts. On the one hand, they demonstrate that a Muslim population is not a "barrier" to modernization and democratization. The causes of the Muslim world's "democracy deficit" or "resistance to modernity" should be sought elsewhere. On the other hand, the Turkish model challenges the assumption that democracy can be "brought" to a country through bypassing the unfolding of historical legacies and the struggle for power of indigenous social actors.

SIX HUNDRED YEARS OF SELF-RULE AND A TRADITION OF STATECRAFT

Unlike other Muslim countries, with the exception of Iran, Turkey was never colonized. Ottoman rule lasted six hundred years, and for much of this period it was remarkably successful in maintaining its sovereignty. Ruling over lands in Asia, Africa, and Europe, the Ottomans built a vast empire that kept the peace within its borders until the advent of nationalism in the nineteenth century.

Implications of the Ottoman Legacy of Multiculturalism and Self-Rule

Ottoman society was ethnically and religiously diverse. That the empire lasted for so long is a testimony to the balance it struck among different ethnic and religious groups. The empire's administrative solution to the heterogeneity of its population was the *millet* (religious community) system that gave semiautonomy to religious communities. Based on the Qur'anic principles involving the *Dimmis* (non-Muslims), the administration of the various non-Muslim communities was left to their respective religious leaders.[3] As İlber Ortaylı argues, the status of the individual under the *millet* system was similar to the division between the *civis* and the *fides* in the Roman Empire, the corresponding statuses under classical Ottoman rule being the *askeri* (military) and the *reaya* (subject). Members of different *millets*, not just Muslims, could hold either the *askeri* or the *reaya* status.[4]

In its classical period, the administration of the empire was based on a model that was blind to ethnic differences. Known as *devsirme*, the Ottoman administration was run by men who had originally been born into Christian families in the empire's European provinces and converted to Islam. Probably constructed to prevent a hereditary ruling class, the *devsirme* system was a curious example of an Islamic empire founded by Turks but ruled, with the exception of the sultan, by an administrative corps made up of people of non-Turkic and non-Islamic backgrounds.

This multiethnic and multireligious setting meant that the population of the empire was open to influences from different cultures, especially in those parts of the empire that were either within Europe or in its proximity, and in Anatolian provinces with large Greek, Jewish, Armenian, and *Levanten* (people of European descent) populations. By the late nineteenth and early twentieth centuries, the everyday life of the Ottoman elite closely resembled that of their European counterparts, as European customs, tastes, languages, music, literature, and philosophy entered their homes.

In addition, long centuries of self-rule meant that Turkey escaped an anti-colonial struggle that positioned itself against the West. When the republic was established in 1923, the earlier debates of the late nineteenth century between the Westernists and the Islamists, which revolved around how much to borrow from the West,[5] continued in the form of a power struggle. Hence, the top leadership's vision of integrating Turkey with the West was not shared by all, not even within the leadership itself. However, the regime consolidated itself within a short period after silencing the parliamentary opposition and suppressing a number of rebellions by Islamist groups and the Kurds. The new republic undertook radical reforms that cut it off from its Islamic-Ottoman past. These unprecedented reforms in a Muslim country had far-reaching consequences in terms of the Turkish road to modernity.

The one-party authoritarian rule that was installed rested on bureaucratic and military cadres loyal to the regime and was backed by local notables.[6] The leading republican elite was monolithic in its vision of a Turkish Republic that would be included among, as they put it, "the civilized nations of the West." This elite shared a common understanding of history, a common language, sense of a common destiny, and a common project for the future—factors considered important by scholars for successful nation building. This early decision to integrate Turkey with the West meant that Turkey was closed to both the socialist and later the Islamist models of republican rule.

Tradition of Statecraft: Institution Building

Political scientists have long talked about "sequences of development" that refer to the timing of systemic shifts conducive to democratization. Although the suggested "sequence" may vary, there is agreement that institution building should precede democratization of the system.[7] The Turkish case fits this sequence.

The Establishment of a Legal-Rational Bureaucracy

The establishment of a Weberian-type legal-rational bureacracy that functions on the bases of merit, rules, regulations, keeping of records, and the separation of official roles and property from their private counterparts was part of the Westernization attempts in the nineteenth century. This resulted in the establishment of modern ministries, an administrative structure, and a merit-based bureaucracy.

Late Ottoman bureaucracy recruited from among the graduates of newly instituted secular schools based on the French *grandes écoles* model that socialized and educated promising students for military and bureaucratic careers.

The republic expanded this merit-based system of social mobility, and the state bureaucracy became an important channel to recruit qualified men and women into administrative and other state jobs. The pattern of social mobility has been strikingly open for people of modest backgrounds. Although favoritism, nepotism, and corruption exist, they takes place mostly through political party ties. Bureaucratic or political rule is not based on class-family-clan-tribe-village ties to leadership. There are no Tikriti families (Saddam Hussein's tribe) in Turkey. This is also true of the military, which recruits from among the lower middle classes, who see the institution as a means of upward social mobility. Neither are there "personal guards" whose loyalty is solely to a leader.

The Development of Rule of Law

Equally important in terms of institution building was the development of the rule of law. It was in the nineteenth century that rule of law based on a codified legal system and a developed legal language emerged. Beginning with the Tanzimat reforms, rule of law increasingly came to be understood as the elimination of arbitrary rules and decisions. The Tanzimat Edict of 1839 recognized the basic rights and liberties of Ottoman subjects. The relatively early experiment with constitutionalism in 1876 and in 1908 laid the foundation for a republican form of government. It was also at this time that Ottoman discourse discovered and invented the *ferd* (the individual), *halk* (the people), and *cemiyyet* (society), as a gradual transition was made from *reaya* (subject) to *ferd* and from *cemaat* (community) to *cemiyyet*.[8] A wealth of political parties, associations, chambers, and the like was established, and political movements became active.[9]

The republic eliminated the multiple legal systems of the Ottomans (the *millet* system) and replaced them with universal law applicable to all citizens. The unification of secular courts under a ministry of justice, the adoption of secular commercial, criminal, and family codes, and the guaranteeing of basic rights and liberties in a written constitution were part of institution building in the early years of the republic. So was the establishment of a parliament in 1920 that later became the seat of democratic politics.

The Establishment of a Professional Army

The establishment of a modern, professional army has its roots in the nineteenth century with the founding of military academies. The military institution played a major role in the modernization of the empire and in the founding of the republic. To this day, it has remained loyal to the republican vision and considers its job to be the "guardian" of the secular, unitary state. Its hierarchical command structure and organization prevent infiltration by political groups deemed dangerous to the foundations of the republic. Its loyalty is to an abstract concept of "nation." Hence, it functions neither as a "revolutionary militia" nor as the "guard of the ruling elite." Strengthened by North Atlantic Treaty Organization (NATO) ties and U.S. military aid, it is one of the most modern, disciplined, and professional armies in the Muslim world.

Like other armies in the Muslim and developing world, the Turkish military has interfered several times in the political process. In 1960 and 1980, it staged two coups against elected governments, and in 1971 and 1997, it forced incumbents out of office although it handed over power to elected governments within short periods of time. The army's self-appointed role as a "guardian" has come under heavy criticism in recent years. Despite its "modernist" origins, it has increasingly become an impediment to the consolidation of liberal democracy in Turkey. It remains to be seen to what extent the legal changes to meet the EU criteria will limit the role of the Turkish military in politics.

CLOSE HISTORICAL TIES WITH EUROPE

A long history of relations with the West is a second distinguishing characteristic of the Turkish case. With the conquering of Istanbul away from the Byzantine Empire in 1453, the Ottomans entered into a new phase of relations with the West. Sultan Mehmet wanted to transform Istanbul into a world city. He gave tax privileges to local Byzantine Greeks who chose to stay; encouraged Greeks and Armenians from other parts of the empire to take residence; revived the Oecumenical Patriarchate; invited Jews, Florentines, Genoese, Venetians, and Franks (West Europeans) to reside in the city; and granted Venice special trading privileges called the "capitulations."[10] These ties were later strengthened and the capitulations were extended to other European countries. By the nineteenth century, the European parts of the empire were more important in shaping the course of its history. For example, the Tercüme Odası (Translation Office) of the late Ottoman administrative system was one of the most influential offices within the bureaucracy. The Ottoman elite spoke French, which was the lingua franca of the Greek, Jewish, Armenian, and Turkish elite circles. Large numbers of students were sent to Europe, and secular educational institutions copying European models, including military academies, were established.[11]

The Influence of the European Enlightenment

The result of these close contacts with Europe was the entering of European Enlightenment ideas into the empire that kindled first the Young Ottoman and later the Young Turk movements for constitutionalism. For example, more than 200 pages were devoted to the French Revolution in secondary school history texts of the period.[12] The Balkans acted as a bridge between the empire and Europe. It was in Salonika that the Young Turks established their revolutionary cells and published journals disseminating ideas of constitutional rule.[13] Enlightenment ideas, especially the emphasis on positivism and progress, became the dominant paradigm for the founding fathers of the republic in their designs for republican education.

After eighty years of republican education and rule, the Turkish public probably differs in its attitudes toward Islam from Muslims in other countries, although the lack of comparative studies on this point makes generalizations difficult. A 1999 nationwide survey shows that although only 2.6 percent of Turkish citizens identify themselves as atheists, 22.9 percent agree with the statement that what is written in the Qur'an is less convincing as a result of progress in science, with 8.7 percent undecided on the subject. Similarly, 34.6 percent believe that Islam should be reinterpreted to accommodate modernity, with 8.8 percent undecided. Together, the two categories make up a little less than half the population. The results of the survey also show that 91.5 percent find tolerance of differences of faith to be important for social peace, and 53.1 percent even agree that there might be good people among the atheists. An overwhelming majority accepts that believers should be considered Muslims even if they do not practice the dictates of religion such as performing the daily *namaz* (prayers), fasting during Ramadan, refraining from alcohol, or wearing headscarves (women). More than 60 percent do not approve of religious political parties.[14]

Secularization

The secularization program of the early republican period was unprecedented for a Muslim country. Although secularization had started a century earlier, it was with the establishment of the republic that a radical program of secularization was put into effect.[15] The *Shari'a* was replaced by a secular code. Polygamy was banned. Women were given equal civic and political rights and equal opportunities in education and employment. A unified secular educational system was established. The sultanate and the caliphate were abolished, a constitutional government based on parliamentary rule was accepted, and legal restrictions were placed on religious involvement in politics and state affairs. Orthodox Islam was put under state control through the creation of a presidency of religious affairs that was tied to the office of the prime minister. All Sufi brotherhoods of "folk" Islam were banned.

The idea that the new republic would look to the West and turn its back to the Muslim world was not readily acccepted by the majority of the population. Originally, this goal was accomplished by force and later through restricting basic rights and freedoms. It was, nevertheless, internalized by the bureaucracy, the military, urban intellectuals, educated strata, and large numbers of notable Anatolian families. Even provincial everyday life changed in the early years of the republic. Later, the middle strata also came to accept these changes.[16]

Today, an overwhelming majority (77.3 percent) of Turkish citizens believe that the early republican reforms have led to Turkey's progress. Only 8.3 percent believe otherwise.[17] More important, support for the establishment of an Islamic state remains limited. Although 21.2 percent in 1999 were in favor of an Islamic state, this percentage is reduced to around 10 percent when specifics are at issue, such as the replacement of the secular civic code with the *Shari'a*. Support for Muslim criminal law is almost negligible, with only 1.2 percent favoring *recm,* stoning to death for adultery.[18]

Emancipation of Women

There was already a nascent feminist movement during the second constitutional period that pushed for women's rights.[19] However, it was after the establishment of the republic that the issue of women gained primacy for the state elite, who linked the emancipation of women to the republican project of integration with the West. Women were given equal rights with men and received the right to vote and to be elected. Primary coeducation became compulsory, and coeducational high schools and universities were opened. At present, there are fifty-three public and twenty-three private universities in Turkey, all of which are coeducational.[20] There was also a concerted effort to open up career and employment opportunities for women. As early as the 1930s, women were employed in the public sector not only in female-oriented careers such as teaching, nursing, secretarial work, and so forth but also in highly prestigious positions such as judge, academician, and doctor.

However, progress in women's rights in later years was not equal to that of the early republican period. Turkey does not fair well in comparative indices about women's development and empowerment.[21] Although feminist organizations have been extremely active and at times effective in furthering women's rights since the 1980s, the rate of progress has been slower than what would be expected from such radical transformation of gender roles. Nevertheless, at least de jure, and in some areas de facto, Turkey is more advanced than other Muslim societies on the issue of women's status.

A Pro-Western Foreign Policy

Turkey was incorporated into the Western security structure as a member of NATO in 1952. Turkey's proximity to the Soviet Union made it a sought-after ally for the United States during the cold war. In the post-Soviet era, its strategic position as a "bridge" for the West, the Middle East, and Central Asia has ensured Turkey's continued value to the United States and the European Union.

Turkey's inclusion in NATO provided it with a defensive shield. Consequently, Turkey escaped the fate of many other Muslim countries that were occupied by the Soviet Union and later by the United States, such as Afghanistan and Iraq, or that had to fight wars of aggression by neighbors, such as Kuwait and Iran. Membership in NATO also meant that Turkey could not engage in warfare without the approval of NATO and, especially, of the United States. The military has been dependent on the United States for its weapons and training and hence has an institutional interest in remaining within these boundaries. The only exception was the Cyprus operation in 1974, which resulted in a UN-imposed embargo. NATO has also prevented the use of force to resolve the Greek-Turkish disputes over the Aegean Islands and national waters.

The fact that Turkey has no oil perhaps also protected the country from direct American and European interference in its domestic affairs as happened in other oil-rich Muslim countries. The U.S.-backed 1953 coup against the Mossadegh regime, in response to the nationalization of Irani oil, closed off Iran's route to democracy, ultimately leading to the Islamic Revolution of 1979. Egypt's president Gamal Abdel Nasser barely escaped Mossadegh's fate in the Suez crisis of 1956 that erupted as a consequence of British-French oil interests. Finally, the economic importance of stabilizing a whole region that is rich in oil should be taken into account as one of the motives behind the U.S. occupation of Afghanistan and Iraq.

This pro-Western foreign policy has contributed to the opening of the Turkish political system. Turkey made the transition from one-party rule to democracy in 1946 at the insistence of the United States in order to join NATO and the United Nations (UN), and later of the European Union to consolidate it for potential membership. In the past few years, Turkey's drive to join the European Union has forced Turkey to correct its record of human rights and extend democratic liberties. Successive governments in recent years have undertaken a series of constitutional and legal reforms. If fully implemented, these legal changes would put Turkey ahead of any other Muslim country in its commitment to democracy.

RELATIVELY EARLY TRANSITION TO DEMOCRATIC POLITICS

Turkish democracy is over half a century old. It made the transition from one party rule to competitive politics in 1946. Except for a few years of military rule following the 1960 and 1980 coups, Turkey has been ruled by elected governments. This, too, distinguishes the Turkish case from other Muslim countries.

Peaceful Transfer of Power

Democracy in Turkey has meant that the struggle for power has been generally carried out within democratic procedures. The idea that governments change through elections has gained legitimacy in the public eye. The military has intervened in civilian politics directly and indirectly several times and still wields power over governmental decisions. These interventions, however, are increasingly seen as illegitimate by the Turkish electorate. Although the military is singled out in public polls as the most trusted institution, it is likely that this trust has less to do with politics than with Turkish citizens' belief that a professional and disciplined army will be able to defend the borders of the country in case of enemy attack. Otherwise, Turkish voters have demonstrated that they prefer parties that are distant from the military. After each instance of military intervention in politics, votes have gone to political parties that the military opposed.

Commitment of the electorate to democratic processes has also meant that Turkish voters do not support political struggles that involve bloodshed. The bloody fight between the Left and the Right in the 1970s, which led to the military takeover of 1980, was largely responsible for the overwhelming support given to the 1982 constitution in a referendum, although in terms of rights and liberties it was the most restrictive constitution of the republican period.

Surveys in the early 1990s confirmed the Turkish public's alienation from ideological politics. When asked whether they would mind a neighbor who was a leftist or a rightist, the majority wanted neither. An overwhelming majority (86.3 percent) supported either change through gradual reform (60.7 percent) or the preservation of the status quo (25.6 percent) rather than revolutionary change.[22] Likewise, the polarization of the electorate by Refah Partisi after it came to power following the 1995 elections and the ensuing political tension were probably responsible for the extremely poor electoral performance in the 2002 elections of Saadet Partisi, founded by the old guard of Refah. A survey conducted in 1999 immediately after Refah's closure by the Constitutional Court found that 67.2 percent of the electorate were against and only 6.9 percent were in favor of religious involvement in politics and state affairs. Similarly, 60.6 percent agreed that there should be no religiously based political parties. Only 24.6 percent thought otherwise, a percentage equal to Refah's support at the time.[23]

Exceptions to peaceful struggle for power were the street fighting between the Far Left and the Far Right in the 1970s and the Kurdish uprising after 1980. The first was largely between the paramilitary organization of the Far Right party Milliyetçi Hareket Partisi (MHP) and the clandestine organizations of the Far Left. Otherwise, the extreme Left parties never mustered more than 3 percent of the votes and the MHP itself received at most 6.4 percent in the 1977 elections.[24] The armed conflict between the separatist Kurdish organization the Kurdistan Workers Party (PKK) and the Turkish army claimed 30,000 dead in more than two decades. The length of the armed conflict was due both to the PKK's refusal to end guerilla warfare and to the Turkish government's refusal to allow organization and representation to the Kurdish minority. However, legislation on ethnic minority rights has been gradually improving in the past few years.

A Moderate Islamic Movement

Turkey's relatively early transition to democracy also helped contain political Islam within democratic boundaries. Turkey was never in serious danger of a change of regime from a secular to an Islamic government. Nor did the power struggle between the Islamists and secular forces turn into radicalism and bloodshed as it did in Algeria. Except for the first two decades of the republic, the struggle for power by the Islamists has been carried out within the democratic process.

Several factors have helped moderate the Islamist movement in Turkey. The first is the role of the staunchly secular military. The military directly or indirectly interferes in the political process when it perceives the movement to pose a threat to the republic's secular foundations. It was the major force behind the resignation in 1997 of Necmettin Erbakan, prime minister and the leader of the Islamist Refah Party, and the subsequent measures taken by the successor government to curtail the Islamists' power and reduce their support base.

The second is the role of the judiciary and the legal system. The secular state is protected by an article in the constitution not subject to amendment. Additionally, a number of articles in the laws on political parties, labor unions, associations, and the criminal code forbid the use of religion for political purposes or private gain. The Constitutional Court has closed a number of parties in the past on the basis of these articles, and a large number of individuals have been imprisoned by criminal courts for violating them.[25] Some of this legislation has been amended in recent years to allow for greater freedom of speech and association, although legal restrictions still remain and the space within which Islamist movements, organizations, and political parties can function is limited.

A third factor is public commitment to the secular state. For many years and especially after the Iranian revolution, the mainstream press and media, the intelligentsia, the universities, the business establishment, labor unions, the majority of the urban educated strata, and a large middle class have been very sensitive to the rising tide of political Islam and have kept a vigil over the secular state. Many within these groups have, over time, adopted more tolerant attitudes. Nevertheless, as mentioned above, the majority of the population opposes the politicization of religion and the granting of a role for Islam in state affairs.

Fourth, the integration of the Islamists to centers of power through the democratic process has helped moderate their views. The republican understanding of laicism had marginalized the Islamists in terms of political power, accumulation of wealth through state favors, social status, and intellectual prestige. This contributed to the emergence of a relatively strong Islamist movement in the early 1970s. It is telling that Erbakan's neo-Islamist Milli Görüş (National Outlook) movement that organized itself in 1970 around Milli Nizam Partisi (MNP) followed Erbakan's unsuccessful attempt to chair the economically powerful Union of Chambers.[26] MNP was closed by the Constitutional Court within a year, and Erbakan founded a new party, Milli Selamet Partisi (MSP), that received 11.8 percent of the votes in 1973. MSP became a coalition partner in several governments in the 1970s.

However, MSP, too, was closed by the military after the 1980 coup. Refah was founded in its place in 1983, following the resumption of civilian politics. Erbakan carried the party to power in the 1995 elections and in 1996 became the prime minister of a coalition government. However, he was forced to resign in 1997, Refah was closed by the Constitutional Court, and Erbakan was banned from political activity. His movement founded the Fazilet Partisi under a different leadership but under his close scrunity. Within a short period, Fazilet was also closed by the Constitutional Court. The movement then split into two groups, both of which were organized around new parties. The younger generation, known as the "reformists," founded the Adalet ve Kalkinma Partisi (AKP), which is now in power following a landslide victory in the 2002 elections. The old guard formed the Saadet Partisi but suffered a major defeat in 2002, gaining only 2.4 percent of the votes.[27]

This saga of Islamist political parties demonstrates the difficulty of suppressing political movements that operate within democratic bounds. This is one of the most important aspects of the Turkish case, with far-reaching consequences for the consolidation of its democracy and with significant implications for Islamist movements in other Muslim countries. Turkey's case shows that within a basically democratic system and despite restrictions, Islamists can participate in politics and even occupy important positions of power. Indeed, since the 1970s, political Islam has produced its own "counter-elites," who have acquired a place in the power hierarchy of Turkish society. These elites are present in national and local politics and administration, big business, the press and the media, and intellectual life. Political Islam has established a network, which has empowered provincial and religiously conservative individuals who were previously marginalized.[28]

This process, in turn, has moderated the movement. Through participation in the electoral process, Islamists discovered that voters expect governments to deliver economically and do not vote on the basis of religious faith alone. The success of Refah rested on its extensive and active grassroots organization, especially in the poor squatter sites surrounding big cities. Party activists performed wide-ranging community activities that delivered help to the urban poor. At the same time, the party became a channel through which some within its ranks could achieve extensive social mobility. However, Refah failed to understand the consensual nature of democracy, and this was a major reason behind its defeat. It polarized the electorate and turned the political arena into a tug-of-war between the secularists and the Islamists. Squeezed between an electorate that the party had helped to radicalize and the necessity to carry on "normal politics" once in power, its leadership became unable to govern.

The young leadership cadres within Refah who founded the AKP understood this second lesson. Even a cursory reading of AKP's party program[29] and the legal changes that the Erdoğan government has accomplished since coming to power in 2002 show the extent to which a political party with roots in the Islamist movement has transformed itself into one of the staunchest defenders of democratic rights and liberties and an enthusiastic supporter of Turkey's entry into the European Union. The AKP is a success story of Turkish democracy.

Development of a Strong Private Sector

The development of a strong private sector and business elites since the 1980s has also contributed to Turkey's democratic consolidation. This elite is internationalist in outlook and favors Turkey's integration in Europe. The powerful organization Turkish Industrialists' and Businessmen's Association (TÜSİAD) has been very active since 1980 in promoting democracy through public statements of its leadership and the publication of reports commissioned to academicians. The Turkish Economic and Social Studies Foundation (TESEV), an independent think tank financed by TÜSİAD members and international nongovernmental organizations, has been equally influential in the proliferation of academic studies that tackle issues of democratization.

Moreover, the shift from import-substitution policies to export-oriented growth and free-market economics in the 1980s has led to the expansion of communication networks such as the Internet, fax machines, television satellite dishes and cables, and direct telephone lines. This expansion has been accompanied by a significant increase in the number of students studying abroad and in international travel. These changes played an important role in opening Turkish citizens to international influence and the liberalization of the political system.

CONCLUSION

This chapter has attempted to show how Turkey's historical experience and evolution have shaped its unique model of secular democracy in the Muslim world. The aim was not to argue for Turkish exceptionalism but to demonstrate how a combination of factors has contributed to the relative success of Turkey's developmentalist model. Some of these factors have historical roots and hence probably cannot be replicated.

The analysis presented here reveals that change occurs through the processes of conflict and consensus among indigenous social forces and the historical legacies that give it direction. However, it does not take place in isolation from leadership choices or independently of international actors. The Turkish experience shows that major transformations take place as a result of the interplay among political leaders, influential social actors, the international community, and historical legacies. Undoubtedly, favorable external conditions, including pressure from the international community to democratize, can play a positive role either during the transition from authoritarian rule to democracy or in the institutionalization and consolidation of new democracies. However, the success of such foreign intervention depends on a number of other factors, which are delineated in this chapter.

Turkey has been struggling to modernize for more than two centuries but still faces problems. On the Turkish political agenda at present are the issues of constitutional, legal, and judicial reform to consolidate its democracy; crackdown on corruption; more autonomy to local governments through administrative reform; strengthening of individual, group, and ethnic rights; redefinition of secularism to allow for greater religious freedom; and, most important, curtailing the role of the military in politics. Turkey's long route to modernization and democratization demonstrates the difficulty of both processes. The analysis presented here challenges expectations that changes from the top down, especially through for-

eign enforcement, can transform the social, cultural, and political landscape of a
country in a relatively short period of time.

NOTES

1. The most representative scholar of this position in recent years is, of course,
Samuel P. Huntington. His essay "The Clash of Civilizations?" *Foreign Affairs* (Summer
1993): 22–49 garnered immediate attention worldwide and drew a host of criticisms in
scholarly journals and elsewhere. For my own critique of it, see Binnaz Toprak, "Prejudice as Social Science Theory: Samuel P. Huntington's Vision of the Future," *Perceptions:
Journal of International Affairs* (March–May 1996): 83–87.

2. Pippa Norris and Ronald Inglehart, "Islamic Culture and Democracy: Testing the
'Clash of Civilizations' Thesis," in Ronald Inglehart, ed., *Human Values and Social
Change: Findings from the Values Surveys* (Leiden: Brill Academic, 2003), 5–34. For details, see Yılmaz Esmer, "Is There an Islamic Civilization?" in Inglehart, *Human Values
and Social Change*, 35–68.

3. H.A.R. Gibb and Harold Bowen, *Islamic Society and the West*, vol. 1, part 2 (London: Oxford University Press, 1959), 207–34.

4. İlber Ortaylı, "The Millet System under the Ottoman Empire: Classical Structure
up to the 16th Century" (research paper, Seminar on Racism and Anti-Semitism, Council of Europe, Strasbourg, December 23, 1994), 3.

5. Tarık Zafer Tunaya, *slamcılık Cereyanı* (Istanbul: Baha Matbaası, 1962).

6. Çağlar Keyder, *State and Class in Turkey* (London: Verso New Left Books, 1987),
chap. 4.

7. Samuel P. Huntington, "The Goals of Development," in Myron Weiner and Samuel
P. Huntington, eds., *Understanding Political Development* (Boston: Little, Brown, 1987),
3–32.

8. On concepts of "individual," "society," and "people" in late Ottoman discourse, see
Zafer Toprak, *Bir Yurttas Yaratmak—Muasır bir medeniyet için seferberlik bilgileri* (Is-
tanbul: Yapı Kredi Kültür Sanat, 1998); "Türkiye'de Toplumbilimin Doğuşu," in Emre
Kongar, ed., *Türk Toplumbilimcileri* (Istanbul: Remzi Kitabevi, 1988), 2:13–29; Emre
Kongar, "Osmanlı'da Toplumbilimin Doğuşu," in Mehmet Ö. Alkan, ed., *Cumhuriyet'ten
Devreden Düsünce Mirası—Tanzimat ve Mesrutiyet'in Birikimi* (Istanbul: İletişim
Yayınları, 2001), 310–27.

9. Tarık Zafer Tunaya, *Türkiye'de Siyasal Partiler: ttihad ve Terakki—Bir Ça ın,
Bir Kusa ın, Bir Partinin Tarihi,* vol. 3 (Istanbul: Hürriyet Vakfı Yayınları, 1989).

10. Philip Mansel, *Constantinople: City of the World's Desire, 1453–1924* (London:
Penguin Books, 1995), 7.

11. Niyazi Berkes, *The Development of Secularism in Turkey* (Montreal: McGill University Press, 1964).

12. Zafer Toprak, "Ali Reşad, Pozitivizm ve Fransız Devrimi," *Tarih ve Toplum* 68 (August 1989): 54–56.

13. Zafer Toprak, "Nationalism and Economics in the Young Turk Era (1908–1918),"
in Jacques Thobie and Salgur Kançal, eds., *Communication et rapports sociaux en Turquie
et en Méditerranée Orientale* (Paris: L'Harmattan, 1994), 260–66.

14. Ali Çarkoğlu and Binnaz Toprak, *Türkiye'de Din, Toplum, ve Siyaset* (Istanbul:
TESEV Yayınları, 2000).

15. Bernard Lewis, *The Emergence of Modern Turkey* (London: Oxford University Press, 1965); Berkes, *Development of Secularism in Turkey,* part 5; Binnaz Toprak, *Islam and Political Development in Turkey* (Leiden: E. J. Brill, 1981).

16. Arzu Öztürkmen, "Remembering through the Material Culture: Local Knowledge of Past Communities in a Turkish Black Sea Town," *Middle Eastern Studies* 39, no. 2 (2003): 179–93.

17. Çarkoğlu and Toprak, *Türkiye'de Din, Toplum ve Siyaset,* table 6.2.1, 59.

18. Ibid., 70–79.

19. Zafer Toprak, "The Family, Feminism, and the State during the Young Turk Period, 1908–1918," in Edhem Eldem, ed., *Premiere Rencontre internationale sur l'Empire Ottoman et la Turquie moderne* (Istanbul: Editions ISIS, 1991), 441–452.

20. *Yüksek Ö retim Kurulu (YÖK,* Ankara Board of Higher Education), www.yok.gov.tr.

21. United Nations Development Programme, UNDP *Human Development Report 2002* (New York: United Nations Development Programmes, 2002).

22. The survey was conducted by Üstün Ergüder, Yılmaz Esmer, and Ersin Kalaycıoğlu. For partial results, see Turk Sanayicileri ve Isadamları Dernegi (TÜSİAD), *Türk Toplumunun De erleri* (Istanbul: TÜSİAD Yayınları, 1991).

23. Çarkoğlu and Toprak, *Türkiye'de Din, Toplum ve Siyaset,* figure 6.2.1, 58, and table 6.2.1, 59.

24. Sabri Sayarı and Yılmaz Esmer, eds., *Politics, Parties and Elections in Turkey* (Boulder, CO: Lynne Rienner, 2002), appendix, table B2.2, 190.

25. For the number of people who were imprisoned between 1949 and 1971 for violating article 163 of the criminal code, which was later repealed, see Mehmet Cemal, "Yüzaltmışüç," *Milli Gazete*, April 10–30, 1974. Based on official statistics, he calculates the number to be 1,971. Seven parties were closed between the years 1924 and 1999 for alleged violations of secular laws.

26. For details of this incident that was to prove an important factor in Erbakan's decision to found a political party, see Necdet Onur, *Erbakan Dosyası* (Istanbul: M Yayınevi, n.d.), 69–75.

27. On the MSP, see Jacob M. Landau, "The National Salvation Party in Turkey," *Asian and African Studies* 11 (1976): 1–57; Binnaz Toprak, "Politicization of Islam in a Secular State: The National Salvation Party in Turkey," in Said Arjomand, ed., *From Nationalism to Revolutionary Islam* (London: Macmillan, 1984), 119–33; Toprak, *Islam and Political Development in Turkey*, chap. 5; Türker Alkan, "The National Salvation Party in Turkey," in Metin Heper and Raphael Israeli, eds., *Islam and Politics in the Modern Middle East* (London: Croom Helm, 1984), 79–102; Mehmet Ali Ağaoğulları, *L'Islam dans la vie politique de la Turquie* (Ankara: Ankara Üniversitesi Basımevi, 1982), chap. 3; Ali Yaşar Sarıbay, *Türkiye'de Modernleşme, Din ve Parti Politikası: MSP Örnek Olayı* (Istanbul: Alan Yayıncılık, 1985). On Refah, see Ziya Öniş, "The Political Economy of Islamic Resurgence in Turkey: The Rise of the Welfare Party in Perspective," *Third World Quarterly* 18, no. 4 (1997): 743–66; Haldun Gülalp, "Globalization and Political Islam: The Social Bases of Turkey's Welfare Party," *International Journal of Middle East Studies* 33 (2001): 433–48; Haldun Gülalp, "The Poverty of Democracy in Turkey: The Refah Party Episode," *New Perspectives on Turkey* 21 (Fall 1999): 35–59; Haldun Gülalp, "Political Islam in Turkey: The Rise and Fall of the Refah Party," *Muslim World* (January 1999): 22–41. For a journalist's view of Refah's internal dynamics, see Ruşen Çakır, *Ne Seriat Ne Demokrasi: Refah Partisini Anlamak* (Istanbul: Metis Yayınları, 1994).

28. For an extensive study of Refah's grassroots activities, see Jenny B. White, *Islamist Mobilization in Turkey: A Study in Vernacular Politics* (Seattle: University of Washington Press, 2002). On the new generation of Islamist intellectuals, see Michael Meeker, "The New Muslim Intellectuals in the Republic of Turkey," in Richard Tapper, ed., *Islam in Modern Turkey: Religion, Politics and Literature in a Secular State* (London: I. B. Tauris, 1999), 121–42; Binnaz Toprak, "Islamist Intellectuals: Revolt against Industry and Technology," in Metin Heper, A. Öncü, and H. Kramer, eds., *Turkey and the West: Changing Political and Cultural Identities* (London: I. B. Tauris, 1993), 237–57.

29. "Adalet ve Kalkınma Partisi Programı 2002," www.belgenet.com.

18

Central Asia and Azerbaijan

Mehrdad Haghayeghi

The dissolution of the Soviet Empire in 1991 led to the emergence of six new republics with a majority Muslim population, namely Azerbaijan, Kazakhstan, Kyrgyzstan, Tajikistan, Turkmenistan, and Uzbekistan. Since these countries, as constituent parts of the Soviet Union (USSR), supposedly had been subjected to economic and political modernization, their postindependence transition to an open economic system and democracy should have been easier compared to other postcolonial states of Asia and Africa. The international environment within which these states were to achieve these goals should also have been more congenial as they did not face the constraints and pressures of the cold war.

The reality, however, has been different. These countries did not become fully modernized under the Soviet system. Rather, certain aspects of the Soviet model of nation and state building stunted the natural development of their sense of nationhood. Other aspects of Soviet-era modernization have also been a hindrance, rather than a help, in their postindependence nation and state building and modernization and democratization efforts.

Other hindrances have been the legacy of tsarist Russian colonialism, the republics' geographical position, resource limitations, and certain aspects of precolonial cultural and political traditions that have survived Sovietization. Meanwhile, the nature of international and regional environments, although better than during the cold war era, have not enhanced the republics' ability to successfully pursue modernization and, more especially, democratization.

THE CURSE OF GEOGRAPHY AND OTHER LIMITATIONS

The landlocked nature of these countries severely limits their economic and commercial options by putting their economic fate largely in the hands of neighboring countries. For example, the export of Turkmen gas and Kazakh oil is determined by Russia's monopoly over the export pipelines. Russia has tried to retain this monopoly by attempting to obstruct the construction of an alternative pipeline thorough Baku-Tbilisi-Ceyhan.[1] Meanwhile, international, especially U.S., pressure has prevented these republics from exporting oil through Iran. At the same time, civil war in Afghanistan throughout the 1990s and volatile conditions following the removal of the Taliban regime in 2002 have made the Afghan option unrealistic. Disagreement among the Caspian Sea littoral states regarding the legal regime of the Caspian has delayed the exploration and development of offshore oil deposits.

The size, resource endowment, and topography of these republics also hinder their economic development. Kyrgyzstan and Tajikistan are mountainous republics with only 7.04 percent and 5.41 percent of arable land, respectively. Both have tremendous potential for the development of hydroelectric industries, but because of the topography their exploration requires large capital investment, which has prevented their full development. The cost of the production and export of Azerbaijani, Turkmen, and Kazak energy is high compared to that of the Middle East. Kazakhstan's large size requires significant investments in infrastructure development to create a viable domestic market, while water scarcity hinders the development of agriculture and agro-industries.

THE PRECOLONIAL ETHNIC, RELIGIOUS, CULTURAL, AND POLITICAL LANDSCAPE IN CENTRAL ASIA AND AZERBAIJAN

On the eve of the Russian advances into Central Asia, the region was largely under the jurisdiction of the two khanates of Khiva and Kokand and the emirate of Bukhara. The territory of Azerbaijan was under nominal control of Iran until Russia annexed it in the aftermath of two wars of conquest (1804–13) and (1824–28). The political structure of the three principalities was authoritarian. Divided into roughly similar administrative subdivisions (*velayat*), these principalities were governed by representatives of the emir or the khan known as *hakim* or *bey*.[2] The tribal Turkmen, Kazakhs, and Kyrgyz were divided into independent federations and led by a single leader under whose authority a tribal council managed the affairs of the tribe.[3]

Loyalty was to the khan or emir and to one's clan, tribe, or ethnic group. There was no sense of a broader identity transcending these divides and commanding the people's loyalty. To the extent that such transcendental identity existed it was based on Islam. Indeed, within the sedentary populations in Central Asia and Azerbaijan, Islam played a prominent role as a component of collective identity and defined the rhythm of life, and it was incorporated into the political and economic structures.

Islamic traditions and the fundamental dictates of *Shari'a* law were skillfully used by the emir or khan to legitimize his rule and the economic and political status quo. Within the traditional elites—the land-owning class, the merchants, and the clergy—the latter played an important role in legitimizing the political structure and shaping the cultural milieu. The clergy ran the public education system and trained the bureaucratic cadre and tax administrators. The khan or emir in turn rewarded the clergy through the allocation of *waqf* (religious endowment land).[4] The landlords provided the khan with manpower for the military and revenue from sharecropping agreements. Wealthy merchants provided the court with luxury items and lent money to the khan in times of need. They supported Islam and its religious and educational network through *zakat* (Islamic tax equivalent to one-tenth of one's annual income). This system was prejudicial to the interests of the peasants, artisans, and urban poor. Educational opportunities were also limited, especially in rural communities and among the urban poor, who remained under the control of the conservative clergy.

Islam's influence among nomadic Kazakhs, Kyrgyz, and Turkmen tribes was weak, and they retained their shamanistic culture and pre-Islamic socioeconomic and political identities, thus permitting their easier assimilation into the Russian empire.

In sum, by the time of the Russian conquest the social and political structures of Central Asia and Azerbaijan had not evolved into forms resembling today's modern states.

RUSSIAN COLONIALISM AND ITS CONSEQUENCES

The Russian conquest of Central Asia began in 1822 and ended in 1887. It had three basic objectives. The first objective was to undermine the military and political power of the traditional political authorities, without totally dismantling it, and to extend Russian political and administrative authority throughout the region. Russia eventually overcame all resistance and established a protectorate over the khanates of Kokand and Khiva, and the emirate of Bukhara.[5]

The second objective—economic—was defined by three factors: to acquire a reliable source of raw material—cotton—for the expanding Russian textile industries; to gain access to new export markets; and to generate enough tax revenue to finance the colonial structure in the region. Russia's needs led to an emphasis on the cultivation of cotton at the expense of other crops. By the end of the nineteenth century Russia had diversified its agricultural policy in Central Asia (Turkistan) by encouraging expansion of production of fruits and silk and by introducing grapevines for commercial production. The bulk of this produce was sent to Russia. Some steppe land was also brought under cultivation. The mineral resources of the region, including oil, were also exploited.[6] Azerbaijan, Kazakhstan, and Turkmenistan became major oil- and gas-producing republics of the Soviet Union following this tsarist colonial policy.

Between 1863 and 1867, Russia increased the value of its exports to the region threefold.[7] By 1894, Russia had effectively blocked out the Indian commodity trade—the only sizable competition to its products. This virtual trade monopoly increased Russia's profit margins and accelerated the production and export of Russian consumer goods, including to Central Asia. Like other European colonizers, the Russians did not build factories to transform the region's raw materials and create an industrial base—an important step in the overall process of modernization. On the contrary, the penetration of Russian goods had a devastating effect on local crafts and industries, which could not compete with their counterparts, thus precluding any possibility of their transformation into more viable industries.

Third, Russia pursued a policy of cultural infiltration and eventual Russification (*russifkatsia*) of Central Asia. The tsarist cultural plan did not call for the disruption of the region's traditional religious and cultural patterns, including the observance of Islamic rituals and practices, partly because earlier attempts to do so had met with stiff resistance. Such efforts had the reverse effect of strengthening indigenous religious traditions. Instead, Russia adopted a strategy of exposing the native population to the great Russian cultural and linguistic heritage through physical contact and education in the native language. It was believed that familiarity with Russian culture would convince the natives of its superiority and generate a desire for cultural assimilation. However, Russia was half-hearted in its Russification policy—which it saw as a civilizing mission. Therefore, no extensive infrastructure of modern education was created, while periodic efforts to weaken the Islamic educational infrastructure undermined the indigenous educational system. As a result, the intellectual quality of the clerical establishment was eroded, the evolution of Islamic learning in a progressive direction was hindered, and local reform efforts were adversely affected.

Economically, by the early twentieth century, the tsarist colonization had transformed Central Asia into a supplier of raw materials and an export market, had caused its loss of self-sufficiency in food production, and had undermined local crafts. The Russian settlement policy in the Kazakh steppe and, to some extent, in Central Asia further contributed to the economic decline of the native population. Politically, the structure of the traditional authority was severely weakened and subordinated to the Russian military-bureaucratic machinery. But no effort was made to create a modern native cadre. Consequently, the traditional political institutions and culture of the region did not evolve.

The Central Asian Response: Rebellion and Reform

The Central Asian response to Russian colonialism followed two distinct patterns. The first was rebellion, which became an increasingly frequent method after the Andijon uprising of 1898.[8] The clerical establishment played a leading role in these rebellions, including the 1916 uprising in Central Asia, thus demonstrating Islam's potential as an anticolonial instrument. Although suppressed expeditiously, these rebellions politicized the population and the religion and alerted St. Petersburg to the volatility of the local situation and to Islam's political potential. The second pattern was one of reform, which involved the adoption of liberal ideas that had become popular in Russia during the reign of Alexander II (1818–81) and continued to flourish after his assassination in 1881. Reform movements in the Ottoman Empire, Iran, and Egypt also influenced the region.

THE JADID MOVEMENT: AN EFFORT TO SYNTHESIZE ISLAM AND MODERNITY

The emergence of the Jadid movement was an Islamic expression of liberal tendencies to which many Muslims had been introduced through indirect and direct—albeit limited—intellectual encounters with the West.

The word *jadid* (new) was taken from the Persian expression *usul-e jadid*, or new method. The term was used in reference to those reformist intellectuals of the region who organized and supported the new-method schools, where reading and writing were taught not by learning Qur'anic verses but by the phonetic method. Pioneered by Ismael Gasprinskii, a Tatar intellectual in the 1880s, these schools operated in Azerbaijan, Crimea, the Volga region, and, by the 1890s, Central Asia. The first Jadid school was opened in Andijon in 1889 and during the following decade spread to all other major cities. The first alphabet in Uzbek by the phonetic method was published in 1900.[9] In his two visits to Central Asia, Gasprinskii advocated the learning of foreign languages and scientific subjects, the creation of modern civic institutions, and improvement in the status of women in Muslim societies.[10]

The Jadid movement intended to rid Islam of its antiprogress elements and appealed to the rationalist and scientific traditions of its golden age. In short, the Jadid movement was part of the broader Islamic reform advocated by figures such as Jamal al-Din al Afghani and Muhammad Abduh, which aimed to reconcile Islamic traditions with the imperatives of modernization. Consequently, the Jadid movement in Central Asia and Azerbaijan was led by progressive members of the clerical establishment together with members of the emerging national bourgeoisie, such as Munnawar Qari, Mufti Muhammad Khoja Behbudi, Mulla Niyaz Sabir-Oghli, Burnash-Oghli, and Said Azambay Muhammadbay, the richest merchant in Tashkent.[11] They believed that political and economic reforms were needed to modernize the region and narrow the gap with the European countries. Indeed, by the early twentieth century some Central Asian Jadidists, in particular those of Bukhara, had realized that "transforming the schools . . . in no way promptly resolved the emirate's problems, for the real obstacle to any genuine evolution of the community lay in the very structure of the state. Altering the social substructure seemed to them an indispensable preliminary to any reform."[12] Subsequently, the Jadid textbooks and publications began to reflect the new political strategy for reform.

Russia's initial response to the Jadid schools was rather positive, and the Russian administration in Central Asia and Azerbaijan encouraged reforms. But once the Russian authorities realized how Jadidism was evolving from a purely educational reform effort into a regional movement for social and political transformation, they withdrew their support and later systematically undermined the movement. These Russian tactics, however, only strengthened the resolve of the supporters of the Jadid movement.[13] Later, the Russians found allies among the local political rulers, the conservative clergy, and other traditional elites in their fight against the Jadidists. These groups, especially the clergy, convinced the emir of Bukhara, an initial supporter of reform, to crack down on the movement's leaders and supporters. The Russians encouraged him in this course and even threatened him with the annexation of Bukhara if he failed to satisfy their demands. These developments heralded the end of the nascent reform movement. A similar fate beset the Azari reform movement. In short, Russia, instead of encouraging modernization in Central Asia, supported the forces of stagnation.

The other reformist trend among some members of the Central Asian upper class was aimed to modernize their societies and political culture in accordance with trends in Russia. Thus, following the revolution of 1905, some natives actively collaborated with the Russian Social Democrats, while others participated in Muslim congresses, hoping to gain more autonomy for Russia's Muslim-inhabited regions.[14]

Soviet Legacy

The fall of the tsarist regime provided an opportunity for the empire's Muslim's to form independence-seeking movements. In Central Asia, such movements included the Alash Orda Movement of Kazakhstan. For a few years, the Bolsheviks and their leader, Vladimir Lenin, were mainly concerned with the establishment of order and the consolidation of power over the European parts of Russia and Central Asia, while the Caucasus remained in the background. During the ensuing civil war (1918–1920), Central Asia became a battleground where the pro-tsarist forces resisted the Bolshevik expansion. Lenin, mindful of anti-Russian sentiments in the region, was careful not to antagonize the local population and the traditional power elite. Additionally, Lenin did not have enough trained cadre in Central Asia and the South Caucasus to carry out his policies, and was therefore dependent on Muslim Communist sympathizers to spread socialist ideas and to distinguish Bolsheviks from the tsarist personnel. Finally, Lenin was aware of Islam and the clergy's power and as a tactical move in the initial phase (1917–1920) adopted a nonconfrontational approach. After consolidating power, however, he embarked on a systematic dismantling of traditional elites' socioeconomic and political powers and launched a war against Islam.

SOVIET MODERNIZATION AND ITS CONSEQUENCES: ECONOMIC DEVELOPMENT

The Soviet modernization of Central Asia and Azerbaijan dates back to the first five-year plan of 1928. The region's agricultural economy, however, had already been transformed under the tsars. By the 1920s, Central Asia had become a significant cotton-producing region, and the Soviets continued the expansion of cotton cultivation.[15] They used the fertile Fergana Valley to generate foreign-exchange revenue through cash-crop production and by reducing dependence on overseas import of citrus, tobacco, tea, rice, and wine.

The Soviets also pursued a comprehensive collectivization program, which caused significant hardship for Kazakhs and largely dismantled their traditional family and clan cohesion, and which disrupted traditional farming practices in Uzbekistan. Forced collectivization eliminated the vestiges of private ownership and free commercial and entrepreneurial practices, thus causing a break in the development of market-based economies.

The Soviet agricultural policies in Central Asia after World War II continued to benefit the European part of the union. An important milestone was the launching, in 1954, of the Virgin Lands Campaign, which transformed northern Kazakhstan into a grain-producing region. The bulk of this grain was exported to other parts of the USSR. The substantial investments required for this project drastically reduced the amount of resources available for those agricultural projects more beneficial to the local economy. The mechanization of agriculture remained lopsided and did not include the cotton fields of Central Asia, where excessive manpower and pesticides were used to reach high yields, to the detriment of industrial development and the health of the population.

The Soviet strategy for Central Asia's industrialization was not driven by concern for sustainable regional development. Rather, it was determined by two considerations. The first was to extract raw materials to be processed and transported to the Soviet European industrial centers. Although by the 1930s a few textile and footwear factories were constructed in Tashkent, no substantial industrial development other than that in the mining sector had taken place in Central Asia. The Baku oil industry was developed in the 1930s not so much to promote the local economy as to satisfy the Soviet Union's growing energy demands in the South.

The second consideration was to save the Soviet industries from falling into the hands of the German army. To this end, whole factories were disassembled and shipped to Central Asia. Some of these industries proved useful, but after the war no significant efforts were made to modernize them, though some were gradually expanded. A number of the relocated factories were later returned to their original sites without regard for Central Asia's economic development. The postwar Soviet industrialization policy, too, was focused on its European parts, and in Central Asia and Azerbaijan only those industries most useful for the development of the Soviet industries outside the region registered higher growth rates.[16]

Some industrial plants were built in those parts of Central Asia and the Caucasus, such as the Issyk Kul Lake in Kyrgyzstan, where the Soviet elite vacationed. Other factories were built to raise the international profile of the Soviet Union as a benevolent socialist empire. These plants, such as the airplane factory in Uzbekistan and the aluminum plant in Tajikistan, defied conventional economic wisdom and were built for propaganda purposes rather than for local economic benefit.

Moreover, the highly centralized nature of the Soviet economic system and the interconnectedness of its various parts created patterns of dependencies that would hinder the progress of these states in the postindependence era. The Central Asian and Azerbaijani economies entered a period of stagnation under Leonid Brezhnev (1964–82), reflecting the overall problems of the Soviet economy. During his long tenure, Brezhnev created a kind of neopatrimonial system in which the relative material well-being of the population was guaranteed by the top leadership in return for their political acquiescence and loyalty. The outcome of this arrangement, involving massive state subsidies and price controls, was a gradual depletion of the Soviet financial power to the point at which it could no longer maintain an adequate productive momentum, which led to a steady decline in its agricultural, industrial, and technological competitiveness.

The lack of discipline in the workforce and widespread corruption at all levels of the state apparatus at both central and republican levels were other causes of decline. The local party bosses were given relative autonomy in return for political loyalty. This led to large-scale agricultural and industrial embezzlement schemes, the most notorious of which, the so-called cotton scandal, was masterminded by the first secretary of the Uzbek Communist Party, Sharaf Rashidov (1976–85). The legacy of the Brezhnev-era institutionalized corruption has proved difficult to uproot.

SOVIET STATE AND NATION BUILDING: SOCIAL, POLITICAL, AND CULTURAL CONSEQUENCES

The Bolsheviks incorporated Central Asia and the South Caucasus into the Soviet Union through military conquest. Nevertheless, the USSR maintained the fiction that the peoples and the nascent states had joined the union voluntarily. The Soviets also embarked on a systematic policy of nation and state building by dividing Central Asia into ethnically based republics. Joseph Stalin did this under the so-called national-territorial delimitation strategy of 1924. He maintained that "in a pre-revolutionary era these countries were torn into fragments and were a convenient field for the exploitative machinations of the internal and external powers. The time is now come when these scattered fragments can be reunited into independent states, so that the toiling masses can be welded with the organs of government."[17] Stalin's argument was based on the Marxist conviction that the prerequisite for a successful transition to socialism was an expeditious conversion of the tribal peoples into modern nations. This was to be done in accordance with four principles enunciated by Stalin as part of his new nationalities policy: unity of territory, language, economy, and culture.

In theory, the creation of these new republics could have provided an opportunity for nation and state building and the flourishing of indigenous cultures.

However, certain internal contradictions of Soviet and republican state and nation building and the way the division of territory was carried out doomed this strategy. The main shortcomings of the Soviet strategy were the following.

Arbitrary Nature of the Republican Borders

In delineating the borders of the new states, Stalin paid no heed to ethnic, linguistic, and cultural factors. Rather, a basic strategy of Stalin was to leave substantial ethnic minorities in each republic, thus enabling the center to better control them. This ethnoterritorial asymmetry has made the development of a strong sense of national identity—an important factor in modernization—difficult, thus perpetuating tribal, clan, and regional identities and loyalties. It has also sown the seeds of interethnic and interstate conflicts. This situation has had a deleterious impact on the postindependence transition to democracy. Fear of interethnic tension and irredentist claims from neighboring states have intensified authoritarian trends and have led to discriminatory policies toward minorities such as the Tajiks in Uzbekistan.[18]

Contradictions Between Socialist Universalism and Ethnoterritorial Nation and State Building

The ultimate goal of the socialist revolution was to create a classless utopian world order. The first step in this direction was to build a socialist system in the Soviet Union and to create a Soviet man, "Homo Sovieticus." A particular characteristic of this new man was his lack of strong ethnic and religious loyalty and an internationalist outlook.[19] Meanwhile, trying to maintain the fiction of the USSR as a voluntary federation of various republics, the Soviet Union encouraged the development of a sense of ethnic and cultural nationalism among its various titular nationalities, while at the same time characterizing expressions of such nationalism as antirevolutionary and against the tenants of socialist internationalism.

A good example of this inherently contradictory Soviet policy is the approach of the authorities to the development of local languages—an indispensable component of cultural autonomy. Despite Soviet claims of wanting to develop national languages and cultures, Soviet policies driven by the principle of Russification undermined them. Policies such as the following reduced the usage of local languages. Expanding Soviet-style education taught exclusively in Russian necessitated the use of Russian settlers and rapid training of local educators with adequate ideological training in communism. The use of Russian as the legal language for all state and local documents forced the majority of the urban inhabitants either to learn Russian or to be excluded from social welfare programs and qualifications for professional jobs. Educational instruction and publication of literature in native languages were directly and indirectly limited.

Kazakhstan and Kyrgyzstan were most severely affected by these policies. The overall result was the erosion of the region's literary heritage and the stunting of the process of national identity formation.

Erratic Approach to Islam

The Soviet approach toward Islam fluctuated between severe repression and periodic tolerance, negatively affecting the evolution of Central Asian Islam. Because of the undermining of the infrastructure of Islamic higher education, the Central Asian countries were deprived of high-quality clerics potentially more open to reformist ideas, such as those who supported the Jadid movement. This situation also opened Central Asian Islam to external influences that were at odds with its traditional Hanafi school. The subordination of the religious establishment to political authorities and the appointment of unqualified clergy to high religious office undermined the credibility and legitimacy of official Islam. This factor has played an important role in the attraction of segments of Central Asian populations to nonindigenous interpretations of Islam, including a variety of extremist ideologies.

Strengthening of Personality-Based and Authoritarian Characteristics of Central Asian Cultures

The nature of the Soviet system meant that instead of altering the traditional authoritarian and personality-based (khan and emir) culture of the region, it strengthened these tendencies, albeit in a new guise. Thus, the cult of the khan was transformed into the cult of the secretary-general of the Communist Party, federal and republican. The pattern of alliances and patronage within the Communist Parties was largely based on family, regional, and ethnic ties. It thus perpetuated the traditional pattern and hindered development of merit-based systems.

In sum, despite some economic and social benefits, Soviet nation and state building in Central Asia did not advance its modernization and hindered the development of even rudimentary forms of democracy.

THE POSTINDEPENDENCE HINDRANCES

In the postindependence era, the Central Asian states and Azerbaijan have faced formidable difficulties in making the transition to a post-totalitarian political system and culture and a market-based economy and in engaging on a path of modernization. Some of these problems are caused by the internal conditions of these countries, while others derive from regional and international dynamics.

The first hindrance is the survival of Soviet-era bureaucratic and political structures and culture, resulting in the exclusion of the newly emerging political forces from the decision-making process. Moreover, corruption, nepotism, organized repression, and the old patronage system still exist.

The second hindrance is the intensification of regional, ethnic, tribal, and clan divisions because of the above factors, thus arresting the process of national identity formation. In some cases, these cleavages have led to civil war, as in Tajikistan. The Nagorno-Karabakh conflict between Azerbaijan and its Armenian minority (supported by Armenia) is another example. There is also a strong economic component to the growing interethnic discord, as more deprived regions, subregions, and clans challenge their better-off counterparts. Although many factors contributed to the Tajikistan civil war, the determination of the Khujandi (Leninabadi) elite, which under Communist rule had dominated the economy and politics of the republic and had kept the clans from the southern and central regions of Kulaib and Qarategin out of the decision-making process, to retain their power was an important cause of its out break. After five years of civil war, an uneasy peace was established in 1997 with the mostly Islamic opposition. However, this has not led to the beginning of a democratic transformation. Rather, the Khujandi predominance has been replaced with that of the Kulaibis.[20]

In Kyrgyzstan, increasingly the impoverished South has been challenging the North's economic and political supremacy.[21] In Uzbekistan, too, power is unevenly divided among several clans, the most powerful having its base in Samarkand, the birthplace of President Islam Karimov. Other clans from Surkhandarya, Kashkedarya, Khorazm, and Fergana have been marginalized since independence.

The third hindrance is the emergence of an ideological vacuum and the appearance of new forms of nationalist and Islamic discourse to shape Central Asia's future evolution. For seventy years, communism provided a framework for all aspects of life throughout the Soviet Union. With the collapse of the Soviet Union and communism, post-Soviet states were left with an ideological vacuum that a variety of political forces espousing different ideologies have tried to fill. The two main ideological discourses that emerged and that pose a potential challenge to the power base and legitimacy of the current power elites have been ethno-nationalism and Islam-based ideologies. Tajikistan is the best example of a group espousing a sociopolitical ideology based on Islam, challenging the existing structure of power, albeit in coalition with other political forces.[22]

This ideological fragmentation, although natural in a post-totalitarian transition, has contributed to the ability of the existing power elites to consolidate their rule. They have co-opted certain Islamic and nationalist symbols while at the same time using the threat of extremist Islam to justify antidemocratic policies. In short, the fact that the Soviet-era elites are more cohesive while the opposition is fragmented has enabled the ruling elite to dispense with any dialogue or bargain with the opposition. This policy of political exclusion has caused a crisis of legitimacy for the Central Asian ruling elites, exacerbated by corruption and nepotism. This crisis of legitimacy could degenerate into political instability, further undermining prospects for modernization and democratization.

This situation has also prevented the development of viable civil society institutions, including political parties, which are necessary requirements of a functioning democracy. Turkmenistan and Uzbekistan have banned organized political opposition, maintaining what resembles a one-party state. In Kyrgyzstan, the opposition party leaders have been subjected to intimidation or imprisonment. In June 2002, Kazakhstan's parliament passed a new law barring the establishment of political parties with fewer than 50,000 members and a nationwide representation.[23] In Tajikistan, President Imomali Rahmonov has effectively marginalized the Islamic opposition. The current presidents have also systematically eliminated opposition forces from power structures, thus arresting the formation of a viable counter-elite that could engage in a discourse on policy options. This has consolidated the institution of presidents for life and created presidential dynasties, as in Azerbaijan, where President Haidar Aliev's son, Ilham, succeeded his father as president in October 2003.

The fourth hindrance, the availability of financial rent based on the actual production of natural resources, notably energy, or the expectation of a large income deriving from their resources in the future, has enabled the ruling elite to ignore the broader society. Other forms of rent have included narcotics trafficking and foreign assistance channeled through existing governments.

FAILURE OF ECONOMIC MODERNIZATION

The postindependence record of Central Asian countries in economic modernization has been equally disappointing. In regard to many socioeconomic indicators there has been a regressive trend, as the living standards for average citizens have deteriorated since the beginning of the 1990s and unemployment levels have remained very high in all republics. Inflation rates have also been high, causing a decline in real incomes and wages, particularly in Tajikistan, Turkmenistan, and Uzbekistan.[24] Although per capita incomes have improved in some republics, there has been a general increase in the poverty level (see Figure 18.1).

A number of economic and political factors have been responsible for this disappointing record, to varying degrees in different cases. Among the political factors, civil strife has played an important role in the case of Tajikistan and Azerbaijan. Among the economic factors, the following have been particularly important. The first factor is the consequences of the collapse of the Soviet Union, which separated these countries from a centrally planned economy, causing serious disruption in their trade patterns and other economic relations.

The second factor is the low level of these countries' integration within the global economic and trade systems, since they had no independent economic and trade relations outside the Soviet Union. Even today, Russia is the region's main trading partner, despite a gradual decline in its commercial interaction with Central Asia.[25] Russia also controls the main routes for oil and gas exports.[26] This situation has made Central Asian countries unduly vulnerable to economic developments in Russia, as demonstrated by the impact of the Russian financial crisis in 1998. This crisis caused an economic recession that took two years for the Central Asian economies to overcome.

Figure 18.1
Percentage of Population Below Poverty Line, 2001

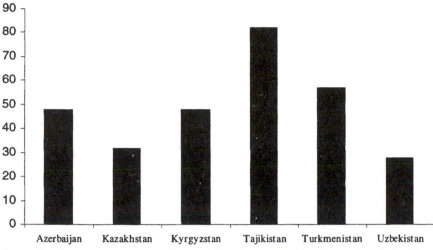

Source: Kazakhstan, Kyrgyzstan, Tajikistan, Turkmenistan, Uzbekistan Country Brief, The World
Bank Group, 2002.

Note: Poverty figures for Turkmenistan and Uzbekistan are underreported by their governments.

The third factor is the limited base of Central Asian economies. Despite some
level of industrialization, Central Asian countries are similar to raw-material-pro-
ducing third world countries, often dependent on the export of one or two products—cotton, oil, natural gas, or gold, for instance. This situation makes them
vulnerable to fluctuations in the price of these commodities and causes uncertainty in the level of their export earnings.

The fourth factor is that because of the lack of an indigenous capital base and
an entrepreneurial class, privatization schemes have resulted mostly in the closure of noncompetitive industries without the establishment of adequate number
of new plants. Meanwhile, as in the case of most third world countries, foreign
investment has been concentrated in extractive industries, especially energy.

The fifth factor is that considerations of state interest, which still control the
economies of Turkmenistan, Uzbekistan, and Tajikistan, plus the fear of the sociopolitical impact of drastic economic reforms have slowed the pace of reform.
The Central Asian countries face the perennial dilemma of third world countries,
namely how to reconcile the goal of economic rationalization with that of social
justice and political stability.

EXTERNAL IMPEDIMENTS

The processes of state building, modernization, and democratization take place
in the context of a dynamic interaction between internal and external forces. As

noted elsewhere in this book, the impact of external factors is more important in the case of politically and economically weak and fragmented states. The Central Asian countries fall within this category. The impact of the external factors—notably great-power competition for empire—in the pre-independence period culminated in Central Asia's absorption into the Russian and Soviet empires.

Among the external factors that have had an adverse impact on Central Asia's postindependence modernization and democratization, the following stand out:

1. Russian desire to retain its influence in the region has led Russia—or certain elements within its leadership—to encourage internal strife in some countries, notably Tajikistan. It has also caused Russia to essentially support the existing power structures.

2. Regional conflicts such as the Afghan civil war and the threat of the spread of Islamic extremist ideas to Central Asia have both contributed to internal strife, as in Tajikistan and to some extent Kyrgyzstan, and have been used by the political establishments to pursue repressive policies. The Afghan conflict has also had negative economic consequences by excluding a southern export route for Central Asian energy through Afghanistan.

3. Growing Western, and especially U.S., interest in the region in the aftermath of September 11 and the Afghan and Iraq wars has meant that Western countries needing the military and political cooperation of Central Asian governments are less willing to pressure them on democratization.[27] With both the West and Russia interested in expanding military cooperation with these countries, there is a risk of their militarization, a condition that has proved detrimental to democratization in other Muslim states in the Middle East and South Asia.[28]

Certain characteristics of the international economic and trading system (see Chapter 11 by Peter Nunnenkamp in this volume) have also adversely affected Central Asia's modernization. The growing external debt problem of these countries is a reflection of these systemic influences (see Table 18.1).

CONCLUSION

The processes of modernization and democratization in the newly independent states of Central Asia have been affected by a multiplicity of internal and external factors. The Central Asian republics' development has been adversely affected by their landlocked geography, thus leaving their economic fate in the hands of their neighbors, especially Russia. Barring a change in U.S.-Iran relations, Russia will have a significant impact in determining the pace of modernization of most of the Central Asian republics.

Second, these republics are still bedeviled by a number of structural dislocations produced by their colonial past. During the Soviet era the development trajectories of these republics were comprehensively redefined, thereby creating distinct forms of political and economic dynamics peculiar to former Soviet republics. Because of the eradication of private property, lack of economic competition and incentive, total absence of a private sector, Russo-centric in-

Table 18.1
Debt to GDP Ratio in Central Asia and Azerbaijan

	2000	2001*
Azerbaijan		
Total Debt/GDP Ratio	22.5 †	n.d.
Present Value of Debt/GDP	n.d.	n.d.
Kazakhstan		
Total Debt/GDP Ratio	64.5	64.2
Present Value of Debt/GDP	36.6	n.d.
Kyrgyzstan		
Total Debt/GDP Ratio	127.3	110.2
Present Value of Debt/GDP	102.6	n.d.
Tajikistan		
Total Debt/GDP Ratio	92.2	82.9
Present Value of Debt/GDP	68.6	71.3
Turkmenistan		
Total Debt/GDP Ratio	50.6	31.7
Present Value of Debt/GDP	n.d.	n.d.
Uzbekistan		
Total Debt/GDP Ratio	56.0	62.0
Present Value of Debt/GDP	55.4	61.3

Source: Development Data Group, World Bank, 2002.

Note: n.d. = no data available.
*Data for 2001 are preliminary.
†This figure is from *Economist Intelligence Unit,* Azerbaijan Country Profile, 2003, 54.

dustrialization, and the politics of totalitarianism, Central Asia faces a more serious set of obstacles to its modernization and democratization compared to other ex-colonies. Most seriously, Soviet colonialism denied these republics the opportunity to experiment with modern state building and socioeconomic reform. It was also to a large extent responsible for dismantling the Jadid tradition, a modernist Islamic movement that potentially could have led to an indigenous Islamic reformation and a synthesis of Islam and modernization. Soviet totalitarianism strengthened the traditional authoritarian tendencies and provided a lasting antidemocratic tradition that still defines the region's political dynamics.

The Soviet economic legacy—notably the cotton monoculture, coerced collectivization, and the lopsided industrialization—has been equally negative. Although the Soviet experience produced a number of positive results, including secularization, high literacy, improved health conditions, and urbanization, the pervasive nature of Communist rule deprived the local population of the spirit of entrepreneurship, an understanding of the workings of a market economy, and any notion of democracy. In short, no single factor, and certainly not cultural or religious peculiarities, can explain the shortcomings of modernization and democratization in the region. In the future, too, a multitude of internal and external variables will determine the shape and pace of the Central Asian states' prospects for modernization and democracy.

NOTES

1. The Baku-Tbilisi-Ceyhan line is currently under construction.

2. Helene Carrere d'Encausse, "Systematic Conquest, 1865–1884," in Edward Allworth, ed., *Central Asia: 120 Years of Russian Rule* (Durham, NC: Duke University Press, 1989), chap. 4.

3. Elizabeth E. Bacon, *Central Asians Under Russian Rule: A Study in Culture Change* (Ithaca, NY: Cornell University Press, 1966), 29–55.

4. Richard A. Pierce, *Russian Central Asia, 1867–1917* (Berkeley: University of California Press, 1960), 143.

5. Earlier, Russia had managed to expand its reign over the Kazakh steppe (1822–54).

6. Pierce, *Russian Central Asia,* 190–99.

7. Seymour Becker, *Russia's Protectorates in Central Asia: Bukhara and Khiva, 1865–1924* (Cambridge, MA: Harvard University Press, 1968), 22.

8. Pierce, *Russian Central Asia,* 226–33.

9. "Jadidism: A Current Soviet Assessment," *Central Asian Review* 12, no. 1 (1964): 33.

10. Adeeb Khalid, *The Politics of Muslim Cultural Reform: Jadidism in Central Asia* (Berkeley: University of California Press, 1998), 90, http://ark.cdlib.org/ark:/13030/ft8g5008rv/.

11. On the leading personalities of the Jadid movement, see Helene Carrere d'Encausse, "Stirring of National Feeling," in Allworth, *Central Asia,* 191–97. Despite the overall similarities of the Jadid movement within the Russian empire, there were differ-

ences of style and approach as to the main direction of the reforms that embodied the Jadid worldview.

12. Helene Carrere d'Encausse, "Social and Political Reform," in Allworth, *Central Asia*, 195.

13. Khalid, *Politics of Muslim Cultural Reform*, 83.

14. For more information on the Young Turks' influence, see Serge A. Zenkovsky, *Pan Turkism and Islam in Central Asia* (Cambridge, MA: Harvard University Press, 1967), chap. 4.

15. Allec Nove and J. A. Newth, *The Soviet Middle East: A Communist Model of Development* (New York: Frederick Praeger, 1966), 24.

16. Ibid., 50.

17. As quoted in Olaf Caroe, *Soviet Empire: The Turks of Central Asia and Stalinism* (London: Macmillan, 1967), 146.

18. Uktum Bekmuhammadov (former head of the Socio-Cultural Association of the Tajiks of Samarkand), interview with the author, Moscow, June 1994.

19. Alexander Zinoviev, *Homo Sovieticus* (New York: Atlantic Monthly Press, 1985); Mikhail Epstein, "Labor of Lust: Erotic Metaphors of Soviet Civilization," http://www.emory.edu/INTELNET/af.lust.html.

20. Mehrdad Haghayeghi, *Islam and Politics in Central Asia* (New York: St. Martin's Press, 1996), 42–47.

21. Alisher Khamidov, "Kyrgyzstan Unrest Linked to Clan Rivalry," *EurasiaNet*, June 5, 2002, http://www.eurasianet.org/departments/insight/articles/eav060502.shtml; "Kyrgyzstan: Focus on Growing Political Instability," Irinnews.org, March 28, 2002.

22. Mehrdad Haghayehgi, "Changing Dynamics of Islamic Politics," *Muslim World* 92, nos. 3 and 4 (Fall 2002): 325.

23. Interfax-Kazakhstan News Agency, Almaty in Russian, BBC Monitoring online, July 19, 2002.

24. Tajikistan, Turkmenistan, Uzbekistan Country Brief, World Bank Group, Country Unit Staff, 2002.

25. *Economist Intelligence Unit,* quarterly country reports on Central Asia and Azerbaijan, statistical appendix, 1995–2002.

26. The Caspian Pipeline Consortium came online in 2001, allowing Kazakh oil from Tengiz field to be exported to Europe through the port of Novorossysk in the Russian Black Sea.

27. Todd Diamond, "US Unilateralism Fuels Great Power Rivalry in Central Asia," *EurasiaNet,* October 1, 2003, www.eurasianet.org/departments/insight/articles/eav 100103_pr.shtml.

28. For more information on the impact of the militarization of Central Asia, see Richard Giragosian and Roger McDermott, "The U.S. Military Engagement in Central Asia: The 'Great Game' or 'Great Gain'?" *Central Asia and the Caucasus, Journal of Social and Political Studies* (Sweden) 25, no. 1 (February 2004).

19

The Roots of Sub-Saharan Africa's Modernization and Democratization Dilemmas

Chuka Onwumechili

Although sub-Saharan Africa is home to 310 million Muslims, in the studies dealing with the causes of the slow rate of the Muslim world's modernization and democratization the region has received little attention. Yet an analysis of the region's successes and failures in the areas of modernization and democratization across the religious divide can shed light on the underlying causes of the Muslims world's modernization and democratization shortcomings and the relative role of religious and cultural factors in this respect. This is because despite some gains in development and modernization such as urbanization, literacy, and growth in communication networks, including an increase in the number of Internet users (see Table 19.1), the region's socioeconomic indicators present a depressing picture and per capita incomes remain low (see Table 19.2).[1]

The region's record in democratization is also mixed. In the late 1980s, sub-Saharan Africa was affected by what Samuel Huntington has described as the third wave of democratization. However, with few exceptions, this democratization trend was short-lived; in some cases it was short-circuited by military or paramilitary interventions, or both, and in others it became the victim of civil strife or state breakdown. Therefore, the experience of the sub-Saharan countries, including those with large Muslim populations (see Table 19.3), forms an important part of the Muslim world's overall modernization and democratization experience. Such an analysis will also allow for a balanced assessment of the actual or potential role of Islam, or some interpretations of it as espoused by various Islamist groups, without falling into the trap of cultural determinism.

In light of the above, the purpose of this chapter is (1) to identify those factors that have been responsible for Africa's modernization and democratization shortcomings irrespective of religious factors; (2) to identify factors specific to those African nations where Islam is the majority religion; and (3) to assess the

Table 19.1
Communication Infrastructure in Sub-Saharan Africa

Medium	1998	2001	2002
Fixed/Mobile Telephones (per 1,000 people)	19.1	40.6	n.d.
Personal Computers (per 1,000 people)	7.3	9.9	12.6
Internet Users	1.5 million	5.3 million	8.9 million

Source: Telecommunications Development Bureau (BDT) of the International Telecommunications Union (ITU), 2003. Available online at www.itu.int/ITU-D/icr/at_glance/af_indicators.html.

Note: n.d. = no data available.

relative impact of various factors. The multiplicity of factors that have affected the process of Africa's modernization and democratization can be broadly divided into two categories: internal and external. Internal factors include the legacy of colonialism, the role of the military, patterns of traditional culture, and dynamics of state building. External factors include the dynamics of the international political and economic systems, notably the impact of the cold war, great-power politics, and the characteristics of the international economic and trading systems.

INTERNAL FACTORS

Certain internal characteristics of African countries, common to both Muslim and non-Muslim countries, have acted as major hindrances to their modernization and democratization. One of these characteristics is the legacy of colonialism. Others are related to the peculiarities of state and nation building in Africa in the past four decades, notably the impact of ethnic strife, the excessive role of the military, and priority given to physical modernization at the expense of building democratic institutions.

Colonial Legacy: Border Disputes

Among the most negative legacies of colonialism in Africa have been the arbitrary boundaries drawn by colonial powers, which sowed the seeds of interethnic, as well as intra- and interstate conflict. The Pan Africanist Congress, held in 1945 in Manchester, U.K., noted that "the artificial divisions and territorial boundaries created by the Imperialist powers are deliberate steps to obstruct the political unity of the . . . African peoples."[2] It is arguable that the drawing of the borders was deliberately undertaken for this purpose, but it is clear that these boundaries have been the cause of numerous interstate and regional wars and irredentist policies. Examples include the territorial dispute between Nigeria and

Table 19.2
Economic Statistics on Sub-Saharan Africa

Country	Population (in millions) Total	Population (in millions) Ages 15-64	Urban Population (% of total population)	Adult Illiteracy Rate (Male/Female % ages 15 and above)	Labor Force (Total in millions/female % of labor force)	Gross Domestic Product ($ in millions)	GDP Real Growth Rate	GDP per capita ($)	% of GDP Agriculture	% of GDP Industry
Benin	7.04	3.3	22	47/75	2.9/48.3	7,380	6.0	380	36	14
Burkina Faso	13.23	5.8	17	65/85	5.7/46.5	1, 451	4.6	1,100	38	21
Cameroon	15.75	8.4	50	20/35	6.2/38.1	2,684	4.0	1,700	43	20
Central African Republic	3.68	2.0	42	39/63	1.8/n.d.	4,296	1.5	1,200	55	21
Chad	9.25	3.7	24	47/64	3.8/44.8	9,297	7.4	1,000	39	14
Congo	56.63	26.1	n.d.	26/48	21.6/43.4	34,000	3.5	600	56	19
Cote d'Ivoire	16.96	9.0	44	40/62	6.6/33.5	24,030	-1.6	1,400	24	22
Djibouti	0.46	n.d.	n.d.	22/42	0.3/n.d.	619	3.5	1,300	n.d.	n.d.
Ethiopia	66.56	33.6	16	52/68	28.3/40.9	48,530	3.0	700	52	11
Gambia	1.50	0.8	31	55/69	0.7/45.1	2,582	5.7	1,800	40	14
Ghana	20.47	10.2	36	19/35	9.4/50.4	41,250	4.5	2,000	36	25
Guinea	9.03	4.0	28	n.d.	3.6/47.2	18,690	3.7	2,100	24	38
Guinea-Bissau	1.36	0.6	32	45/75	0.6/40.5	901	-4.3	700	56	13
Kenya	31.64	16.6	34	11/23	15.9/46.1	32,890	1.1	1,100	19	18
Liberia	3.32	1.7	45	29/62	1.3/39.6	3,116	2.0	1,000	n.d.	n.d.
Madagascar	16.98	8.3	30	26/39	7.6/44.7	12, 590	-11.9	800	30	14
Malawi	11.65	5.5	15	25/52	5.1/48.5	6,811	1.7	600	34	18
Mali	11.63	5.5	31	63/83	5.4/46.2	9,775	4.5	900	38	26

Cameroon over Bakassi, which began in 1994; the rival claims of Angola and the Democratic Republic of Congo over the Cabinda enclave; and the post–World War II border disputes between Somalia and Kenya, Somalia and Ethiopia, and Ghana and Togo. These disputes have encouraged the establishment of authoritarian national governments, leading to a weakening of internal democratic institutions and the diversion of funds from developmental purposes.

Table 19.2 (continued)

Mozambique	17.48	9.6	33	39/70	9.4/48.4	19,520	7.7	1,100	22	26
Niger	11.06	5.4	21	76/91	5.3/44.3	8,713	2.9	800	40	17
Nigeria	133.88	69.4	45	27/42	51.6/36.6	112,500	3.2	900	30	46
Republic of Congo	2.95	1.6	66	12/24	1.3/43.5	2,500	0.0	900	6	66
Rwanda	7.81	4.3	6	26/38	4.7/48.8	8,920	9.7	1,200	40	22
Senegal	10.58	5.2	48	52/71	4.4/42.6	15,640	2.4	1,500	18	27
Somalia	8.03	4.5	28	n.d.	3.9/43.4	4,270	3.5	600	n.d.	n.d.
Sudan	38.11	18.0	37	30/52	12.7/29.8	52,900	5.1	1,400	39	19
Swaziland	1.16	0.6	27	19/21	0.4/37.8	5,542	1.6	4,800	17	44
Tanzania	35.92	18.0	33	15/32	17.7/49.0	20,420	6.1	600	45	16
Togo	5.43	2.4	34	27/56	1.9/40.0	7,594	2.9	1,400	39	21
Uganda	25.63	11.2	15	22/42	11.2/47.6	30,490	5.5	1,200	36	21
Zambia	10.31	5.4	40	14/27	4.4/44.7	8,240	2.3	800	22	26

Sources: *World Development Indicators 2003* (Washington, DC: IBRD/The World Bank, 2003); Central Intelligence Agency, *CIA World Factbook 2003* (Washington, DC: Central Intelligence Agency, 2003).

Interethnic Tensions

Colonial borders often divided a single ethnic group or "ethnic nation" into two or more modern states. The Ewe in West Africa, who saw themselves as a self-contained nation, were split into the modern states of Togo and Ghana; the Yorubas were divided into the Benin Republic and Nigeria. African nations were against these policies because they delinked people from their ethnic and traditional political leaders, including kings. This policy of forcing rival ethnic nations to cohabit within a new state has been a major cause of interethnic tensions within African countries and a source of chronic instability. The colonial powers ignored the long history of ethnic nations that had existed long before the advent of colonialism. Pamela Mbabazi notes that "the modern nationalist in the African context is an alien concept, which was imported and transplanted by the colonial powers. Groups were torn apart and others brought together by the colonial demarcation of states and, arguably, this has resulted in the creation of pluralistic communities, with many disparities."[3] These ethnic nations continue to exist as separate "nations" within the ethnically plural modern state. Long after independence the identity of ethnic nations within African modern states remains

Table 19.3
Statistics on Islam in Sub-Saharan Africa

Country	Total Population (millions)	Muslim Population (millions)	Muslim Population (% of total population)	Country	Total Population (millions)	Muslim Population (millions)	Muslim Population (% of total population)
Benin	7.04	1.41	20	Malawi	11.65	2.33	20
Burkina Faso	13.23	6.61	50	Mali	11.63	10.47	90
Cameroon	15.75	3.15	20	Mozambique	17.48	3.5	20
Central African Republic	3.68	0.55	15	Niger	11.06	8.85	80
Chad	9.25	4.72	51	Nigeria	133.88	66.94	50
Congo	56.63	5.66	10	Republic of Congo	2.95	0.06	2
Cote d'Ivoire	16.96	6.36	38	Rwanda	7.81	0.36	4.6
Djibouti	0.46	0.43	94	Senegal	10.58	9.95	94
Ethiopia	66.56	31.62	48	Somalia	8.03	8.03	100
Gambia	1.50	1.35	90	Sudan	38.11	26.68	70
Ghana	20.47	3.28	16	Swaziland	1.16	0.12	10
Guinea	9.03	7.68	85	Tanzania	35.92	12.57	35
Guinea-Bissau	1.36	0.61	45	Togo	5.43	1.09	20
Kenya	31.64	3.16	10	Uganda	25.63	4.1	16
Liberia	3.32	0.6	20	Zambia	10.31	2.47	24
Madagascar	16.98	1.19	7				

Source: Central Intelligence Agency, *CIA World Factbook 2003* (Washington, DC: Central Intelligence Agency, 2003).

stronger than that of the states, in the sense that people relate more to their ethnic kin than to fellow citizens of other ethnic groups. This phenomenon has prevented the development of postindependence countries into strong modern states where a more civic sense of identity unites the people across ethnic divides.

Ethnic crises have primarily been manifested in two ways. The first manifestation is competition for scarce resources, at times culminating in full-blown wars, as demonstrated by the conflicts between the Hutus and the Tutsis in Rwanda, the most serious of which occurred in April 1994, and between the Lendu and Hema in the Democratic Republic of Congo in 1972, 1985, and 1996. Paradoxically, these types of tensions and conflicts can often be exacerbated by the practice of democracy. Burundi is a classic example of this paradox. There is deep-seated distrust between the majority Hutus and the minority Tutsis, who control the military.[4] Consequently, as Seyoum Y. Hameso points out, the multiparty democracy in Burundi, which led to the election of a Hutu president in 1993,[5] set in motion a chain of events that culminated in a tragic war. Five months after the 1993 elections, Tutsi soldiers assassinated the president, and another Hutu was elected to replace him. But shortly afterward, he was killed in a suspicious plane crash. The national assembly then elected yet another Hutu as the interim president, but this time the Tutsi-dominated army overthrew the interim president and installed a Tutsi as president. The Burundi case is an extreme example of ethnic rivalry, but other cases that undermine the consolidation of democracy abound. The second manifestation of these ethnic cases are the separatist movements that seek to reshape the state along ethnic lines. For example, the Igbos of Nigeria, citing a pattern of ethnic persecution, fought a three-year separatist war from 1967 to 1970. Ethiopia fought the Eritrean separatists from 1962 to 1993.

These crises, too, divert scarce funds from developmental purposes, and "in a few African countries, the ethnicization of politics" has led to total state breakdown.[6]

Patterns of Colonial Development

The pattern of colonial development did not facilitate the modernization of postindependence countries. On the contrary, because of its basic features it may have made modernization more difficult. According to the colonial pattern, the development of infrastructure such as transportation and communication was to serve the needs of the colonial administration and the colonial center rather than those of the colonies. Nor did the colonial powers use Africa's abundant natural resources to create an industrial base. Rather, Africa served as a source of raw materials and as an export market for the enrichment of the colonial metropolis. Meanwhile, colonial development disrupted the traditional pattern of economic life as well as causing environmental damage and undermining certain sectors. For example, according to one author, British colonial policy in Kenya, which required forced confinement of African peasants in crowded reservations in order to provide cheap labor for English planters in the highland, caused the impoverishment of Kenyan peasants and soil exhaustion.[7] Little was done in terms of education and health. This meant that the postindependence states faced a gigantic developmental task.

In the political arena, the colonial powers did little to encourage real democracy. Rather, their policy was based on exploiting various divisions within the society, utilizing traditional power structures with their tribal and personality-based characteristics, or using force to subdue the recalcitrant natives. Thus, as noted by one author, "colonial rule was by no means a preparation for post-independence democratic government." The problem was not so much a failure by

Africans to learn the lessons of parliamentary government; rather, the lessons of authoritarian colonial rule were learned too well.[8]

In short, colonial rule did little to prepare the African nations for democracy. Anticolonial struggles carried out under the leadership of charismatic leaders such as Mzee Jomo Kenyatta, Kwame Nkrumah, and others strengthened Africa's personality-based traditional political cultures, thus prejudicing its future democratic development.

Excessive Role of the Military

The extensive and constant interference of the military in internal politics since the last days of colonial rule has been another impediment to modernization and democratization. In the early days of independence these countries were mostly under civilian rule. However, civil rule lasted a short period and the military interventions began by the early 1960s. Several reasons account for this phenomenon. Civil rulers had moved away from the multiparty democratic systems that had brought them to power and had adopted single-party systems. For instance, after independence in 1960 and 1962, Muslim-majority Senegal and Mali and Christian-majority Uganda quickly adopted one-party systems. Their rational was that African states should concentrate on national development and modernization instead of being locked into eternal bickering and debates characteristic of a multiparty democratic system.

The vision of these postindependence leaders proved wrong, as significant national development and modernization remained elusive, thus providing the justification for subsequent military coups. Military leaders cited economic decline and failed national development to justify the taking over of the government,[9] a practice described as the "development thesis" of military coups.[10] This thesis was applied in the case of the coups in Mali and Niger. Hamani Diori of Mali, who had ruled the country since independence in 1960, was removed in a military coup in 1974. The coup was carried out on the pretext of saving people from economic hardship.

However, the military was no more successful in achieving developmental goals and improving people's living conditions than the civilian rulers had been. Rather, it introduced new complexities in state-military relationships. It undermined the military's professionalism and exacerbated authoritarian tendencies. Most of Africa's military establishments remain professionally weak. Nor is the trend toward militaries' intervention in internal politics declining. On the contrary, in some countries, such as Côte d'Ivoire, where the military has traditionally been professional and largely apolitical, the use of the military for internal police action in 1989 and 1990 eventually presaged a greater interest on the part of the military in state politics. Indeed, the military's opportunity to become involved in governing the state came in 1999, when civil unrest in Côte d'Ivoire helped justify General Robert Guei's overthrow of President Henri Konan Bedie's government. The threat of military intervention becomes particularly high when social policies, changes, or economic disturbances threaten the military's interests. In 1994, Gambia's military mutinied because of complaints about food and accommodation in the barracks and because payment was not getting through to Gambian peacekeeping forces in Liberia.[11]

The excessive role of the military not only hinders modernization and democratization but can lead to the state's complete breakdown, as illustrated by the cases of Sierra Leone and Liberia. In Sierra Leone, the military's interference quashed democratic rule and led to a debilitating war. With incidences of military mutinies and chronic nonpayment of military wages, there is growing concern among observers of African affairs that there may be an increase in the level of military intervention. In Liberia, military confrontations also led to the breakdown of the state. The military dictatorship of Samuel K. Doe was crushed by an insurgent military band led by Charles Taylor in the 1990s. Taylor's victory was Pyrrhic, however, and it led to a chaotic state where military fought each other while the state's welfare suffered. The above demonstrates the kind of vicious circle many African countries are caught in: developmental failure encourages authoritarianism and militarism, while the latter further complicates the task of modernization and democratization.

STATE BUILDING AND DEMOCRACY

The preoccupation with state building often impeded democratization (see chapter 12 in this volume by Mohammed Ayoob). This preoccupation derived from the fact that postindependent African states were multiethnic and their survival was by no means certain. Even today, most of these states consider state building and national survival their highest goals. In this context, authoritarian practices rather than democracy have been seen as necessary to state survival.[12] In line with a view popular in the 1960s and 1970s among some development experts and political scientists, it was believed that a strong authoritarian one-party state would be more effective in advancing modernization. Consequently, postindependence Africa from the 1960s to the early 1980s was ruled by authoritarian civilian regimes, often espousing socialist economic models of development, or by military dictatorships. These types of governments achieved some success in education and urbanization, but they retarded modernization in other important areas. For instance, the lack of citizen participation in national debate hampered the growth of civil society, democracy remained a national mirage, and there was little success in nurturing national identities transcending ethnic loyalties.

OTHER OBSTACLES

The high population growth rates in most of the African countries have hampered modernization.[13] Many of these countries have limited resources, and the increase in population has meant that states have not been able to sustain their modernization and state-building plans. Instead, they have become preoccupied with providing basic needs such as food and focusing on job creation. Newly created jobs, however, have been intended merely to disburse wages to stem the rise in poverty and have not been focused on maximizing productivity. In the process, governments have become the largest employers, and the private sector has remained undeveloped. The latter has delayed the emergence of a strong middle class independent from the state, which is important in the process of democratization. Meanwhile, festering corruption, intended to build individual empires of wealth to the detriment of the state, has weakened the state. These factors combined to create an unstable situation—the result of the absence of not only a strong state but a private sector and a middle class as well. This situation has also deepened ethnic and class cleavages and has contributed to civil strife. The Democratic Republic of the Congo is a good example of the devastating consequences of widespread and high-level corruption. In addition, the prevalence of a patriarchal culture in both Muslim and non-Muslim Africa has hindered the advancement of women—a necessary factor for modernization.

EXTERNAL FACTORS

External factors, notably the continuing influence of colonial powers, the fallout of the cold war, the impact of the international economic system, and the policies of new international actors, have adversely affected the course of Africa's modernization and democratization.

The ex-colonial powers, especially France and, to a lesser extent, Britain, still maintain a significant presence in Africa and actively intervene in its politics. French and British intervention has at times been positive, especially in preserving the state. For instance, French support was critical to the defeat in the Chadian crises of the Libyan-backed groups that supported of Hissene Habré in 1982. Britain was involved in the Nigerian civil war, to help forestall the attempt of the Igbos of eastern Nigeria to secede from the country, and in Uganda Britain helped to restore professionalism in the army after a long period of decay. However, on other occasions France and Britain have supported military and other corrupt and nondemocratic rulers.[14] France supported Jean-Bedél Bokassa of the Central African Republic (1966–79), who in 1972 declared himself emperor, and Britain was initially in favor of Idi Amin. At times, France has acted against the maintenance of the state. In the Democratic Republic of the Congo in 1997, France supported Denis Sassou-Nguesso and his Cobra militia in an uprising against the elected government. France's main motive was to protect its economic interests. The French had been angered by the Congolese government's opening of its oil market, then dominated by French companies, to American competition.[15]

THE IMPACT OF THE COLD WAR

In his *From the Congo to Soweto*, Henry F. Jackson cites a declassified U.S. government document, which in 1960 clearly stated, "What we [the United

States] do . . . or fail to do . . . in Africa [in the next year] will have a profound effect for many years. . . . We see Africa as probably the greatest open field of maneuver in the worldwide competition between the [Communist] Bloc and the non-Communist world."[16] That signified the beginning of the cold war in Africa between the West and the Soviet Union (USSR). This became a major hindrance to Africa's modernization and democratization. It encouraged high levels of state dependency on external powers and opened several war fronts on the continent. It also led external powers to support authoritarian regimes of either the Right or the Left. The negative examples of the cold war in Africa include Congo.[17] In Ethiopia, the Soviet-supported revolution in 1974 had devastating consequences. The East-West rivalry in Somalia contributed to the country's later problems.

In Angola, the West and the USSR fought a proxy war by supporting the rival Angolan parties—the People's Movement for the Liberation of Angola and the National Union for the Total Independence of Angola, respectively. Despite Angola's oil riches—which incidentally continued to flow during the war—there was no economic or human development, as resources were used to buy weapons.

Since the end of the cold war, the neglect of African problems by the international community has become a negative factor in its modernization. For example, it took the international community nearly two years before intervening in Rwanda to stop the civil war. International response to Africa's other crises, such as the AIDS epidemic, has also been slow. This has been because, with the elimination of the Soviet threat, Africa has lost its strategic importance. In short, both the wrong type of engagement and neglect on the part of major actors have adversely affected Africa's modernization and democratization.

EXTERNAL ECONOMIC INFLUENCES

As noted earlier, poor economic performance of postindependence governments contributed to military coups and authoritarianism in Africa. In turn, the failure of the authoritarian leaders caused an economic decline in most of the sub-Saharan African nations in the 1980s, which resulted in widespread street uprisings challenging authoritarian governments. Following these protests there was a wave of democratization, with the possibility of economic improvement through market liberalization, widespread employment, and economic growth. If the governments fail to realize these expectations, democracy will be endangered. Fortunately, in the late 1990s the economic growth rates of African countries steadily increased. However, African scholars warn that such growth may be unsustainable because of Africa's low investment and savings rates.[18] Another problem is the undiversified base of African economies and their dependence on the export of a single or few commodities highly vulnerable to fluctuating prices. Thus, the fall in the price of coffee or other agricultural commodities can be devastating to African economies.

Policies of international financial institutions such as the International Monetary Fund (IMF) and the World Bank also threaten the survival of democracy and continued modernization in sub-Saharan Africa. De Walle maintains that "donor conditionality is corrosive of democratic practices and values."[19] The stringent loan policies of international financial institutions often force African states to make significant adjustments, which may include suspension of government subsidies that are provided as part of public services. The example of Côte d'Ivoire in the post-Boigny era is quite instructive. The long-serving Houphouët-Boigny and his party (Parti Democratique de Côte d'Ivoire) had encouraged the influx of foreigners into the North of the country to support a booming agricultural economy. Most of these immigrants were Muslims from Burkina Faso, Mali, Niger, and Guinea. The boom went bust in the 1980s when the United States' interest rates rose and exacerbated Côte d'Ivoire's problems because its debts were pegged to U.S. dollars.[20] Côte d'Ivoire sought to survive through structural adjustment programs proposed by the World Bank. These programs forced the state to reduce its development and modernization programs in the impoverished North, sparking massive demonstrations against the state, which ultimately brought to the fore a simmering hatred between the southerners and the northerners. The military, led by General Robert Guei, was called in to quell the internal uprising. As noted earlier, military involvement in internal police actions is usually a harbinger for future military coups, as it was in the Côte d'Ivoire. General Guei was to return in 1999 to carry out a coup and use martial law to quash longtime democratic practices. Thus, while international financial institutions' policies and adjustments may make fiscal sense, they often generate massive suffering and lead to mass protests against the governments, which, in turn, provide opportunities for military intervention or force the government to use brute force to quell the protests. None of these options help democracy building, and some may lead to full-blown war, the introduction of martial law, and even state breakdown, thus also making modernization nearly impossible.

The character of the international trading system has also adversely affected Africa's economic development. For instance, the Multifiber Arrangement (MFA) was designed to set up quotas for textiles and apparel imported from developing to developed countries. The MFA adversely affected countries such as Mauritius and Kenya, which depended on such exports. Mauritius became subject to the U.S. quota in 1985. In 1994, Kenya also became subject to the quota. The quota forced Kenya to lose 40 percent of its exports to the United States, and 75 percent of jobs in its textile industry were lost, with more than thirty companies having to close down.[21]

Developed countries have unjustly used health and safety concerns to create barriers for trade with Africa. In December 1997, the European Union (EU) banned the importation of Mozambican fish, claiming that cholera could be transmitted to European consumers, although Japan, the largest importer of such fish, had imposed no such restrictions. Besides, the World Health Organization (WHO) had clearly testified that the European Union had no justification for such a decision.[22]

Agricultural subsidies in the United States and the European Union also adversely affect African states. A good example is cotton subsidies in the United States. At the Cancun conference in September 2003, Mali, Burkina Faso, Benin Republic, and Chad filed a complaint with the World Trade Organization (WTO) about cotton subsidies offered to U.S. and EU farmers.[23] These subsidies amounted to $5.8 billion in 2001–2 alone. The subsidies caused Mali to lose $43 million in expected cotton revenues. This constitutes a substantial loss in a country where cotton provides 40 percent of the entire export revenue. It is also noteworthy that the $3 billion worth of subsidies granted to U.S. cotton farmers outstripped the entire economic output of Burkina Faso. The subsidies thus impoverish the African nations, denying them needed revenue. In short, the global trading system has not helped Africa, and African demands for more favorable trading conditions have received a cold response from the industrial countries. A new phenomenon is the position of those multinational companies involved in extractive activities. Some of these companies seem willing to deal with armed groups engaged in civil wars as long as their business interests are protected. A good example is the behavior of companies engaged in the diamond trade. According to one author, "companies such as De Beers and others have directly contributed to the death and strife caused in many parts of Africa, in particular Sierra Leone and Angola. These two countries in particular continue to suffer the effects of civil war which are greatly funded through diamonds trade."[24] Illicit sales of diamonds have also helped fund conflicts in Congo and Liberia, leading the United Nations to try to put an end to these unlawful transactions.[25]

THE IMPACT OF NEW ACTORS

Since the early 1970s new actors such as Libya, Egypt, Iran, and Saudi Arabia have tried to influence developments in sub-Saharan Africa. One impact of their activities has been the export of various ideologies, including more puritanical or revolutionary forms of Islam.

The activities of these countries partly account for the recent rise of Islamism in sub-Saharan Africa. However, many of these activities have been carried out by private organizations that have tried to gain influence through Islamic education and similar activities.[26]

These actors have created new divisions and problems for a number of African countries by exacerbating religious differences. Some states such as Libya have also used religion to advance other territorial and ideological interests. For instance, Libya's interest in Chad was based on territorial claims.[27] In sum, the activities of the new actors have further fragmented African societies, making the task of modernization and democratization more difficult.

THE CASE OF THE MUSLIM STATES

There are two types of Muslim states in sub-Saharan Africa:[28] (1) those such as Senegal, Mali, Djibouti, Gambia, Guinea, and Niger, where Islam is practiced by well over half of the population, and (2) mixed states, where no one religion is adhered to by 50 percent of the population. These include Nigeria, Côte d'Ivoire, Ethiopia, and Tanzania, where 40 percent, 41 percent, 45 percent, and 30 percent, respectively, of the populations are Muslims. Tanzania is also home to about two-thirds of all Muslims in East Africa.

The major barriers to modernization and democratization that African states with a Muslim majority face are similar to those facing non-Muslim states. However, the rise of Islamist movements and groups that ask for the establishment of a government based on a strict interpretation of *Shari'a* creates additional problems for some Muslim states. According to Nicholas Colombant, in Mali, the number of Islamist associations has risen to 150 from just a handful, and these groups can pose a threat to Mali's nascent democracy.[29] In Nigeria the insistence of some Muslim groups on a government based on *Shari'a* is putting stress on its constitution and efforts to make a transition to democracy.[30]

Certain Islamic traditions, as interpreted by the Islamists, coupled with indigenous African traditions limit the role of women and thus impede modernization and democratization. However, Islam per se is not a barrier to democratization, as the success of Mali and Senegal illustrates. In Senegal, an opposition candidate was elected to the presidential seat over an incumbent president in March 2000. In Mali, a candidate from one of the opposition parties won the presidential election over the candidate of the ruling party in May 2002. Also, in Senegal females occupied as many as fourteen parliamentary seats in 2000.[31] More Senegalese women have entered the workforce as well.

The successes of these countries have been due to their ability to curb the role of the military, reduce ethnic tensions, develop strategies for integrating Islamic practices with state laws, stabilize the economy, and build a vibrant civil society.

Senegal's case has shown that the smaller the size of the active military the better the chance of establishing civilian control over it. The Senegalese military does not serve as a career for a significant number of youths. Moreover, the military is not the only armed force in the country. It can easily be opposed by a paramilitary gendarmerie with relatively the same force strength and also by a resident French battalion that is just as well equipped. The presence of the French military discourages coup attempts.

The ability to reduce ethnic tensions has also been important in consolidating democracy, while democratization has helped mitigate ethnic problems. Scholars have attributed Mali's recent success in democratic consolidation to increased governmental administrative transparency, accountability, opportunities for policy pluralism, and citizen participation. These measures have allayed the fears of ethnic minorities of being dominated by the largest ethnic groups. Since 1995, Mali has organized annual national open forums with unencumbered citizen participation. Meanwhile, transparency has helped break down the barriers of distrust and bond ethnic groups together to achieve the higher goal of nation building within a democratic context.

Economic progress has contributed to these success stories. The gains in Senegal and Mali have coincided with economic growth. Vengroff and Kone describe Mali's transformation from authoritarian to liberal democracy as "extraordinary."[32] However, to sustain growth these countries need the help of the international community, especially in the form of better trading terms and access to U.S. and European markets, as well as more favorable development loans. Without these measures, the fledgling African democracies may not survive. In fact, De Walle warns, "If [African] democratic regimes cannot overturn the recent pattern of declining real wages, rising levels of poverty, and inadequate public spending on physical infrastructure and social services, they may lose their popular legitimacy and eventually fall prey to political instability."[33]

Senegal and Mali's development of a vibrant civil society has been another contributing factor to their success. Mali has a network of organizations committed to democratic participation. These include women's organizations such as the Coordination of Women's Organizations, the Women's Peace Movement, and the Association of Women Lawyers. The result is that women's access to power has been greatly improved in Mali. In 1997, as many as six women occupied ministerial-level positions in Ibrahim Keita's government, and scores of others remain active in Mali's civil society and nongovernmental organizations.[34] Most of Mali's democratization projects are linked to the masses through grassroots development, which includes training offered to women's groups, general advocacy training, and anticorruption workshops, among others. Many of these projects have helped support the development of a vibrant civil society, and they encourage further democratization. Mali's case should serve as an example for other states within the sub-Saharan region.

CONCLUSIONS

The foregoing discussion has illustrated that a number of internal and external factors continue to impede sub-Saharan Africa's modernization and democratization. These range from interethnic tensions often leading to intra- and interstate wars, to the excessive role of the military in national life, to discriminatory aspects of the international economic system. These factors equally affect Muslim and non-Muslim states because the states share similar historical experiences and have similar economic and political profiles. In the case of some Muslim states, conservative and extremist interpretations of Islam are complicating aspects of modernization such as improvement in women's situation and democratization. In some countries, such as Nigeria, these interpretations of Islam are exacerbating interethnic tensions. However, there are success stories in Africa as well that provide a glimpse of what is needed to help Africa's modernization and democratization. Senegal and Mali—both Muslim-majority countries—are cited as examples of democratic consolidation in sub-Saharan Africa. These cases are proof that a multiplicity of factors and not merely religious and cultural peculiarities account for the success or failure of modernization and democratization.

NOTES

1. United Nations Educational, Scientific, and Cultural Organization figures show that while literacy rates for females over fifteen years of age in sub-Saharan Africa have risen from 36 percent to 50 percent between 1990 and 2000, the equivalent figures for males have been 60 percent and 70 percent, respectively.

2. George Padmore, *History of the Pan-African Congress* (London: Hammersmith Books, 1963), 130–34.

3. Pamela Mbabazi, "Ethnicities in Crises of Governance in Africa: The Case of Uganda in the Great Lakes Region," in Sandra MacLean, Fahimal Quadir, and Timothy Shaw, eds., *Crises of Governance in Asia and Africa* (Burlington: Ashgate, 2001), 227–44.

4. Hutus form over 75 percent of Burundi's population.

5. Seyoum Hameso, "Issues and Dilemmas of Multiparty Democracy in Africa," *West Africa Review* 3, no. 2 (2001), www.icaap.org/iuicode?.

6. Marina Ottaway, "Ethnic Politics in Africa: Change and Continuity," in Richard Joseph, ed., *State, Conflicts, and Democracy in Africa* (Boulder, CO: Lynne Reinner, 1999), 299–317.

7. Samir Amin, *Imperialism and Unequal Development* (New York: Monthly Review Press, 1977), 141.

8. Barry Munslow, "Why Has the Westminster Model Failed in Africa?" *Parliamentary Affairs* 36 (Spring 1938): 224–27.

9. Samuel Decalo, *Coups and Army Rule in Africa: Motivations and Constraints,* 2nd ed. (New Haven, CT: Yale University Press, 1990); Staffan Wiking, *Military Coups in Sub-Sahara Africa: How to Justify Illegal Assumptions of Power* (Uppsala, Sweden: Scandinavian Institute of African Studies, 1983).

10. Chuka Onwumechili, *African Democratization and Military Coups* (Westport, CT: Praeger, 1998), 38. I describe this phenomenon by noting that "the development thesis arrogates the title of people's representatives to military coup leaders, who claim to have militarily intervened on behalf of downtrodden citizens."

11. Alex Thomson, *Introduction to African Politics* (London: Routledge, 2000), 129.

12. Kidane Mengisteab, "Democratization and State Building in Africa: How Compatible Are They?" in Kidane Mengisteab and Cyril Daddieh, eds., *State Building and Democratization in Africa: Faith, Hope, and Realities* (Westport, CT: Praeger, 1999), 21–39.

13. United Nations Development Programme, *UNDP Demographic Indicators 1950–2025*, rev. 1992 ed. (New York: United Nations Development Programme, 1993); Population Reference Bureau, *World Population Data Sheet* (Washington, DC: Population Reference Bureau, 2001). These reports indicate that nine out of the top ten countries with high population growth rates are African countries. These countries, including Benin Republic, Mali, and Niger, experience over 3 percent average annual growth change in population. Growth rates of 1.9 percent and higher mean that populations would double in about thirty-five years if the rates continue. More than 90 percent of African countries are growing at a rate of 1.9 percent or more annually.

14. Thomson, *Introduction to African Politics*, 129.

15. Onwumechili, *African Democratization*, 80–81.

16. Henry F. Jackson, *From the Congo to Soweto: US Foreign Policy Toward Africa Since 1960* (New York: William Morrow, 1982), 21–52; R. Craig Nation and Mark Kauppi, *The Soviet Impact in Africa* (Lexington, MA: Lexington Books, 1984), 1–8, 44.

17. In the Congo (former Zaire), the cold war led to the Soviet support for Patrice Lumumba while the United States supported Joseph Kasavubu. This support rivalry between the United States and the Soviet Union led to an intractable civil strife, which distracted from Congo's postindependence goal of modernization and development. Jackson, *From the Congo to Soweto,* noted that Congo's dependence on cold war support led to the long personality rule of Mobutu Sese Seko, who plundered the state but was assured of his hold on power by the support of the United States.

18. United Nations Department of Public Information, "Africa's Growth Slowed in 1998," *Africa Recovery* 12, no. 2 (1998).

19. Nicholas van De Walle, "Globalization and African Democracy," in Joseph, *State, Conflicts, and Democracy in Africa,* 109.

20. Cyril Daddish, "Elections and Ethnic Violence in Cote d'Ivoire: The Unfinished Business of Succession and Democratic Transition," *African Issues* 29, nos. 1 and 2 (2001): 14–19.

21. Brenda Jacobs, "H.R. 1432 Could Propel Sub-Saharan Sourcing," *Bobbin* 38, no. 11 (July 1997), 88–89; Micheal Phillips, "US Rethinks Trade Policy with Africa," *Wall Street Journal,* sec. A, 2, July 15, 1996.

22. "UN Agency Opposed to EU Ban on Mozambican Fish," March 3, 1998, http://panafricannews.com; Richard Mshomba, *Africa in the Global Economy* (Boulder, CO: Lynne Rienner, 2000), 105.

23. Amadou Toure and Blaise Campaore, "Your Farm Subsidies Are Strangling Us," *New York Times,* sec. A, 17, July 11, 2003, www.newfarm.org/International/. The two authors are the presidents of Mali and Burkina Faso, respectively. Additional information can be obtained from "International Agricultural Subsidies are 'Destructive' to African Agriculture, Payne Says," http://usinfo.state.gov/regional/af/trade/.

24. Laurent Crenshaw, "Diamonds, De Beers, and Destruction: How Conflict Diamonds Have Ravaged Africa," June 7, 2002, http://www.stanford.edu/class/e297c/war_peace/africa_struggles_with_slavery_colonialism_and_hiv_aids/lcrenshaw.html.

25. BBC News, "UN Targets 'Blood Diamonds' Trade," August 2003, http://news.bbc.co.uk/go/pr/fr_12/hi/africa/311742.stm.

26. Adeline Masquelier, "Debating Muslims, Disputed Practices: Struggles for the Realization of an Alternative Moral Order in Niger," in John Comaroff and Jean Comaroff, eds., *Civil Society and the Political Imagination in Africa* (Chicago: University of Chicago Press, 1999), 219–50; Adeline Masquelier, "Identity, Alterity, and Ambiguity in a Nigerian Community: Competing Definitions of 'True' Islam," in Richard Werbner and Terence Ranger, eds., *Postcolonial Identities in Africa* (Atlantic Highlands, NJ: Zed Books, 1999), 222–44.

27. Sulayman Nyang, "The Islamic Factor in Libya's Africa Policy," *Africa and the World* 1 (January 1988): 13–23; Raymond Copson, *Africa's Wars and Prospects for Peace* (Armonk, NY: M. E. Sharpe, 1994), 62–64.

28. See the *Worldmark Encyclopedia of Nations: Africa,* vol. 2 (Farmington Hills, MI: Gale Research, 2001) for a graphic taxonomy of religion and states.

29. Nicholas Colombant, "Mali's Muslims Steer Back to Spiritual Roots," *Christian Science Monitor* February 26, 2002, 8.

30. Abubakar Dauda, "Ethnic Identity, Democratization, and the Future of the African State: Lessons from Nigeria," *African Issues* 29, nos. 1 and 2 (2001): 31–36. These groups have succeeded in forcing several Nigerian administrative states to be run under *Shari'a* law. Such states include Zamfara, where the *Shari'a* code is strictly enforced.

31. United Nations Development Programme, *Human Development Report 2000* (New York: United Nations Development Programme, 2000).

32. Richard Vengroff and Moctar Kone, "Mali: Democracy and Political Change," in J. Wiseman, ed., *Democracy and Political Change in Sub-Saharan Africa* (New York: Routledge, 1995), 45–70; R. James Bingen, David Robinson, and John Staatz, eds., *Democracy and Development in Mali* (East Lansing: Michigan State University Press, 2000).

33. Nicholas van De Walle, "Globalization and African Democracy," in Joseph, *State, Conflicts, and Democracy in Africa*, 95.

34. Robin-Edward Poulton and Ibrahim Youssouf, *A Peace of Timbuktu: Democratic Governance, Development, and African Peacekeeping* (New York: United Nations, 1998), 108.

Conclusion and Suggested Remedies

Shireen T. Hunter

The foregoing analysis of the various factors affecting the process of modernization and its outcome—notably, whether it leads to the establishment of democratic forms of government—together with the case studies, yields a number of conclusions. These conclusions, in turn, suggest a number of measures that could encourage modernization and democratization in the Muslim world and, indeed, other non-Western countries.

- *Modernization and democracy are not static and uniform phenomena*, but rather dynamic processes bounded by time and space, hence the importance of a historical approach to the study of modernization and democracy.

- *Modernization and democracy are contested concepts subject to varying interpretation*, hence the question of whether there are different types of modernity and democracy and, if so, whether they are equally valid.

- *Timing is crucial in determining the shape, process, agents, and outcome of modernization* and, in particular, whether it is accompanied by democracy. Available evidence shows that those countries that have undergone modernization earlier have done so more through the agency of private actors than through that of states. By contrast, in the case of the latecomers to the process of modernization, which include all non-Western countries, the state has had the primary role. This situation, in turn, has affected the political structure of the various late-modernizing countries. In particular, it has either prevented the establishment of democratic rule or has delayed it.

- *The level of backwardness* of a country at the time of modernization influences the character of its modernization process, its agents, and its outcome, including whether modernization leads to democratization.

- *Serious disruption in the process of modernization* because of wars and revolution or external intervention affects its pace and outcome. A majority of Muslim countries have suffered from such disruptions.

- *There is no causal relationship between modernization and democratization* in the sense that one would inevitably lead to the other. Indeed, historically some of the most technologically and organizationally modern societies, such as Nazi Germany and the Soviet Union, have been undemocratic. A number of other countries, such as Meiji Japan, Communist China, Taiwan, South Korea, Singapore, and some Latin American countries, have achieved modernization under various shades of totalitarian and authoritarian regimes. Meanwhile, there are examples, albeit not numerous, of countries with low levels of modernization, which have more or less democratic forms of government. Nevertheless, the evidence also shows that the most modernized societies are also those with democratic systems.

- *Democracy is neither monolithic nor static.* In particular, the present Western-style liberal democracy is a relatively novel phenomenon and is the result of the gradual widening of the popular base of Western democracies and its shifting ethical foundations.

- *The relationship between culture, on the one hand, and modernization and democracy, on the other, is at best ambiguous.* Certainly, historical evidence does not support a culturally determinist explanation for either modernization or democracy. Nor does it support a view of culture as static. On the contrary, historical evidence points to cultural transformation as a result of modernization and various indigenous and exogenous influences.

- *Islam is neither monolithic nor impervious to change.*

- *Islam per se is neither antimodern and antimodernization nor antidemocracy.* However, certain readings of Islam and certain interpretations of the "modern" can render the two incompatible. However, Islam is not unique in this regard, and, in reality, a reductionist reading of any religion makes it incompatible with modernity and democracy. Moreover, there are elements in Islam and its intellectual tradition that make it compatible with modernization and democracy. Therefore, in discussions of the role of Islam in hindering or helping modernization, it must be clear *which* Islam and *which* modernity and democracy are at issue. Clearly, reductionist and radical readings of Islam are incompatible with liberal democracy and with modernity if the latter is defined as complete secularization of the society and denial of any public role for religion.

- *The importance of the external environment.* Historical evidence shows that the character of the external environment within which states have had to modernize and democratize has played an important role in determining the success or failure of both processes. The early European modernizers enjoyed a favorable or at least neutral external environment. The European expansion to other parts of the world, beginning as early as the sixteenth century, provided Europe with raw materials, including gold and silver, and later markets for its burgeoning industries. European migration to the New World (the Americas) and other colonies eased demographic pressures and prevented the upsurge of instability. Through their expansion into other lands, the Europeans created the international system in a way that suited their own interests. Other nations that wanted to join the system had to do it on European terms.

  Meanwhile, colonialism negatively impacted the evolution of non-European countries—though to varying degrees. In some cases, notably that of Iran, colonial rivalries hindered indigenous efforts at modernization and democratization. Perhaps the two most damaging aspects of colonialism were the haphazard delineation of borders without any concern for ethnic and religious affinities, and the distortion of the intellectual evolution of the colonies and semicolonies. The first dimension sowed the seeds of intra- and interstate conflicts, many of which are still bedeviling the Muslim world, and the second, by giving modernization a reactive and defensive aspect, aroused resistance.

Anticolonial struggles, often requiring militias and charismatic leadership, also left a legacy of large military establishments and personality-based politics, both of which have hindered the establishment and consolidation of democratic forms of government.

The character of the European-centered and later global interstate system, with fierce competition among key members, also adversely impacted non-Western and, especially, Muslim countries, because of the latter's important geopolitical location.

In particular, the East-West rivalry in the context of the cold war (1946–89) had serious negative consequences for the Muslim countries. The nature of the international economy, with its uneven and highly skewed distribution of wealth and power, has also had an inhibiting effect on the Muslim world's modernization and, consequently, its prospects for democratization. Trade barriers and the high cost of capital and technology are some of the most damaging aspects of the international economic system.

- *A number of internal characteristics of Muslim countries* have also adversely affected the process of their modernization and democratization. These include the excessive role of the state in the economy and the concomitant weakness of the private sector, the rentier nature of some Muslim states—such as the actually or potentially energy-rich countries—and the undue power and influence of the military in all aspects of national life.

Certain cultural traits of Muslim societies not directly linked to religion, such as extended families, gender gaps, and patriarchal relationships, also impact negatively on the twin processes of modernization and democratization.

SUGGESTED REMEDIES

The foregoing conclusions suggest a certain line of action to overcome the obstacles to modernization and democratization in the Muslim world.

- Modernization and democratization should be viewed as ongoing processes rather than one-off projects to be implemented and then forgotten.
- It must be realized that although modern societies have a number of traits in common, historically there have been multiple modernities because every process of modernization is influenced by time and space and preexisting economic, political, social, and cultural realities. As Muslim countries continue their process of modernization, an Islamic version of modernity will also emerge. Culturally relevant projects of modernization and democratization have a greater chance of success because they will not be perceived as alien and thus be rejected or elicit a negative reaction.
- Muslim countries and peoples should not reject modernity and democracy because of their supposed foreign origins. Rather, they should develop their version of modernity through a process of selective adoption of essential elements of modernization and by translating them into culturally acceptable models.
- Islam's own traditions of rationalist and scientific thinking and products should be revived and propagated, thus proving that rationalism and, hence, modernity are not in opposition to Islam.
- The balance of power between the state and society must be altered in favor of society by encouraging the growth of the civil society, by reducing the role of the state, especially in the economic area, and by the concomitant expansion of an independent pri-

vate sector. The role of the military in politics and economy should also be reduced. Given the economic realities of the Muslim world, the state will continue to have an important role in the process of modernization. However, the developmental strategy of the state should be such as eventually to empower the society and create a more favorable equilibrium between the two.

- Greater emphasis should be put on education and health, both necessary for a productive population.

- There must be greater efforts to close the gender gap through appropriate legislation and public education.

- There must be greater efforts at resolving regional and interstate disputes, which are manipulated to justify large militaries and the importance of the military in national life. Paramount among these disputes is the Arab-Israeli conflict.

- Key international actors must view the modernization and democratization of the Muslim world as being in their own long-term interest. Therefore, they should refrain from supporting unrepresentative governments and should lend their support to democratic forces.

- The international economic system should be reformed in order to make it more congenial to all developing states, including those with a majority-Muslim population. In this context, discriminatory trade practices should be eliminated and access to capital and technology should be made easier.

Selected Bibliography

Abdalla, Ahmed, ed. *The Army and Democracy in Egypt* (in Arabic). Cairo: Sinai Publishers, 1990.

Abduh, Muhammad. *The Theology of Unity*. Trans. Ishaq Musa'ad and Kenneth Cragg. London: George Allen & Unwin, 1966.

Abou El Fadl, Khaled. "Islam and the Challenge of Democracy." *Boston Review* (April–May 2003).

Abrahamian, Ervand. *The Iranian Mujahedin*. New Haven, CT: Yale University Press, 1984.

Abu Bakar, Ibrahim bin. *Islamic Modernism in Malaya: The Life and Thought of Sayid Sheikh Al-Hadi, 1867–1934*. Kuala Lumpur: University of Malaya Press, 1994.

Abu Nasr, Julinda, A. Khoury, and H. Azzam, eds. *Women, Employment, and Development in the Arab World*. The Hague: Mouton/ILO, 1985.

Afshar, Haleh. "Women, State and Ideology in Iran." *Third World Quarterly* 7, no. 2 (April 1985).

Ağaoğulları, Mehmet Ali. *L'Islam dans la vie politique de la Turquie*. Ankara: Ankara Üniversitesi Basımevi, 1982.

Ahmad, Ahrar. "Islam and Democracy: Text, Tradition, and History." *American Journal of Islamic Social Sciences* 20, no. 1 (Winter 2003).

Ahmad, Mumtaz. *State Politics and Islam*. Indianapolis, IN: American Trust Publications, 1986.

Ahmed, Akbar S., and Hastings Donnan. *Islam, Globalization and Postmodernity*. London: Routledge, 1994.

Akbarzadeh, Shahram, and Abdullah Saeed, eds. *Islam and Political Legitimacy*. London: RoutledgeCurzon, 2003.

Akhavi, Shahrough. *Religion and Politics in Contemporary Iran: Clergy-State Relations in the Pahlavi Period*. Albany: State University of New York Press, 1980.

Al-Banna, Gamal. *Demokratiya Jadida* [New Democracy]. 2nd ed. Cairo: Dar al-Fikr al-Islami, 2000.

Alesina, Alberto, and David Dollar. "Who Gives Foreign Aid to Whom and Why?" *Journal of Economic Growth* 5 (March 2000).

Algar, Hamid. *Mirza Malkum Khan: A Study in the History of Iranian Modernism.* Berkeley: University of California Press, 1969.

―――. *Religion and State in Iran, 1785–1906: The Role of Ulema in the Qajar Period.* Berkeley: University of California Press, 1969.

Al-Hibri, Azizah. "Islam, Law, and Custom: Redefining Muslim Women's Rights." *American University Journal of International Law & Policy* (1997).

Al-Jabri, Mohammed ʿAbed. *Arab-Islamic Philosophy: A Contemporary Critique.* Trans. Aziz Abbassi. Austin: University of Texas Center for Middle Eastern Studies, 1999.

Al Khoei, Sayyed Abdol Majid. "Islam and Secularism." *islam21* 3 (December 1997).

Allworth, Edward, ed. *Central Asia: 120 Years of Russian Rule.* Durham, NC: Duke University Press, 1989.

Almond, Gabriel, and James Coleman, eds. *The Politics of Developing Areas.* Princeton, NJ: Princeton University Press, 1960.

Amin, Samir. *Imperialism and Unequal Development.* New York: Monthly Review Press, 1976.

―――. *Unequal Development: An Essay on the Social Formations of Peripheral Capitalism.* New York: Monthly Review Press, 1976.

Amirahmadi, Hooshang. "Emerging Civil Society in Iran." *SAIS Review* 16, no. 2 (1996).

―――. *The Revolution and Economic Transition: The Iranian Experience.* Albany: State University of New York Press, 1990.

Ansari, Zafar Ishaq, and John L. Esposito, eds. *Muslims and the West: Encounter and Dialogue.* Islamabad: Islamic Research, 2001.

Arjomand, Said, ed. *From Nationalism to Revolutionary Islam.* London: Macmillan, 1984.

Arkoun, Mohammed. *Rethinking Islam: Common Questions, Uncommon Answers.* Trans. Robert D. Lee. Boulder, CO: Westview Press, 1994.

Atabaki, Turaj, and Margreet Dorleijn, eds. *Kurdistan in Search of Ethnic Identity.* Utrecht: Houtsma Foundation, 1990.

Ayoob, Mohammed. "The Third World in the System of States: Acute Schizophrenia or Growing Pains?" *International Studies Quarterly* 33, no. 1 (March 1989).

―――. *The Third World Security Predicament: State Making, Regional Conflict, and the International System.* Boulder, CO: Lynne Rienner, 1995.

Ayubi, Nazih N. *Over-Stating the Arab State: Politics and Society in the Middle East.* London: I. B. Tauris, 1995.

Bacon, Elizabeth E. *Central Asians Under Russian Rule: A Study in Culture Change.* Ithaca, NY: Cornell University Press, 1966.

Bakar, Osman. "Islam and the State in Malaysia." *Journal of the Institute of Diplomacy* (forthcoming).

Bakhash, Shaul. *The Reign of the Ayatollahs: Iran and the Islamic Revolution.* Rev. ed. New York: Basic Books, 1990.

Banani, Amin. *The Modernization of Iran, 1921–1941.* Stanford, CA: Stanford University Press, 1961.

Baranski, Zygmunt G., and Robert Lumley, eds. *Culture and Conflict in Post War Italy: Essays on Mass and Popular Culture.* Basingstoke: Macmillan, 1990.

Barkey, Henry. "Why Military Regimes Fail: The Perils of Transition." *Armed Forces and Society* 16, no. 2 (Winter 1990).

Barlas, Asma. *Believing Women in Islam: Unreading Patriarchal Interpretations of the Qur'an.* Austin: University of Texas Press, 2002.

Barro, Robert J., and Rachel McCleary. "Religion and Economic Growth." NBER Working Paper 9682. National Bureau of Economic Research, Cambridge, MA, 2003.

Bauer, Peter T. *Dissent on Development: Studies and Debates in Development Economics.* Cambridge, MA: Harvard University Press, 1972.

Beblawi, Hazem, and Giacomo Luciani, eds. *The Rentier State.* London: Croom Helm, 1987.

Beck, Lois, and Nikki Keddie, eds. *Women in the Muslim World.* Cambridge, MA: Harvard University Press, 1978.

Bell, Daniel. *The Cultural Contradictions of Capitalism.* New York: Basic Books, 1976.

Bellin, Eva. *Stalled Democracy: Capital, Labor, and the Paradox of State-Sponsored Development.* Ithaca, NY: Cornell University Press, 2002.

Berdal, Mats, and David M. Malone, eds. *Greed and Grievance: Economic Agendas and Civil Wars.* Boulder, CO: Lynne Rienner, 2000.

Berger, Peter L., ed. *The Desecularisation of the World: Resurgent Religion and World Politics.* Grand Rapids, MI: William B. Eerdmans, 1999.

Berghahn, Volker. *Militarism: The History of an International Debate, 1861–1979.* Cambridge: Cambridge University Press, 1981.

Berkes, Niyazi. *The Development of Secularism in Turkey.* Montreal: McGill University Press, 1964.

Berman, Harold. *Law and Revolution: The Formation of the Western Legal Tradition.* Cambridge, MA: Harvard University Press, 1983.

Berman, Paul. *Terror and Liberalism.* New York: W. W. Norton, 2002.

Bernstein, Henry, ed. *Underdevelopment and Development: The Third World Today.* Harmondsworth, UK: Penguin Books, 1973.

Bhagwati, Jagdish. *The Economics of Underdeveloped Countries.* London: Weidenfeld and Nicolson, 1966.

———. *The New International Economic Order: The North-South Debate.* Cambridge, MA: MIT Press, 1977.

———. "The New Thinking on Development." *Journal of Democracy* 6, no. 4 (October 1995).

Bill, James, and Robert Springborg. *Politics in the Middle East.* London: Little, Brown, 1990.

Billington, R., et al. *Culture & Society.* Basingstoke: Macmillan/Palgrave, 1991.

Binder, Leonard, et al. *Crises and Sequences in Political Development.* Princeton, NJ: Princeton University Press, 1971.

Bingen, R. James, David Robinson, and John M. Staatz, eds. *Democracy and Development in Mali.* East Lansing: Michigan State University Press, 2000.

Birand, Mehmet A. *Thirty Hot Days.* Nicosia, Cyprus: K. Rustem & Bros., 1985.

Black, E. C. *The Dynamics of Modernization.* New York: Harper & Row, 1966.

Böttcher, Annabelle. *Syrische Religionspolitk unter Asad.* Freiburg: Arnold-Bergstrasser-Institut, 1998.

Bozeman, Adda B. "Iran: US Foreign Policy and the Tradition of Persian Statecraft." *Orbis* 23 (Summer 1979).

Brackman, Arnold. *The Communist Collapse in Indonesia.* New York: W. W. Norton, 1969.

Braga, Carlos A. Primo. "The Doha Agenda: Opportunities and Challenges for Developing Countries." Mimeo. World Bank, Washington, DC, 2003.

Bromley, Simon. *Rethinking Middle East Politics.* Cambridge: Polity Press, 1994.

Brown, Edward G. *The Persian Revolution of 1905–1909.* Cambridge: Cambridge University Press, 1910.

Brown, Michael E., ed. *The International Dimensions of Internal Conflict.* Cambridge, MA: MIT Press, 1996.

Brynen, Rex. "Economic Crisis and Post-Rentier Democratization in the Arab World: The Case of Jordan." *Canadian Journal of Political Science* 25, no. 1 (March 1992).

Çakır, Ruşen. *Ne Seriat Ne Demokrasi: Refah Partisini Anlamak.* Istanbul: Metis Yayınları, 1994.

Çarkoğlu, Ali, and Binnaz Toprak. *Türkiye'de Din, Toplum ve Siyaset.* Istanbul: TESEV Yayınları, 2000.

Caroe, Olaf. *Soviet Empire: The Turks of Central Asia and Stalinism.* London: Macmillan, 1967.

Case, William. *Politics in Southeast Asia: Democracy or Less.* London: RoutledgeCurzon, 2002.

Caville, Thiery. *L'economie de l'Iran Islamique l'entre ordre et desordres.* Paris: Hartman, 2002.

Chartouni-Dubarry, May, ed. *Armée et nation en Égypte: Pouvoir civil, pouvoir militaire.* Paris: Institut Français des Relations Internationales, 2001.

Chaudhry, Kiren A. *The Price of Wealth.* Ithaca, NY: Cornell University Press, 1997.

Chilcote, Ronald H. *Theories of Comparative Politics: The Search for a Paradigm Reconsidered.* Boulder, CO: Westview Press, 1964.

Choudhury, Masudul Alam. *Islamic Economic Co-Operation.* London: Macmillan, 1989.

Choueiri, Youssef M. *Islamic Fundamentalism.* London: Pinter, 1990.

Chouet, Alain. "L'espace tribal Alaouite à l'épreuve du pouvoir: La désintégration par le politique." *Maghreb-Machrek* 147 (Winter 1995).

Cinar, Mine, ed. *The Economics of Women and Work in the Middle East and North Africa.* Amsterdam: Elsevier/JAI Press, 2001.

Clapham, Christopher. *Third World Politics.* Madison: University of Wisconsin Press, 1985.

Cohen, Stephen P. *The Pakistan Army.* 1984. Reprint, London: Oxford University Press, 1998.

Cohen, Youssef, Brian R. Brown, and Abramo Fimo Kenneth Organski. "The Paradoxical Nature of State Making: The Violent Creation of Order." *American Political Science Review* 75, no. 4 (1981).

Collier, Paul, and David Dollar. "Can the World Cut Poverty in Half? How Policy Reform and Effective Aid Can Meet International Development Goals." *World Development* 29, no. 11 (2001).

Comaroff, John, and Jean Comaroff, eds. *Civil Society and the Political Imagination in Africa.* Chicago: University of Chicago Press, 1999.

Cook, Michael, ed. *Studies in the Economic History of the Middle East.* Oxford: Oxford University Press, 1970.

Cordonnier, Isabelle. *The Military and Political Order in Pakistan.* Geneva: Programme for Strategic and International Security Studies, 1999.

Courriére, Yves. *Les feux du désespoir: 1960–1962—des barricades à l'abime.* Paris: Marabout, 1971.

Cowan, C. D., and O. W. Wolters, eds. *Southeast Asian History and Historiography: Essays Presented to D. G. E. Hall.* Ithaca, NY: Cornell University Press, 1976.

Cox, Brian C., and Anthony E. Dyson, eds. *The Twentieth Century Mind: History, Ideas, and Literature in Britain.* Oxford: Oxford University Press, 1972.

Curzon, George N. *Persia and the Persian Question.* Vol. 2. London: Longman, 1892.

Daddish, Cyril. "Elections and Ethnic Violence in Cote d'Ivoire: The Unfinished Business of Succession and Democratic Transition." *African Issues* 29, nos. 1 and 2 (2001).

Dauda, Abubakar. "Ethnic Identity, Democratization and the Future of the African State: Lessons from Nigeria." *African Issues* 29, nos. 1 and 2 (2001).

Dawisha, Adeed. *Syria and the Lebanese Crisis.* New York: St. Martin's Press, 1980.

DeFronzo, James. *Revolutions and Revolutionary Movements.* 2nd ed. Boulder, CO: Westview Press, 1996.

Descartes, Rene. *The Philosophical Writings of Descartes.* i and ii. Trans. J. Cottingham, R. Stoothoff, and D. Murdoch. Cambridge: Cambridge University Press, 1985.

Desrues, Thierry, and Eduardo Moyano. "Social Change and Political Transition in Morocco." *Mediterranean Politics* 6, no. 1 (Spring 2001).

Deutsch, Karl W. *Nationalism and Social Communication.* New York: John Wiley & Sons, 1953.

Diamond, Larry. *Developing Democracy: Towards Consolidation.* Baltimore: Johns Hopkins University Press, 1999.

———, ed. *Political Culture and Democracy in Developing Countries.* Boulder, CO: Lynne Reinner, 1993.

Diamond, Larry, Juan J. Linz, and Martin Seymour Lipset, eds. *Democracy in Developing Countries: Asia.* Vol. 3. Boulder, CO: Lynne Rienner/Adamantine Press, 1989.

Diamond, Larry, Marc F. Plattner, and Daniel Brumberg, eds. *Islam and Democracy in the Middle East.* Baltimore: Johns Hopkins University Press, 2003.

Dudley, Leonard, and Ulrich Blum. "Religion and Economic Growth: Was Weber Right?" *Journal of Evolutionary Economics* 11, no. 2 (2001).

Duner, Bertil, ed. *Turkey. The Road Ahead.* Stockholm: Swedish Institute of International Affairs, 2002.

Durkheim, Emile. *The Elementary Forms of Religious Life.* London: George Allen and Unwin, 1976.

Easterly, William, and Ross Levine. "Tropics, Germs, and Crops: How Endowments Influence Economic Development." NBER Working Paper 9106. National Bureau of Economic Research, Cambridge, MA, 2002.

Economic and Social Commission for Western Asia. *Impact of Economic Reform Policies on Poverty in Selected ESCWA Member Countries: Egypt, Jordan and Yemen.* Beirut: Economic and Social Commission for Western Asia, 1998.

Eisenstadt, Michael. "The Armed Forces of the Islamic Republic of Iran: An Assessment." *Middle East Review of International Affairs* 5, no. 1 (March 2001).

Eisenstadt, Shmuel N., ed. *Patterns of Modernity.* Vol. 2, *Beyond the West.* New York: New York University Press, 1987.

———. "The Reconstruction of Religious Arenas in the Framework of 'Multiple Modernities.' " *Millennium: Journal of International Studies* 29, no. 3 (2000).

El Ghoul, Bernard. "De la cité-marchande à la cité-globale—Pouvoir et société à Doubai." Ph.D. diss., Institut d'Etudes Politiques de Paris, 2003.

El Said, Rifaat. *Alliberaliya al Misriyya* [Egyptian Liberalism]. Cairo: Al-Ahli, 2003.

Embong, Abdul Rahman. *State-Led Modernization and the New Middle Class in Malaysia*. New York: Palgrave Macmillan, 2002.

Emmanuel, Arghiri. *Unequal Exchange*. London: New Left Books, 1972.

Enayat, Hamid. *Modern Islamic Political Thought*. Austin: University of Texas Press, 1982.

Esposito, John L. *Islam and Politics*. 4th ed. Syracuse, NY: Syracuse University Press, 1998.

Esposito, John L., and John O. Voll. *Islam and Democracy*. New York: Oxford University Press, 1996.

———. *Makers of Contemporary Islam*. New York: Oxford University Press, 2002.

Fahmy, Khaled. *All the Pasha's Men*. Cairo: American University in Cairo Press, 2002.

Farcau, Bruce W. *The Coup: Tactics in the Seizure of Power*. Westport, CT: Praeger, 1994.

———. *The Transition to Democracy in Latin America: The Role of the Military*. Westport, CT: Praeger, 1996.

Farouk-Sluglett, Marion, and Peter Sluglett. *Iraq Since 1958: From Revolution to Dictatorship*. London: I. B. Tauris, 2001.

Fasano, Ugo, and Quing Wang. "Fiscal Expenditure Policy and Non-Oil Economic Growth: Evidence from GCC Countries." IMF Working Paper WP/01/195. International Monetary Fund, Washington, DC, December 2001.

Fehér, Ferenc, Agnes Heller, and Gyorgy Markus. *Dictatorship Over Needs: An Analysis of Soviet Societies*. Oxford: Basil Blackwell, 1983.

Finkle, Jason L., and Richard W. Gable, eds. *Political Development and Social Change*. New York: John Wiley & Sons, 1966.

Fisher, Sydney N., ed. *The Military in the Middle East*. Columbus: Ohio State University Press, 1963.

Frank, Andre Gunder. "The Development of Underdevelopment." *Monthly Review* 18 (September 1966).

Fromkin, David. *A Peace to End All Peace: The Fall of the Ottoman Empire and the Creation of the Modern Middle East*. New York: Henry Holt, 1989.

Fujita, Masahisa, Paul R. Krugman, and Anthony J. Venables. *The Spatial Economy: Cities, Regions, and International Trade*. Cambridge, MA: MIT Press, 1999.

Fukuyama, Francis. "Confucianism and Democracy." *Journal of Democracy* 6, no. 2 (April 1995).

Funston, John. *Malay Politics in Malaysia: A Study of the United Malays National Organization and Party Islam*. Kuala Lumpur: Heinemann Educational Books (Asia), 1980.

Gallie, W. B. *Philosophy and the Historical Understanding*. London: Chatto & Windus, 1964.

Galwash, Ahmad A. *The Religion of Islam: A Standard Book*. 5th ed. Cairo: Imprimerie Misr, 1958.

Gause, Gregory F., III. *Oil Monarchies: Domestic and Security Challenges in the Arab Gulf States*. New York: Council on Foreign Relations, 1994.

Gellner, Ernest. "Civil Society in Historical Context." *International Social Science Journal* 43, no. 3 (1991).

Gerschenkron, Alexander. *Economic Backwardness in Historical Perspective*. Cambridge, MA: Belknap Press of Harvard University Press, 1962. Reprint, New York: Praeger, 1965.

Gershevitch, Ilya, ed. *The Cambridge History of Iran*. Vol. 2, *The Median & Achaemenian Periods*. Cambridge: Cambridge University Press, 1985.

Ghatak, Subrata. *Introduction to Development Economics*. 3rd ed. London: Routledge, 1995.

Ghoussoub, Mai. "Feminism—or the Eternal Masculine—in the Arab World." *New Left Review* 161 (January–February 1987).

Gibb, H.A.R., and Harold Bowen. *Islamic Society and the West*. Vol. 1, part 2. London: Oxford University Press, 1959.

Giddens, Anthony. *The Nation-State and Violence*. Cambridge: Polity Press, 1985.

Gleason, Abbott. *European and Muscovite*. Cambridge, MA: Harvard University Press, 1972.

Griffin, Keith, and John Gurley. "Radical Analyses of Imperialism, the Third World, and the Transition to Socialism: A Survey Article." *Journal of Economic Literature* 23, no. 3 (1985).

Guibernau, Montserrat, and John Hutchinson, eds. *Understanding Nationalism*. Cambridge: Polity Press, 2001.

Guiso, Luigi, Paola Sapienza, and Luigi Zingales. "People's Opium? Religion and Economic Activities." NBER Working Paper 9237. National Bureau of Economic Research, Cambridge, MA, 2002.

Gülalp, Haldun. "Globalization and Political Islam: The Social Bases of Turkey's Welfare Party." *International Journal of Middle East Studies* 33 (2001).

Gülen, Fethullah. "A Comparative Approach to Islam and Democracy." *SAIS Review* 21, no. 2 (2001).

Gullick, J. M. *Rulers and Residents: Influence and Power in the Malay States, 1870–1920*. South-East Asian Historical Monographs. Singapore: Oxford University Press, 1992.

Guveli, Asli, and Serdar Kilickaplan. "A Ranking of Islamic Countries in Terms of Their Levels of Socio-Economic Development." *Journal of Economic Cooperation* 21, no. 1 (2000).

Haggard, Stephan, and Robert R. Kaufman. *The Political Economy of Democratic Transitions*. Princeton, NJ: Princeton University Press, 1995.

Haghayeghi, Mehrdad. "Changing Dynamics of Islamic Politics." *The Muslim World* 92, nos. 3–4 (Fall 2002).

———. *Islam and Politics in Central Asia*. New York: St. Martin's Press, 1996.

Hall, John A., ed. *Civil Society: Theory, History, Comparison*. London: Polity Press, 1995.

Hall, Stuart, et al., eds. *Modernity: An Introduction to Modern Societies*. Cambridge, MA: Blackwell, 1996.

Halpern, Manfred. *The Politics of Social Change in the Middle East and North Africa*. Princeton, NJ: Princeton University Press, 1963.

Hameso, Seyoum. "Issues and Dilemmas of Multiparty Democracy in Africa." *West Africa Review* 3, no. 2 (2002).

Hamzeh, A. Nizar. "Lebanon's Hizbullah: From Islamic Revolution to Parliamentary Accommodation." *Third World Quarterly* 14, no. 2 (1993).

Harik, Iliya F., and Denis Sullivan, eds. *Privatization and Liberalization in the Middle East*. Bloomington: Indiana University Press, 1992.

Harper, Timothy N. *The End of Empire and the Making of Malaya*. Cambridge: Cambridge University Press, 1999.

Hashim, Muhammad Yusoff. *The Malay Sultanate of Malacca: A Study of Various Aspects of Malacca in the Fifteenth and Sixteenth Centuries in Malaysian History.* Kuala Lumpur: Dewan Bahasa dan Pustaka, 1992.

Held, David. *Models of Democracy.* Cambridge: Polity Press, 1987.

Henry, Clement, and Robert Springborg. *Globalisation and the Politics of Development in the Middle East.* Cambridge: Cambridge University Press, 2001.

Heper, Metin, and Raphael Israeli, eds. *Islam and Politics in the Modern Middle East.* London: Croom Helm, 1984.

Heper, Metin, A. Öncü, and H. Kramer, eds. *Turkey and the West: Changing Political and Cultural Identities.* London: I. B. Tauris, 1993.

Herb, Michael. *All in the Family: Absolutism, Revolution and Democracy in the Middle Eastern Monarchies.* Albany: State University of New York Press, 1999.

Hill, Hal. *Indonesian Economy Since 1996: Southeast Asia's Emerging Giant.* Cambridge: Cambridge University Press, 1996.

Hilley, John. *Malaysia: Mahathir, Hegemony, and the New Opposition.* London: Zed Books, 2001.

Hirschman, Albert. *Exit, Voice, and Loyalty: Responses to Decline in Firms, Organizations, and States.* Cambridge, MA: Harvard University Press, 1970.

Hirst, Paul Q. *Associative Democracy: New Forms of Economic and Social Governance.* Amherst: University of Massachusetts Press, 1994.

Hofheinz, Roy, Jr., and Kent E. Calder. *The East Asia Edge.* New York: Basic Books, 1982.

Hofstede, Geert. *Culture's Consequences: Comparing Values, Behaviours, Institutions, and Organisations Across Nations.* 2nd ed. Thousand Oaks, CA: Sage, 2001.

Honderich, Ted, ed. *The Oxford Companion to Philosophy.* Oxford: Oxford University Press, 1995.

Hourani, Albert. *Arabic Thought in the Liberal Age.* Rev. ed. Cambridge: Cambridge University Press, 1983.

Hudson, Michael. *Arab Politics: The Search for Legitimacy.* New Haven, CT: Yale University Press, 1977.

Hunter, Shireen T. *Iran After Khomeini.* Washington, DC: Center for Strategic and International Studies, 1992.

Hunter, William W. *The Indian Musalmans.* London: Trübner, 1871.

Huntington, Samuel P. *The Clash of Civilizations and the Remaking of World Order.* New York: Simon and Schuster, 1996.

———. *Political Order in Changing Societies.* New Haven, CT: Yale University Press, 1968.

———. *The Soldier and the State: The Theory and Politics of Civil-Military Relations.* Cambridge, MA: Belknap Press, 1957.

———. *The Third Wave: Democratization in the Late Twentieth Century.* Norman: University of Oklahoma Press, 1993.

Hussein, Freda, ed. *Muslim Women.* London: Croom Helm, 1984.

Ibn Khaldun. *The Muqaddimah.* Trans. Franz Rosenthal. Princeton, NJ: Princeton University Press, 1974.

Ibrahim, Ahmad, Sharon Siddique, and Yasmin Hussain, eds. *Readings on Islam in Southeast Asia.* Singapore: Institute of Southeast Asian Studies, 1985.

Ibrahim, Ibrahim, ed. *Arab Resources: The Transformation of a Society.* London: Croom Helm, 1983.

Ibrahim, Saad Eddin. *Egypt, Islam, and Democracy*. Cairo: American University in Cairo Press, 2002.

Ibrahim, Safie bin. *The Islamic Party of Malaysia: Its Formative Stages and Ideology*. Kuala Lumpur: Nawi Ismail, 1981.

Inglehart, Ronald, ed. *Human Values and Social Change: Findings from the Values Surveys*. Leiden: Brill Academic, 2003.

Inglehart, Ronald, and Pippa Norris. "The True Clash of Civilizations." *Foreign Policy* (March–April 2003).

Inglehart, Ronald, Pippa Norris, and Christian Welzel. "Gender Equality and Democracy." *Comparative Sociology* 1, nos. 3–4 (2003).

International Crisis Group. "Pakistan: Transition to Democracy?" ICG Asia Report 40. Islamabad: International Crisis Group, October 3, 2002.

International Studies and Programming, Macalester College. "Malaysia: Crossroads of Diversity in Southeast Asia." *Macalester International* 12 (Autumn 2002).

Issawi, Charles. "Economic and Social Foundations of Democracy in the Middle East." *International Affairs* 32, no. 1 (1956).

———, ed. *The Economic History of Iran: 1800–1914*. Chicago: University of Chicago Press, 1971.

"Jadidism: A Current Soviet Assessment." *Central Asian Review* 12, no. 1 (1964).

Jaffar, Kamarudin. *Dr Burhanuddin Al Helmy: Pemikiran dan Perjuangan*. Kuala Lumpur: IKDAS SDN BHD, 2000.

Jaffrelot, Christophe. *Pakistan: Nationalism Without a Nation?* London: Zed Books, 2002.

Janowitz, Morris. *The Professional Soldier: A Social and Political Portrait*. New York: Free Press, 1971.

Jansen, Marius. *The Making of Modern Japan*. Cambridge, MA: Harvard University Press, 2000.

Jesudason, James. "Statist Democracy and the Limits to Civil Society in Malaysia." *Journal of Commonwealth and Comparative Politics* 33, no. 3 (1995).

Johan, Khasnor. *The Emergence of the Modern Malay Administrative Elite*. Singapore: Oxford University Press, 1984.

Johns, Anthony. "From Coastal Settlement to Islamic School and City: Islamization in Sumatra, the Malay Peninsula and Java." *Hamdard Islamicus* 4, no. 4 (1981).

Johnson, Chalmers. *MITI and the Japanese Miracle: The Growth of Industrial Policy*. Stanford, CA: Stanford University Press, 1982.

Jones, Eric L. *The European Miracle*. 2nd ed. Cambridge: Cambridge University Press, 1987.

Jones, Owen Bennet. *Pakistan: Eye of the Storm*. New Haven, CT: Yale University Press, 2002.

Joseph, Richard, ed. *State, Conflicts, and Democracy in Africa*. Boulder, CO: Lynne Reinner, 1999.

Kaldor, Mary. *New and Old Wars: Organized Violence in a Global Era*. Stanford, CA: Stanford University Press, 1999.

Kamarck, Elaine Ciulla, and Joseph S. Nye, Jr., eds. *Governance.com: Democracy in the Information Age*. Washington, DC: Brookings Institution, 2002.

Kamrava, Mehran. "The Civil Society Discourse in Iran." *British Journal of Middle Eastern Studies* 28, no. 2 (2001).

Kanbur, Ravi, Kevin M. Morrison, and Todd Sandler. "The Future of Development Assistance: Common Pools and International Public Goods." Policy Essay 25. Overseas Development Council, Baltimore, 1999.

Kanet, Roger E., and Edward A. Kolodziej, eds. *The Cold War as Cooperation*. Baltimore: Johns Hopkins University Press, 1991.

Karabelias, Garassimos. "The Evolution of Civil-Military Relations in Post-War Turkey, 1980–95." *Middle Eastern Studies* 35, no. 4 (1999).

Karl, Terry L. *The Paradox of Plenty: Oil Booms and Petro-States*. Berkeley: University of California Press, 1997.

Katouzian, Homa. *The Political Economy of Modern Iran: Despotism and Pseudo-modernism, 1926–1979*. New York: New York University Press, 1981.

Katzman, Kenneth. *Warriors of Islam: Iran's Revolutionary Guards*. Boulder, CO: Westview Press, 1993.

Kaufmann, Daniel, Aart Kraay, and Pablo Zoido-Lobatón. *Governance Matters, II: Updated Indicators for 2001–02*. Washington, DC: World Bank, 2002.

Keddie, Nikki R. *An Islamic Response to Imperialism: Political and Religious Writings of Sayyid Jamal ad-Din "al-Afghani."* Berkeley: University of California Press, 1983.

———. *Qajar Iran and the Rise of Reza Khan*. Costa Mesa, CA: Mazda Publishers, 1999.

———. *The Roots of the Revolution: An Interpretive History of Modern Iran*. New Haven, CT: Yale University Press, 1981.

Kedourie, Elie. *Democracy and Arab Political Culture*. Washington, DC: Washington Institute for Near East Studies, 1992.

Keen, David. *The Economic Functions of Violence in Civil Wars*. Adelphi Paper 320. Oxford: Oxford University Press for IISS, 1998.

Kepel, Gilles. *Jihad: The Trail of Political Islam*. Cambridge, MA: Harvard University Press, 2002.

———. *The Prophet and Pharaoh: Muslim Extremism in Egypt*. London: Al Saqi Books, 1985.

Keyder, Çağlar. *State and Class in Turkey*. London: Verso New Left Books, 1987.

Khadduri, Majid. *War and Peace in the Law of Islam*. Baltimore: Johns Hopkins University, 1955. Reprint, New York: AMS Press, 1979.

Khalid, Adeeb. *The Politics of Muslim Cultural Reform: Jadidism in Central Asia*. Berkeley: University of California Press, 1998.

Khatami, Mohammad. *Islam, Liberty, and Development*. Binghamton, NY: Institute of Global Cultural Studies, Binghamton University, 1998.

Khosrokhavar, Farhad, and Olivier Roy. *Iran: Comment sortir d'une revolution religieuse*. Paris: Editions du Seuil, 1999.

Kienle, Eberhard. *A Grand Delusion: Democracy and Economic Reform in Egypt*. London: I. B. Tauris, 2000.

———. "More than a Response to Islamism: The Political Deliberalization of Egypt in the 1990s." *Middle East Journal* 52 (Spring 1998).

Kim, Khoo Kay, and Mohd Fadzil Othman, eds. *Tamadun Islam di Malaysia*. Kuala Lumpur: Persatuan Sejarah Malaysia, 1980.

Kim, Youn-Suk. "Korea and the Developing Countries: Lessons from Korea's Industrialization." *Journal of East Asian Affairs* 11, no. 2 (1997).

King, Charles. "The Benefits of Ethnic War: Understanding Eurasia's Unrecognized States." *World Politics* 53, no. 4 (July 2001).

Kongar, Emre, ed. *Türk Toplumbilimcileri.* Vol. 2. Istanbul: Remzi Kitabevi, 1988.

Korany, Bahgat, Rex Brynen, and Paul Noble, eds. *The Many Faces of National Security in the Arab World.* Montreal: Macmillan, 1993.

———. *Political Liberalization and Democratization in the Arab World.* Vol. 1, *Theoretical Perspective.* Boulder, CO: Lynne Rienner, 1995.

———. *Political Liberalization and Democratization in the Arab World.* Vol. 2, *Comparative Experiences.* Boulder, CO: Lynne Rienner, 1998.

Krieger, Silke, and Rolf Trauzettel, eds. *Confucianism and the Modernization of China.* Mainz: Hase & Koehler Verlag, 1991.

Kurzman, Charles, ed. *Liberal Islam: A Sourcebook.* New York: Oxford University Press, 1998.

Landau, Jacob M. "The National Salvation Party in Turkey." *Asian and African Studies* 11 (1976).

———. *Radical Politics in Modern Turkey.* Leiden: Brill Academic, 1974.

Landes, David. *The Wealth and Poverty of Nations: Why Some Are So Rich and Some So Poor.* New York: W. W. Norton, 1998.

Lane, Jan-Erik. *Constitutions and Political Theory.* Manchester, UK: Manchester University Press, 1996.

Langhammer, Rolf J. "The WTO and the Millennium Round: Between Standstill and Leapfrog." Kiel Discussion Papers 253. Institute for World Economics, Kiel, Germany, 1999.

Laqueur, Walter Z., ed. *The Middle East in Transition.* New York: Frederick A. Praeger, 1958.

Laroui, Abdulla. *Azmat al-Muthakafin al-Arab* [Crisis of Arab Intellectuals]. Beirut: Dar al Talia'a, 1970.

Lawson, Fred. *Why Syria Goes to War.* Ithaca: Cornell University Press, 1996.

Leong, Ho Khai, and James Chin, eds. *Mahathir's Administration: Performance and Crisis in Governance.* Singapore: Time Books International, 2001.

Lerner, Daniel. *The Passing of Traditional Society: Modernizing the Middle East.* Glencoe, IL: Free Press, 1958.

Leveau, Rémy. *Le sabre et le turban.* Paris: François Bourin, 1993.

Lewis, Bernard. *The Emergence of Modern Turkey.* London: Oxford University Press, 1965.

———. *Islam and the West.* New York: Oxford University Press, 1993.

———. "The Roots of Muslim Rage." *Atlantic Monthly,* September 1990.

———. *What Went Wrong? Western Impact and Middle Eastern Response.* New York: Oxford University Press, 2002.

Linz, Juan J., and Alfred Stepan, eds. *The Breakdown of Democratic Regimes.* Baltimore: Johns Hopkins University Press, 1978.

———. *Problems of Democratic Transition and Consolidation: Southern Europe, South America, and Post-Communist Europe.* Baltimore: Johns Hopkins University Press, 1996.

Lipset, Seymour Martin. "Some Social Requisites of Democracy: Economic Development and Political Legitimacy." *American Political Science Review* 53, no. 1 (March 1959).

Litwak, Robert S., and Samuel F. Wells, Jr., eds. *Superpower Competition and Security in the Third World.* Cambridge, MA: Ballinger, 1988.

Lobmeyer, Hans Günter. *Opposition und Widerstand in Syrien.* Hamburg: Deutsches Orient-Institut, 1995.

Looney, Robert E. *Economic Origins of the Iranian Revolution.* New York: Pergamon Press, 1982.

Lowi, Miriam. "Algérie 1992–2002: Une nouvelle economie politique de la violence." *Maghreb-Machrek* 175 (Spring 2003).

Luciani, Giacomo. "Economic Foundations of Democracy and Authoritarianism: The Arab World in Comparative Perspective." *Arab Studies Quarterly* 10, no. 6 (1988).

Lummis, C. Douglas. *Radical Democracy.* Ithaca, NY: Cornell University Press, 1996.

Maaruf, Shaharuddin. *Malay Ideas on Development: From Feudal Lord to Capitalist.* Singapore: Times Book International, 1988.

MacIntyre, Alasdair. *Marxism and Christianity.* London: Pelican Books, 1971.

MacLean, Sandra, Fahimal Quadir, and Timothy Shaw, eds. *Crises of Governance in Asia and Africa.* Burlington, VT: Ashgate Publishing, 2001.

Madelung, Wilferd. *The Succession to Muhammad.* Cambridge: Cambridge University Press, 1997.

Makaruddin, Hashim, ed. *Islam and the Muslim Ummah: Selected Speeches of Dr Mahathir Mohamad.* Subang Jaya: Pelanduk Publications, 2001.

Mansel, Philip. *Constantinople: City of the World's Desire, 1453–1924.* London: Penguin Books, 1995.

Mariategui, Jose Carlos. *Siete ensayos de interpretacion de la realidad Peruana.* 1928. Reprint, Mexico, DF: Serie Popular Era, 1988.

Martinez, Luis. *The Algerian Civil War, 1990–1998.* New York: Columbia University Press, 2000.

Martinez, Patricia. "The Islamic State or the State of Islam in Malaysia." *Contemporary Southeast Asia* 23, no. 3 (December 2001).

Marty, Martin, and Scott Appleby, eds. *Fundamentalisms Observed.* Chicago: University of Chicago Press, 1991.

Marx, Anthony W. *Faith in Nation: Exclusionary Origins of Nationalism.* New York: Oxford University Press, 2003.

Maududi, S. Abul A'la. *Khutabat* [Fundamentals of Islam]. 2nd ed. Chicago: Kazi Publications, 1977.

Mauzy, Diane K., and R. S. Milne. "The Mahathir Administration in Malaysia: Discipline through Islam." *Pacific Affairs* 56, no. 4 (Winter 1983).

Mazrui, Ali A. *Cultural Forces in World Politics.* London: James Currey, 1990.

McClelland, David C. *The Achieving Society.* New York: John Wiley & Sons, 1976.

McDaniel, Tim. *Autocracy, Modernization, and Revolution in Russia and Iran.* Princeton, NJ: Princeton University Press, 1991.

McVey, Ruth T., ed. *Southeast Asian Transition: Approaches through Social History.* New Haven, CT: Yale University Press, 1978.

Means, Gordon P. *Malaysian Politics: The Second Generation.* Singapore: Oxford University Press, 1991.

Melia, Thomas O. "What Muslims Want: In Afghanistan, and Elsewhere—Democracy." *Georgetown Journal of International Affairs* 4, no. 1 (Winter–Spring 2003).

Mengisteab, Kidane, and Cyril Daddieh, eds. *State Building and Democratization in Africa: Faith, Hope, and Realities.* Westport, CT: Praeger, 1999.

Mernissi, Fatima. *Beyond the Veil: Male-Female Dynamics in Modern Muslim Society.* Rev. ed. Bloomington: Indiana University Press, 1987.

Middle East Watch. *Syria Unmasked: The Suppression of Human Rights by the Asad Regime.* New Haven, CT: Yale University Press, 1991.

Milner, Anthony C. "Islam and Malay Kingship." *Journal of the Royal Asiatic Society of Great Britain and Ireland* 1 (1981).

Minces, Juliette. *The House of Obedience: Women's Oppression in Algeria.* London: Zed Books, 1982.

Moghadam, Valentine M., ed. *Democratic Reforms and the Position of Women in Transition Economies.* Oxford: Clarendon Press, 1993.

———. *Modernizing Women: Gender and Social Change in the Middle East.* 2nd ed. Boulder, CO: Lynne Rienner, 2003.

———. *Women, Work, and Economic Reform in the Middle East and North Africa.* Boulder, CO: Lynne Rienner, 1997.

Moghissi, Haideh. *Feminism and Islamic Fundamentalism: The Limits of Postmodern Analysis.* London: Zed Books, 1999.

Mohamed, Alias. *PAS Platform: Development and Change, 1951–1986.* Petaling Jaya: Gateway Publishing House, 1994.

Mohd Yasin, Norhashimah. *Islamization/Malaynization: A Study on the Role of Economic Development of Malaysia, 1963–1993.* Kuala Lumpur: A. S. Noordeen, 1996.

Moore, Barrington, Jr. *Social Origins of Dictatorship and Democracy: Lord and Peasant in the Making of the Modern World.* Boston: Beacon Press, 1966.

Moosa, Ebrahim. *Islam and Cultural Issues.* Victoria: University of Victoria, Centre for Studies in Religion and Society, 2002.

Morgan, Theodore, and Nyle Spoelstra, eds. *Economic Interdependence in Southeast Asia.* Madison: University of Wisconsin Press, 1969.

Mouffe, Chantal, ed. *Dimensions of Radical Democracy: Pluralism, Citizenship, Community.* London: Verso, 1992.

Moussaoui, Abderrahmane. "De la violence au Djihad." *Annales HSS* 6 (November–December 1994).

Nasr, Seyyed Vali Reza. *Islamic Leviathan: Islam and the Making of State Power.* New York: Oxford University Press, 2001.

Nation, R. Craig, and Mark Kauppi. *The Soviet Impact in Africa.* Lexington, MA: Lexington Books, 1984.

Nawang, Adnan Hj. *Za'ba and the Malays* (in Malay). Kuala Lumpur: Berita Publishing Sdn. Bhd., 1998.

Nevins, Allan. *The War for the Union: War Becomes Revolution 1862–1863.* Vol. 6. New York: Charles Scribner's Sons, 1960.

Noland, Marcus. "Religion, Culture, and Economic Performance." International Economics Working Paper WP03-8, Institute for International Economics, September 2003.

Norton, Augustus Richard, ed. *Civil Society in the Middle East.* New York: E. J. Brill, 1995.

Nouri, Abdullah. *Shokhran-e-Islah: Defaiatal-e-Abdullah Nouri.* 1378. Reprint, Tehran: Tarh-e-Naw, 1999.

Nove, Allec, and J. A. Newth. *The Soviet Middle East: A Communist Model of Development.* New York: Frederick A. Praeger, 1966.

Nunnenkamp, Peter. "Liberalization and Regulation of International Capital Flows: Where the Opposites Meet." Kiel Working Papers 1029. Institute for World Economics, Kiel, Germany, 2001.

———. "Shooting the Messenger of Good News: A Critical Look at the World Bank's Success Story of Effective Aid." Kiel Working Papers 1103. Institute for World Economics, Kiel, Germany, 2002.

————. "To What Extent Can Foreign Direct Investment Help Achieve International Development Goals?" Kiel Working Papers 1128. Institute for World Economics, Kiel, Germany, 2002.

————. "Wachstumsdivergenz zwischen Entwicklungsländern: Hat die Entwicklungsökonomie versagt?" *Zeitschrift für Wirtschaftspolitik* 52, no. 2 (2003).

Nunnenkamp, Peter, and Manoj Pant. "Why the Case for a Multilateral Agreement on Investment Is Weak." Kiel Discussion Papers 400. Institute for World Economics, Kiel, Germany, 2003.

Nyang, Sulayman. "The Islamic Factor in Libya's Africa Policy." *Africa and the World* 1 (January 1988).

Nyerere, Julius. *Ujamaa: Essays on Socialism*. London: Oxford University Press, 1968.

O'Donnel, Guillermo. *Modernization and Bureaucratic-Authoritarianism: Studies in South American Politics*. Berkeley: Institute of International Studies, University of California, 1973.

O'Donnel, Guillermo, and Philippe Schmitter. *Transitions from Authoritarian Rule: Tentative Conclusions About Uncertain Democracies*. Baltimore: Johns Hopkins University Press, 1986.

Omar, Ariffin. *Bangsa Melayu: Malay Concepts of Democracy and Community, 1945–50*. Kuala Lumpur: Oxford University Press, 1993.

Öniş, Ziya. "The Political Economy of Islamic Resurgence in Turkey: The Rise of the Welfare Party in Perspective." *Third World Quarterly* 18, no. 4 (1997).

Onur, Necdet. *Erbakan Dosyası*. Istanbul: M Yayınevi, n.d.

Onwumechili, Chuka. *African Democratization and Military Coups*. Westport, CT: Praeger, 1998.

Organski, A. E. *Stages of Political Development*. New York: Alfred A. Knopf, 1965.

Ortaylı, İlber. "The Millet System under the Ottoman Empire: Classical Structure up to the 16th Century." Research paper, Seminar on Racism and Anti-Semitism, Council of Europe, Strasbourg, December 23, 1994.

Ottaway, Marina. *Democracy Challenged: The Rise of Semi-Authoritarianism*. Washington, DC: Carnegie Endowment for International Peace, 2003.

Ouda, Mohammed. *al-Demokratiya al-Urabiya* (Urabi Democracy). Cairo: Al-Ahali, 1982.

Öztürkmen, Arzu. "Remembering through the Material Culture: Local Knowledge of Past Communities in a Turkish Black Sea Town." *Middle Eastern Studies* 39, no. 2 (2003).

Parla, Taha. "Mercantile Militarism in Turkey." *New Perspectives on Turkey* 19 (1998).

Parry, Vernon J., and M. E. Yapp. *War, Technology, and Society in the Middle East*. London: Oxford University Press, 1975.

Parsons, Talcott. *The Structure of Social Action*. New York: Free Press, 1968.

Patai, Raphael. *The Arab Mind*. New York: Charles Scribner's Sons, 1973.

Perlmutter, Amos, ed. *The Political Influence of the Military*. New Haven, CT: Yale University Press, 1980.

Picard, Elizabeth. "Authoritarianism and Liberalism in the Reconstruction of the Lebanese Armed Forces." Paper presented at the Fourth Mediterranean Social and Political Research Meeting, Montecatini Terme, March 19–23, 2003.

Pierce, Richard A. *Russian Central Asia, 1867–1917*. Berkeley: University of California Press, 1960.

Polanyi, Karl. *The Great Transformation: The Political and Economic Origins of Our Time*. Boston: Beacon Press, 1944.

Polk, William R. *The Development Revolution: North Africa, the Middle East, and South Asia*. Washington, DC: Middle East Institute, 1963.

Poot, Huib, Arie Kuyvenhoven, and Jaap Jansen. *Industrialization and Trade in Indonesia*. Yogyakarta: Gadjah Mada University Press, 1990.

Population Reference Bureau. *World Population Data Sheet*. Washington, DC: Population Reference Bureau, 2001.

Posusney, Marsha Pripstein. *Labor and the State in Egypt: Workers, Unions, and Economic Restructuring*. New York: Columbia University Press, 1997.

Prebisch, Raul. *Towards a New Trade Policy for Development*. New York: United Nations, 1964.

"President Bush Discusses Freedom in Iraq and Middle East." Remarks by the president at the twentieth anniversary of the National Endowment for Democracy. United States Chamber of Commerce, Washington, DC, November 6, 2003. http://www.whitehouse.gov/news/releases/2003/11/20031106-2.html.

Preston, Peter W. *Political/Cultural Identity: Citizens and Nations in a Global Era*. London: Sage, 1997.

Qutb, Sayyid. *Islam: The True Religion*. Trans. Ravi Ahmad Fidai. Karachi: International Islamic, 1981.

Radelet, Steven. "Indonesia: Long Road to Recovery." Development Discussion Paper 722. Harvard Institute for International Development, Cambridge, MA, 1999.

Rahim, Abdur. *Principles of Muhammadan Jurisprudence*. Madras, 1911.

Rahman, Fazlur. *Islam and Modernity: Transformation of an Intellectual Tradition*. Chicago: University of Chicago Press, 1982.

Ramadan, Tariq. *To Be a European Muslim*. Leicester, UK: Islamic Foundation, 1998.

Ramazani, Rouhallah K. *The Foreign Policy of Iran: A Developing Nation in World Affairs 1500–1941*. Charlottesville: University of Virginia Press, 1966.

Randall, Vicky, and Robin Theobald. *Political Change and Underdevelopment: A Critical Introduction to Third World Politics*. 2nd ed. Durham, NC: Duke University Press, 1998.

Rhodes, Robert I. *Imperialism and Underdevelopment: A Reader*. New York: Monthly Review Press, 1970.

Richards, Alan, and John Waterbury. *A Political Economy of the Middle East*. 2nd ed. Boulder, CO: Westview Press, 1996.

Riddell, Peter. "The Diverse Voices of Political Islam in Post-Suharto Indonesia." *Islam and Christian-Muslim Relations* 13, no. 1 (2002).

Rigby, Andrew. "Lebanon: Patterns of Confessional Politics." *Parliamentary Affairs* 53, no. 1 (2000).

Rodinson, Maxime. *Islam and Capitalism*. London: Allen Lane, 1974.

Rostow, Walt W. *Politics and Stages of Growth*. Cambridge: Cambridge University Press, 1971.

———. *The Stages of Economic Growth: A Non-Communist Manifesto*. Cambridge: Cambridge University Press, 1962.

Roy, Oliver. *The Failure of Political Islam*. Cambridge, MA: Harvard University Press, 1994.

———. *L'islam mondialisé*. Couleur des idees. Paris: Seuil, 2002.

Rueschemeyer, Dietrich, Evelyne Huber Stephens, and John D. Stephens. *Capitalist Development and Democracy*. Chicago: University of Chicago Press, 1992.

Sachedina, Abdulaziz. *The Islamic Roots of Democratic Pluralism*. Oxford: Oxford University Press, 2001.

Sadowski, Yahya. "Cadres, Guns, and Money: The Eighth Regional Congress of the Syrian Ba'th." *Middle East Report* 134 (July–August 1985).

———. *Scuds or Butter? The Political Economy of Arms Control in the Middle East.* Washington, DC: Brookings Institution, 1993.

Sadri, Mahmoud, and Ahmad Sadri, trans. and eds. *Reason, Freedom, and Democracy in Islam: Essential Writings of Abdolkarim Soroush.* Oxford: Oxford University Press, 2000.

Salamé, Ghassan, ed. *Democracy without Democrats? The Renewal of Politics in the Muslim World.* London: I. B. Tauris, 1994.

Sarıbay, Ali Yaşar. *Türkiye'de Modernlesme, Din ve Parti Politikası: MSP Örnek Olayı.* Istanbul: Alan Yayıncılık, 1985.

Sayarı, Sabri, and Yılmaz Esmer, eds. *Politics, Parties, and Elections in Turkey.* Boulder, CO: Lynne Rienner, 2002.

Sayigh, Yezid. "Security and Cooperation in the Middle East: A Proposal." *Middle East International* 429 (1992).

Selat, Nordin. *Kelas Menengah Melayu.* Kuala Lumpur: Utusan Melayu Bhd., 1976.

Seng, Philip Loh Fook. *Seeds of Separatism: Educational Policy in Malaya, 1874–1940.* Kuala Lumpur: Oxford University Press, 1974.

Sfakianakis, John, and Robet Springborg. "Civil-Military Relations in Egypt." *Journal of Arabic, Islamic, and Middle Eastern Studies* 5, no. 2 (1999).

Shayegan, Daryush. *Cultural Schizophrenia: Islamic Societies Confronting the West.* Syracuse, NY: Syracuse University Press, 1997.

Shuster, W. Morgan. *The Strangling of Persia.* New York: Century, 1912. Reprint, Westport, CT: Greenwood Press, 1968.

Siddiqa-Agha, Ayesha. "Power, Perks, Prestige, and Privileges: Military's Economic Activities in Pakistan." Paper presented at the international conference Soldiers in Business: Military as an Economic Actor. Institute for Policy and Community Development Studies, Jakarta, October 16–19, 2000.

Siddiqui, Kalim. *Issues in the Islamic Movement, 1983–84 (1403–04).* London: Open Press, 1985.

Simensen, Jale. "Democracy and Globalization: Nineteen Eighty-nine and the 'Third Wave.'" *Journal of World History* 19, no. 2 (1999).

Singer, Hans W. "Dualism Revisited: A New Approach to the Problems of Dual Society in Developing Countries." *Journal of Development Studies* 7, no. 1 (1979).

Sivard, Ruth Leger. *Women . . . A World Survey.* Washington, DC: World Priorities, 1985.

Smith, Donald Eugene, ed. *Religion and Political Modernization.* New Haven, CT: Yale University Press, 1974.

Solzhenitsyn, Aleksander, ed. *From Under the Rubble.* Washington, DC: Regenery Gateway Editions, 1981.

Soroush, Abdolkarim, in Mahmoud Sadri and Ahmad Sadri, eds. and trans. *Reason, Freedom, and Democracy in Islam: Essential Writings of Abdolkarim Soroush.* New York: Oxford University Press, 2002.

Springborg, Robert. "The President and the Field Marshal: Civil-Military Relations in Egypt Today." *Middle East Report* 147 (July–August 1987).

Sukarno, President. *Toward Freedom and the Dignity of Man.* Jakarta: Department of Foreign Affairs, 1961.

Sundaram, Jomo K. *Mahathir's Economic Policies.* Kuala Lumpur: INSAN, 1988.

—————. *A Question of Class: Capital, the State, and Uneven Development in Malaysia.* Singapore: Oxford University Press, 1986.

Surush, Abulkarim. "Shariati va Jameeshenasi-e-Din." Author's translation from the Persian original. *Kian* 3 third year, no. 13 (June–July 1994).

Talmon, Jacob L. *The Origins of Totalitarian Democracy.* New York: Frederick A. Praeger, 1960.

Tapper, Richard, ed. *The Conflict of Tribe and State in Afghanistan.* London: Croom Helm, 1983.

—————. *Islam in Modern Turkey: Religion, Politics, and Literature in a Secular State.* London: I. B. Tauris.

Teitelbaum, Joshua. "Dueling for *Da'wa*: State vs. Society on the Saudi Internet." *Middle East Journal* 56, no. 2 (2002).

Telhami, Shibley, and Fiona Hill. "Does Saudi Arabia Still Matter?" *Foreign Affairs* 81, no. 6 (November–December 2002).

Teymouri, Ibrahim. *Asr-e-Bikhabari Tarikh-e-Imtiazat Dar Iran.* 1332. Reprint, Tehran: Chap-e-Eghbal, 1953–54.

Thobie, Jacques, and Salgur Kançal, eds. *Communication et rapports sociaux en Turquie et en Mediterranée Orientale.* Paris: L'Harmattan, 1994.

Thomson, Alex. *Introduction to African Politics.* London: Routledge, 2000.

Tilly, Charles, ed. *The Formation of National States in Western Europe.* Princeton, NJ: Princeton University Press, 1975.

Tinker, Irene, ed. *Persistent Inequalities: Women and World Development.* New York: Oxford University Press, 1990.

Todaro, Michael P. *Economic Development in the Third World.* 4th ed. New York: Longman, 1989.

Toprak, Binnaz. *Islam and Political Development in Turkey.* Leiden: E. J. Brill, 1981.

—————. "Prejudice as Social Science Theory: Samuel P. Huntington's Vision of the Future." *Perceptions: Journal of International Affairs* (March–May 1996).

Toprak, Zafer. "Ali Reşad, Pozitivizm, ve Fransız Devrimi." *Tarih ve Toplum* 68 (August 1989).

—————. *Bir Yurttaş Yaratmak—Muasır bir medeniyet için seferberlik bilgileri.* Istanbul: Yapı Kredi Kültür Sanat, 1998.

—————. *Premiere rencontre internationale sur l'Empire Ottoman et la Turquie moderne.* Istanbul: Editions ISIS, 1991.

"Towhidi (Divinely Integrated) Populism Versus Vulgar Populism." *Mojahed* 1, no. 6 (June 1980).

Tunaya, Tarık Zafer. *slamcılık Cereyanı.* Istanbul: Baha Matbaası, 1962.

—————. *Türkiye'de Siyasal Partiler: ttihad ve Terakki—Bir Ça ın, Bir Kuşa ın, Bir Partinin Tarihi.* Vol. 3. Istanbul: Hürriyet Vakfı Yayınları, 1989.

Turner, Bryan S. *Orientalism, Postmodernism, and Globalism.* London: Routledge, 1994.

TÜSİAD. *Türk Toplumunun De erleri.* Istanbul: TÜSİAD Yayınları, 1991.

United Nations. *The World's Women 2000: Trends and Statistic.* New York: United Nations, 2000.

United Nations Department of Public Information. *Africa Recovery* 12, no. 2 (1998).

United Nations Development Programme (UNDP). *The Arab Human Development Report 2002: Creating Opportunities for Future Generations.* New York: UNDP, 2002.

—————. *Arab Human Development Report 2003: Building a Knowledge Society.* New York: UNDP, 2003.

————. *Human Development Report 2000*. New York: UNDP, 2000.

————. *Human Development Report 2002*. New York: UNDP, 2002.

————. *UNDP Demographic Indicators 1950–2025*. Rev. 1992 ed. New York: UNDP, 1993.

van Bruinessen, Martin. "Genealogies of Islamic Radicalism in Post-Suharto Indonesia." *Southeast Asia Research* 10, no. 2 (July 1, 2002).

Van Creveld, Martin. *The Transformation of War*. New York: Free Press, 1991.

Van Dam, Nikolaos. *The Struggle for Power in Syria: Politics and Society under Asad and the Ba'th Party*. 1979. Reprint, London: I. B. Tauris, 1996.

Van Dewalle, Dirk. *Libya Since Independence*. Ithaca, NY: Cornell University Press, 1998.

Vatikiotis, Panayiotis J. *The Egyptian Army in Politics: Pattern for New Nation*. Bloomington: Indiana University Press, 1961.

Viorst, Milton. *In the Shadow of the Prophet: The Struggle for the Soul of Islam*. New York: Doubleday, 1998.

von der Mehden, Fred. *Religion and Modernization in Southeast Asia*. Syracuse, NY: Syracuse University Press, 1986.

Waldner, David. *State Building and Late Development*. Ithaca, NY: Cornell University Press, 1999.

Watt, W. Montgomery. *Islamic Political Thought: The Basic Concepts*. Edinburgh: Edinburgh University Press, 1968.

Weber, Max. *The Protestant Ethic and the Spirit of Capitalism*. Trans. Talcott Parsons. New York: Charles Scribner's Sons, 1958. Reprint, London: Unwin University Books, 1974.

————. *The Sociology of Religion*. 5th ed. Boston: Beacon Press, 1969.

Wedeen, Lisa. *Ambiguities of Domination: Politics, Rhetoric, and Symbols in Contemporary Syria*. Chicago: University of Chicago Press, 1999.

Weeks, John. "The Demography of Islamic Nations." *Population Bulletin* 43, no. 4 (December 1988).

Weiner, Myron, and Samuel P. Huntington, eds. *Understanding Political Development*. Boston: Little, Brown, 1987.

Weiss, Linda. *The Myth of the Powerless State*. Ithaca, NY: Cornell University Press, 1998.

Welch, Claude E., Jr., ed. *Political Modernization*. Belmont, CA: Wadsworth Publishing, 1967.

White, Jenny B. *Islamist Mobilization in Turkey: A Study in Vernacular Politics*. Seattle: University of Washington Press, 2002.

Wickham, Carrie Rosefsky. *Mobilizing Islam: Religion, Activism, and Political Change in Egypt*. New York: Columbia University Press, 2002.

Wiking, Staffan. *Military Coups in Sub-Sahara Africa: How to Justify Illegal Assumptions of Power*. Uppsala, Sweden: Scandinavian Institute of African Studies, 1983.

Witte, John, Jr., and Johan D. van der Vyver, eds. *Religious Human Rights in Global Perspective: Religious Perspectives*. The Hague: Martinus Nijhoff Publishers, 1996.

Wittfogel, Karl A. *Oriental Despotism: A Comparative Study of Total Power*. New Haven, CT: Yale University Press, 1957.

Wolff, Kurt H., ed. *Essays on Sociology and Philosophy by Emile Durkheim*. Columbus: Ohio State University Press, 1960.

Woo-Cumings, Meredith, ed. *The Developmental State*. Ithaca, NY: Cornell University Press, 1999.

Woodward, Mark. "Indonesia, Islam, and the Prospect for Democracy." Southern Methodist University Asian Symposium, Dallas, 2001.

World Bank Group. *Middle East and North Africa Development Report. Gender and Development in the Middle East and North Africa: Women and the Public Sphere.* Overview. Washington, DC: World Bank, 2003. http://lnweb18.worldbank.org/mna/mena.nsf/Attachments/GenderReport-overview/$File/GENDER-REPORToverview.pdf (accessed February 17, 2004).

———. *World Development Indicators 2003*. Washington, DC: World Bank, 2003.

Wright, Dennis. *The English Amongst the Persians*. London: William Heinemann, 1977.

Wright, Mary. *The Last Stand of Chinese Conservatism*. Stanford, CA: Stanford University Press, 1957.

Yarshater, Ehsan, ed. *The Cambridge History of Iran*. Vol. 3, *The Seleucid, Parthian and Sasanid Periods*. Cambridge: Cambridge University Press, 1983.

Yinger, Milton J. *The Scientific Study of Religion*. New York: Macmillan, 1970.

Zabih, Sepehr. *The Communist Movement in Iran*. Berkeley and Los Angeles: University of California Press, 1966.

Zakaria, Fareed. *The Future of Freedom: Illiberal Democracy at Home and Abroad*. New York: W. W. Norton, 2003.

———. "The Rise of Illiberal Democracy." *Foreign Affairs* 76, no. 6 (November–December 1997).

Zartman, I. William, ed. *Political Elites in Arab North Africa*. New York: Longman, 1982.

Zenkovsky, Serge A. *Pan-Turkism and Islam in Central Asia*. Cambridge, MA: Harvard University Press, 1967.

Zinoviev, Alexander. *Homo Sovieticus*. New York: Atlantic Monthly Press, 1985.

Zonis, Marvin. *The Political Elite of Iran*. Princeton, NJ: Princeton University Press, 1971.

Zubaida, Sami. *Islam, the People, and the State: Essays on Political Ideas and Movements in the Middle East*. London: I. B. Tauris, 1993.

———. "The Politics of the Islamic Investment Companies in Egypt." *British Society for Middle Eastern Studies* 17 (1990).

Index

About the Editors and Contributors

MOHAMMED AYOOB is distinguished professor of international relations at Michigan State University. His articles have appeared in such journals as *World Politics*, *Foreign Policy*, and *International Affairs*, and he is the author of ten books, including most recently *The Third World Security Predicament* (1995).

OSMAN BAKAR is professor and Malaysia Chair of Islam in Southeast Asia, Center for Muslim-Christian Understanding at Georgetown University. He has authored twelve books and 120 articles on various aspects of Islam. He is the author of *Islam and Political Legitimacy in Malaysia* (2003).

HEATHER DEEGAN is professor of comparative politics at Middlesex University. Her areas of expertise include governance, political legitimacy, and globalization in the African context. Her publications include *The Middle East and Problems of Democracy (Issues in Third World Politics)* (1994) and more recently "Critical Issues in African Elections" (*Wilton Park/FCO Report*, 2003).

BRUCE W. FARCAU is a retired foreign service officer and professor at University of Central Florida. He has authored four books on Latin American politics and history, including *The Transition to Democracy in Latin America: The Role of the Military* (1996).

MEHRDAD HAGHAYEGHI is professor and the director of Master of International Affairs at Southwest Missouri State University. His research and teaching interests include comparative politics and Middle Eastern and Central Asian studies. He is the author of *Islam and Politics in Central Asia* (1995).

SHIREEN T. HUNTER is the director of the Islam Program at the Center for Strategic and International Studies. Her areas of expertise include the Middle

East, especially the Persian Gulf region, and Islam, including Russia, Europe, and the United States. Her latest publications are *The Future of Islam and the West: Clash of Civilizations or Peaceful Coexistence?* (1998), *Islam: Europe's Second Religion* (ed.; 2002), and *Islam in Russia: The Politics of Identity and Security* (2004).

SAAD EDDIN IBRAHIM is professor of political sociology at American University in Cairo. He is the founder and the first secretary-general of the Arab Human Rights Movement and the founder and chairman of the Ibn Khaldun Center for Development Studies, Cairo. Because of his advocacy for democracy, he was recently imprisoned by the Mubarak regime in a highly publicized case (2000–2003).

MEHRAN KAMRAVA is professor and chair of the Department of Political Science at California State University. He has written extensively on Middle Eastern issues. Recent publications include *Democracy in the Balance: Culture and Society in the Middle East* (1998) and *The Modern Middle East: A Political History Since World War I* (2005).

GIACOMO LUCIANI is professor of political economy and codirector of the Mediterranean Programme at the European University Institute, and Professorial Lecturer of Middle East Studies at the Johns Hopkins University, Bologna Center. He is editor and coauthor of *The Arab State* (1990).

HUMA MALIK is a fellow in the Center for Strategic and International Studies Islam Program. Her research focuses on ethnic and sectarian conflicts in South Asia. She is the coeditor of two reports, *Islam in Europe and the United States: A Comparative Perspective* (2002) and *Integrating Muslim Communities in Europe and the United States* (2003).

TIMOTHY McDANIEL is professor of sociology at University of California, San Diego. He is a specialist in Russia and cultural roots of large-scale social change. His is the author of *Autocracy, Modernization, and Revolution in Russia and Iran* (1991) and *The Agony of the Russian Idea* (1996).

VALENTINE M. MOGHADAM is professor of sociology and the director of women's studies at Illinois State University. She is the author of *Modernizing Women: Gender and Social Change in the Middle East* (2003). She lectures widely and consults for international organizations and UN agencies on gender, development, and the Middle East.

PETER NUNNENKAMP is a senior economist at the Kiel Institute for World Economics. His research and publications focus on the economic implications of globalization, the determinants and effects of foreign direct investment, and financial crises and reforms of the international financial architecture.

CHUKA ONWUMECHILI is professor and chair of the Department of Communications at Bowie State University. He has published several books, including *African Democratization and Military Coups* (1998). He also has published several book chapters and articles and has appeared on television programs to discuss African issues.

ELIZABETH PICARD is the director of research at the Centre National de la Recherche Scientifique. She is a specialist in security and identity politics in the Middle East. She is the author of *La nouvelle dynamique au Moyen-Orient* (1993) and *Lebanon: A Shattered Country* (2002).

TAMARA SONN is professor of humanities in the Department of Religious Studies at College of William and Mary. She is a specialist in Islamic intellectual history and Islam in the contemporary world. Her most recent works are *Comparing Religions through Law: Judaism and Islam* (with J. Neusner; 1999) and *A Brief History of Islam* (2004).

BINNAZ TOPRAK is professor of political science at Bogazici University. She has published widely on political Islam in Turkey. Her publications include *Islam and Political Development in Turkey* (with Ali Çarkŏlu; 1981) and *Türkiye'de Din, Toplum ve Siyaset* (2000).

JOHN O. VOLL is professor of Islamic history and the director of the Center for Muslim-Christian Understanding at Georgetown University. He specializes in Islamic history, modern Islamic movements, Sudanese history, and world history. He is the author of *Islam: Continuity and Change in the Muslim World* (1994) and co-author of *Islam and Democracy* (1996).

FRED R. von der MEHDEN is professor of political science at Rice University. He has written and lectured widely on religion and politics in Southeast Asia. Among his publications are *Religion and Nationalism in Southeast Asia* (1968) and *Religion and Modernization in Southeast Asia* (1986).

Holy Family
UNIVERSITY